Advance praise for

FIVE RING CIRCUS

Chris Shaw brilliantly and grippingly uncovers the looting of Vancouver, how the IOC and its drug-fuelled Games poison our democracies, award government licenses to land speculators, and dump the bill on taxpayers. It's a story of grotesque deceit confronted by heroic protests and citizen-driven corruption investigations that shame the co-opted media. A must-read for any community under threat from the Olympic boosters.

— ANDREW JENNINGS, investigative reporter and filmmaker

We are told that the slogan of the Olympics is Faster, Higher, Stronger. But for far too many host cities, it's been Greed, Guns, and Graft. Chris Shaw's *Five Ring Circus* is a remarkable contribution to unmasking what really goes down when the Olympics come to town — in Vancouver and beyond. This is an urgent must-read, and the best sporting expose I've read in years.

— DAVE ZIRIN, author *A People's History of Sports in the United States.*

A crucial tale, told under pressure on the fly, of public-spirited citizens standing up for shared truths forged in the teeth of the blizzard of lies pumped out by Olympic industry media. A gripping epic about corporations sociopathically obsessed with re-colonizing our sacred places as subsidized outdoor malls for bored and lonely tourists to go to for retail therapy. Read it and realize that local networks of citizens can be re-invigorated in the struggles against these place invaders.

— MARTIN SLAVIN, gamesmonitor.org.uk

The Olympic juggernaut must be stopped! I wholeheartedly agree with Christopher Shaw, and you will, too, after you read this book. This is the real Olympic story, a careful and passionate documentation of every hidden detail behind the Vancouver bid and organizing committees'"feel good" facade.

— HELEN JEFFERSON LENSKYJ, author of *Inside the Olympic Industry: Power, Politics and Activism, The Best Ever Olympics: Social Impacts of Sydney 2000* and *Olympic Industry Resistance: Challenging Olympic Powers and Propaganda*; Professor Emerita, University of Toronto

The Olympic Games are often regarded as a gift to host cities. In his thoughtful but impassioned *Five Ring Circus*, Chris Shaw succeeds in tearing away the public relations wrapping and IOC ribbons. With well-worded precision, he examines the real prize inside, meant for developers and insiders: a countdown clock wired to a civic incendiary device.

— GEOFF OLSON, *Common Ground* magazine

Ten minutes of this book is enough to throw one inside a world once known by only a handful of people. Shaw describes the true face of this private leviathan, the IOC: its deep and consolidated fascist roots, and the unbeatable string of financial disasters left after the rodeo has gone from town. If you want to know exactly what the *olympics* are, and what they absolutely are not, just don't miss it.

— STEFANO BERTONE, co-founder of the Turin 2006 Antiolympics' Committee.
Member of the Worldwide Opposition to the "olympic games".

In the public mind, the Olympics are all about international brotherhood, and friendly contests among amateur athletes from around the world. Well-researched and important, *Five Ring Circus* reveals the realities of how this world really works and what it's really about — greed and money. *Five Ring Circus* is about more than just the Olympics; it's a vehicle, a microcosm, that can open people's minds to looking beneath the surface of *the spectacle* of fantasy media reality.

— RICHARD MOORE, author *Escaping the Matrix:*
How We the People can change the world

This book is the IOC and VANOC's worst nightmare. *Five Ring Circus* is a well-researched and challenging examination of how the Olympics is, at its heart, all about real estate mega deals, and making rich developers even richer. Christopher Shaw should get a gold medal for investigative journalism.

— DAVID EBY, lawyer, Pivot Legal Society

Everything you wanted to know about the Olympic Games is in *Five Ring Circus*. Shaw exposes the massive corporate corruption surrounding the Games, and names our British Columbian politicians who align themselves with the vile, wretched schemes of corporate vandals to defraud the rest of us of our public lands, waters, and money. A must-read for every Canadian. Or for that matter, for citizens everywhere who may be in danger of being conned into giving up their birthright by these economic terrorists.

— BETTY KRAWCZYK, Citizen Granny

In 2003 they promised us a world class city. Instead the people of Vancouver got a doubling of the homeless rate, erosion of civil liberties, surveillance cameras, an ever-increasing crime rate, increasing rents, evictions, an ecological disaster and, to make matters worse, we will be paying for this for the next 30 years. If you are wondering how this mess came about, this book is an essential read.

— CONRAD SCHMIDT, director "Five Ring Circus" documentary film;
founder, Work Less Party; and author, *Workers of the World Relax*

Five Ring Circus

MYTHS *and* REALITIES
of the OLYMPIC GAMES

Christopher A. Shaw

NEW SOCIETY PUBLISHERS

CATALOGING IN PUBLICATION DATA:
A catalog record for this publication is available from
the National Library of Canada.

Cover design by Diane McIntosh.
Images: 123RF/Sean Gladwell; Punchstock/IZA stock

Printed in Canada. First printing June 2008.

New Society Publishers acknowledges
the support of the Government of Canada through the
Book Publishing Industry Development Program (BPIDP)
for our publishing activities.

Paperback ISBN: 978-0-86571-592-9

Inquiries regarding requests to reprint all or part of *Five Ring Circus*
should be addressed to New Society Publishers at the address below.

To order directly from the publishers, please call toll-free (North America)
1-800-567-6772, or order online at www.newsociety.com

Any other inquiries can be directed by mail to:

New Society Publishers
P.O. Box 189, Gabriola Island, BC V0R 1X0, Canada
(250) 247-9737

New Society Publishers' mission is to publish books that contribute in
fundamental ways to building an ecologically sustainable and just society, and
to do so with the least possible impact on the environment, in a manner that
models this vision. We are committed to doing this not just through education,
but through action. This book is one step toward ending global deforestation
and climate change. It is printed on Forest Stewardship Council-certified
acid-free paper that is **100% post-consumer recycled** (100% old growth
forest-free), processed chlorine free, and printed with vegetable-based, low-
VOC inks, with covers produced using FSC-certified stock. Additionally,
New Society purchases carbon offsets based on an annual audit, operating
with a carbon-neutral footprint. For further information, or to browse our full
list of books and purchase securely, visit our website at: www.newsociety.com

NEW SOCIETY PUBLISHERS
www.newsociety.com

For my children,
Ari and Emma,

in honor of the living memory of
Colleen McCrory and Harriet Nahanee

and for that unrepentant,
indomitable champion of Mother Earth,
Betty Krawczyk.

*The Olympic Games
are the great Circus Maximus of planet Earth.*

Varda Burstyn,
from the foreword to Helen Lenskyj's
Inside the Olympic Industry[1]

Contents

Part 4.
The Fourth Ring: Olympic Myths and Realities

Part 5
The Fifth Ring: Resistance to the Olympics

Acknowledgments

The motto of my mother's family is this: *Vincit veritas* — truth prevails.

Because I believe this to be true, this project was begun.

The book may have begun with this belief alone, but it could not have been completed without the contributions both large and small of numerous people. Space and propriety precludes me from naming them all, but notably there are the following individuals to whom I owe my gratitude: my street medic friends, Jill, Bella, Crimson and Cara who helped me first see what the Olympics really was all about.

To Phil LeGood for friendship and insight and for picking up a huge role as one of the main NO GAMES 2010 spokespersons. My friend and colleague Conrad Schmidt of the Work Less Party played a major role; it was with him that I first broached the topic of a documentary movie and a book. Charlie Smith, Editor of the *Georgia Straight*, deserves special mention since this project really arose during a conversation with him when he suddenly said, "You know a lot about the Olympics, you should write a book." He may have been mistaken about my knowledge base, but the seed was sown.

My thanks especially to Carolyn Wong who did much of the background research to fill in gaps that I left behind in my mad dash to deadline. Others who provided information or feedback included: David Maidman, Gordon Flett, Ian Gregson, Yolane Beyens, Greg Hamilton, David Eby and Anna Hunter. Many others served as sounding boards for topics raised in the book, particularly my long-time friends Denis Kay and Jill McEachern who offered critical advice at various junctures. Jill, pregnant with our daughter Emma in the year leading to Prague, was particularly supportive at a very difficult time.

Other support came from Rosalin Sam and Chief Garry John and others of the St'at'imc, Matt Burrows of the *Georgia Straight*, Bella and Crimson, Chuck Gould, Franklin Lopez and Cara Goldberg. Prof. Helen Lenskyj, Andrew Jennings and Stefano Bertone provided important insights on past Olympic Games or the IOC generally. Philippe Praz of the Swiss Embassy in Ottawa provided the much-needed information about the IOC's tax status in that country. Information was also supplied by members of the Fourth Estate, notably, Bob Mackin, Wendy Cox, Vaughn Palmer and Daphne Bramham.

I am grateful also to my erstwhile colleagues in the provincial Green Party for tolerating my obsession with the Games for so long, notably, Adriane Carr and the late environmental champion, Colleen McCrory. In addition, there were many NO GAMES supporters who were constant sources of encouragement. Many others who never got officially involved nevertheless sent letters or e-mails or sometimes just left telephone messages, usually saying "thanks for what you are doing." A few souls who will remain nameless sent secret information that helped move the opposition along. A number of members of the media helped in various ways. Sometimes, they directed me to information that I might have missed. Other times, their contribution came when the microphones switched off, and they said, "I'm really glad you are doing what you are doing…someone has to keep the bastards honest." I can't name them since I don't want them to get into trouble with their editors, but they know who they are. I hope someday they will write their own stories.

Two organizations that I'm formally involved with also deserve acknowledgement. My employer, the University of British Columbia, and my department, Ophthalmology, generally trusted me to keep to the guidelines for faculty members involved in political advocacy and always respected my right of academic freedom. The Canadian Forces Reserve in British Columbia usually showed the same trust.

I also want to thank the Canadian citizenship judge who, back in 1990, told me, "I want to see you involved in the political life of your new country." I promised to do so. This book is one part of keeping that promise.

I am grateful to Chris Plant, at New Society Publishers (NSP) for seeing the potential of this project, and for his support at all stages of the work. Also from NSP, Ingrid Witvoet, Sue Custance, EJ Hurst and Ginny Miller were most helpful. Diane McIntosh created the vibrant original cover for the book. My gratitude also goes to Judith Brand for her expert copy editing, fact checking and numerous suggestions for improvements.

My gratitude and love go to my children, Ari and Emma. Ari got dragged to endless meetings, listened to me rant, provided important critical feedback and did it all with a grace rare in a teenager. Emma gave up her daddy far too many nights, often sitting quietly on my lap or being held in my arms while I was being interviewed. This book is really for them in the hope that one day in their lifetimes the Olympic Games will really be about international sport acting for the true enrichment of community and the human endeavor, rather than a corrupting business enterprise that impoverishes both.

Needless to say, any errors or omissions found in these pages are inadvertent, and are solely my own.

— Chris Shaw
Deep Cove
November 2007

Preface

The important thing in life is not the victory but the contest;
the essential thing is not to have won but to have fought well.

BARON PIERRE DE COURBERTIN (1863–1937),
FOUNDER OF THE MODERN OLYMPICS

My own Olympic adventure — oddly enough begun in the original spirit of Pierre de Courbertin — began with a long car ride home to Vancouver from Calgary. My fellow street medics and I had gone to provide medical support for anti-globalization protesters at the June 2002 G8 Summit in Kananaskis, Alberta. The event itself had been relatively calm. Neither the police nor the demonstrators wanted a repeat of the street battles of Quebec City two years earlier. As medics, we hung out on the outskirts of the various demonstrations, watching our fellow activists and hoping all the while that nothing would go sideways that would require us to pull out the first aid kits.

While we waited, we spent our time chatting up the locals, always hopeful that somehow we'd be able to reach out to average people and explain what we thought wrong with the G8's agenda. Calgarians are generally friendly folks; some of them noticing our medic vests had come over to talk, mainly to ask what the demonstrations were all about. At one demonstration in a downtown mall, a protest group composed of naked people covered with mud (I forget why) was targeting a Gap clothing store. A pretty woman in her twenties approached us and asked my fellow medic Crimson and me what was happening. "I don't get it," she said, pointing at the mud people congregating outside the store. "What have they got against the Gap? They made nice clothes." We agreed that maybe the clothes were fine, but that to make them, the company exploited factory workers in the developing world, a practice condoned if not encouraged by the World Trade Organization and the G8. "But they make nice clothes," she reiterated, the look on her face segueing from innocent confusion to insipient panic. Could we possibly be some of the dangerous "radicals" the Calgary press had been warning everyone about? She must have concluded that indeed we were because after her pained third "But they make nice clothes," she scurried away from us toward a knot of Calgary police who

were keeping a wary eye on the demonstration. We watched as she spoke to
them while gesturing animatedly in our direction. The police nodded at her,
turned in our direction and smiled; one constable even nodded a vague greet-
ing. That was that, no harm done, but also no knowledge about globalization
transferred to someone from outside the circle of those already amongst the
converted.

     This encounter, like so many others, drove home a point that many of us
had been struggling with: How do you reach out to ordinary people who have
been bombarded by media and government pronouncements on the "benefits
and inevitability" of globalization? Years before, Edward Herman and Noam
Chomsky had coined the term "manufacturing consent" [1] to describe the process
by which a corporation-controlled government and media endlessly hammer
home their messages, selling, in this case, "free market reforms" in just the same
way as they might pitch any other product. To create "balance," the media might
let in the odd opposing view, but it was always careful to make sure that such
heresies were surrounded by still further pro-globalization pronouncements.
What is the average citizen to think? Well, if all the mainstream political parties
agree, if all the mainstream media agree as well, the pro-globalization worldview must be correct, right? The end result for much of the 1980s and 1990s had
been a largely compliant citizenry composed of people who — if they thought
about it at all — concluded that they had examined the evidence critically and
made up their own minds that globalization was for the economic good of everyone, that the "rising tide lifts all boats," that free trade formed the bedrock
of democracy. Everyone says so, so it must be true. Confronted by globalization's opponents, the notion that economic or social realities are not as they
seem sounds a frankly discordant note to the background pronouncements
of politicians and news anchors. The possibility that a corporation-controlled
and globalized world economy is far more likely to generate poverty than universal wealth goes against a firmly implanted and well-nourished worldview.
For many like the woman in Calgary, the very fact that anyone might question
the received wisdom is profoundly unsettling and definitely something to be
avoided if at all possible. Economics can be confusing and boring enough at the
best of times; getting past years of psychological conditioning to try to displace
preprogrammed views is pretty difficult. Certainly the chance of doing so in a
thirty-second encounter is unlikely in the extreme.

     Now on the long drive home, Jill, Crimson, Bella and I found ourselves
contemplating an article in a newspaper that had found its way into Opal, our
van and part-time home. The paper had been used as a placemat for the food
bowl of our accompanying furry friend, a three-legged dog named Indy. Indy

didn't seem to mind if we borrowed the paper for a while. Other than that the news was days old, one article caught our attention. The report noted that Vancouver was hoping to be shortlisted by the International Olympic Committee (IOC) for the 2010 Winter Olympic Games. Eight cities were in the running with four finalists soon to be chosen for the *honor* of submitting formal bids. The article listed some of the key players in Vancouver's bid, including real estate baron Jack Poole. It also reported that the Vancouver Bid Committee had the support of all levels of government. Opinion in the van was mixed: Someone said, "Cool"; someone else said "Corporate scam." As we thought about it further, we realized that we didn't really understand the Olympic Games or what they meant very well at all. What kind of beast was the IOC? Was it a benevolent organization that promoted elite sports for the stated goals of peaceful competition amongst the nations, or was it a big multinational business? Could it be both? Then there was the question of what to make of the fact that all levels of government were all onside with the likes of a developer like Poole. Maybe we'd all had too much tear gas in our diet over the previous years, but our skepticism was rapidly rising. After all, if the governing BC Liberal party (not really very "liberal") and the developer-ridden Vancouver city government were onside, then there had to be a rat in there somewhere. Maybe the Olympics overall, as well as the particular Games at the local level, were the same globalization phenomenon we had been fighting in Kananaskis and elsewhere? If so, maybe exposing it could be our "wedge" issue, one that we could use to broach the flaws of globalization to an apathetic or uninformed audience: Very few people seemed to be anti-Olympics. The rest, conditioned all their lives to love the Games, might just be curious why anyone wouldn't be completely onside. It would be like hating Santa Claus, for some a notion so weird that they'd just want to know why.

Taking an anti-Olympics stand was only a vague notion, but one that germinated on the long drive home. Opal kept breaking down, and when we arrived home some 20 hours later, the idea of looking in more detail at the Olympics and Vancouver's bid was firmly rooted. We had no idea where it would take us. Perhaps had we known, we would have given the paper back to Indy and forgotten the whole thing.

What I didn't realize then was that Vancouver's bid would come to dominate my life and that, for good or ill, exploring worldwide Olympic myths and realities was going to be a path I'd be on for years to come. This book is the culmination of that journey...so far.

Readers will quickly notice that the focus of *Five Ring Circus* is on Vancouver's Olympics and the way it has impacted the citizens of this city and region. I've tried to make it clear that Vancouver's "geocentric" bid, both in its origin and evolution, was not unique. In fact, as I began to look into the IOC and Olympic cities in more detail, startling similarities became apparent. The pattern that finally emerged clearly showed that bids are all "imagineered" and controlled in the same way. Moreover, all "successful" bids produce comparable crops of lies, broken promises, debt, social displacement and environmental destruction. Vancouver's bid history is thus like that of Sydney, Salt Lake City, Athens and Torino in the past and is utterly predictive of London and Sochi in the future.

The first caveat to the material that follows is that getting a firm grip on Olympic numbers — for example, the costs of the Games, including security, the environmental impacts and the like — is subject to numerous assumptions and a host of variables not available to those outside Olympic inner planning circles. In all cases, I have tried to make a minimal number of assumptions, using primary source material as often as possible. This procedure led me to come up with figures that are likely in the low-end range, hence an underestimate of the true costs and impacts. The real numbers, if they are known at all, are available only to those in government and the Olympic organizing committees. For reasons that will become clear, neither is telling.

The second caveat is that I have gone far beyond the "official" Olympic industry sources for information, focusing on primary news sources and the dissident publications of authors such as Professor Helen Lenskyj and the investigative reporter Andrew Jennings. While traditional Olympic writers and scholars have produced an impressive body of articles and books, they also tend to "toe the party line," and few offer anything that can be considered critical of any aspect of the Olympic enterprise. There are, however, some unexpected gems to be found in this literature when one reads between the lines.

There is an old adage that to know history is to predict the future. Nowhere is this truer than with the Olympics. To citizens of the cities now competing for 2016 and beyond, take note: The events that I describe here are in your future if you listen to the siren songs of the IOC and your local bid boosters. It may be too late to prevent the worst of the outrages from occurring in Vancouver, but you can still save your own cities from a similar fate.

Whether you do so or not is, remarkably, really up to you.

THE FIRST RING

The Cult of the Olympics, Vancouver 2010 and the Opposition

· · · · ·

Olympism is not a system — it is a state of mind.
This state of mind has emerged from a double cult:
that of effort and that of Eurythmy —
a taste of excess and a taste of measure combined.

PIERRE DE COUBERTIN[1]

I am always amazed when I hear people saying that sport creates
goodwill between nations, and that if only the common peoples of
the world could meet one another at football or cricket,
they would have no inclination to meet on the battlefield.
Even if they didn't know from concrete examples
(the 1936 Olympics, for instance) that international
sporting contests lead to orgies of hatred, one
could deduce it from general principles.... At the
international level sport is frankly mimic warfare.

GEORGE ORWELL[2]

CHAPTER 1

Jack Poole's Smile

*If the Olympic bid wasn't happening
we would have to invent something.*

Jack Poole[1]

*Like all con tricks, it works best by arriving suddenly in the
locality, promising "fantastic" outcomes to the greedy and the
needy, getting a binding contract signed by the "urban elites"
of the host cities (a contract which clearly says "the IOC is
not responsible for the overspend, you are"), raising a political
storm of protest amongst a vocal minority (who are eventually
worn out from the effort of challenging the juggernaut), then
departing to a new city to work the old con on a fresh set of
startled punters. That's why the Olympics is always on the
move. No-one would let them do it twice in their lifetime.*

Martin Slavin[2]

Once upon a Time in Vancouver

THIS BOOK traces the history of Vancouver's bid and ultimate success obtaining the 2010 Winter Olympic Games.
The early stages of the bid and the nascent opposition were only
the beginning of a saga that would span more than ten years and
ultimately prove to have immense consequences for Vancouver and
British Columbia long into the future. Vancouver's Olympic bid and its
cultish and often curious collection of supporters, the bid's opposition, the
media, the politicians and a still uncertain public had a long way to go before
it was all done.

In the following pages, I will probe the hidden aspects of Vancouver's bid,
explore the history of the IOC in order to put the Vancouver Olympics into a

wider context and examine the events after Vancouver "won" the bid in 2003. In particular, I will expose the true nature of the Olympics — Vancouver's in particular — and finish with a discussion of the continuing local and international opposition to the Olympics. Thus, while the focus will be on the Vancouver Games, what's happened in my own city simply mirrors what inevitably transpires in all Olympic host cities: The same real estate developers organize and drive the Olympic bid, a litany of promises — all later broken — are made about people and the environment to garner public support, and once the bid is won, costs escalate wildly out of control. The names of people and places may differ, but the pattern is clearly recognizable across time and space. In fact the similarities are so striking that it will become obvious that host cities are simply following a generic recipe, one that gets sold time and time again to a public largely ignorant that they are being manipulated for private ends.

We've a long way to go...it's time to consider the path to Vancouver's "time to shine" in 2010.

In the Beginning

One of the enduring myths about the Olympic Games is that they are actually about sports. It shouldn't come as a surprise that much of the world — at least the part of it that depends on the corporate press for their information — accepts this as being basically true. Fifty years of saturation advertising tends to have a considerable impact, dulling the background drumbeat of scandals and misspent public funds, International Olympic Committee (IOC) members on the take, corrupt judges and doped-up athletes. Of course not all IOC members are corrupt and not all athletes use drugs, but public funds are almost always misspent, and the hidden area where most of this money goes is into real estate projects for private developers. What sports has to do with the Olympic Games for the IOC beyond the television rights is a serious question, but there's no doubt that behind every Olympic Games of the last quarter century were real estate deals in the making. This may surprise many readers who suppose that the awarding of the "privilege" to host the Games originates with the IOC. In fact it originates with the candidate cities that will do virtually anything and everything to get the Games simply as a device to promote projects that taxpayers would otherwise refuse, usually those that have lurked in the wings for years, soundly rejected because they made little or no economic or social sense. And, in every potential Olympic city, the actual Games drivers are real estate developers. How often is this true? Always. Viewed in this light, the IOC is less the predator than the scavenger, a ravenous corporate vulture endlessly circling the globe, waiting for the local developers in the various countries to bring down the prey, the local taxpaying citizenry. If enough magic Olympic pixie dust falls on the citizenry, the IOC and developers hope that the good burghers will abandon all reason and give their blessings and dollars willingly. Tying the Games to such projects suddenly imbues them with a different aura, and all previous rationality about real costs versus potential benefits goes out the window. The IOC and local bid boosters spend considerable funds to ensure that this occurs. If absolutely nothing else in this book takes hold, remember this: *The Olympic Games at the local level are all about real estate.*

Jack Poole's Smile

In the world of Vancouver real estate, there may be many players, but there is only one éminence grise, the legendary baron of Daon Corporation, Vancouver Land Corporation, Greystone Properties and now Concert Properties, holder of the Order of British Columbia and Order of Canada, none other than Mr. Jack W. Poole.

Jack Poole is a well-kept elderly gentleman, looking far younger than his 74 years, tall and slim, with close-cropped gray hair. But, look at any picture of Poole and you see the same curious half smile. I've seen him wear it while presenting his Olympic fantasies to gullible Vancouverites. It was there when he was escorting Britain's Prince Edward at an Olympic booster event in Vancouver. It was even plastered on his face when he received his Order of Canada from the Governor General, Michaëlle Jean. Actually, it's less a smile than a smirk, a curious twisting of the lips that seems to suggest he knows something you don't. And, true enough, he does: He and his colleagues at VANOC have conned an anxiety-ridden Vancouver into bidding for and accepting the 2010 Winter Olympic Games. He and his insider group are going to make billions, and he knows it. Vancouverites and British Columbians, just like the citizens in past Olympic cities, are going to lose billions but don't know it…yet. By the time they do, it will be a done deal, too far advanced to stop, with no paper trail, nothing concrete that could incriminate Poole and his friends in a scam of gargantuan proportions.

Poole was originally a farm boy from Saskatchewan, an aspiring hockey player whose career path was cut short by a freak traffic accident. He has since risen from failed entrepreneur to be Chairman of Concert Properties, one of the most successful real estate/development companies in North America. Along the way, he bankrolled the current premier of British Columbia, Gordon Campbell, first as mayor of Vancouver, later in the bid to become the leader of the Liberal Party of BC and finally into the Premier's office. Poole was Chairman of the Vancouver-Whistler 2010 Olympic Bid Corporation, the second stage of Vancouver's Olympic bid for the 2010 Games and now serves in the same role for VANOC, the Vancouver Organizing Committee for the Games.

Finally, the smirk is a statement: Even if you do know what's going on, what can you do about it? The answer is you can't do anything, and Poole knows this too. If you were he, sitting in the catbird seat, Chairman of VANOC and Concert Properties, with a passel of medals pinned to your chest, you'd smirk too.

Vancouver's bid to host the Winter Olympics has come a long way from some premature notions back in the 1960s and '70s that Whistler could use a boost that only an Olympic audience might provide. Whistler back then was not particularly well known as a ski resort, pretty much nowhere-ville in the world of sports tourism. Then, as always, the notion of bidding on the Olympics (for 1972 and 1976) came into the minds of local businessmen as a means to propel Whistler into the big leagues. And as a notion, it wasn't a bad one, provided they'd had the wherewithal to sell it. Whistler didn't then and, although it had tried to bid for the 1976 Winter Games, wound up turning down an offer from the IOC to host the latter after Denver bailed out following a negative outcome in a statewide referendum.

The idea of a Vancouver Olympics was to remain dormant for almost 30 years before resurfacing with a group of the local business and real estate elite who decided to run the Olympic Jolly Roger up the flagpole one more time. By the late 1990s, the idea had taken shape in the form of an organization called the Vancouver-Whistler 2010 Bid Society, a shortlisted who's who of developers, business interests and politicians.[3] There were even former Olympic athletes to lend the proper aura to the organization as one really about sports. The difference this time around with the Olympic venture was that Vancouver was no longer a sleepy burg on Canada's left coast; it had become a thriving metropolis fueled by the massive Asian immigration of the late 1980s and early '90s. Expo '86 had been a huge success at selling Vancouver to the world, and Whistler was booming, so much so that it had become the number one ski resort in North America. The idea that Vancouver could actually be in the running to get the Games didn't seem so outlandish this time around, especially for an emerging Vancouver civic identity that was one part exuberant overconfidence and two parts angst, composed of the palpably aching need to feel "world class." The world-class rubric is merely shorthand for a playground for rich tourists, but for many Vancouverites it was a title they desperately craved. Poole and his colleagues read this audience well, sized up the market and knew they had a potential winner if they could play to civic pride. All it took was grease, soon to be provided by the provincial government of the time, the New Democratic Party (NDP), notionally a strange bedfellow for Poole and his developer colleagues.

In the highly connected world of insider politics, getting the NDP onside wasn't as strange as it seemed. The conventional wisdom that corporations like Poole's Concert Properties would only dance with those of the right was a holdover of a political age long since past. The truth was much more curious and an insight into the true nature of British Columbia's politics, namely that Poole and other developers had a huge in with both the BC Liberals, ostensibly conservative and pro-business, *and* with the NDP, supposedly socialist-leaning and anti-business. Consider this: Poole had a number of labor union stalwarts, notably Ken Georgetti and Tony Tennessy, on Concert's board of directors, and the working capital of the company was solidly in the hands of various union pension funds. This arrangement was a carry-over from Concert's previous existence as Greystone Properties, and before that Vancouver Land Corporation (VLC). VLC had managed to secure city land from Vancouver's then Non-Partisan Association (NPA) mayor and future BC Liberal premier, Gordon Campbell, as well as money from the provincial NDP government of Premier Mike Harcourt. Both land and funds were to construct "social housing," a long-term project that never in fact went to completion. It didn't matter: VLC did very well and bided its time. By the time Concert was up and running, the main chance had come into view, a shot at the absolute mother of all gravy trains: development projects bankrolled by Olympic dreams and compliant taxpayers.

The Bid Society was incorporated in BC in 1998 and in its relatively short life managed to grab over $50,000 from the NDP government of new Premier Glen Clark.[4] The Society chugged along, lining up support from business and government and managing to convince almost anyone who would listen that the Olympics would be great for the economy. The fact that the most cursory survey of past Games shows that host cities tend to lose money wasn't on the table yet, and most Vancouverites, if they knew about the project at all, seemed vaguely in awe of the possibility that Vancouver could actually be in the running. In some ways, the pitch was oddly reminiscent of those old Mickey Rooney musicals from the 1940s and '50s, the ones where he turns to his gang and says, "Hey, kids, let's put on a show." This was all still before the hype started in earnest, and although relatively low-key, the Bid Society did get the ball rolling before conveniently vanishing. The Bid Society had served its role as placeholder, and no one on the board seemed to protest when the provincial government revoked their incorporation status for failing to file financial reports. The over $50,000 of provincial taxpayers' money was never accounted for.[5]

The Bid Society's replacement was a far slicker machine, the Vancouver-Whistler 2010 Bid Corporation, which suddenly appeared on the scene in 1999.

Far more robust in structure, it was replete with a board of directors that was indeed a who's who of BC and Alberta real estate and corporate interests.[6] Included were Stanley Kwok and Caleb Chan, the latter having also served on the Bid Society, and numerous others who orbited within the real estate solar system dominated by Li Ka Shing, multi-billionaire Hong Kong businessman and a key developer with huge interests in the 2008 Beijing Summer Games. Many on the Bid Corp stood to gain handsomely from an Olympics-driven real estate boom, especially one propelled up the Sea to Sky highway toward Whistler and the Callaghan Valley, the latter the proposed site of the Nordic events.

There were a few former Olympic athletes tossed in, as with the Bid society, to make it seem as if it were really about the sports, but there were also a number of curious appointees at the national level, appointees who made no sense from either sports or a business perspective. As an example of the latter, France Chrétien Desmarais, daughter of Prime Minister Jean Chrétien, was on the board. Another attribute that would play a role in her selection was that she was the wife of André Desmarais, CEO of the Ontario megacorporation Power Corp, and daughter-in-law of Paul Desmarais, a major mover and shaker. The link between Power Corp and the Olympic Technical Team will be dealt with in a later chapter, but suffice it to say here that at the time this appointment seemed discordant except as a sop to her father.

Jack Poole headed up the Bid Corp as their Chairman and used the resources of Concert Properties to push the bid, even seconding Concert's CEO, David Podmore, to run the 2003 plebiscite campaign. The latter had been the high-stakes effort to win over Vancouverites and get them to vote yes to the Olympics. Putting Podmore in the driver's seat had been a strategic as well as a tactical choice. First, Poole needed some space between his history as a failed real estate guru and his new shiny role as Bid Chairman: Considerable tax dollars were potentially on the line; reminding the public about the failure of previous companies would not fly if the public were to be convinced that Olympic projects would come in "on time and on budget." Poole's hard-edged persona was also a particularly compelling reason not to put himself in front of an audience of ordinary Vancouverites, both the smirk and the body language conveying contempt for anyone not instantly on his side.

Poole made another wise choice in hand-picking the new front man for the Bid Corp, pulling in former Olympian John Furlong to be the CEO and the smiling face the public and media saw. Furlong had managed Vancouver's exclusive Arbutus Club for years before taking the job at Bid Corp. He was far smoother than Poole and less likely to be ruffled, at least in public, and unlikely to utter the threats to the City that Poole would later come to regret. Furlong, all things considered, seemed an able and willing torch carrier for the cause, one whose "I have seen the light" zeal peculiar to so many who have competed in the Games projected the notion of true believer and loyal follower. Furlong's job was to sell the emerging "frame" that the Games were about nothing more than elite athletics and Vancouver's "time to shine" for the rest of Canada, and sell it he did.

The choice of Furlong as Bid Corp CEO and later in the same role with the successor organization VANOC was almost purely in the hands of Poole who never actually relinquished the reins of power in either organization. Comparing the relationship between Poole and Furlong to that of US Vice President Dick Cheney and George Bush wouldn't be far wrong. The last thing a potentially jumpy public needs to see is that damned smirk that, oddly, Poole and Cheney seem to share. Furlong had one additional advantage: He was largely unknown to the media. Then there was simply the optics of having a company that stood to gain financially from the Games being so obviously involved in pushing the bid forward. Poole adroitly stickhandled his way past all of this in the bid period with his choice of Furlong. The façade began to slip in 2005 when some in the media began questioning his motives when Poole slipped up and Concert tried to bid on the construction of the Athletes' Village. But this was still far in the future.

Vancouver Gets Shortlisted

By the early summer of 2002, the Bid Corp had all three levels of government firmly onside, each ready to help cough up the bulk of the $34 million in cash and untold amounts in services and staff time that made up the Bid Corp's war chest in its campaign to win the 2010 Games. Their slick "Bid Book" produced that same summer highlighted for the IOC and British Columbians why they thought Vancouver's bid was best of all the candidate cities.

The original list of cities competing for 2010 had stood, including Vancouver, at eight: Salzburg (Austria), Bern (Switzerland), Pyeongchang (South Korea), Andorra la Vella (Andorra), Harbin (China), Jaca (Spain) and Sarajevo (Bosnia and Herzegovina). In late August 2002, the IOC's short list was out, and Vancouver's name was on it. The field was now cut in half, and Vancouver was in a race against Salzburg, Bern and Pyeongchang. The Canton of Bern would soon hold a referendum on hosting the Games, or more precisely on whether the citizens wanted to spend the money. They didn't. Considering that Switzerland is home to the IOC, the resulting No vote leading to Bern dropping out must have been a shock to IOC officials. But it was good news for Vancouver's Bid Corp and its followers who saw their odds go up accordingly.

The hype from the Bid Corp and the mainstream media began to crank up to full throttle.

Many Vancouverites became giddy at the prospect: The city hoisted Olympic banners on every street pole, and "I'm backing the Bid" and "It's our time to shine" bumper stickers seemed to be everywhere. It was wild overkill meant to impress the IOC and perhaps stifle any murmur of local opposition, the latter an odd notion since up to then there had been no opposition to speak of. The Bid Corp, however, had learned from TOBid, its sister organization in Toronto, and its failed attempts to snag the 1996 and 2008 Games and didn't want to have any serious dissent crawl out from under their bid.

The Bid Corp Campaign Begins

The Bid Corp's initial focus was based on the supposed economic benefits of hosting the Olympic Games. British Columbia's economy was then in a slump, and the bid boosters assured the public that Olympic mojo was the ticket to a brighter future. The argument went something like this: The total cost of hosting the 2010 Games will be just over a billion dollars, just over half of it for construction of the various sports venues. These venues would be paid for out of the public purse but would pay back the economy many times over in jobs and resulting taxes flowing into the treasury. Most of the operating costs would be paid by private sponsors and would generate windfall profits in actual Games revenues. The resulting surplus would be tossed about like confetti for all to share. Hence, for British Columbians, it was all a "win-win" proposition. That most of this was not true will be addressed in the next chapter and later in the book.

The Bid Corp also began a very successful campaign to remove any potential opposition by the simple expedient of buying it off: Vancouver's bid would be socially aware, would aid the poor by creating job opportunities and social housing, would be the greenest Games ever and it would enhance First Nations financial dreams and showcase their culture. The arts community would have arts legacies and an "arts Olympics," their own chance to shine in the eyes of the world. The business sector and its chief cheerleader, the Vancouver Board of Trade, never exactly a hard sell, were promised a bigger convention center and a raft of goodies, including enhanced tourism. Organized labor got promises of unionized jobs raining down from the sky. Not that labor needed much of a push either, especially with the NDP solidly backing the scheme and bigwigs Georgetti and Tennessy on Concert Properties board of directors hammering any skeptical union members into line.

It looked like a slam dunk, at least from the perspective of community support, something the IOC claims to care about. Just to make it appear that it wasn't completely a cooked deal, the Bid Corp even arranged to have a tame opposition, a group calling itself the Impact of Olympics on Communities Coalition (IOCC). The IOCC had been the brainchild of Jim Green, one of the councilors of the opposition civic party, the Coalition of Progressive Electors (COPE). The IOCC looked in some ways like an opposition, and it made noises of concern like one. But, as we will see, it was another front, merely a means to divide any potentially honest opposition by creating the notion that this was a real-with-teeth watchdog organization, committed to the poor, willing and able to monitor all aspects of the Games and ensure that all the golden promises were kept. It was nothing of the sort, but it did its job well and, for a time, blunted the emergence of real opposition groups. And, when such groups finally arose, the IOCC would show its true colors and line up on the side of the Bid Corp.

All of this was still in the future.

CHAPTER 2

Saying No to 2010: The Fledgling Opposition to the 2010 Games

*Only those who want to see their hometowns bankrupted,
militarized and flattened should pine for the Olympic Games.*

DAVE ZIRIN, WELCOME TO THE TERRORDOME:
THE PAIN, POLITICS, AND PROMISE OF SPORTS

The Birth of Vancouver's Real Olympic Opposition

IT WAS IN THE early summer of 2002 on a long road trip home
from Kananaskis, Alberta, in a dusty white van that I got interested in Vancouver's Olympic bid for the 2010 Winter Games. The
initial bid had gone in to the IOC in the spring, but, like most people, I hadn't paid much attention. Now, in a discarded newspaper
in the back of the van, I saw a short story that the IOC would release
the 2010 short list of finalist cities at the end of August.[1] Opinion in
the van was mixed: "What's up with this Olympic shite?" combined
with "I think the games are cool." In fact we had no clue what sort of creature we were looking at. On one side, we — like most of those on the planet
with a TV — had the received version firmly locked into our brains by half a
century of cumulative saturation advertising: Hot young bodies doing incred-
ible athletic feats, peaceful competition, the brotherhood/sisterhood of hu-
mankind, good for the economy, an inspiration to youth...*ad nauseum.* Against
this wave of warm fuzzy images, we had only a nagging suspicion arising from
years working with the anti-globalization movement: When something is being sold so hard by the corporate media, watch out. Our second cautionary
thought also arose from our experience with the often bizarre political machinery of our home province of British Columbia: If both the main provincial
parties — the Liberals and the NDP — support the Vancouver Olympic bid,
if the two main Vancouver civic parties (NPA and COPE) do likewise, then

the Olympic Games must be like the cure for cancer and Mother Teresa all rolled up together, or...there was something else afoot. Perhaps we were just too damned suspicious and paranoid after too many years of breathing tear gas vapors; or perhaps we were missing something.

There was only one thing to do about it: Do some research and find out. It was relatively easy to find generally heart-warming information about the Olympics, much harder to distill facts from the endless hype and purple prose that seemed to clothe the Games like a toga. There were thousands of personal achievement stories about the Games on the Web, the "agony of defeat, the thrill of victory" kind of things about athletes who had won gold or those who saw medals slip away. The athlete stories had a uniform slickness, a well-rehearsed aura that seemed to emerge in waves during the bid period when all was still up in the air, during the pre-Games period when local enthusiasm was supposed to mount to a fever pitch and, naturally, during the running of the Olympics themselves. There were also a number of stories on the various financial and doping scandals that plague the Games time and time again. These too were slickly done, branding those deemed responsible for any malfeasance as bad apples, minor stains on an otherwise pristine enterprise, while at the same time managing to titillate the audience's need for scandal. No matter how egregious the scandals became, the personal stories of athletic prowess and determination always trumped any sleaze. Then there were the pro-business stories, the sort put out by local boards of trade, extolling the economic benefits accruing to cities that host the Games.

And yet, in the background of this onslaught of pro-Olympic verbiage, there were some real hard facts waiting to be uncovered. For example, there were a number of papers and articles by academics and journalists who had actually looked at the financial outcomes of hosting the Olympics and found the results wanting.

In Vancouver's bid alone, there were a number of fallacious assumptions and half-truths that were pretty obvious. First the Bid Corp's assertion that Vancouver's overall costs would be restricted to sports venues and operating costs was misleading: Apart from the historical observation that these always escalated, the Bid Corp had refused to acknowledge the infrastructure costs for the projects that were nevertheless essential to clinching the bid: among them, a new convention center, an expanded highway to Whistler and a light rail system, partially underground, to the airport. How could these be essential to Vancouver's bid yet not be Olympic costs? Although there was much semantic wrangling by the Bid Corp and the provincial government on this topic, insisting that "they were going to be built anyway," the simple questions to answer were these: Are these projects essential to the bid succeeding? Have the priorities or timelines of these projects been changed by the bid or the Olympics? If the answer to either of these questions was yes, then they were true Olympic costs and had to be recorded as such.[2] The Bid Corp and the government had also downplayed the usually massive security bills that other Olympic host cities had run up, especially post 9/11. As for the other economic arguments put forward, did the economy boom when the Games were awarded? Well, yes, there were construction jobs during the building period, but what happened afterwards? What, for example, was the difference between building a convention center or a hospital? The same jobs might be created by the infusion of government money into any infrastructure project, but the first created a structure to be used by a small segment of society, the other by many. What about dollars tricking into the economy and taxes flowing into the treasury? The same answer applied. Increased tourism? Actually, tourism traditionally experienced a "spike" during the actual events but then returned to the same level as before the bid.[3] Finally the argument that the actual Games revenues exceeded costs and generated a surplus was often simply not true. Weighed against the infrastructure costs, it was demonstrably not true. Finally there were some sobering stories about what usually happens to the poor and the environment.

It didn't take long for us to see the big picture: The IOC and the local Games organizers were selling dreams, not facts. Games critics — academics and investigative journalists — labored mightily to provide a solid base of countervailing facts and figures but were simply incapable of disconnecting the Olympic dreams in the minds of most of the citizenry from Olympic realities on the ground. Much of the public simply didn't seem to care that facts didn't match the glowing expectations and promises. It was simply surreal, as if there were two parallel Olympic worlds that never coincided. Indeed, these were very different worlds, not in the sense of geography, but rather as rhetorical domains: The dominant one belonged to the IOC and its coterie of camp followers, the bid cities' Games organizers, a compliant media, politicians of all stripes and, not least, the special business interests with the most to gain. In due course, the latter would literally own terrain, but to get there they needed to piggyback on the IOC's ownership of something more fundamental: the "frame."

Building the Olympic Frame

The frame of any debate is composed of the boundaries, the premises and assumptions, the very rules about how existing or alternative paradigms will be viewed and by which new information can be accepted or rejected. Numerous examples of frames can be drawn from politics; we need examine only a few to see how they dictate the nature of a debate before we consider the accepted frame for the Olympics. A current example of a highly successful frame, at least until recently, was brought forward by the United States government within minutes of the September 11 attacks: "Bin Laden and Al-Qaeda did it because they hate our rights and freedoms and are creatures of pure evil. You are with us, or with them." Whether you accept or reject the morality of the various wars that have ensued since 9/11, as long as you accept the frame, you are playing in their rhetorical ballpark. If you don't want to be fighting in Afghanistan or Iraq for all of the multiple reasons that these are immoral and unwinnable wars, you are still stuck if you accept the frame: Do you want the terrorists to win? The 9/11 Truth movement has attempted, recently with some success, to turn the frame, or at least to broaden it to include the notion that the US government was somehow culpable in the slaughter. Or consider a more successful frame shift from an earlier century: In January 1776 a largely unknown English advocate of American independence, Thomas Paine, published his revolutionary tract, *Common Sense*. Considerable American and British blood had already been shed in the preceding year at Lexington and Concord and more recently outside of Boston at the Battle of Bunker Hill.[4] The insurrection was already ugly enough, but the frame of the debate up to that point was about the innate rights of Englishmen, those in the American colonies in relation to those in England. Paine's *Common Sense* broke the frame by deconstructing the historical and legal basis of the British monarchy and forcing Americans to reconsider if they wanted to be part of such an illegitimate and corrupting enterprise. You are not fighting to be some kind of Englishman living under a mad monarch, Paine wrote, your blood has been shed to be something new, an independent nation based on a different concept of government. Up until this point, the number of Americans who supported outright independence likely wouldn't have filled an average-sized pub. After the publication of *Common Sense*, a solid proportion of Americans wanted nothing less. Paine had shifted the frame of the debate. Six months later, the Continental Congress declared independence.

With the notion of the frame in mind, let's turn back to the Olympics. The carefully constructed frame is that the Olympic Games from their inception thousands of years ago right up to the present day have been about the power of elite athletics to promote peace and understanding amongst the nations. As the official IOC history has it, wars stopped to allow athletes to travel to the Olympic Games in peace. Today the Olympics carry on this sacred task, unifying the world for 17 glorious days in a celebration of athletic perfection. On ice rinks and basketball courts, luge runs and swimming pools, the youth of the world come together in a magical land whose only language is the language of pure sport. Israelis and Arabs, Croats and Serbs, any and all of those who normally face each other across barbed wire and through gunsights, break bread together in the Athletes' Village. It is, admittedly, a beautiful image and even to some extent true. The official mantra that the redemptive power of the Olympics makes possible human interactions that otherwise would not occur, however, is simply incorrect.[5]

Correct or not, the Olympic frame as reinforced for over 100 years constrains any debate about the Games. The usual pro-Olympic argument goes something like this: "So what if the Games cost more than we said they would? So what if there was corruption by a few bad-apple officials or if some misguided athletes used banned drugs? Whatever the problems, the ideal remains pure. Or are you against sports for youth and a model of peaceful competition?" The failure to challenge the frame sets in motion the paradox that whatever arguments Olympics opponents muster about the numerous financial and ethical failings of the Games — from the IOC right down to the local bid committees and politicians — they are firmly stuck in rhetorical quicksand: The overriding goals of the Olympic movement take precedence over petty concerns about squandered money or environmental destruction each and every time. One environmentally focused group in West Vancouver relentlessly refused to make any statements that sounded even remotely anti-Olympic, utterly bought into the existing Olympic frame and fatally undercut any hopes they might have had of stopping the extinction of the environmental treasure of Eagleridge Bluffs. A negotiating position that began with "We're not against the Olympics, but we just want them to be the best/greenest they can be" was a recipe for self-imposed defeat and the destruction of the Bluffs. Indeed, this was precisely what happened, as we'll see later.

The framing of the Olympics as the Mother Teresa of global events is no accident: The IOC has assiduously built the frame over decades, using local organizing committees and a compliant media to sell it to the world's inhabitants. Each two years, at alternating Summer or Winter Games, the world gets its booster shot of saturation exposure. The official frame not only has the huge advantage of massive repetition, but also plays strongly into the basic human emotional response to spectacle and pageantry. Opening and closing ceremonies are classic examples of how the emotions of average people can be manipulated to create a bond between the audience and the Olympics. Athletes and spectators alike speak of being "transformed" by the Olympic experience, and no doubt they are totally sincere in the belief that the Games have changed their lives and that of their community, at least for the duration. One woman I know attended the Nordic Games in Eastern Canada years ago and still speaks about the experience with near mystical fervor. Much of this explains the often cult like response of Olympic boosters when faced with any opposition, no matter how mild, to the Games. For many of these people, economic and social facts are largely irrelevant, and the bad things that happen are virtually inconsequential to the overall sweep and majesty of the Olympic experience.

There is no particular novelty to any of this. Organized religion and the state have manipulated the same set of human emotions for millennia, and the Olympics merely capitalizes on the same psychological source.[6] The Nazis understood this perfectly in 1936. No doubt China's rulers do as well, and the Olympic spectacle they will put on in 2008 will have the same intent and likely outcome.

The Olympic frame was something I didn't understand very well back in 2002, and even though the reading I had done showed any potential gains from hosting the Games to be illusory, I was loathe, as were most of my emerging colleagues, to suggest any outright anti-Olympic sentiments. I also didn't understand very well the emotive power of the Olympic spectacle and why so many people I talked to would simply tune out any negative information. During the next year, reporters would often start their interviews with questions that asked what my problems were with Vancouver's bid, then would segue into, "You aren't against the Olympics themselves, are you?", their voices tinged with the potential horror of confronting a true heretic. Like so many others, I was not ready to read beyond the frame, not ready to take the leap into outright blasphemy and so dutifully said that, no, I wasn't against the Games *per se*, merely how they were being carried out. Those fighting to save Eagleridge Bluffs made the same mistake. For them, and for me, this was a fatal error. If I could go back in time, I would reverse my choice. It's Monday-morning quarterbacking to be sure, but a clearer denunciation of all things Olympic back when the opposition started might have done far more to stop Vancouver's 2010 Games than anything else that followed.

Scrolling back to the late summer of 2002, it all seems to have happened to a different person. I was still naïve, still uncertain about the frame and how hard to push, uncertain if anything I might say could have any impact on the emerging events. However, having done some research and now armed with some solid facts, I contacted the Canadian Broadcasting Company (CBC) about doing a radio commentary. By this time it was September and Vancouver was on the short list. My commentary, run at 7 AM, was only five minutes long and merely served to ask two questions: Are we being asked to pick up the tab for a losing financial project that can only benefit the developers? Are we just being taken for suckers? Both my answers were a clear "Yes."

The commentary didn't get much attention at first. It was just too early, most Vancouverites really had little idea that the machinery was already in motion under their feet, and the Bid Corp had already siphoned off any potential dissent by including members of the First Nations and poverty groups on their board of directors.

NO GAMES 2010

My friends and I, the core group from Kananaskis, had now formed a loose organization that we called NO GAMES 2010. What we'd do with this group, we didn't know. Whether we'd find allies, we also didn't know. In the fall, however, things were picking up politically, and the pros and cons of hosting Olympics were starting to be discussed. Admittedly, it was all within the usual frame, but at least there was discussion.

It was not long after this that I heard a CBC Radio interview with Jim Green, then a COPE city councilor and a founding member of the IOCC. For a man who claimed to represent a watchdog organization, his lack of skepticism about all things Olympic seemed rather profoundly disingenuous. Indeed he sounded more like a closet Games booster. Charlie Smith, then a lead writer at the *Georgia Straight*, had heard my CBC commentary and called to get my opinion of Green's comments. I said they sounded wishy-washy and were leading me to question the very nature of the IOCC as an opposition. I gave the name of our group as an alternative.

My comments as reported in the *Straight* caught the attention of Rafe Mair, then the host of a talk show on the local radio station CKNW. Mair, bearded and crusty, no-nonsense, unwilling to take tripe from anyone, had been a BC provincial government cabinet minister for a right-of-center party before becoming a radio celebrity.[7] Over the years he had built up a wide and devoted following, one that stayed with him each time a station got squeamish about the topics he raised for discussion and gave him the boot. Mair invited me to be on his morning show a few days later, a daunting prospect for the relative media novice I was at the time. Not only was I going out of town the weekend before and hence would have little time to prepare, the topic was the Olympics and why I was against Vancouver's bid. Mair's reputation left me with concerns that I would be roasted alive for being an idiot…and all in front of a live audience of tens of thousands of British Columbians. This was not the way I wanted an anti-Olympic opposition to start. I was so nervous, in fact, that I tried to pawn the interview off to my colleague Crimson from NO GAMES.

Alas, Crimson had to work that morning, so this left me as the sacrificial lamb. So there I was one bright Monday at 8 AM, ready for my encounter with Mair's razor-sharp scorn.

Mair opened with one of his characteristically typical spiels, in this case offering his opinion about the wisdom of hosting the Games, then launched into the costs of previous Games and the fact that if the Games came they would mess up the highway near his home in Lions Bay just north of West Vancouver. Mair, had in fact, made the key points I was going to raise: The costs would be astronomical and the disruption to peoples' lives not worth the bother. All I had to do was amplify Mair's comments with a few facts and figures before we were into commercial break. The commercials were followed by callers, most of them highly sympathetic to the notion that the Games were an extravagance that BC couldn't afford. This was, after all, still in 2002 when the provincial Liberal government was happily cutting schools and hospitals to balance the books. Half an hour later, I was out of the studio, unscathed and realizing that there might be some depth to the potential opposition. The key was to find it.

This interview did get heard, not only in Vancouver, but also across the province. I started to get calls, letters and e-mails from both bid backers and bid opponents. The reaction of the backers was pretty typical: What kind of moron would refuse the economic opportunity that hosting the Games offered? Didn't I know that the Games made bags of money? Why look at Calgary's success in 1988. What about the boom created by Expo in 1986? Didn't I want BC to come out of the economic slump left over by a decade under the fiscally incompetent NDP? These questions followed the trajectory laid out by the Bid Corp and the provincial and civic governments that were flogging the Games as an economic miracle in the making. Patiently, at least at first, I tried to reason with the bid backers: Study after study by respected academics showed that mega-sporting events, the Olympics in particular, made no overall profit for the jurisdiction that hosted them. The infrastructure costs alone were huge, security costs were growing by leaps and bounds with each successive Games, and there were shopping lists of hidden expenses. Any profit was solely during the actual running of the Games, that is, during the 17 days of actual competition. Then — and only then — if you subtracted Games profits from Games debits during this limited operating period, could the numbers come out in the black. Even so, they rarely did. I tried to point out that Enron-style accounting was far too common with Games financial projections in which organizing committees tried to off-load infrastructure costs to government while claiming financial benefits that could never be proven to be Games related. Some *Vancouver Sun* columnists, notably Vaughn Palmer and

Daphne Bramham, had already done the math and realized the likely financial "legacy" of any potential Vancouver Games was going to be a whopping
debt. The golden example of Calgary, so often tossed into the mix as the proof
of Olympic profitability, turned out to be anything but. Several years after the
1988 Winter Olympics, *Toronto Star* reporter Thomas Walkom had visited
Calgary to sift fact from fiction, and he had come away with a clear picture of
what had actually transpired: The Calgary Winter Olympic Games had cost
taxpayers close to $1 billion in extra costs, so the Games were not actually prof-
itable in total.[8] Indeed, much of the cost borne by taxpayers was for the infrastructure, over $451 million for luge runs and ski jumps, and so on, later sold
off to a private company for $1.

The notion so prevalent in Vancouver booster circles that Calgary had
made a bundle was, like so many things Olympic, an illusion. Most bid boosters simply refused to believe it or indeed to accept any countering figures put
forward by me or anyone else. The refusal to look at established facts was my
first introduction to an amazing facet of Olympic psychology: the almost cultlike adherence to official mythology: Calgary had declared the Games a fiscal
success, and hence it must be so. When I wouldn't give ground on Calgary, out
came Expo 86, Vancouver's earlier attempt to hype the city to the world. Hadn't
it put Vancouver on the map? Hadn't it made lots of money? Yes, maybe, but it
had also spurred some nasty uncontrolled growth, goosed the housing market
out of the range of many in the middle class and displaced a considerable number of the city's poorest and most desperate residents. Leaving aside the pros
and cons of such events, comparing the 6-month-long Expo to a 17-day party
was the logical equivalent of comparing gorillas and bananas: Sure, both live in
the jungle, but that's where the similarity ends.

Some boosters were not just the average "I love everything Olympic" types,
but solid businessmen, seemingly mystified that I couldn't — or wouldn't —
see the financial potential of the Games for Vancouver. One in particular, a
former University of British Columbia (UBC) member of the Board of Governors, Robert H. Lee, was particularly perturbed. Once he found out I was
on the faculty of his alma mater, his shock turned to something akin to outrage. Wouldn't I reconsider? Professors, after all, have an enviable reputation
with the general public, a public that to him was far too easily led astray. I tried
to call him back to explain my position but could never get past his switch-
board. It seemed he was a real estate baron with numerous projects in the past
at UBC…and potential ones in Whistler, the future venues for many Olympic events. He had also been a major business partner of Bid Corp Chairman
Jack Poole.

Some of the Vancouver boosters never went into the economic arguments: Either the value of the Games was too much a given to bother with or was sort of irrelevant to the big and overriding issue of civic and national pride. This was where the comments began to get nasty: Where was my pride in the city, the province, or the country? Maybe, I wasn't really a Canadian at all, certainly not a very patriotic one.

In contrast to the boosters, the opposition comprised a more diverse lot. A few opposed the bid out of the knowledge that the Olympics are a sham and the frame itself an illusion. Others, who might better be classified as a "soft opposition," were honestly confused about what the Olympics represented, yet wanted to believe the Olympic dream: They were skeptical about the involvement of the different levels of government and suspicious of the motives of the developers that seemed to be driving the bid, yet hopeful. Perhaps the largest fraction of opponents had very specific concerns with some aspect of the bid and wanted their particular issues dealt with before finally giving thumbs up or down. Environmental groups, including many members of the BC Green Party, fell into this category, as did some members of anti-poverty organizations. Lastly, a lot of people simply worried about the final bill and what it would really cost taxpayers when the Games had come and gone. Except for the small fraction that opposed the Olympics out of principle, most people drawn to the early opposition simply wanted the Games to be about what they claimed to be. In other words, the frame had to reflect reality. Regardless of the reason for opposing the bid, all of them wanted me to keep asking questions. NO GAMES 2010 had become the vehicle for their disquiet, and I had become their *de facto* spokesperson.

The most curious aspect of finding myself a spokesperson for disgruntled citizens was that some mysterious information started sliding into my e-mail inbox or slipping under my office door in brown envelopes. The first was from an environmentalist living in the Interior who was fighting a proposed ski resort slated for her area. In a story that would become common, the resort proponents hoped to piggyback on Olympic momentum to get government approval and maybe the cash to build the infrastructure. Somewhere during her attempts to block the resort, this woman had stumbled on an agreement between the Bid Corp and the Squamish and Lil'wat native bands. In payment for their support of the Games being held in their traditional territories, the bands would receive a cash payment and a cultural center. To me this was for all intents and purposes a bribe to bring about First Nations approval. I called the woman to verify the facts and found that her interpretation of this document was the same as mine. She didn't want to reveal where she had acquired the material, but wanted it made public. And the best way to do this, we agreed, was to release the material to the press.

I had begun to know some of the media in Vancouver and called one reporter I knew, Damian Inwood of the *Province*. Inwood, tall, stocky, very much the typical Brit in appearance and demeanor, was — and still is — unabashedly pro-Games. Indeed his stories would provide some of the most positive spin of any of those I saw over the next few years. Still, he had interviewed me briefly following the Rafe Mair show and had been friendly enough, if dismissive of the chances of the opposition to change the outcome. When I told him about the secret agreement, he wanted to see it. Pro-Games or not, payoffs were news, and the *Province* was interested. He did a telephone interview with me to get my reaction about what I thought the agreement meant, then arranged for a photo shoot to go with the story. The idea was that I'd hand a copy of the agreement to the *Province* photographer. The photo was duly taken in front of the Molson Brewery near Vancouver's Burrard Bridge, a site chosen because Molson had become one of the first corporate bid boosters. Molson's giant neon sign, visible to everyone crossing the bridge, urged Vancouverites to support the bid. I was still learning to play the media game and just wanted the story out. If this meant posing for a staged shot, I was ready to do so. A few days later, the story came out with a photo of me giving the Molson 2010 Bid sign a big thumbs-down. Officials of the two native bands in question reacted with predictable outrage at the suggestion that they had been bought off. They even sent representatives to a NO GAMES meeting to find out where we were going with the whole thing. The public reaction had also been swift: Most people were not all that happy with bribes being paid. A few *Province* readers weighed in with the race card: Just more damned "Indians" getting more handouts. While I was satisfied that we had given the Bid Corp a black eye, no one in our group wanted to give any impression that we were in any way anti-native, an impression that the Bid Corp would have been only too happy to exploit. NO GAMES issued a press release slamming the secrecy of the deal, while making it clear that we supported native aspirations. The message was not lost on many traditional members of the various bands, some of whom would become our strongest supporters and allies.

One of these was Rosalin Sam of the St'at'imc (pronounced Stat'lee'um) from a reserve near Mt. Currie, 45 minutes northeast of Whistler. Sam, a woman with a gentle open face and long dark hair, had been a traditionalist for most of her life. She believed that the correct path for her people was to conserve the land and animals and not try to mimic the development-at-all-costs frenzy so typical in white Canadian society. Her views were widespread amongst the St'at'imc, although both the Mt. Currie band and St'at'imc on other reserves certainly had enough people who felt the opposite way. Along with others, Sam had submitted a formal complaint to the IOC concerning their fears about the potential for harm to native land, culture and the environment that the Olympics would bring.[9] Their concern arose from their experience over the previous two years fighting a ski resort development within their territory. St'at'imc band members had blocked an old logging road to the east of Mt. Currie at a place they called Sutikalh (Melvin Creek on provincial maps). It was here that a former Canadian Olympic gold medal skier, Nancy Greene Raine, and her developer husband, Al Raine, hoped to build the new resort. The problems with this scheme in the traditionalist view was that these mountains and valleys were part of their historical territory, valuable both in a practical sense for the plants and wildlife they contained and in a spiritual sense as some of the last unspoiled wilderness of St'at'imc territory. The last thing Sutikalh and the St'at'imc needed was yet another resort for rich foreigners. Opposition within the St'at'imc grew and led to a blockade that the RCMP had tried and failed to break.[10] Arrests were made and the activists targeted for harassment, yet the blockade held and remains in place to this day.

With the Olympic bid now coming up for consideration, Sam's concerns were twofold. First, she worried about the spillover effect of a successful bid and the impetus it might give the proposed resort at Sutikalh. She was also concerned that the Callaghan Valley, part of St'at'imc traditional lands, would be destroyed by the proposed Nordic events and would later be gobbled up by developers. Her concerns were well founded. The Bid Corp's own projection for the area called for a four-season resort complete with golf courses and hotels.[11] For Sam and the other traditionalists, this was something to be avoided at all costs. During our first telephone conversation, she had made it clear to me that many band members had opposed the Games coming to their land. She related the story of how the Bid Corp had made a presentation to extol the notion, only to find at the question and answer period that most in the audience were opposed. This widespread opposition had not saved the Callaghan from the jaws of the Bid Corp, and Sam believed, as did I, that the money handed out to the band leaders had a lot to do with this outcome.

Not too long after I met Rosalin Sam, I found a message on my telephone giving me some information about the proposed development in the Callaghan Valley and how it ran afoul of a previous claim dating back to the 1980s. Some research uncovered a story about a mother-and-daughter team who had dreamed of making the Callaghan Valley a new ski mecca but who had seen a submission already accepted scrapped by Victoria bureaucrats who had other plans, plans that involved another collection of developers (for details, see chapter 9). Having talked to Rosalin Sam, I wasn't sure that the traditionalists would like the older Callaghan plan any more than VANOC's, but it led to a stunning revelation: Many of the bureaucrats involved in the earlier event were now actively working for the Bid Corp.

This was the part that got me thinking about the reality behind the Games: What Sutikalh/Melvin Creek and the Callaghan had in common was the obvious fact that some non-natives wanted native land for ski resorts and saw in the Olympics the means to get it. This wasn't about sports at all; it was, however, all about real estate, pure and simple. As we would later see, this pattern persisted in all aspects of the Vancouver Games: Whether in the mountains or in the city, real estate was the mystery ingredient. And the real estate connection was not only in Vancouver, but everywhere the Olympic machine had gone in the past and would go in the future.

NO GAMES 2010 had now demonstrated a public presence. Our ability to find "newsworthy" material and to push it out into the mainstream media made people realize that there was indeed an opposition, however fragmentary and unorganized it might be. And, we were about to get both more coverage and more supporters. All it would take would be a lawsuit.

Suing the Crown Corporations Behind the Bid

Another surprise phone call once again added to the NO GAMES campaign. This one was from a Vancouver lawyer, Larry Pierce. He wanted to meet with me and Chuck Gould, another fellow I hadn't met before. Gould — bookish, opinionated and sometimes abrupt — ran an advertising company in the nearby city of Surrey. His first words to me were memorable: "I guess your friends and you are a bunch of lefties and I'm more right wing than Attila the Hun, but we might have something in common about this Olympics crap." It turned out that Gould had smelled a rat in the Olympic hype, done his own homework and concluded that we were all being hosed. He had also discovered something I didn't know, namely that various Crown corporations, the BC Lottery, the Insurance Corporation of BC, the Pavilion Corporation (the agency responsible for provincial buildings and facilities) among them,[12] had been using their publicly derived money to back the bid. Gould had contacted Pierce to see if this was legal. Pierce clearly thought not and suggested a lawsuit against the Crown Corporations and the directors of the Bid Corp to force the latter to give the money back. I agreed and Pierce filed the suit in BC Provincial Court. The Bid Corp went into spin mode…and the press went wild.

We were soon on Rafe Mair's show again, this time pitted against John

Furlong, Poole's loyal sidekick, and Bid Corp CEO. Furlong, long, lanky with close-cropped blond hair going gray, was chosen because he was considered smooth — at least smoother than Poole. Now he was going ballistic when Gould tried to pin him down on all the free advertising the Bid Corp was getting from the mainstream media. Such advertising was costly, as Gould well knew from his own business, so his question to Furlong was this: What are you promising in return for the freebies? Furlong dodged on-air, turned beet-red, then at the commercial break threatened to come across the table separating us to punch Gould out. Unruffled, Gould merely adjusted the glasses that made him appear like a high-school guidance counselor and kept hammering away in his quiet way with more probing questions. Mair for his part simply laughed at the spectacle of an outraged Furlong threatening violence. When we went back to air, Furlong was still red-faced and fuming.

The NO GAMES 2010 Coalition

With the disclosure of the First Nations bribe and our lawsuit against the Crown corporations and the Bid Corp, NO GAMES had disrupted the carefully choreographed plan of the Bid Corp, and we had started to generate momentum. Various subgroups now wanted to ally with us. It was a diverse list. The group at Sutikalh with Rosalin Sam was one. Another was the Leaky Condo Coalition, a group who had been fighting for years for stronger government regulations and for compensation from developers who built shoddy condominiums. Their spokesperson, James Balderson, was a flamboyant character, well known to local media for colorful speeches that often descended into rants. Balderson and his group feared that a successful Vancouver bid without new regulations would simply create a building boom leading to future leaky — and moldy — condos as part of the real Olympic "legacies."

One outcome of all the media attention we had generated was that we were now joined by a social activist named Phil LeGood who agreed to take on a piece of what was becoming a major part of my daily life: spokesperson for NO GAMES. I hadn't known LeGood personally before this, but knew that his reputation as an Olympic opponent was solid. He had been on the radio damning the Games, and his arguments were always carefully covered by facts and a solid analysis of what the Games were actually about. LeGood, tall, sandy haired and fiercely articulate, was a commanding presence in public meetings. His history with COPE and as a union member brought him particular credibility with both groups, and his passionate denunciation of the bid often drew prolonged applause. He was to become a valued colleague and friend and one of the most powerful opponents of the bid. Back in 2002, however, he brought something else to the table: He had been in contact with the leader of the BC Green Party, Adriane Carr. She and her husband, the environmentalist Paul George, wanted to meet with us to discuss the Games and what position the BC Greens should take. I was happy to oblige.

The BC Greens Join the Coalition

LeGood and I met Carr and George at a restaurant near the University of British Columbia (UBC). Carr, a former college geography professor, looked like her televised pictures: a pleasant, middle-aged woman of medium height, a typical soccer mom, which, in fact, she really was. Carr had an incisive intelligence that was backed with a detailed knowledge of BC's quirky politics. The story she was to hear from us about the people behind the bid came as no surprise. George was a stocky bearlike man with a short, white beard and a shock of medium-length white hair. His ursine intensity frightened some people, but for us he was crucial: Carr relied on him as a sounding board and as a judge of people and positions. If George thought we were the real thing and worthy of support, Carr and the BC Greens would be willing to provide it.

As we sat down to dinner, Carr told us that the Greens were not sure where they wanted to be on the issue. Both she and George knew enough to be skeptical of the claims of the government and Bid Corp, but many Greens liked the Olympics out of general principle. Others saw joining the Olympic opposition as political suicide. Carr had taken the party to its highest ever showing in the 2000 provincial election, and some party strategists saw opposing the Games as a potentially fatal mistake. Carr, however, was — at least at that time — a risk taker and, as dinner progressed, warmed to the idea of joining the Coalition.

Having the Green Party come onside was going to be our first political endorsement, and it brought with it the potential for using the Green Party machinery to reach out to many more people. Unknown to the Greens at the time, it was also to prove one of their most astute political moves and gave them a real opposition status as the only political party to come out against the bid. We cemented the deal with a toast to the now linked fortunes of NO GAMES and the provincial Greens.

Civic Politics and the Bid

In the fall of 2002, a civic election was looming in Vancouver, and the opposition "left-wing" party, the Coalition of Progressive Electors (COPE), seemed poised to take over the city for the first time. COPE had been founded in 1968 by a coalition of left-wing activists, including legendary Vancouver radical Harry Rankin. Originally called the Committee of Progressive Electors, at its origin it had strong links to both organized labor and the provincial and federal NDP, thus providing a solid left-wing alternative to the center-right Non-Partisan Association (NPA) that had run Vancouver for decades. COPE drew the bulk of its support from working-class East Vancouver and, although they hadn't ever held power, had come close and continued to have some influence at city council.

For NO GAMES, this seemed too good to be true. The ruling NPA, a party of developers and the elite, were, to say the least, wildly in support of the bid. Bumping them from the roost seemed at best a long shot. Still, LeGood and I were convinced that if COPE came to power we could derail the bid completely. This was, however, before we began to understand the curious nature of what passes for left-wing politics in Vancouver and that COPE, just like the NPA, would be almost completely in bed with the bid organizers.

Many of the more progressive COPE candidates for city council at the time seemed likely to be sympathetic to the anti-Vancouver bid opposition or, at the least, willing to listen to the concerns of NO GAMES. These included new councilors Anne Roberts and Ellen Woodsworth. In addition, there were two previously elected councilors, Dr. Fred Bass and lawyer Tim Louis, both well known for their left-leaning positions on various issues. COPE was also running a number of young activists from the anti-globalization movement for positions on the school and parks board. Not all was roses, however. David Cadman had solid progressive credentials, but as we were later to discover, his ties to organized labor would make him a solid bid supporter. There was also Jim Green, long-time COPE politico and former mayoral candidate, who had made his reputation in activist circles as an anti-poverty campaigner. Others in the anti-poverty groups saw him as a "poverty pimp," using his position as advocate for the poor to advance his own agenda. Green had pretended to be neutral about Vancouver's Olympic bid but would turn out to be one of its strongest supporters. Finally, trying to be a broadly based coalition of the left of center, COPE was also fielding some very questionable progressives. One was Tim Stevenson, a recently defeated provincial NDP minister. Another was Raymond Louie, a relative unknown.

For those of us in NO GAMES, Jim Green had an additional reputation that concerned us: He had founded a group that billed itself as the Olympic watchdog, the Impact of Olympics on Community Coalition (IOCC). We didn't see that they were watching much of anything, particularly developers about to get rich off Olympic deals. NO Games labeled them the Olympic "watch poodles," perhaps in hindsight, an insult to poodles. As we'll see later, until almost five years after their founding, they wouldn't even utter a yip of protest.

Most curious of all was COPE's choice for their mayoral candidate, the political neophyte and former RCMP officer and Vancouver coroner, Larry Campbell. His work as coroner had spawned a popular television show. The dapper Campbell, silver hair combed straight back, was like everyone's favorite but slightly smarmy uncle. Snappy repartee and a taste for expensive suits had swayed a press corps that seemed prepared to love him.

Campbell had made a career of leverage, somehow sliding between jobs without really having any particular credentials that one would normally expect as essential. Why, for example, would a cop make a good coroner, or a coroner a good politician? Whatever Campbell lacked in job credentials however, he displayed a wealth of glibness and self-promotion as coroner and later in his neat segue into civic politics. In 2002 he had gone cruising the political circuit, offering his services to the various civic parties in the run up to the municipal election. Most had turned him down. COPE, however, saw an opportunity to rebrand themselves as something other than doctrinaire lefties and to capitalize on Campbell's notoriety as city coroner. The grassroots members of COPE may have been concerned by this choice, but party strategists saw in Campbell the means to attract the squishy center vote. The outcome of the election proved them right.

I had been in Edmonton, Alberta, the weekend of the civic election in November 2002. Hearing the news played out over the jubilant celebrations of COPE supporters, I was sure that the writing was on the wall for the bid. Mayor-elect Campbell stunned the Bid Corp by promising a citywide referendum on the Olympic bid, triggering an angry outburst from Jack Poole. On my return to Vancouver, some reporters found me to get my opinion about the sea change in Vancouver politics and what this boded for Vancouver's Olympic chances. I thought it meant they were dead in the water if there was an honest, binding referendum. Some of the reporters, notably Charlie Smith of the *Georgia Straight*, were more experienced than I in the curiously twisted nature of Vancouver's civic politics. Smith's reply to me was less than sanguine: Sit down, son; it's never quite so simple.

Smith and the others were quite right: It wasn't simple. It turned out that Campbell was offering a plebiscite, not a referendum. To many, this meant the same thing, but the two couldn't have been more distinct, a plebiscite being non-binding, essentially a public opinion poll. On top of this, most of the new city council, including the two NPA survivors, remained solidly in favor of the bid. The future fracture lines in COPE that would become a schism by 2005 were already present: Campbell, Stevenson, Louie, Cadman and Green instantly lined up with the pro-bid yes side. The other four COPE councilors

sat on the fence until near the end, finally, and we thought reluctantly, supporting the "no" side. Getting them to this position had taken Phil LeGood and me
many hours of patient explaining why the bid was a scam. Their opposition
in the end was at best lukewarm. In one meeting, they had told us that they'd
have to seek the guidance of those they considered to be the most able political
"strategists": elected members of the provincial and federal NDP. Considering
that the provincial NDP had been behind the bid from the beginning, this did
not bode well for a strong opposition position — and indeed none was forth-
coming.

Weird Political Groupings:
The Yes and No Sides Form Up

With most of the city councilors behind the bid and the city staff putting
up pro-bid banners on every available lamppost, we knew our work was cut
out for us to even the balance if we had any hopes of winning the plebiscite.
Making our lives more difficult was that we had three levels of government to
overcome: Not only was the city demonstrably not neutral about the bid, the
provincial government was an active booster. To top this off, the federal government was pimping for the bid as well by holding a series of public "education" events designed to persuade Vancouverites that they should vote yes.

Just as we in NO GAMES were beginning to realize that the bid was not
really about sports but real estate, we were also learning that in politics left
and right were not what they seemed to be. In interviews with Rafe Mair, I'd
frequently get asked the question, Why can't you lefties get it together. This
would have been a good question if the terms really meant anything then (or
now). As I was beginning to discover, "left" and "right" were meaningless titles
when describing the pro- and anti-bid groups. The pro-bid side consisted of
the supposedly left-of-center COPE leadership, the neo-conservative Liberal
provincials and the center-left federal Liberals. Big labor supported the bid
and would support the "yes" side in the plebiscite, taking its orders from the
union bosses and the NDP. Some anti-poverty groups had been co-opted onto
the pro-bid side by having at least one leader elevated to the Bid Corp's board
of directors.[13] Arts groups were mostly onside as well, having been promised
endless goodies including a cultural "Olympiad." First Nations leaders were
also officially supporters.

In opposition, there was a loose coalition of groups ranging from focus
groups like the Leaky Condo people, some in the anti-globalization community, the provincial Greens and some libertarian types who objected to the use
of taxpayer money for what was surely a corporate welfare scheme. A number

of union activists were clearly on the NO GAMES side, sensing something distinctly odd in organized labor's curious relationship with Jack Poole's Concert Properties and Gordon Campbell's Liberals, but their support was largely secret and taken with some risk. First Nations traditionalists were with us.

In conventional political spectrum terms, the groupings made little sense. To those of us in NO GAMES, it was a revelation that the parties were not what we thought they were, rather only flags of convenience: Those on the side of the developers — if not their payroll — were for the Games. Those who thought we were going to get screwed were against. Charlie Smith had his own theory: "It seems that the difference is one of shoes: Those with nicely polished shoes are in favor of the bid; those with scruffy shoes, against." Whatever the real reason, it clearly was not a simple left–right thing because when it came to this issue the left–right thing broke down completely. This raised the question in our minds of whether traditional political grouping meant anything anymore? Our answer then was that they didn't, a conclusion not altered since then by other strange political events.[14]

What made it all so damned weird for us in the opposition was that individuals and groups that really should have seen through the Olympic hype instead found themselves divided, confused by the frame of the argument and by the position of their official and unofficial "leaders." That many of the latter had a vested interest in the outcome seems to never have entered the brains of many people who normally would have found it more than passing strange to find "progressive" Vancouver Mayor Larry Campbell and "conservative" Liberal Premier Gordon Campbell on the same side. Somehow, for many so-called progressives, this was not nearly as strange as the official pedigrees of NO GAMES supporters — that is, were we pro-NPD enough to support. These divisions in the end created the conditions for what can only be described as a self-imposed defeat. It was not that the left in BC was unused to defeat, just particularly odd that they didn't recognize it when it came barreling down the pike toward them once again.

When Politics Get Really Weird

What had started as a simple anti-globalization exercise had become a "red pill" excursion down the bizarre rabbit hole of BC's politics. It was more than weird enough for my tastes already, but the universe obviously thought I needed more lessons in the strange and unusual. About midway through the plebiscite campaign, I started to get late-night phone calls from a mystery man. The first had come one night when I was still out at a NO GAMES meeting. My partner had taken the call from a man who refused to identify himself, except to say that he had some information I would be interested in. By now I was used to secret sources, so this was nothing particularly unusual. A few nights later, he called back, claiming to have information about the forces backing the bid. He knew this because he used to work with the developers and tame politicians, including Premier Gordon Campbell. The story he spun seemed quite credible and reinforced the emerging view I had that the official political groupings and public perception of the same had nothing to do with political reality. The Olympics had never been a left–right thing in Vancouver: It was all about the special interests, and these special interests could — and would — fly flags of the left or right at will. Their loyalty, however, was not to the flag, rather to the cabal of developers who had run BC politics for generations. Added to the mix was a relative newcomer, the Hong Kong billionaire Li Ka Shing and his numerous business partners in Vancouver. The source claimed to fear for his life because of what he was telling me. Over the next weeks he would provide me material at secret drop-offs, in one case to a newspaper box with documents hidden under local real estate ads. I was innately suspicious, but what the source told me made sense and checked out. In the end, I got to meet him in person and discovered that his brother had been one of the original Bid Society directors and a man who had wielded considerable official influence at the university where I worked. This last caused me considerable concern as an associate professor soon up for promotion. In the NO GAMES group, I was now the principal spokesperson; the University was firmly pro-bid having been promised a new hockey rink for free.[15] A former UBC member of the Board of Governors was a top real estate developer; UBC's new chancellor, Allan McEachern, served as the Bid Corp's ethics commissioner; and Larry Bell of the Bid Corp Board of Directors was the Chairman of UBC's Board of Governors. The possibility for a serious career misstep seemed very real.

It was to get even stranger and more surreal: The source, although bang on about the people and events behind the Games bid, had his own agenda: He was a con man looking for his main chance. At first his help to me and to NO GAMES stemmed from a basic motive of revenge: He had fallen out with his brother and the latter's developer friends and wanted to get even. Telling me about the secret brotherhood of developers was one way to do so since he knew I could get the stories out to the media. At the same time, having a grateful UBC professor as a friend might just pay off financially. It didn't, but the outcome highlighted yet another feature of the Olympics: Everyone involved in promoting the Olympics is in it for something, the gold, the main chance, whatever; it's never as it seems, never just about sports and peace. In the end, there is the dream of dollar signs at the end of every Olympic rainbow.

CHAPTER 3

"Our Time to Shine"

*Everything we have been told about the Olympic legacy turns
out to be bunkum. The Games are supposed to encourage us
to play sport; they are meant to produce resounding economic
benefits and to help the poor and needy. It's all untrue.
As the evictions in London begin [for the 2012 Summer
Games], a new report shows that the only certain Olympic
legacy is a transfer of wealth from the poor to the rich.*

GEORGE MONBIOT,
"THE OLYMPIC GAMES MYTHS BUSTED," MONBIOT.COM

Real Estate
and Olympic Bids

OLYMPIC BIDS, as we've seen, are constructed by and for real
estate developers. Virtually every bid of the last 25 years,
likely longer, has had a major development project at its core. With
the Summer Games, the projects are usually in the inner cities, usually in areas developers have been eyeing for some time. This was true
in Barcelona (1992), Atlanta (1996), Sydney (2000), Athens (2004) and is
abundantly true in Beijing where the total reshaping of the city for the 2008
Games has displaced up to 2 million people.[1] London in the run up to the 2012
Games will be no different, with a chunk of East London being morphed into
a new ritzy yuppie haven to be called Stratford City. One can even see the potential developments in cities whose bids "failed." Toronto failed twice in its
bids for 1996 and 2008, but developers still eye the harbor waterfront and keep
waiting for their chance. In New York's bid for 2012 it was the Hell's Kitchen
district that was due for the wrecking ball with upscale apartments to follow.
Winter Games may have a city component — Vancouver's does, as we will see
later — but the usual thrust is on ski resort development: Nagano (1994), Salt

Lake City (2002), Torino (2006)[2] and now Vancouver for 2010 all followed the same pattern. (The forests that will fall in Sochi, Russia, for the 2014 Games will be discussed in the epilogue). The rule of thumb for evaluating any Olympic bid is to ask what land is up for grabs, land that just might need the extra boost that taxpayer acquiescence and dollars can help put on the market.

The process usually starts at the local level with a few good old-boy developers schmoozing local politicians to get the ball rolling. After that, it's all about leverage. Developers and their friends get a few city officials onside, then go after those higher up the food chain in state or provincial politics before signing on national level politicians. Each level needs the next for more funding since the Games are ferociously expensive to produce. City councils are asked to provide not only active support but usually land, if not also cash. The big money comes in at the state/province level since it is here that the expenses will really blossom for mega-sized infrastructure projects and, crucially, for security. In regard to infrastructure, roads will have to be built, subways constructed and airports and ports expanded. Most of all, someone has to be willing to sign on the dotted line for any cost overruns. The national level support may not kick in initially if there are several cities in one country vying for the same Games. However, once the national Olympic committee has chosen the city they will support, the push for funds moves to the national government as bid organizers seek promises to pony up the remainder of the funding. Helen Lenskyj's studies on the Sydney and Atlanta bids are perfect examples of how all bids are basically identical in origin, structure and promotion.[3]

Vancouver's bid followed the classic model, all the steps outlined above following in sequence. As we've seen, it all began with local developers who, along with a director from Jack Poole's Concert Properties, created the Vancouver-Whistler 2010 Bid Society. The provincial government kicked in $50,000 to help out while the Society continued to leverage like mad. Once the Canadian Olympic Committee had chosen Vancouver, the federal government came onside, and with this, all the ducks were in a row for a run at 2010. All one really has to do is change the place names, and Vancouver's bid sounds exactly like earlier and later ones.

From Bid Society to Bid Corp

Vancouver's bid between 2000 and the summer of 2002 was unremarkable in most respects. Very few Vancouverites seemed aware that their city was even in the running; fewer still seemed to care much one way or the other whether it won or lost. The response in the rest of the province ranged from lukewarm to outright hostile, the latter from people quite rightly suspecting that the Olympics would do nothing at all for their regions, or worse, might even suck up money needed for local schools and hospitals. Which of course, it ultimately did.

The Vancouver-Whistler 2010 Olympic Bid Society quietly evaporated before the Province could de-list them for failing to file any financial reports during their entire existence. By 1999 the replacement organization, the Vancouver-Whistler 2010 Olympic Bid Corporation, was in place and ready to roll. As documented in the previous chapter, the organization's board of directors was a virtual shopping list of BC's developer elite. It also had the requisite key political figures, some former Olympic athletes tossed into the mix to give it a measure of sports credibility and some individuals whose potential contribution was unclear. Of the latter, the inclusion of the daughter of Canada's Prime Minister was particularly unusual and therefore notable.

The Vancouver Bid Corp had a war chest of some $34 million as they came out of the gate in the summer of 2002, most of this contributed by the Province of British Columbia. The Bid Corp also had considerable in-kind contributions from the City of Vancouver, the federal government and the private sector. Each level was not only supposed to kick in financial or material support, it was also supposed to actively contribute to the selling of the bid to the citizenry and, more crucially, to the IOC. The first signs of this in Vancouver were the suddenly ubiquitous "I'm backing the Bid" bumper stickers and buttons. "It's our time to shine" bumper stickers came in a close second. The federal government hosted a Canadian culture festival at Granville Island, a popular tourist spot in the center of Vancouver, and just happened to have on hand a number of hired boosters to pass out bumper stickers and buttons extolling the bid. The City of Vancouver donated considerable staff time behind the scenes and plastered lampposts with flags of Olympic symbols and sports. So far, it was all the pretty standard type of Olympic buzz and one that the IOC would read as popular support when they came to visit.

All candidate bid organizations have to file an application with the IOC along with a non-refundable payment of $150,000. Usually, there are half a dozen or more cities in the running at this time, although only a few of them will actually have the juice — or grease — to make it to the next stage. As detailed by British investigative journalist Andrew Jennings[4] throughout the entire process of initial bid to final decision, the IOC shamelessly eggs cities on, flattering each for their unique culture and environment, encouraging those falling behind to try harder, hinting incessantly that each city really, really has a good chance to win the gold if they will only do a tiny bit more, make that extra effort to make their bid the "best ever."·

Reading Jennings's books and being a veteran of the opposition to Vancouver's bid, I couldn't help but think that perhaps the IOC is helping in even more direct ways. Somewhere in Lausanne, I suspect there is the equivalent of "Bidding on the Olympic Games for Dummies," in which the IOC lays out suggestions for how to run a bid, how to deal with the press, how to talk to politicians, what to say to jittery citizens and how to undercut any opposition. Whether or not such information exists in written form, the corporate knowledge certainly does, and it is reinforced by the frequent visits of IOC officials to every shortlisted city in the months leading to the final choice. Organizers in each bid city also study past successes and failures in great detail.

It clearly serves the IOC well to have multiple cities in the running: Every city is paying the IOC for the privilege, and it would hardly serve its bank account to have too few competing, in other words to have a repeat of the bid for the 1984 Summer Games when Los Angeles was the only city in the race. LA's single-city phenomenon also put the IOC in a bind since part of their leverage to get extra goodies for themselves lies in playing off one city against another. LA was in a vastly stronger bargaining position when it came down to negotiating the crucial legal agreement with the IOC, the so-called Host City Agreement.

But this was a fluke: The IOC typically has multiple candidate cities chomping at the bit in the race for the Games. Eventually, however, the IOC has to begin the process of shortlisting the cities, eliminating about half. For the survivors, the pressure now really begins to build. It's also at this point that some of the citizenry begin asking impertinent questions about the economics of it all, and the IOC and local bid organizations trot out their standard rejoinder, "If the Games weren't great for a city in all ways, why would cities be lining up to bid on them?" It's a neat rhetorical trick and a perfectly circular one to boot. Yes, cities do line up to bid for the Games, although not as many as in years past, given the staggering overall costs of recent Games. The reason cities bid on the Games is not because they generate money for local government or community — they don't — but because they generate fabulous real estate development opportunities. Since, invariably, bidding cities are controlled by city councils chock full of current or former real estate developers, the motivation to bring on the Games is apparent. And, it usually turns out that some of these same folks just happen to have pet projects in mind.

The costs go way, way up once a city is shortlisted. To go on to the next round, it has to cough up $500,000 as an entry fee for the IOC. Why the cost is so high and what the IOC does with the money exactly is unclear, but this fee eats a considerable part of any bid city's budget. Much of the rest goes into two crucial items: First, to produce a slick "Bid Book" designed to persuade the IOC that their city, "X," is the best. Direct financial incentives to IOC members are also common "expenses," as we will see in chapter 6. Second, an advertising blitz becomes a "must have" item in order to convince the locals that they really, really want to host the Games. The IOC claims to monitor public opinion and the level of support for the bid, and indeed it is likely that they do, but not quite the way one might expect. Carefully constructed polls of highly selected target audiences are designed to give a desired result. Such opinion poll manipulation was obvious in Vancouver's bid: City residents who had been promised all the benefits but no financial pain seemed to show support. Canadians in general who had no clue what it was likely to cost them also were supportive. Curiously, most Bid Corp and BC government polls religiously stayed away from the rest of British Columbia, especially the Interior whose citizens were being clobbered by cutbacks in government services and watching in shock as hospitals and schools were closed in their communities.

The IOC knows the polling game well and is not unduly worried about early soft support for the Games. What they are worried about is potential embarrassment if an overtly hostile opposition exists. Berlin's opposition groups successfully created a sense of fear in IOC hearts by threatening direct action before and during the Games and by actually carrying out minor sabotage of IOC vehicles during the bid period. The combination of radical theory and practice were likely contributing factors that doomed Berlin's bid. Similarly, the strong opposition mounted by Bread Not Circuses in Toronto certainly made their city seem a poor choice from the IOC's vantage point.

The Continuing Opposition to Vancouver 2010

Up to the fall of 2002, there had been little real opposition to the Bid Corp. The pretend opposition, the IOCC, had managed to create the impression that they were on the ball and watching out for everyone. NO GAMES was still in its infancy and no real threat, although some of our actions were starting to put us on the map. I continued to act as NO GAMES spokesperson, occasionally in demand on talk shows and for media interviews. I even received several media names: Rafe Mair of the radio station CKNW dubbed me the "Olympic Sourpuss"; his successors nicknamed me "Dr. No." NO GAMES continued to put out fact sheets on the bid examining the myths and realities that preceded and followed each Games. We held parties at which we made anti-2010 buttons and worked on designs for bumper stickers and leaflets.[5] It was all pretty low-key, and the presence of an opposition to the bid remained largely unknown to many Vancouverites.

The nicknames I got during this period were mostly meant in good humor by the radio talk-show hosts but underneath lay a theme that was prevalent in the pro-bid camp: Those opposed to the Games were simply a bunch of anti-fun naysayers. Didn't we realize what a great party the Olympics would be? We answered with this analogy: Let's say you're a parent, but instead of making sure your kids are fed, clothed, see the doctor when necessary and get to school on time, you spend all your time partying with your buddies, totally neglecting your children in the process. Are you a good parent or a bad one? Clearly the latter, right? The Ministry of Children and Family Development will take your kids away faster than you can say "I'm backing the Bid," and rightly so. Now, let's up the scale. Your government decides it's more important to host a 17-day party than take care of the needy, the homeless and the dispossessed. Is this the action of a responsible or a corrupt and/or thoughtless government in thrall to special interests? In the view of NO GAMES, the clear answer was the latter. To us it seemed simple: No one is saying that there shouldn't ever be a party, just that individual and social responsibilities had to be met *before* the party began. In later chapters, the cumulative impact of Olympic partying versus other social priorities will be discussed in detail.

The Plebiscite Campaign

The obscurity of NO GAMES 2010 changed abruptly with the bombshell of November 2002: In the Vancouver civic election, the long-ruling NPA was booted out and the left-leaning COPE was in. Worse, Vancouver's new COPE mayor, Larry Campbell, announced the City would call a referendum to let Vancouverites decide if they wanted the Games or not, a move that triggered a significant sea change in the Olympic debate.

The call for a referendum sent the Bid Corp and Jack Poole into a frenzied combination of panic and bluster. Poole went on record threatening that Vancouver could get sued by the Canadian Olympic Committee if the vote went sideways, that is, if voters freely rejected the bid. This was nonsense since other cities had dropped out of bids before without consequence: Denver had *won* the bid for the 1976 Games, but fell victim to a referendum in Colorado two years *afterwards* and dropped out of hosting the Games. The IOC passed the Games to Innsbruck without batting an eye;[6] Bern had dropped out of the 2010 competition following a referendum in the Canton of Bern, again with no fallout from the IOC or national Olympic committee.

Poole's comments got some people's backs up, but the new COPE majority didn't want a fight and quickly began backpedaling. In fact, Campbell and much of the COPE leadership didn't want a negative outcome at all. What they wanted was *an illusion* of choice followed by the outcome they had in mind. In no time, the referendum, defined as a legally binding vote on a single question by the electorate, was recrafted as a "plebiscite." A referendum is a dangerous option if you want a predictable outcome. A plebiscite in contrast is a "public expression of community's opinion, with or without binding force."[7] Since the last thing that either the Bid Corp or Larry Campbell wanted to risk was a wrong choice by Vancouverites (and only they got to vote), a referendum was out, the plebiscite was in. And it was to be non-binding, in essence an opinion poll. Watching City Council members, in particular Fred Bass, trying to massage the definitions was eerily reminiscent of Bill Clinton's prevarications about sex. We at NO GAMES were aware that the City and IOC were free to ignore the outcome if we won…and likely would, not that our chances of winning were all that good. Yet not contesting it would give the Bid Corp a free ride. Thus, for good or ill, the die was cast and we launched into the No campaign with whatever meager resources we could scrounge.

Poole and the Bid Corp put their least threatening faces forward, using CEO John Furlong as the official spokesman. At the same time, Poole brought in his colleague and Concert's CEO, David Podmore, a short, stocky, middle-aged man who sported dyed white-blond heavily gelled hair as the official head of the Yes committee. Maybe the notion was that Podmore's mod look would appeal to youth voters who might otherwise be turned off by a buttoned-down sort of guy.

The playing field had never been level; now it was tilted at 90 degrees. The Bid Corp had $34 million in the bank, most of it public money to be used as necessary to convince the same public that it was a good idea to host the Games. They had three levels of government actively working on their behalf, all actively contributing staff time and likely move direct and indirect funding as well. The press was not only pumping out stories with a positive spin, but it was donating free advertising to boot. Most active of all was the new mayor, Larry Campbell, who fell into his role as Olympic booster with gusto. His flagrant support of the bid was clearly a key factor helping to convince Vancouverites that it really was a great idea that wouldn't cost them "one penny." The city put up banners and provided endless staff time to help the Yes campaign. The full extent of the behind-the-scenes contributions has never been revealed.

Not only were all levels of government firmly onside with the bid, even the main opposition parties helped out. The corporate media bombarded Vancouverites and British Columbians endlessly with editorials and glowing testimonials from past Olympic cities. The Bid Corp signed up celebrities like Rick Hanson to pump for the Games. Rock bands sang the praises of the bid, and former Olympians, some of them getting on in years, were trotted out to emphasize the legacy of Olympic sports for youth. The Yes team even brought out former NDP Premier Mike Harcourt who had resigned in disgrace in 1996 after a NDP fundraising scandal was revealed. A few months prior to joining the bid team, Harcourt had taken a bad fall and was now in a wheelchair. Getting him to show up now to cheerlead for the bid was cheesy in the extreme, but it worked to gain support. Organized labor was largely on the Yes side for reasons that can be summed up by few simple considerations: union pension funds bucking up Concert Properties, the fact that the NDP had allowed this whole scam to get going in the first place and the dangled carrot of lots of unionized jobs. The pro-bid message, hammered home with each TV or radio ad, every newspaper editorial, each promotion by a celebrity was this: The Olympic Games are the embodiment of human cooperation, they won't cost us a penny (and they will make us rich)…and we really can't understand why a few naysayers are against this remarkable event. Just how many pennies it will end up costing the City of Vancouver and the Province we will see in a later chapter.

The "Bid Book" that came out in the fall of 2002 was the usual collection of Olympic platitudes, a description of the venues and, crucially, some promises the Bid Corp made to Vancouverites and British Columbians. The first of these promises was of financial accountability: Not only would the Games cost exactly what they said now, but the process would be fully transparent. A second promise was for social "inclusivity," meaning that Vancouver's poor would not bear the brunt of the Games through evictions or rent increase. Finally, the Bid Corp, mirroring the IOC's own "third pillar of Olympism," were suggesting the Games would be "environmentally sustainable," whatever that term was supposed to mean.[8] They made much of these promises and likely swayed numerous votes their way during the plebiscite battle.

The Bid Corp began churning out bumper stickers ("I'm backing the Bid" and "It's our time to shine") by the tens of thousands and handing out buttons, lapel pins and banners to anyone who would take them. The Bid Corp's official watchdog, IOCC, was also pumping for the bid in spite of being officially neutral, often sharing the same side of the stage with the Bid Corp during some of the debates between bid supporters and opponents.

We on the naysayer side were running on financial empty, trying to get our messages out through a few meager buttons and bumper stickers ("Healthcare before Olympics" and "If you're backing the Bid, you're spending my money, so back off") and scrambling to go wherever and whenever the media invited us. As a coalition of organizations with varied interests and reasons to oppose the Games, we had a tough time sticking to a simple message. The end result was that the emerging message was necessarily diffuse and our limited financial resources were spread too thinly to keep the message in public view. During the campaign we spent maybe $1,500 against at least a million by the Bid Corp, not counting the millions more of in-kind contributions they received from all levels of government and from the private sector. We did have some in-kind contributions from various union members acting on the sly, but this could never compensate for official union support for the Yes team. On top of this, the coalition really only had three spokespersons able to get in front of the media on a moment's notice: me, Phil LeGood of NO GAMES and Adriane Carr of the provincial Green Party.

The consequence of this tilted field was that we were literally run off our feet. I've never asked how the others handled it, but my life had become absolute hell on wheels: Not only did I have my demanding day job with my lab and teaching, but my partner was pregnant, and I was taking a high-level army reserve staff course that alone consumed dozens of hours per week. My typical routine was: Get to my office by 8 am, deal with crucial administrative laboratory issues; talk to the press for part of the day, all the while scratching out time to run the lab and do my teaching. The consequence was that I was rarely on my way back home until 8 or 9 at night, and that was only if there weren't any NO GAMES meetings scheduled. After household chores, there was reading for my army course, followed by preparations for media releases and NO GAMES planning until the wee hours. The next day this would all be repeated. The campaign went on from mid November 2002 until February 22, 2003. After one appearance on Vaughn Palmer's *Voice of BC* show up against David Podmore, a reporter for a community newspaper noted that I looked tired and drawn. No doubt I did.

In spite of being tired, we all felt we were having an impact. Perhaps one way to measure this was that the tenor of some Yes supporters began to wander into direct attacks on the patriotism of the No side, with me as the key whipping boy. An incident that stands out was when the CEO of the ski hill at Grouse Mountain send out a chain e-mail to all his contacts naming me as a prominent "American anti-globalization activist" out to derail BC's chances for 2010. The clear implication was that I was some sort of "Black Block" member, as likely to throw a Molotov cocktail as not, and an unpatriotic foreigner to boot. This e-mail touched off a series of nasty incidents. On three occasions during the plebiscite campaign, letters arrived at my home address with notes that said, "This is what you will get," swastikas drawn below the words. The not-so-veiled message: "We know where you and your family live," the swastikas an obvious message about my Jewish family background.

The threats and innuendo did not stop when the Yes side won the plebiscite, but actually increased as the IOC's decision in Prague loomed. One driver saw the NO GAMES bumper stickers on my car, drove alongside me, seemed to recognize me, then got right on my bumper and tailgated me for kilometers. When I pulled over to let him pass, he stopped too, waited for me to resume driving, then got back within feet of my bumper and followed me all the way home. The host of a Vancouver radio sports show threatened to beat me up if Vancouver lost the bid, and anonymous threats were e-mailed to me daily.

The debates during the plebiscite were particularly revealing, not only for the absurd bias shown by the media in setting them up so that the balance was completely skewed in favor of the Yes side, but by the way they were framed by the backdrops. In one Canada-wide broadcast on the Canadian Broadcasting Corporation (CBC), not only was it a 5:1 ratio of Yes versus No advocates with me in the lone spoiler role, but CBC put in endless clips in the background of happy athletes going for gold. CBC would claim that this was because the subject was the Olympics, and hence showing pictures of athletes was completely appropriate, but from our view at NO GAMES, this was subliminal advertising at its worst (or best, depending on which side you're on). Our more-sarcastic supporters wondered why CBC didn't show a dark hole with money being dumped into it if they needed a realistic backdrop to show what the Games were really about.

By the end of the campaign, the Yes side had spent their million plus to give Vancouverites the full glory of saturation advertising. The outcome should never have been in question, but deep inside the Bid Corp and City Hall there must have been a few souls who thought that some extra insurance would be wise. The City had installed Global Election Systems' AccuVote voting machines in 1996, and they would be used in the plebiscite. Global was later bought out by the infamous Diebold Election Systems. The plebiscite was 21 months before the use of Diebold machines would cast a long shadow over the outcome of the 2004 US presidential election. And as with the machines in 2004, although diagnostics were run on the Global machines, there was no way to check if a vote-stealing virus could have been inserted by means of the memory card.[9] In addition, although Vancouver's official protocols called for the ballots to be manually counted to ensure that the number cast matched with the number recorded on the printout tape, no such count was apparently made to see if the final tallies matched.[10]

During the early voting and on plebiscite day, companies that were enthusiastic bid supporters bused their workers to the polling stations. Pro-bid politicians worked to get their supporters out. The media ran pro-bid editorials.

On the night the results of the plebiscite were to be announced, the venues chosen for the post-results party typified just how different the two sides were. The Yes side had rented the ballroom of a fancy downtown Vancouver waterfront hotel. We in the No Games Coalition had taken over an upstairs room at a pizzeria in Vancouver's Gastown district.

On February 22, after anxiously waiting for hours, the polls closed, and by 8 PM, the results were in: The Yes side had won with 63.4%; No trailed with 36.6%. The number of those voting was higher than in previous city votes, approximately 40% of Vancouver's eligible voters. This outcome was later touted as a resounding victory for the bid and the interest it had generated. We noted, however, that it merely asked an opinion of 12% of all BC voters (Vancouverites), and of this, only about 45% cared to express one. The Yes side's supposedly vast sweep thus only represented 3% of BC voters, yet all British Columbians were going to pay for the Games. We pointed this out and called for a binding, province-wide referendum on a clear question. For the media, however, it was over: They were off to cover the victory celebrations, filming ecstatic Bid Corp boosters back-slapping Jack Poole, while David Podmore, Jim Green and the Campbell twins (Mayor Larry and Premier Gordon) exchanged bear hugs and high-fives.

For those of us on the No side watching the spectacle on television from a few blocks away, the Yes side celebration typified all that the Games had come to symbolize: Big corporations, big real estate interests and big labor, all in bed together and preparing to ride the Olympic gravy train at the expense of average British Columbians.

Later, as we scrutinized the voting patterns of the different ridings, we noted how odd it was that so many voters in East Vancouver had gone for the Yes side. Well, it could have been the influence of Jim Green and his COPE faction. Then again, in hindsight, it might have been less the ham-handed bonhomie of Mr. Green than the magic of electronic voting. We couldn't prove it then, we can't now, but the thought lingers that maybe, just maybe, some of the happy dancing folks at the Yes party had made very sure that they'd have an outcome to celebrate. For sure there were some funny things afoot during the plebiscite campaign. One of the No supporters would later write me the following:

I did some postering leading up to the plebiscite on whether people were in favor of holding the Winter Olympics in Vancouver to be held on February 22, 2003. I was the only one doing this in Kitsilano, putting up a very simple "Vote No to the Olympics" poster. Being a one-person operation, I just did it using the method that would be the fastest and easiest, stapling them (the posters) to telephone poles. I then took a walk around the next day and was shocked to find not one poster still up, somebody had done a clean sweep of the 150 or so I'd posted. There were other posters up, mostly business oriented, but also many for an upcoming peace march, but none of these were touched, only mine. I remembered thinking that the people who wanted a Yes vote were very well organized indeed. It was a very smooth, clinical operation, all my efforts erased, like they'd never been done at all, but leaving everything else intact. They'd "neutron bombed" me.

I went to Henry Hudson Elementary School on the day of the plebiscite, and when I finished marking my voting card, I went and stood in line to hand it to the man inserting them into the voting machine. I was giving it to him when he told me that it was upside down, and I had to hand it to him the other way up. Then he said very loudly, seemingly for the benefit of the people around us and standing in line behind me, "I don't have to see how many times you voted YES." This was the person actually putting the voting cards in the machine, loudly and unashamedly shilling for the YES vote right in the polling station. I'd never seen anything like that, and I haven't since. It was shocking.[11]

With the plebiscite over and "won" by the Bid Corp, the opposition was expected to accept the "will of the people" and fade away. In many cases, bid boosters actually went further, demanding that opponents now "get onside" with the winners and join them in supporting the bid, an attitude that reinforced the cultlike nature of all Olympic bids. Any failure to do so was going to be seen as highly unpatriotic and, it was darkly hinted, would "have consequences." The Vancouver City councilors who had voted No promptly switched over to the bid camp, in the process abandoning the 36.6% of those who had opposed the Games in Vancouver, not to mention all those in opposition across the province.

The NO GAMES Coalition refused to kowtow to these demands. The plebiscite had been deliberately chosen to be non-binding, had disenfranchised 88% of the population who would ultimately pay for the Games if Vancouver won, and had been won not by facts or reason, but by the financial power of the Bid Corp and three levels of government. We didn't see any reason to cease educating people about Vancouver's bid or to stop trying to derail it. There were still many months to go before the IOC's final decision in Prague, and a lot could still happen. We weren't going anywhere except back into the trenches to take the fight to the next level.

"The Games Are Ours"...
and We Do Mean Ours, Not Yours

*We will never again award the Games in [the] future to a
city which has no significant public sector commitment.*

RICHARD POUND. QUOTED IN *THE NEW LORDS OF THE RINGS*[1]

*We should not be pursuing any open ended contracts. They
[the NDP] don't even know what the final cost will be, and if
you can't guarantee the cost, I guarantee you it will go up.*

GORDON CAMPBELL[2]

The Road to Prague

WITH THE PLEBISCITE "won," the Bid Corp now really only
had the greed of the IOC to contend with. The IOC gleefully followed the Bid Corp and the various BC politicians in declaring the plebiscite a great victory for the Olympic spirit and for
Vancouver, but must have been mightily relieved. Had Vancouver
followed Bern and backed out, the franchise would have been looking shaky. Then again, maybe they knew about the black box voting machines and slept well in the days before the plebiscite. With the fuss officially
over, the IOC's Technical Team was coming to town to visit the Bid Corp's
proposed venues and decide if they were up to the IOC's "standards." Roughly
translated, this meant would they be convenient for the Olympic family and
for TV coverage of the Games?

Bella from NO GAMES and I had written an open letter to IOC President Jacques Rogge asking if our group could meet with the Technical Team
and present our reservations about the Vancouver bid. We mentioned in the
letter that they had previously met with Games opponents in Toronto and

elsewhere and that it would be best if they heard what we had to say directly, rather than reading it later in the newspapers. Not long after this, I received a call from Paul Manning, Jack Poole's main administrative assistant from Concert Properties who had followed him to the Bid Corp. Manning informed me he was in charge of scheduling any meetings with the Technical Team and that he would try to get us a short meeting. He mentioned that some First Nations leaders from a band in the Fraser Valley also wanted to meet with the Team members. My response was that any meeting needed to include the various faces of the opposition: me representing the NO GAMES Coalition; Phil Le-Good; Rosalin Sam from the St'at'imc; Adriane Carr as provincial Green Party leader; a representative of the arts community; and Nan and Diane Hartwick with their complaints about the theft of their project in the Callaghan Valley. Manning accepted all but the Hartwicks, citing time constraints. Only later was I to learn that he had been briefed by Poole to keep them away. Apparently, Poole knew all about the skullduggery in the Callaghan project, having heard it directly from the Hartwicks. Clearly, having this can of worms opened in front of the IOC was the last thing Poole wanted to have happen, and it had the potential to derail the use of the valley for the Nordic venues and, with that, the bid itself.[3] Poole was not the only squeamish one: The RCMP had quietly shelved an investigation into a charge of abuse of process brought by the Hartwicks.[4]

The meeting was scheduled for the Wosk Centre for Dialogue located in downtown Vancouver. On the way in, I had to push through a media scrum, making it past after some brief comments and a promise to answer questions after the event. A few minutes later, the delegation and I were ushered into the meeting room by Manning and introduced to the Technical Team. Their leader, Gerhard Heiberg, had headed up Lillehammer's successful 1994 bid for the Winter Olympics, and he now had his eyes firmly fixed on a glorious future within the IOC hierarchy: He was planning to run for one of the IOC vice-presidencies in July 2003. The team also included Charmaine Crooks, a former Canadian Olympian and, crucially, also a member of the Bid Corp's board of directors, the latter a clear conflict of interest. Most of the other members of the team were unknown to us.

Heiberg was the one who interested me the most. I had walked into the meeting with briefing notes for all the members of the team and planned to talk about all items but one. This last item linked Heiberg through his former association with Norwegian offshore oil and gas giant Aker Kvaener ASA to various members of the Vancouver Bid Corp board of directors. I wanted this to be our leverage with Heiberg: I wouldn't mention it in my presentation, but it would be there for them to see and would demonstrate that bringing the Games to Vancouver carried the risk that we would raise a stink and embarrass both the Bid Corp and the IOC.

Each of us in turn presented our arguments. LeGood and I stressed the fiscal aspects, the impact on the poor and the environment. Rosalin Sam dealt with the spillover effects on St'at'imc traditional territories. Adriane Carr mirrored my points and emphasized the lack of transparency and accountability the Bid Corp had shown so far. It was a cordial meeting overall; the team members asked a few perfunctory questions, thanked us for coming and that was that. They had done the official *pro forma* act of pretending to listen to the opposition and now could get on with the business at hand. Carr and I went outside and jumped into the midst of a second press scrum. Heiberg walked out of the building, and according to one witness, wandered off down the street, seemingly lost in thought.

The next day saw the Technical Team drive up to Whistler to view future venues. On arrival, Heiberg stressed that the drive had been a long one and that it would really be a good idea to fix the road to make the trip faster. Shortly thereafter, Heiberg abandoned IOC "recommendations" and went for a private ski run with Prime Minister Chrétien. What they may have talked about was not revealed to the press, but they both mentioned how great the skiing had been.

What they didn't mention was that the Prime Minister also had a link to both the bid and to Heiberg, through Power Corp of Ontario. Power Corp just happened to have two key officers connecting them directly to Vancouver's bid. André Desmarais (co-CEO) was married to Chrétien's daughter, France. She had been appointed to the Bid Corp in 2002. André's father, Paul Desmarais, was the former president of the company and was, and still is, Chairman of the Executive Committee and the company's majority shareholder. The elder Desmarais also served on the Board of Directors of Bombardier, a Montreal firm whose Chairman, Laurent Beaudoin, was also on the Bid Corp's board of directors. Bombardier was one of the companies listed as potential builders of the future Vancouver airport subway system.

Aker Kvaener was all over oil and gas projects projected to occur off the coast of British Columbia. Aker Kvaener also had a number of projects with Li Ka Shing's omnipresent empire, as did Power Corp, both working with Shing's Husky Energy. In May 2003, just two months after the Technical Team's visit, the European consortium TotalFinaElf gave a $300 million contract to Aker Kvaener.[5] Power Corp is the major shareholder in TotalFinaElf. Aker Kvaener is a huge company, so it should come as no surprise that they would have deals all over the place, including with Power Corp, but the contract via TotalFina-Elf just seemed remarkably timely and convenient. Maybe it was just another way of keeping it all in the family, both literally and in a global sense.

My initial perception that the IOC was merely another international mega-corporation, albeit a remarkable one, was not dissuaded by these connections, rather the opposite. Seeing how all the players were linked up behind the scenes merely reinforced my anti-globalization perspective, showing yet again that the cabal of multinationals who control economies do it for their benefit, not ours. The IOC was merely showing another of its many faces as liaison between the main players. Should I have been surprised? No, because the business world works, in large measure, based on such contacts, even tax-payer funded ones, and I knew this. The IOC, however, was like a sleeper cell, the public not even aware that it provided an additional service to sweeten the pot: If you help us take your city, we'll help you in various other ways too.

As the IOC vote in Prague approached, the Bid Corp became oddly quiet. The media kept the public in a frenzy, at least that part of the public that seemed to give a damn. Of the two remaining competing cities, Salzburg was considered the one to beat: It had the infrastructure already in place, the public was generally supportive, and much of their financing was private. Pyeongchang had some big plusses too. Their transportation scheme was a masterpiece using bullet trains to move people around. Even better, they proposed that the Games would serve as a future impetus for the peaceful reunification of North and South Korea.

The decision in Prague by the IOC was held on July 2, 2003. The NO GAMES supporters and members of the provincial Greens had gathered at a coffee shop in Kitsilano to wait out the result. The Yes side had rented the vast General Motors (GM) Place and filled it with Games boosters. My "spidey" senses weren't telling me which way the vote would go, so I had prepared two statements, one if Vancouver won, another if it lost. I had to decide what my role would be if Vancouver got the nod. Would I just say congratulations, accept it as a done deal and fade away? Some reporters had posed the question to me in the days and weeks after the plebiscite, asking if I would now get "onside" with the bid. The same question arose in the weeks leading to Prague. My answer in February and since had been that no, I wouldn't. As the day of decision approached, my answer remained the same. I was still convinced that the Olympics were a scam in general and for Vancouver in particular. There was no way I could ever lend my support to something so innately corrupt. But, if I was going to continue to oppose the Games, what would my role be? Could the Games be stopped in some way? Should I restrict myself to a watchdog role in the absence of any other group doing this job? These were the questions that kept me up the night before the vote, and as I walked into the coffee shop I still didn't know the answer. Life for me would be so much easier if Vancouver lost, although I'd still have to contend with the verbal threats and perhaps physical assaults I'd been threatened with.

In Prague the IOC was set to vote with 107 members present. The first ballot gave a surprising lead of 51 votes to Pyeongchang, long considered to be the underdog. Vancouver was in second place with 40 votes. Poor Salzburg, long considered the front-runner, got only a measly 16 votes and was forced to drop out. It now became a race between Vancouver and Korea for the prize, booby or otherwise. The TV cameras covering the reaction in Vancouver cut away to an anxious pro-Games crowd on the other side of town. At the No gathering we were still cautiously optimistic that Pyeongchang would keep its commanding lead, helping us in the process duck the Olympic bullet.

After a brief break, the balloting continued. While waiting for the results to come in, I juggled two slips of paper, my victory and my defeat speeches. Finally, the results were in: IOC President Jacques Rogge mounted the stage and with the showmanship of an Academy Awards host, held up a piece of paper and solemnly intoned, "The winner is...Vancouver." Vancouver had won by 3 votes, 56 to 53. One hundred and seven IOC delegates had taken a coffee or pee break after the first ballot, but 109 returned to vote in the second round. Taking the two new votes (presumably those from one of the competing countries who couldn't vote) plus the 16 who had voted for Salzburg in the first round, this meant that 16 of the 18 up-for-grabs votes had gone to Vancouver. The possibility that this had happened by chance seemed remote.

The TV cameras scanned the jubilant Bid Corp delegation, then cut away to bid supporters at GM Place cheering themselves stupid. A pall had descended on the No side gathering. As usual, Adriane Carr and I were into a media scrum. What would we do now, the media wanted to know. Carr said something vague about watchdogging the process and hoping the Games would be as green as promised. I read a statement thanking our supporters and vowed to keep scrutiny on all Bid Corp doings and promises. Months of work trying to stop the machine had failed. It was now over and time to return to normal life.

After Vancouver was chosen, the IOC continued their internal business in Prague. Heiberg, in part due to our role linking him to the Bid Corp, went down to defeat in his battle against Korean Un Yong Kim for one of the IOC's vice-presidencies. A few months later, Un Yong Kim would be charged with corruption back home in Korea and would have his vice-presidency revoked.[6]

The Korean media even suggested that Un Yong Kim had betrayed Pyeong-chang in favor of Vancouver as part of an overall deal to get him the vice-presidency. Looking behind the curtain of the IOC's internal machinations is always difficult, and we were never able to confirm if the story was true. Still, what was true was that the Chinese had strongly supported Vancouver's bid, perhaps with some help from Li Ka Shing, the Hong Kong and Vancouver real estate baron and a major player behind Beijing's 2008 Summer Games.

The Ongoing Resistance
to Vancouver's Olympic Games

I took the summer off from politics and Olympics and got reacquainted with my partner, my son and my new daughter. Later that summer I was called up for firefighting with the Army Reserve in the Interior, and the events of the previous year were pushed out of my mind with the realities of this task. Meanwhile, Ian Gregson, a Green Party organizer and supporter of NO GAMES, had organized a watchdog website called "2010 Watch."[7] This became the start of an ongoing monitoring and education effort by those of us still interested in fighting on.

After the summer I was back to my role as watchdog as I had promised after the Prague decision. Working with 2010 Watch as their main spokesperson, I continued to expose the litany of broken promises that would become more obvious as the Olympic projects began to unfold. Fiscal accountability, transparency, protection of the poor and providing the "greenest Games ever" were not promises meant to be kept. Many Vancouverites had bought into them hook, line and sinker, but for the Bid Corp and its successor organization, VANOC, these were only words to be mouthed from time to time. The provincial government didn't seem particularly eager to make them do more. With each pronouncement from VANOC, members of the media would look to me to provide "balance."

The BC Green Party had left the scene, their own promises to help watch-dog the Olympics worth about as much as the Bid Corp's. In their place, we found new allies in a new political grouping called the Work Less Party (WLP). Their founder, Conrad Schmidt, was a fellow NO GAMES member who had turned his activism to the task of educating the public about the insanity of our hyper-consumerist culture. The Olympics were the perfect example of mindless consumerism, and Schmidt and WLP became a major part of anti-Olympic activity in Vancouver. Schmidt was later to produce a widely acclaimed anti-Olympics documentary film called *Five Ring Circus* to bring the message to the widest possible audience.[8]

The New Face of the Bid Corp: VANOC

Meanwhile the Bid Corp had now become the Vancouver Organizing Committee for the Olympic Games (VANOC) and was looking for a CEO. Oddly, they didn't seem to be in any rush. Finally, in 2004 after a series of *in camera* meetings at a Vancouver waterfront hotel, the selection committee chaired by Jack Poole chose none other than John Furlong. Members of the media trying to cover the meetings had been not only denied access to the deliberations, but were literally frogmarched out by the hotel security staff. This event was not a good omen for future transparency, in fact it was a prescient glimpse of future VANOC inscrutability.

John Furlong had been an Olympic athlete himself, competing for his native Ireland. He eventually immigrated to Canada, starting off his new life as the director of Parks and Recreation for the City of Prince George in northern British Columbia. He later moved on to a similar position in the Vancouver Island community of Nanaimo. Furlong's sports credentials included membership in the Canadian Olympic Committee and chairing BC's Summer and Winter Games and Sport BC. From there he had taken over as the manager of the tony and exclusive Arbutus Club, a position he held for 14 years until hand-picked by Jack Poole to be President and CEO of the Vancouver Bid Corp. The Arbutus Club belongs to Caleb Chan, the rich developer who had been a member of the Bid Corp's Board of Directors.

The choice of Furlong drew considerable flack, most notably from Canadian Olympic Committee boss and IOC member, Dick Pound, who had pronounced Furlong unfit for the job of CEO saying, "Mr. Furlong is a perfectly capable person and a nice person, but he doesn't have the experience that you need for this job."[9] Indeed, it is hard to argue with Pound's initial assessment. Furlong had decent enough sports credentials and had officially led the Bid Corp to its successful outcome in Prague, but did this qualify him to run a multibillion-dollar enterprise? Over the coming years, many citizens and media pundits would have reason to wonder if the order of magnitude jump in job responsibility was really warranted by Furlong's skills or had more to do with Jack Poole's apron strings.

It really didn't matter what Pound or anyone else beside Poole wanted. In the end, the selection of Furlong prevailed, Pound apologized and Poole had his loyal water boy as VANOC's point man.

Vancouver's Hidden Costs

Jack Poole went on to promise to "account for every penny," a sentiment echoed by Vancouver Mayor Larry Campbell, soon off for greener pastures.

Campbell had also promised Vancouverites during the plebiscite campaign that the Games wouldn't cost them "one penny." Both sets of penny promises were empty. The Bid Corp never released the full financials of how they had used $34 million of mostly taxpayer money, and VANOC would eventually issue unaudited financial reports and call this transparent and accountable reporting.

Larry Campbell's promises about the costs to Vancouver are also worth reexamining, simply because they were such blatantly lies. Campbell had made his "not one penny" statement claiming that any and all cost overruns would be picked up by the Province. This was not exactly correct, for while British Columbia held the bag for major venue and security costs, they did not own those that were purely within Vancouver's turf. Some examples will suffice to show just how the bag was pulled over Vancouverites' eyes: The curling facilities and aquatic center cost was to rise by $19.26 million. The practice ice hockey rink at the Killarney Community Centre would rise by $11.5 million; the Trout Lake ice practice facility would jump by $7.5 million. All of this happened just in the first three years after Prague.[10]

There was worse to come: A curious deal between the City of Vancouver and a company then called Millennium Properties Ltd. to build the Vancouver Athletes' Village was also in the works. The City's spreadsheets for the project talked about an overall $64 million best-guess profit on the entire Southeast False Creek lands. The authors of the study conveniently made it nearly impossible to separate out the cost of the Village from the entire 80-acre parcel.[11] What, in fact, they had done was take the revenue from the purchase by Millennium ($193.2 million) of the 23-acre Village site and subtract the cost of remediation and improvement of the total 80 acres. What they hadn't added on as a cost was the $82.5 million to be paid to Millennium for the 250 housing units the City was going to own. This discrepancy reduced the profit to a debit of some $18.5 million. Added to the costs cited above, the bill for Vancouver taxpayers was now passing $57 million and growing, and staff days spent on Olympic issues both before and after Prague remained unaccounted for.

All of this was rapidly adding up, but this was not the whole cost to Vancouverites, not by a long shot. The elephant in the living room was 2010 Olympic security. How much would this cost the taxpayers? The provincial and the federal governments will pick up the bulk of this, but they surely won't be paying the salaries and overtime of the Vancouver Police Department. As of this writing, the Vancouver Police Department refuses to release either their costs to date or projected expenses for the actual Games themselves.

All in all, it was a lot of pennies that Larry Campbell hadn't owned up to before the plebiscite vote in 2003. One might think that voters would have held him to account at the next municipal election as the bills began to roll in. Well, they might have, but Campbell was far smarter than anyone had thought.

What Ever Happened to
Larry Campbell and COPE?

In fact Campbell never had to account for his weak math skills at all. Maybe he just looked at his to-do list and saw that his work in Vancouver was done: Olympics delivered? Check; convention center delivered? Check; Richmond Airport Vancouver subway (RAV) line delivered? Check. Well then Tonto, it was "Hi-yo Silver, away," and in a cloud of dust, Campbell was off before the 2005 civic election, leaving the hapless Jim Green and the rest of COPE scratching their heads and wondering, "Who was that masked man?" In short order, his reward was in the mail, and Campbell got posted to the cushiest of patronage jobs in Canada: the unelected federal Senate, home to numerous political hacks of the major parties since Canada became a nation in 1867. How does one join the 105 lucky folks who get to sit in the Senate's Red Chamber? Delivering major real estate projects is obviously as good a way as any.

Sadly there was to be no soft landing for COPE: All of their kowtowing to the Olympic machine couldn't save them from what was to come. The left-leaning part of COPE, called by some COPE Classic (David Cadman, Tim Louis, Fred Bass, Ellen Woodsworth and Anne Roberts), had been finding it increasingly difficult to get along with their more developer-friendly siblings, the COPE Lite faction led by Jim Green. Green and two other Lites (Raymond Louie and Tim Stevenson) had consistently supported Campbell in boosting the Olympics and all major development projects, Olympics-related and not. They now split to form a new party called Vision Vancouver, parking themselves near the NPA's part of the spectrum, becoming in essence what they had actually been all along: NPA Lite.[12] Vision chose Green as their mayoral candidate and filled out their ranks with like-minded developer-friendly types. What was left of COPE decided to run their own slate for city council while supporting Green for mayor. They didn't want, they explained, to split the "progressive" vote.

COPE got thoroughly thrashed in 2005 by a re-energized NPA under former councilor and now mayor-elect Sam Sullivan. COPE was reduced to one councilor (Cadman), Vision held on to two seats (Louie and Stevenson) and picked up two newcomers (Heather Deal and George Chow), but Green was out of a job. It was a victory for the NPA's moneyed backers and a stunning reversal of fortunes only three years after COPE's 2002 sweep. Money alone couldn't explain it, however. It took real stupidity too. COPE's courting of the city's developers and the bid hadn't endeared them to many of the working poor or those who saw through the Olympic scam, so many may just have stayed home. Vision Vancouver, running in the middle of the road, pretty much divided what COPE supporters remained, letting the NPA slither through the gap.

There was still a long way to go before 2010. Vancouver's win in Prague was going to have a dramatic effect on the city and its residents. But before we consider the full impact of the Olympic machine, we need to understand the beast in more detail.

Thus, we now turn to an unsanitized history of the Olympic Games and the IOC.

THE SECOND RING

The Hidden History
of the Olympic Games

• • • • •

*The modern Olympic Games began in 1896 as a place for
the imperial rivals — in the process of carving up the world
from Cuba to the Congo to the Philippines — to spur fevered
nationalist frenzies through sports. In an age when people
like Teddy Roosevelt expounded on the redeeming values of
empire and the development of "muscular Christianity" through
sports, the Olympics provided the perfect place for the rulers of
imperialist nations to assert their right to symbolic domination.*

DAVE ZIRIN,
WELCOME TO THE TERRORDOME:
THE PAIN, POLITICS, AND PROMISE OF SPORTS

"Faster, Higher, Stronger": The Myth of the Olympic Games and the Hidden History of the IOC

No nation since ancient Greece has displayed a more truly national public interest in the Olympic spirit than you find in Germany. We can learn much from Germany!

QUOTE ATTRIBUTED TO AVERY BRUNDAGE,
PRESIDENT OF US OLYMPIC COMMITTEE AND LATER IOC PRESIDENT,
BEFORE THE 1936 OLYMPIC GAMES, HOSTED BY NAZI GERMANY

I really thought the American Olympic officials simply weren't aware of the problem, and that once it was called to their attention they would do the right thing. Why would they care who's on the one big team from South Africa? I mean, if they discovered it was an all-white team, and an 80 percent Black country, what's the problem? But they cared because they realized that the whole Olympic thing was a club; a men's club of wealthy racists. The whole notion of sports and sportsmanship was a scam. These guys were effectively using the Olympics to travel high on the hog, with international trips, and I'm sure they went very first class, I'm sure they brought their wives and girlfriends. Or both. I'm sure they lived it up, toasting with dictators and potentates.

JIM BOUTON OF THE NEW YORK YANKEES, QUOTED IN DAVE ZIRIN'S,
WELCOME TO THE TERRORDOME: THE PAIN, POLITICS, AND PROMISE OF SPORTS

The Mythology Begins:
The Olympic Games in Ancient Greece

MENTION ANCIENT Greece and what come to mind for most people are the stories of the warriors and gods who populate Greek mythology.

The next thing that pops up is the Olympics. Curiously, we have been led to believe that the history of the Olympic Games is somehow more factual than the "other" mythology, when in fact much of what passes for Olympic history is just as much myth-based as the stories of Zeus, Heracles (Hercules), Achilles and all the rest. There are many detailed accounts from official and unofficial sources about the history of the ancient Olympic Games and their modern sequels. Readers interested in exploring this history should refer to these sources.[1] The following is only meant to provide some general milestones and a background against which we can better understand the current Games, including Vancouver's 2010 Winter Olympics.

One version for the origin of the Olympics is that it started as a festival dedicated to the Earth goddess Gaea some 3,200 years ago near an the eponymous Mount Kronos, where legend holds that Kronos was defeated by his son, Zeus. Then, as now, the River Alpheios arose to the southeast in Arkadia, passed through Elis (now Ilia) in the west, then flowed past Olympia before ending in the Ionian Sea. It was there in a lush grove where the Alpheios and its tributary Kladeos meet that local inhabitants held an agricultural festival celebrating the harvest during the second full moon after the summer solstice.[2] Informal foot races were part of the festivities.

It was these same legendary rivers that figured prominently in the fifth of Heracles' many labors. Heracles, half deity, half human, had been ordered by his uncle King Eurythius to clean the cattle stables of King Augeias of Elis. Augeias had one of the largest herds of cattle in Greece, all kept in one massive stable that had never been mucked out. Heracles offered to do this crappy job in one night for a payment of one tenth of the herd. If he failed, his labor would be free. A deal was struck and Heracles set to work. He first knocked a hole in each end of the stables, then dug a trench from both the Alpheios and Kladeos to the stables and used the rushing waters to wash away years of accumulated manure. The task completed, Heracles approached King Augeias to demand his reward, but the old king refused to honor the deal. Obviously, ancient Greece was no different than the modern world in what happened next: Heracles sued. He took King Augeias before the local judges who ordered the king to pay up.

According to the Greek poet Pindar writing in the 4th century BC, Heracles used some of the revenue from his reward to construct a temple at Olympia. The temple had six altars and was dedicated to his father, Zeus. Olympia, in turn, became the site for a series of religious festivals and athletic games held every four years and similarly designed to honor the chief of the gods. Legend has it that Heracles planted the first olive tree at Olympia, a tree whose branches were later woven into wreaths to be worn by the victors. These games eventually took their name from the site where they were held, becoming the Olympic Games of antiquity. The first formal Games were organized by the city-state of Elis whose cattle baron rulers became the first judges, heralds and ambassadors. Athletes were required to come to Elis 30 days before the Games to train. Those arriving late and without a valid excuse were fined. The failure to pay the fine earned the miscreant a flogging.

A peace treaty between the city-states of Elis and Pisatis (now Pisa, Greece) eventually expanded to encompass the Games themselves. From this came the Olympic truce (*ekecheiria*, literally "holding of hands"), a three-month-long period that was announced before and during each of the Olympic festivals to allow visitors to travel safely to and from Olympia. According to historical record, during the ekecheiria, wars stopped and no military forces were allowed near Elis (although the truce did not apply elsewhere). Legal disputes and actions were also suspended, including the imposition of the death penalty.[3] With ekecheiria, the Games became synonymous with peace, a theme the IOC would later exploit to the hilt.[4]

The first written report of the Olympics is from the 776 BC Games, which consisted of a single event, the stade, a 192-meter race, which was won by Coroebus, a hometown boy, making him the first recorded Olympic champion. As the Games continued, other races were added, along with boxing, wrestling and the *pankration*, the latter a variant form of mud wrestling in which there were no real rules. Basically the opponents tried to hurt each other badly enough to force one of them to surrender. It really didn't pay to be a loser, because for the ancient Olympians, death was preferable. Another popular event was the four-horse chariot race, a contest that sometimes resulted in the death of the competitors.

The Olympic Games eventually totaled a dozen or so events and grew to become the largest contests of their time, attracting an estimated 40,000 and 50,000 spectators to Olympia and maximally straining the local resources and environment. Current popular mythology envisions pious athletes competing fairly and in peace for the honor of Zeus while women in white tunics look on adoringly. The reality was not quite so pristine. In fact, the Games were the "Super Bowl, Woodstock, Mardi Gras, a holy pilgrimage and Chippendale dancers all rolled into one…a sanctuary of soaring marble temples and a foul, drunken shantytown plagued by water shortages, campfire smoke and sewage."[5]

The only real inn was reserved for ambassadors and officials, the Olympic "family" of the day. Everyone else had to camp wherever they could find space;

toilets were wherever people chose to squat. Married women were barred from the Games as it was considered immodest for them to view the naked, olive oil-coated athletes. Prostitutes and unmarried women, however, were allowed, the former capitalizing on the presence of men without their wives and apparently finding considerable gold in the process. Married women camped on the opposite side of the Alpheios River, holding their own contests dedicated to the goddess Hera.

All athletes swore an oath in the temple of Zeus to follow a strict Olympic regimen that consisted of training for a ten-month period before the Games and refraining from the use of "potions," the latter the ancient equivalent of today's "doping." Those found to have broken the oath were fined and required to erect statues, *zanes*, inscribed with pious statements. In spite of the Olympic oath, cheating was endemic. The first zane was erected by Eupolus of Thessaly after the 388 BC Games. Eupolus apparently bribed three opponents to take dives in the boxing competition. His zane was by no means the last. One of the biggest scandals of the ancient Games occurred under Roman rule when in 67 AD the judges awarded Emperor Nero the olive leaf crown for the chariot race. The only problem was that Nero had been thrown from his chariot and didn't even finish the race. Nero also bribed the judges to include poetry reading as an Olympic event.

Successful athletes were well rewarded for their efforts, so much so that many professional athletes included the Olympic Games as part of their circuit of local contests. Athens gave out 500 drachma awards,[6] a considerable sum, along with the keys to the city to Olympic winners. Olive oil, free food and sex were some of the other rewards. The losers, in contrast, did not fare so well and were expected to slink off in disgrace.

In total, 293 successive five-day-long Games were held four years apart at Olympia, spanning the period of the Greek city states, through the period of the Roman Empire and up to 393 AD when Emperor Theodosius I of Constantinople, a Christian, banned pagan worship along with the Games in 393AD. The Olympic Games were not to return for over 1,500 years.

The Renaissance of Greek Culture
and the Origin of the Modern Olympic Games

The modern Olympic Games really began in the 19th century with the rediscovery of the glories of ancient Greece, its philosophy, science, art and, finally, the Olympics. *Philhellenism*, "the love of Greek culture," became a societal fad in Western Europe, galvanized in part by the 1821 rebellion of the Greeks against their Ottoman rulers.

Intervention by the British, French and Russian navies crushed the Ottomans at the Battle of Navarino in 1827. The Treaty of Constantinople in 1832 ended the Greek War of Independence and created the modern Greek nation as a monarchy. Athens became its capital in 1833. That same year, the poet Panagiotis Soutsos wrote his epic "Dialogue with the Dead," in which the author conversed with Plato and called for the revival of the Olympics and the other hallmarks of ancient Greece. The poem inspired a wealthy merchant, Evangelis Zappas, to write to Greece's King Otto in 1856, offering to finance the revival of the Games.

In 1859 the first version of the modern Olympic Games was held in Koumoundourou Square in Athens as part of an agricultural and industrial fair. One of the cash prizes given to the victors was sponsored by the Wenlock Olympic Committee of England.

Zappas funded the excavation of the Panathenian Stadium, a venue used for Games held in 1870 and 1875; the latter was open only to university students, and the outcome was considered to be inferior to the Games of 1870. In 1888 the Greek Olympic Games were suspended. Meanwhile, in England the Wenlock Olympian Committee, founded by doctor/magistrate William Penny Brookes, held their own "first" Games in 1861. The National Olympian Association (NOA) was formed in 1865, and the British National Olympics were held at the Crystal Palace in London also that year. Brookes attempted to interest the Greek government in a new Olympic Games without success. In 1889 he began corresponding with a French nobleman, Baron Pierre de Coubertin, and in 1890 invited de Coubertin to England to observe the British Olympics.

Pierre Fredy de Coubertin was born in Paris in 1863, four years after the first unofficial games of the modern era were held. De Coubertin held the strong belief that sports made for a well-rounded and vigorous person. Although the sources of his inspiration were diffuse and likely not solely his own, de Coubertin conceived of an international competition to promote athletics, his vision giving rise to the modern Olympic Games. In 1890 he founded the Union des Sociétés Françaises de Sports Athlétiques (USFSA) and pitched the idea of revitalizing the ancient Olympics. With this as his goal, de Coubertin organised an international congress that was held at the Sorbonne in Paris in 1894. The congress had 79 delegates, representing nine countries. Of these, five were nobles, two were generals, and nine were leading industrialists. By 1900 de Coubertin had added ten more barons, princes and counts. Pierre de Coubertin was, after all, a nobleman himself, and the Games were not really for the little people.

The outcome of the congress was twofold. First, the congress agreed to establish the International Olympic Committee (IOC) and named Demetrius Vikelas, a Greek businessman, as its first president. De Coubertin became the general secretary and, after Vikelas, the IOC's second president in 1896. Second, the new organization decided to hold the first "official" modern Olympics in Athens, to be officially known as the Games of the First Olympiad with sequels to follow every four years just as in ancient Olympia. The Athens Games proved a success, but soon faltered in the shadows of the World's Fairs in 1900 and 1904. A reversal of fortune came with the stellar success of the Summer Games of 1906.

The Olympic ideal had also caught the attention of more than the aristocracy. Many ordinary people saw in the Games the possibility of a popular people's Olympics. In 1925, 150,000 spectators gathered for the first "Workers' Olympics"; 100,000 showed up at a similar gathering in Vienna in 1931. Barcelona was to be next in 1936, but the civil war instigated by Franco's fascists ended the "People's Olympics," an irony that would not be lost on future IOC President Juan Antonio Samaranch.

The International Olympic Committee Carries on: From Baron Pierre De Coubertin to Count Jacques Rogge

Godefroy de Blonay, a Swiss baron, took over the role as "acting" president when De Coubertin joined the French Army to fight in World War I. De Courbetin took back the reins in 1919 and held them until he stepped down for good after the 1924 Games in Paris. In spite of the fact that he was not really the first to organize the modern Games, the IOC and many Olympic historians continue to view him as the founder of the modern Olympics by virtue of the organization he founded. De Coubertin was followed in the presidency by Count Henri de Baillet-Latour from Belgium (1925 until 1942). The Games came to a halt during the war years, but soon afterwards, de Baillet-Latour was succeeded by Swedish industrialist J. Sigfrid Edström, who ran the IOC from 1946 to 1952.

Nineteen fifty-two brought in the American Avery Brundage who held the post until 1972. He was against the idea of women competing in the Games and, during the rise of the Nazis in Germany, was one of Hitler's most ardent supporters. A member of the IOC, Brundage praised the Führer and the Nazi regime, denied that there was any possibility that Jews were being persecuted in Germany and utterly refused to countenance cancelling the Berlin Games of 1936. His unwillingness to challenge fascism while an IOC member continued during his tenure as IOC president, when he also refused to take action to ban openly repressive regimes from competing. During his presidency, he firmly opposed the exclusion of either apartheid-era South Africa or the openly racist government of Rhodesia (now Zimbabwe). Perhaps he was simply against taking actions that could be seen as "politicizing" the Games. If so, the Nazis had no compunctions about doing so, and the 1936 Games were a huge propaganda victory for a country bound and determined to achieve world conquest for the Aryan race. The Nazis squeezed the Games for every ounce of publicity and credibility possible. During World War II, German U-boats adorned their conning towers with the five interlocked Olympic rings, perhaps making these the last sights that many Allied sailors saw in this lifetime. Brundage's open support for the Nazis and his later refusal to act against South Africa and Rhodesia simply made a mockery of the Olympic ideal of universal brotherhood, a fact not lost on non-white athletes and spectators. The extent of Brundage's — and the IOC's — hypocrisy became readily apparent during the Summer Olympic Games in Mexico City in 1968. Just days before the Games were to open, Mexican police and the army massacred as many as 500 student protesters in the Plaza de las Très Culturas in the Tlatelolco section of Mexico City. As Helen Lenskyj notes,

> The Tlateloloco killings were fatally intertwined with the oncoming Olympics. This was a time of mass struggle from the Yucatan to Tijuana. Student strikes had rocked Mexico throughout the year. As part of a rising tide of protests, students vowed to challenge the coming Olympic leviathan. They raised chants like "Justice, yes! Olympics, no!"[7]

The protesters had been primarily concerned with poverty and the endemic corruption of the ruling Institutional Revolutionary Party (PRI), but had also clearly made a link between the exploitation and ongoing neglect of the poor with the amount of money being lavished on the Games.

The IOC refused to allow the massacre to "politicize" the 1968 Games, but what followed next highlighted the extent to which the mechanics of running the Games trumped every other concern, social or ethical. African-American sprinters Tommie Smith and John Carlos had captured the gold and bronze medals, respectively, in the 200-meter race. To highlight ongoing racism in the United States, and in a gesture of solidarity with the slain Mexican students, Smith and Carlos raised black-gloved fists during the playing of the American anthem. This event outraged Brundage and the IOC, and the response was immediate: Smith and Carlos were summarily expelled from the Athletes'

Village as well as from the Games. The sprinter who took the silver medal, Australian Peter Norman, supported Smith and Carlos in their protest. Norman later said:

> There is often a misunderstanding of what the raised fists signified. It was about the civil rights movement, equality for man…. The issues are still there today, and they'll be there in Beijing [in 2008], and we've got to make sure that there is a statement made in Beijing, too. It's not our part to be at the forefront of that; we're not the leaders of today, but there are leaders out there with the same thoughts and the same strength.[8]

Brundage remained president until 1972, departing soon after the disastrous Munich Summer Games at which Palestinian terrorists of the Black September organization slaughtered 11 Israeli athletes. Brundage, true to form, refused to halt the Games to honor the dead Israelis. Once again, the Games as an institution was blind to the real world, its own interests always paramount, always superseding the lofty words about peace and brotherhood. The IOC's frequent contention that the Games are above politics has historically simply ignored reality and common sense. Even if the IOC was truly oblivious, host countries and their enemies are not. The Nazis demonstrated this in 1936, as did the killings in Mexico City, the US-led boycott of the Moscow Games in 1980 and the Soviet reverse boycott of the Los Angeles Games in 1984. Beijing in 2008 promises much of the same as it uses the Summer Games to gloss over brutal repression in Tibet, to their appalling human rights record throughout China, the persecution of Falun Gong, and the displacement of over 1.5 million Beijing residents. Those opposed to any or all of these, including those incensed by Chinese support for the Sudanese and Burmese governments, will find ample reason to make the 2008 Games a political event as well.

Michael Morris, third Baron Killanin of Ireland, was next in line for the IOC presidency, holding the office from 1972 until 1980 when Juan Antonio Samaranch from Spain took over. Samaranch, the son of a wealthy factory owner, was born in Barcelona in 1920 and was still a teenager when the Spanish Civil War erupted in 1936. In spite of his youth, he was already a dedicated fascist youth organizer and strike-breaker. After the Civil War, Samaranch rose in the fascist movement of dictator Generalissimo Francisco Franco, eventually becoming a national government minister, president of the Catalan Regional Council and member of the Barcelona City Council. Samaranch never repented his open support of fascism, at least not the Spanish variant, declaring during Franco's lifetime that he remained "one hundred percent Francoist."[9] His tenure as president of the IOC showed that he had not abandoned such allegiances either in spirit or practice. As detailed by Andrew Jennings, Samaranch was a dictatorial president, obsessed with the Francoist concept of "sacred unity" that he applied to the Olympic movement, and secretive to a fault. He also shared with his hero Franco one more trait: He was an egomaniac.

Samaranch presided over some of the more egregious Olympic scandals of the late 20th century, including that of Salt Lake City, detailed in the next chapter. With sponsors threatening to pull out, Samaranch's time was done, and the IOC scrambled to institute at least the semblance of reform.

In 2001 the race to choose the eighth official president was on between three candidates: Belgian count, orthopedic surgeon and Olympic yachtsman, Jacques Rogge; former South Korean military intelligence officer of a corrupt and brutal military dictatorship, Un Yong Kim; and Canadian lawyer Richard (Dick) Pound. After the years of Samaranch and the endless drumbeat of scandals, the IOC's feral survival senses kicked in with a life-saving choice as they picked Rogge, the ultimate "gray man," the complete apparatchik. Un Yong Kim came in second, but had he won the presidency, it could have ended the IOC itself, for he was soon to be implicated along with his son in the ongoing Salt Lake City bribery scandal. Even after weathering that storm, Kim just couldn't seem to keep his paws out of the trough. After the 2003 Prague decision to award the 2010 Games to Vancouver, Kim was charged by the South Korean government with corruption. It was also widely believed back home that he had deliberately sabotaged Pyongchang's bid for the 2010 Games, working behind the scenes in aid of Vancouver[10] in exchange for Chinese support in his race to win an IOC vice-presidency.

The "bronze" in the presidency race went to Dick Pound, a man whose career both in and out of the IOC has taken some interesting paths. A Montreal lawyer and partner in the firm of Stikeman Elliott,[11] Pound is a former Olympic swimmer (1960), a former vice-president of the IOC (1987 to 1991; 1996 to 2000) and currently the Chancellor of Montreal's McGill University.

Pound became secretary-general of the Canadian Olympic Committee, rising to the presidency in 1977. In 1978 Pound was elected to the IOC and put in charge of negotiating television and sponsorship deals. In this role, he may have revolutionized the Olympic movement by striking huge agreements with multinationals such as Visa, McDonald's, Kodak and Coca-Cola, in the process helping to transform the IOC into a multi-billion-dollar enterprise. In 1983 Pound was voted to the executive board of the IOC, and President

Samaranch asked him to negotiate the IOC's biggest-ever television broadcast deal. Pound's first deal brought in $325 million for worldwide TV rights to broadcast the 1988 Calgary Winter Games. The last deal Pound undertook for the IOC was for the 2008 Summer Games in Beijing, with a projected windfall profit for the IOC of $1.7 billion.

In 1998, after a scandal involving doping at the Tour de France touched the IOC peripherally, President Samaranch looked to Dick Pound for help in finding a solution. Pound's proposal was to create an international authority, the World Anti-Doping Agency (WADA), which was to be "independent" of the IOC and any international sports governing bodies. WADA's role was to conduct investigations into alleged drug use in sports, in essence acting to regulate and police the sporting world; Pound would go on to become its Chairman. In 2003 a World Anti-Doping Code was issued and is adopted for all Olympic sports, requiring all athletes to follow a universal set of regulations, including abstinence from a list of banned drugs. WADA proposed a set of standardized laboratory protocols and laid out judicial and appeals process for those accused of being in violation of doping policy. Pound finally retired as Chairman of WADA in 2007. When he addressed the IOC for the last time in his role as WADA's chief, Pound observed that doping in professional sports was "organized, systematic, well-financed, well-researched cheating.… This is not going to go away by holding hands and having a zen thing going 'ommmm.'"[12]

Doping was only part of the problem plaguing the IOC near the end of the 20th century. In 1999 Samaranch again turned to Pound to lead an internal investigation into the bribery of IOC members prior to the decision that gave the 2002 Winter Games to Salt Lake City. The investigation led to ten IOC members being expelled or resigning.

Unlike during the Samaranch years, the IOC seems to have since avoided the major scandals that almost brought it down in the late 1990s. This near-death experience has certainly led IOC members to more scrupulously mind their p's and q's, yet the endemic corruption behind the Games remains unchecked and largely unobserved by most of the mainstream press. Rogge is no Samaranch, yet what can one conclude about a man who must know that the insane costs of hosting the Olympic Games (estimated at $60 billion for Beijing) put cities and countries into near penury, that environmental destruction is a constant feature of the Games' true "legacy" in spite of the IOC's pledge "to encourage and support a responsible concern for environmental issues, to promote sustainable development in sport and to require that the Olympic Games are held accordingly" (see chapter 15) and that the ongoing displacement of the poor and homeless is getting worse, not better (chapter 13).

Clearly, the IOC as an organization simply does not care about such things. In the course of just over 100 years, the IOC has repeatedly shown its true colors. Were they ever a democratic, egalitarian organization promoting sports for the masses? Well, no. Of nine actual or acting presidents, the IOC had put three barons, two counts, two businessmen, an overt fascist and a fascist sympathizer in its top job. With leaders like this, are the outcomes surprising?

The Formal Structure of the IOC

The IOC's current roster consists of 116 members, including the President (currently Jacques Rogge), representing 79 nations (the number varies). In 1998 the list of IOC members showed that they had come from a number of previous occupations: business, the military,[13] various bureaucracies, the diplomatic corp...and, oh yes, there were some sports officials from the various allied sporting organizations, National Organizing Committes (NOCs), or from International Sporting Federations (ISFs). Sixteen IOC members are women. Only 15 of the members can be active athletes. In terms of IOC membership by nationality, the Western world holds a disproportional share: Five each are from Switzerland, Great Britain, Sweden, Australia and Russia; the Netherlands has four members; the US and France each have three members. Under regulations revised after the Salt Lake City scandal, members are elected for an eight-year term but can be re-elected and serve until age 70. IOC candidates for membership are voted in by existing members, usually following the direction of the president. The IOC's governing body, the Executive Council, is headed by a president and has four vice-presidents along with ten members elected by secret ballot. The president serves an eight-year term and can be re-elected once for four more. The current IOC has many internal "commissions," including an Athletes' commission, a Sport and Environment commission, one on Finance and another on Ethics.[14]

The IOC is formally related to the 205 current and largely self-regulating NOCs and some 28 ISFs, including the International Ski Federation and the International Basketball Federation. The World Anti-Doping Agency is affiliated with the IOC as an advisory body.

The so-called Olympic movement consists of the IOC and the above NOCs and ISFs, bid and city organizing committees and, one hopes, the athletes. The term "Olympic family" refers to IOC officials, members, judges, NOC and sports federation officials and their secretaries, staff and guests and members of their real families. A more precise term than the above would be Helen Lenskyj's "Olympic industry" which encompasses all of the above and adds all those who profit from the international Olympic gravy train, including the sponsors and others who use the Games to peddle their products, the media and the Boards of Trade and real estate developers who hope to capitalize on Olympic spending.[15]

Pillars of Olympism

The IOC defines their underlying credo, "Olympism," in the following manner:

> Olympism is a philosophy of life, exalting and combining in a balanced whole the qualities of body, will and mind. Blending sport with culture and education, Olympism seeks to create a way of life based on the joy found in effort, the educational value of good example and respect for fundamental ethical principles.[16]

Two of the longest-standing such pillars are those of sports and the arts. The first seems rather obvious, given what the IOC is supposed to be about. The view that arts and culture should also figure into the equation can be traced back as far as de Coubertin, but the IOC merely encourages rather than de- mands an arts component, sometimes called an "Arts Olympiad," for each Olympic Games. This feature plays a large role in getting arts groups onside with any city's bid, but since the funding has to arise from within the organiz- ing committee's intrinsic budget, the extent to which arts have a significant role is debatable. In 1994 the IOC added their third Olympism pillar: the "environ- ment and sustainable development." How much of this pillar and its politically correct sentiments is merely greenwash will be discussed in chapter 15.

The Bid Procedure for Candidate Cities

As laid out in the IOC's Olympic Charter (chapter 5, rule 34),[17] the bidding process for any city that wants to try its luck begins with a submission applica- tion to the IOC by the country's NOCs, which then chooses the candidate city from a list that may include more than one aspirant. Since 1999, the process has been conducted in two stages. First, applicant cities answer a questionnaire covering themes of importance to the IOC, notably the organizing committee's plans to make the Games a success. The answers allow IOC evaluators to mea- sure the strengths and weaknesses of the general plan, along with the actual or potential capacity to carry it out. A weighted-average score for each city is de- rived from the questionnaire's 11 themes: " political and social support, general infrastructure, sports venues, Olympic Village, environment, accommodation, transport, security, past experience, finance, and legacy." The IOC's Executive Board selects the cities that are qualified to proceed to the next stage, the short list. This marks the true candidature phase. At round two, the official "candidate cities" are required to complete and submit a second questionnaire in the form of an extended, more detailed candidature file that will be scrutinized by the IOC Evaluation Commission (consisting of: IOC members, representatives of ISFs, NOCs, athletes, the International Paralympic Committee and other international "experts"), followed by a visit to the city by members of the Evaluation Commission/Technical Team to obtain a first-hand look at proposed Olympic venues and probe details of the bid more closely. The Evaluation Commission sends their report to IOC members at least a month before an IOC electing session.

The final decision is made by the assembled active IOC members, each with one vote. Those members whose countries are in the running abstain while their respective city is still in the competition. Because an absolute majority is required, this process often takes multiple votes, the city with the lowest tally being eliminated in each round.

The IOC's Revenue Stream

The IOC derives its riches from various sources. Its website[18] contains a partial list of revenues that includes: television broadcast rights for the reporting period of 2001 to 2004 (US$2,229 million [53% of the total]), sponsorships and partnerships (US$1,459 million [34%]), ticketing (US$441 million [11%]) and direct marketing and/or licensing of Olympic products (US$86.5 million [2%]). Some of these numbers reflect the total value of the item before splitting the revenues with the host city's organizing committee (for example, television rights); other items seem to be purely IOC profits during the reporting period.

Not included are the fees paid by bid candidate cities for the different stages of the bid process. For the 2010 Games, Vancouver initially faced off against seven other cities. At $150,000 each, this generated $1.2 million directly into the IOC's bank accounts. At the end of round one in the 2010 competition, half the cities were eliminated. The remaining four submitted the second-stage bid with a filing fee of $500,000 for a total of $2 million more to the IOC. For the 2012 Summer Games, nine cities were initially in the running, down to five in round two. Thus for one Winter–Summer Games cycle, this process generated a minimum of $7 million for IOC coffers. Assuming that the application fees paid by bid cities in the 2014 Winter–2016 Summer Games cycle are equivalent to those of 2010–2012 Games cycle, then the total going to the IOC for the privilege of bidding on the Games is about $14 million for any four-year period. The income from these fees, small though they may be in relation to television broadcast rights, is not insignificant and maybe one key reason why the IOC encourages as many cities as possible to go through the bid process. Overall, what this gives us after half of the television broadcast revenues have been divided up with the host city's organizing committee is something just over $3 billion for all the revenue streams that are officially listed.

Just as real estate is the driving force behind local bid organizers, the marketing of products is the IOC's reason for being. The biggest and best products they produce are the athletes, sold to television in the form of broadcast rights for their performances. In turn, television broadcasters use the images of the athletes to sell advertising opportunities. Sponsors, who usually have their own products to peddle, thus pay twice: first, to the IOC to link their stuff to the magic of the five rings…and it is not cheap; next, to the broadcasters to run their ads. It's all one more happy, interconnected family.

Television rights are now the big money earners for both the IOC and the local organizing committees. Indeed it is difficult to see how the organizing committees would come anywhere near breaking even on operating costs without them. Some recent examples show the magnitude of TV broadcast revenues and how they have grown over the last decade: 1993–1996: $1.251 billion; 1997–2000: $1.845 billion; 2001–2004: $2.229 billion. The Athens Summer Games alone had television broadcast revenues of nearly $1.5 billion; Beijing is expected to top $1.7 billion. The Winter Games are no slouches either: Torino in 2006 pulled in $833 million; Vancouver in 2010 is expecting over $ 1 billion.[19] Under current agreements, the IOC keeps 51 percent of these funds, the rest go to the organizing committees.

It's worthwhile looking in a bit more detail at what one of the networks, NBC, which has held US television rights since 2006 and will keep these through 2012, is paying: 2006 Torino, $614 million; 2008 Beijing, $894 million; 2010 Vancouver, $820 million; 2012 London, $1.81 billion. Since the latter is for NBC alone, the total television broadcast revenues from all sources is likely to be vastly higher.

NBC is a subsidiary of General Electric (GE), interestingly, one of the major sponsors in the IOC's TOP program (The Olympic Partner). GE, which also makes weapons for the US military, was said to expect revenues of at least $900 million and an operating profit of $20 million from the broadcasts from Athens in 2004. Later reports suggested that revenues from advertising were closer to the $1.5 billion mark.

The other areas of the IOC revenue stream are more than respectable as well. The TOP sponsorships generated $279 million in 1993–1996, $579 million in 1997–2000 and $663 million from 2001–2004. Domestic sponsorships of which the IOC gets a cut were: $534, $655 and $796 million, respectively; licensing was $451, $625 and $411 million in the same periods. Vancouver's organizing committee is expected to get $201.4 million of the total for 2010 alone.[20] Finally, ticket sales brought in $115, $66 and $87 million respectively. The total of all revenue streams was $2.630, $3.77 and 4.187 billion for these years.[21] As above, the fraction that is the IOC's alone is unclear.

The IOC also sells more mundane things — such as toys, mascots, pins and coins — and this merchandise is also actively promoted by the local organizing committee. Keeping it all in the Olympic family and guarding against so-called "ambush marketing" becomes a key demand that the IOC makes to all levels of government in their Host City Agreement, one that makes the absolute demand that the organizing committee and all levels of government enforce with the ferocity of fiends from hell.

Much of the IOC's marketing strategy, which just so happens to dovetail nicely with that of the TOP sponsors, is brand marketing with an emphasis targeting children. The IOC seeks to instill brand loyalty not only for the Games themselves, but also for the products being advertised. For example, during the Athens Olympics, McDonald's seamlessly segued actual swimming events into commercials featuring Ronald McDonald jumping off a diving board. Clearly the intent was to suggest that Ronald was part of the event, the hidden message being, "If you want to be an Olympic athlete, a Big Mac a day will help you get there." Such advertising was also designed to indoctrinate children into consumer culture. As Helen Lenskyj notes in relation to the Sydney Olympics in 2000,

> The cynical exploitation by sponsors and the IOC alike of "Olympic spirit" rhetoric and pseudo-educational initiatives were key components of the campaign to reach children and youth. On a broader scale, it could be argued that any Olympic education program serves to promote not only sport-related values…but also the values of the Olympic industry and its corporate partners, thereby socializing children to become "global consumers."[22]

What does the IOC do with its billions? First, it's important to realize that they pay no taxes apparently anywhere on the planet. A key component of the Host City Agreement with any city is that the IOC will not be taxed on any aspect of Games or Games-related profits. In Australia for the 2000 Summer Games, state and federal legislatures passed special legislation to make this happen. In Canada, Federal tax exemption was, in fact, granted to the IOC in a clause of the 2007 budget. Under both the provincial and federal tax legislation, only charities, non-profit organizations and religious bodies can claim tax-free status; it remains unclear under which umbrella the IOC fits: It's certainly no charity, is definitely a "for-profit" organization and, although it exhibits and elicits cultlike behavior, is not a religion. Curiously, however, in Swiss law, the IOC is considered a "non-profit" entity. What this means was explained to me by a Mr. Philippe Praz, the first secretary at the Swiss embassy in Ottawa, who wrote in an email:

> Regarding the fiscal status of the IOC in Switzerland, I can mention the following aspects. The Swiss Government and the IOC have signed an agreement on November 1, 2000, describing the status of this ONG [non-governmental organization, or NGO] in Switzerland. Article 3 of this agreement mentions that *the CIO [IOC] is federal income tax exempt. The same exemption exists for the cantonal and communal income tax as well as for the wealth tax* [italics mine]. On the other hand, the CIO [IOC] is paying all other taxes like VAT (value added tax).[23]

The latter is not strictly true as it turns out, and the IOC constantly seeks exemptions from such taxes, much to the disgust of some Swiss lawmakers.

Regardless of what status it slides in under, it is clear that the IOC will pay no taxes on its enormous profits. This returns us to our question: If the IOC pays no taxes on its wealth, where does it go? To its hundred plus employees?[24] Unlikely. The IOC in fact claims that, of the revenues derived from the marketing of the various Games rights and products cited above, 92% goes to the various NOCs, city organizing committees and ISFs. Is there any independent auditing to prove that this is true? No. However, *assuming* it is true, this still leaves them 8% of the total, income-tax free. If the IOC's take over a four-year block is about $3 billion (a low-end estimate), this means that they have revenues of $750 million per year. Of this, based on an 8%:92% split, they keep $60 million for coffee and croissants...and whatever else they want. This $60 million does not include their own revenues from the sale of Olympic products such as stamps, coins, pins and other Olympic paraphernalia.

As we'll see in the next chapter, the IOC leadership and members do very well with this "fraction" of the profits. It also doesn't hurt that bidding cities pick up almost the entire costs of having the IOC visit, including hotels, transportation and entertainment, both during the bid phases and during the actual Games. What the IOC actually does with their overall profits is anyone's guess...and the IOC isn't telling.

Sponsors, Partners and Official Suppliers:
Marketing the Olympic Rings

The TOP sponsor companies pay the IOC top dollar to receive exclusive world-wide marketing rights and opportunities within their designated product categories. They can also develop marketing programs with the various members of the Olympic Movement — the IOC, the NOCs and the organizing committees. Partners also receive a number of marketing aids.[25] TOP partners at the Torino 2006 Winter Games represented a host of powerful multinationals: Coca Cola, Atos Origin, General Electric, Johnson-Johnson, Kodak, Lenovo, Manulife, McDonald's, Omega, Panasonic, Samsung and Visa. It's difficult to see how Coca-Cola and McDonald's whose junk food is surely part of what's driving the current North American obesity epidemic could be considered part of a healthy sporting lifestyle, a supposed goal of the IOC. McDonald's role in the destruction of tropical forest for range land is just as surely not environmentally sustainable, in violation of the third "pillar" of Olympism. The sins of the other multinationals are no less: Coca Cola is financing a war in Columbia, General Electric produces weapons of mass destruction for the US military, and newcomer DOW Chemical took over Union Carbide without expressing any residual responsibility for the world's worst industrial accident: The poison gas leak at the Union Carbide plant in Bhopal, India, killed thousands and left many thousands more with permanent disabilities. While the IOC says very politically correct things about the world, many of these statements even inspiring, when it comes to action, the IOC best personifies the Biblical observation, "By their deeds ye shall know them."

Another serious money-maker for the IOC is the licensing of products including film, video games and other multimedia presentations. For example, the Sydney Games in 2000 had over 100 licensees with more than 3,000 different product lines later sold across Australia with a total revenue stream of $500 million. Within the licensing schemes there are three tiers: the IOC itself, the organizing committees and the NOCs. The IOC has a revenue-sharing formula to determine their percentage of royalties and that of the other partners.

The Olympic "Movement"
Becomes the Olympic "Industry"

The IOC from the days of Baron Pierre De Coubertin onwards has never been democratic or egalitarian. Neither has it been particularly accountable to the public or even to governments, for that matter. In the days before the IOC needed vast financial contributions of taxpayer dollars, it may not have been particularly problematic that they operated as an elite private club. If their attitude hasn't changed, what has? Simply this: What was once a relatively modest venture, more or less focused on sports, has become an international megacorporation, and with it, the corporate persona has blossomed.

Tracing the trajectory of the IOC's wealth and power from its relatively humble origins to today reveals more than a casual similarity to the growth of many multinational corporations during the same period. Less than 50 years ago, the IOC was still struggling financially, operating as a small organization with a skeleton staff, never quite sure if the next Games would get off the ground.[26] If an athlete in those days had to be "amateur," so too was the IOC. Then, during the 1980s, it was seriously discovered by the television industry, which saw the Games as the perfect backdrop for advertising everything from cola to cameras, credit cards to telecommunications. And with television came the serious sponsors, all willing to shell out vast sums to link their names, and products, to the Games. In a very few years, the athletes had become a product line, and the Olympics itself had become a brand. As Naomi Klein documents in her book *No Logo*,[27] the corporate shift from marketing products to marketing brand names has utterly changed the business world. The IOC as owners of an international business brand — the Olympics — was solidly into this emerging trend, and a mighty profitable one it was turning out to be. Up until the 1960s the IOC had been a relatively modestly funded organization. In the 1980s the shift happened, and the wealth started to roll in. After 2000, with its new income-tax-free status in Switzerland, the sky was the limit. Only the IOC now knows how much money they really have, but it surely ranges from hundreds of millions to billions.

Somewhere something else had begun to change. The IOC may have been casual in the extreme about the so-called Olympic ideals of brotherhood, but at least one could still argue it was still focused on elite sports as an expression of human achievement. But by the 1980s the IOC was beginning to be about more than sports and Greek Olympian ideals, whatever the latter might really have been. By the time Samaranch took over in 1980, the IOC was well on its way to being a completely different beast. What Simson and Jennings would describe in their expose, *The Lords of the Rings*, published in 1992 was already clearly established: "All Olympic gatherings are a constant and glittering round of first-class travel, five-star hotels, champagne receptions, extravagant banquets, mountains of gifts and lavish entertainments. And frequently, there's not even an athlete insight."[28]

Finally, it's also important to realize that, above and beyond the greed of today's IOC, there is another agenda at play: Once a city has embarked on the path to win the Games, especially once it has been successful, the IOC sets the agenda for the next seven years: Virtually everything done in the city and surrounding region is done for the Olympics, for the profits of the IOC and for those driving the local organizing committee. Dave Zirin, whose words opened this chapter, summarized it best: "Only those who want to see their hometowns bankrupted, militarized and flattened should pine for the Olympic Games."[29]

What makes the lust of bid cities to acquire the Olympics all the more remarkable is that the IOC's agenda frequently comes wrapped up in scandals of various shapes and sizes. The fact that they are perennial, occurring every two years, should serve as our wake-up call. The fact that they don't highlights the power of the IOC, in concert with a compliant media, to keep the Olympic frame intact.

But before we consider the role of the media, we need to look at some of these Olympic scandals in detail.

No Games Without a Scandal...
or Two...or More

*I told the senators how the IOC had tried to jail me a few
years back, for saying what everyone now accepted as the truth:
that there was a culture of corruption in the Olympics.*

Andrew Jennings,
The Great Olympic Swindle,
When the World Wanted Its Games Back

BRITISH INVESTIGATIVE journalist Andrew Jennings and his
co-author, Vyv Simson, published their blockbuster expose of
the IOC, *The Lords of the Rings*, in 1992.[1] In what may have been
the first honest mainstream portrayal of the secret doings of the
IOC, Simson and Jennings showed how the Olympic system had
been corrupted at all levels, from the egotistical former Falangist
official who served as the IOC's president in the last decades of the
20th century, down through the ranks of IOC members on the take, corrupt judges and drug-enhanced athletes. It all made for good, hard-hitting
journalism, the kind that investigative reporters are *supposed* to do. As Jennings noted in his latter book, *The New Lords of the Rings*,[2] the response from
the IOC was swift and harsh. Using Swiss law designed to protect the rich
and powerful from "defamation" and attacks against their "honor," IOC President Samaranch requested that the Lausanne State prosecutor bring criminal
charges against Jennings and Simson for criminal defamation. If convicted, the
penalty, could have been up to six months in jail for each of the journalists. Jennings recounted how the Swiss Ministry of Justice subsequently triggered the
European convention on mutual assistance in criminal matters. This in turn
involved the British Home Office that duly passed the injunction to Scotland
Yard, which served the injunctions on Jennings and Simson. The reporters

faced trial in Switzerland, but both declined to attend what they anticipated would be a kangaroo court in a country they felt answered "how high" when the IOC said "jump." After being tried *in absentia*, the reporters were convicted, sentenced to five days in jail (suspended for three years) and fined $1,000 for court costs. Later Jennings recounted these events in his testimony before a US Senate committee investigating the bribery scandals that exposed the IOC and host city organizers before the 2002 Salt Lake Games. In his book, Jennings wrote:

> I told the senators how the IOC had tried to jail me a few years back, for saying what everyone now accepted as the truth: that there was a culture of corruption in the Olympics. I told them how astonished I had been to learn that the Olympics are controlled by a man who joined Spain's youth fascists in 1936 and kept on doing that right-arm salute until the dictator General Franco died in 1975. I introduced them to some of the characters Samaranch has chosen to run the world's biggest festival of goodwill — the man who destroys rainforests for a living, the man who served as Idi Amin's defence minister and some other nice guys.[3]

The Olympic and Paralympic Movements: A World of Contrasts

Before getting into the IOC's frequent scandals, it is appropriate to contrast the IOC with what it is not: the Paralympic Games, the latter perhaps the last bastion of "pure" sports at an international level. The name "Paralympic" is derived from the Greek *para* meaning "beside," since these Games are held alongside (actually three weeks after) the IOC's Winter or Summer Olympic Games. The Paralympics are thus held each two years in the same host cities, usually using the same facilities. Cities competing to host the Olympic Games must include the Paralympic Games, thus signalling their acceptance of the responsibilty to organize and conduct these Games.

Although their origins go back to the early 1950s, the first official Paralympic Games were held in Rome in 1960. Since 1988 the Summer Paralympics have followed the Summer Olympics Games; the Winter Paralypmics started to follow the Winter Olympics in 1992.

The Paralympics' governing body, the International Paralympic Committee (IPC), is a legally distinct entity from the IOC, with its own structure, logos and even flag. The IOC has been adamant that the IPC not use its five-ring logo because of marketing concerns, in fact on occasion making quite a stink about it.[4] This behaviour perfectly illustrates the IOC's attitude to the IPC as one of wary suspicion, as if somehow the disabled might steal their thunder... or product line. On the flip side, the IOC's affliation with the IPC, however loose, allows them significant credits in the "political correctness" department. For very little effort on their part — most of the organization of the events is done by the host city organizing committee — the IOC can pretend to accept the notion that the disabled are just as good as their own elite athletes. Tossing a scrap of acceptance to the IPC reaps for the IOC the worldwide perception that they are inclusive. It is the latter, more than anything, that allows the IOC to tolerate this unwanted sibling.

How the IOC really feels about the IPC is revealed by the refusal to allow the latter to use the five rings. Talk about brand protections: the IOC wouldn't even let them use five symbols, let alone interlocking rings. After all, a market logo is a market logo, and this means big bucks. As a consequence, the IPC flag is distinct, featuring three semi-ovals of red, blue and green on a field of white. These symbols are the Korean *tae-geuks*, symbolizing what the Paralympic movement considers as the most significant components of a human being: mind, body, spirit. The IPC's vision statement is "To enable Paralympic athletes to achieve sporting excellence and to inspire and excite the world"; their motto, "Spirit in motion."

The fact that the Paralympics occur weeks after the IOC's Games serves to limit their audience, locally as well as with the national and international media. In particular, television coverage of the Paralymics is a tiny fraction of that devoted to the regular Olympics. The consequences of this lack of attention are twofold, one "bad," one decidedly good: The Paralympics don't make anywhere near the money that the IOC does, but this means that they do it for the love of sports, rather than for the profits that can be made by marketing athletes as products for a worldwide television audience.

It's hard not to see in the Paralympic Games that which the IOC may have started out to be back in 1896 but lost along the way. If the Olympic Games are going to survive the next decades, they will only do so if they start to look and act a lot more like the Paralymics.

The IOC'S Official and Unofficial Scandals

In Wikipedia's online dictionary, a scandal is defined as "a widely publicized incident involving allegations of wrong-doing, disgrace, or moral outrage. A scandal may be based on reality, or the product of false allegations, or a mixture of both." Sport, like many other aspects of life, is riddled with scandals large and small. Given the stakes for fame and treasure in professional sports in general, not least those of the Olympics, it may not be surprising that human nature succumbs to the temptation to cheat. In this context, it is interesting to note how often the Olympics crops up in any list of the top scandals of the last 100 years. *Times Online* recently listed their top 50 sporting scandals, and the IOC scored a whopping 25% of these, three in the top ten alone. Some of the more glaring examples: Canadian sprinter Ben Johnson's loss of the gold medal in Seoul in 1988 after testing positive for a banned sterol; American figure skater Tonya Harding conspiring to injure her fellow teammate and competitor, Nancy Kerrigan, in 1994; a fixed boxing match that gave the gold medal to Korean Park Si-Hun in 1988 when clearly he had lost the bout; 10 of 12 Spanish Paralympic basketball players found not to be disabled in 2000 (even the Paralympics falls victim to the same mentality, albeit not as often as the Olympics); Greek athletes testing positive for drugs in 2004; a French figure skating judge who was pressured by her national organization to award the gold to the Russian pair over the clear Canadian winners; Olympic boycotts for various reasons in 1976, 1980 and 1984; and, finally, the massive IOC vote-buying scandal that managed to include corrupt IOC members *and* an equally corrupt bid committee colluding to deliver the 2002 Winter Games to Salt Lake City.[5]

Scanning the above — really only a partial list — allows us to see the general categories of Olympic scandals, scandals that come in a remarkable variety of flavors and combinations. The obvious ones are: misconduct by IOC members or officials, misconduct by bid and organizing committees, bribes offered and/or taken by judges to affect outcomes, and doping and other forms of outright cheating by athletes, coaches and others. The less obvious scandals, including the outright fraud on society with its attendant costs in all domains will be described later in this chapter. In regard to the outright scandals, it would be safe to say that each Olympic Games has at least one; some have a number of overlapping scandals of all categories. Some of the most famous of these are those discussed in more detail below.

Scandals Involving the IOC

The largest scandal directly involving the IOC in recent memory, one that almost blew the organization out of the water, occurred during the bidding process for the 2002 Winter Games. Salt Lake City ultimately won, but how they did so involved IOC members, the local bid organizers and the IOC's hierarchy, the latter for the most part wallowing in a pit of massive denial that anything was wrong at all.

It began this way: After Salt Lake lost the 1998 bid to Nagano, the Salt Lake Olympic Bid Committee (SLOBC) decided that it had to be a bit more aggressive in how it encouraged IOC members to vote for their city. Before 1998 IOC members were free to visit bid cities, a practice that encouraged some members to seek favors and made the candidate city eager to offer them. In SLOBC's case, this took the form of "humanitarian aid" in which the children of IOC members were offered scholarships at local universities. SLOBC was apparently more than generous with some 13 such scholarships handed out in the bid period.[6] SLOBC members justified the scholarships, not to mention the lavish gifts and entertainment showered on visiting IOC members, as the result of "friendships" that had arisen with bid committee members. When the allegations broke in the media, the IOC went into damage control, hired a major public relations firm to deal with the mess and tried to pretend that it was all business as usual with nothing untoward happening at all.[7]

It turned out that they were half right: It *was* business as usual, and many past bid cities, those successful and those not, had done much the same. National Public Radio newscaster Howard Burkess confirmed this when he called Swiss IOC member Marc Hodler who promptly spilled all the beans. Hodler claimed that up to 25 IOC members were open to bribes. Moreover, one of them, along with three other "agents," could have influenced the outcomes of the bid process that gave the Games to Atlanta in 1996, Nagano in 1998, Sydney in 2000 and the latest at Salt Lake City. Toronto's failed bid for 1996 also came under scrutiny when it was revealed that the Toronto Olympic Committee (TOOC) had provided special jobs for Finish IOC member Pirjo Haeggman. Overall Toronto had paid out something to the tune of $900,000 for travel and in cash.[8] Not only did bid committees typically behave in this manner in trying to win friends and supporters amongst IOC members, it also became clear that most committees closely monitored IOC members and created detailed dossiers of their habits and desires.[9] Sydney's 2000 Games committee was similarly tarred with claims that Australian Olympic Committee President John Coates had promised cash to Kenyan and Ugandan IOC members in return for their votes. In 1998 IOC President Samaranch first tried to cover up the mess, then turned to tortured attempts to justify the Salt Lake City scandal. His successor, Jacques Rogge, later called the actions of Coates in the Sydney scandal "perfectly correct."

Hodler's unusual candor created a firestorm in the media and led to a US Senate investigation of Olympic corruption. The stench of Olympic bribery was not only embarrassing to the IOC and the US NOC, but it was also threatening something far more drastic: a whack to their pocketbooks when key sponsors threatened to pull out unless reforms were instituted. The sponsors included John Hancock Financial Services, NBC and Time Inc. Embarrassment was one thing, a hit to the revenue stream quite another, so reluctantly the IOC tried to cobble together a reform package that included a ban on IOC members visiting candidate cities.[10] Helen Lenskyj would call these reforms "new wine in old bottle."[11] One consequence of the Salt Lake City disclosures was that a number of SLOBC members thought to be involved either resigned or were fired. It was another case of a few presumably bad apples being cleaned out of the barrel, but the stories coming from other bid cities made it clear that the problem was systemic, rather than merely an isolated incident in an otherwise pristine enterprise. After Sydney won the 2000 Summer Games, an independent examination of the bid was conducted by retired Auditor General Tom Sheridan. Sheridan reported that the bid had featured "aggressive marketing" by the Sydney Olympic Bid Committee (SOBC), which had included the provision of plush accommodations, entertainment, financial "assistance" and "gifts" to curry favor with IOC members. SOBC had also used professional lobbyists to develop "friendships" with IOC members. Just as in Salt Lake City, employment and scholarships were offered to the families of IOC members and athletes. In addition SOBC members actively lobbied for votes during their own promotional visits to the countries of IOC members.[12]

Sheridan concluded that there were three major deficiencies in IOC guidelines, including the lack of monitoring of compliance with existing regulations, a lack of clarity and, crucially, "the potential for significant support (benefits) to be made available outside the guidelines through government-to-government support or NOC support." The Sheridan report reinforced the notion that such behaviors had been part of Olympic bids for years. Sheridan wrote,

> It soon became clear that the Salt Lake case was not an isolated example of impropriety, but part of a complex system of relationships among bid committees in the United States, Canada and Australia, and links between members of bid committees and the IOC.[13]

Scandals Involving Bid Corps/Organizing Committees

The Salt Lake City scandal touched both the IOC and the bid committee at the same time, and showed that bid cities often used the same methods. However, some cities did even more.

Sydney's Olympic bid had a number of points of similarity with that of Vancouver. Many of these will be discussed later in chapter 13, but one glaring point to mention here is conflict of interest: In both Sydney and Vancouver,

IOC and NOC members also sat on the bid committee. Sydney added to the vote buying cited above by continuing to pander to those it considered special. It reserved between 60 and 80 percent of the tickets for the top 2000 Olympic events for themselves, for the Olympic Committee of Australia and, of course, for Olympic "family" members.

Nagano (1998) engaged in the same pre-bid shenanigans with payments of thousands of dollars for any IOC members with their hands out. To keep it all on the hush-hush, the organizing committee later burned their books.[14]

Construction scandals also figure prominently in the histories of several Olympic Games. Most recently, Beijing's 2008 Summer Games projects have shown massive levels of corruption. Beijing Vice-Mayor Liu Zhihua, in charge of construction for the Games, was fired in 2006 for taking something like $1.4 million worth of bribes from various construction firms. The services of prostitutes seemed to have been an additional incentive. Three other officials were also fired for taking bribes.[15] Other cities have had much the same experience, but perhaps none more so than during the construction for Montreal's 1976 Summer Olympics, with the outright theft forever branding Montreal as the "Mafia Olympics." Investigative journalists had done some digging and found that Montreal's Mayor Jean Drapeau, the man who had infamously said that the Olympics "could no more lose money than a man can have a baby," had chosen some unusual "partners" to have his Olympic baby with. Drapeau had set up a public-private partnership with a company headed by one Joe Zappia, a man later charged with fraud and conspiracy for falsifying Olympic Village construction costs. Zappia was eventually acquitted: The key witnesses had died before they could testify.[16] As for the "man having a baby" claim, Drapeau left Montrealers (and Quebecers) over $2 billion in the red, a debt taxpayers only finally retired some 30 years later in 2006. The Olympic stadium, the "Big 'O,'" that he had hoped would be his legacy, became jocularly known as the "Big Owe." It was not used after the Games, its crumbling remains reminding Montrealers daily of the folly of chasing the Olympic Games.

Bribery and Doping Scandals

As cited above, it is a rare Olympics that doesn't feature judges taking bribes to provide a predetermined outcome or athletes testing positive for banned substances. The IOC's typical response is to label the offender a "bad apple," while strenuously denying that there is any general corruption or doping problems in Olympic sports. Another response is outright denial. One of the funnier examples of the latter occurred during the Salt Lake City Winter Games in the pairs figure skating competitions. The Canadian pair, Jamie Sale and David

Pelletier, "lost" the gold medal after putting in what most observers thought was a far superior performance to that of the Russian team of Yelena Berezhanya and Anton Sikharulidze. Sale and Pelletier refused to take the decision lying down; the Canadian team got involved, and the IOC soon faced a growing rebellion. Desperately ducking and weaving, the IOC first tried to deny that any funny business had occurred. The result had been so egregious, however, that denial alone wouldn't work this time, so the IOC came up with a truly novel plan: Rather than change what was obviously a fraudulent result, the IOC issued as second set of gold medals! How two pairs of skaters could both take gold was never explained.

Doping crops up perennially in the Games, and those so inclined to cheat are rarely caught in spite of the efforts of agencies such as WADA. Although the actual level of doping in Olympic sports is not known, it is estimated to vastly exceed the number of miscreants so charged in any Olympic year. Readers interested in more details about Olympic judging and doping scandals can find these in the books of Andrew Jennings.[17]

The IOC's Safeguards (for Itself)

The IOC makes no provision for actually addressing any negative outcomes arising from the Games, apart from politically correct words that is. In fact the IOC tries to protect themselves from any liability whatsoever while micromanipulating the overall staging of the Games. For example: IOC Rule 40 says that they will not accept any level of economic liability for host city deficits; Rule 61 states that the IOC controls all publicity and advertising; Rule 17 demands that all levels of government and the organizing committee guard against "ambush marketing"; Rule 38 maintains the IOC's veto over other meetings and events in the host city, neighboring areas and Olympic sites for a four-week period. As always, it's "What's mine is mine, what's yours is mine."

Endemic Corruption:
The Olympic Games and the General
Impact on Host Cities

As detailed in the preceding sections, corruption in various disguises is a fellow traveler to the Olympic circus. Sometimes corruption is the good old-fashioned kind, for example, the organizing committee getting caught in sleazy financial deals or kickbacks before or during the Games. Sometimes those on the take are IOC officials or judges. In regard to the IOC members themselves, the regulations (or more precisely "recommendations") passed after the Salt Lake City meltdown now make it more difficult — but not by any means impossible — to influence how members vote. Bid cities can still find creative ways to "develop friendships" with IOC members as long as they manage to do so more discretely than in the past. The IOC's official position on the issue of members on the take was that they dumped all of their corrupt members after 2002, but this is hard to credit in an organization in which institutional graft appears to be so firmly rooted.

Given the nature of the parent, should we expect the kids will turn out differently? No, and they don't. The IOC has made its priorities clear: Profit (for them) no matter what, and organizing committees follow suit in spades. Given this, the athletes can hardly be ignorant about how the system works, and for many the thought of going home medal-less is simply unthinkable. Thus those inclined to cheat do so the only way they really can: with banned performance enhancing substances and methods. The perception amongst a fraction of athletes that those who take drugs have at least a quantitative advantage over those who don't combines with prospects of the enormous rewards for those who go home with golden baubles. Pretty much everyone involved also knows that the chances of detection are relatively low, that cheaters actually caught by urine tests are a small fraction of those whose pee really is dirty. Like a lollypop dangled in front of a toddler, or a "scholarship" waved at an IOC member, the temptations placed in the path of Olympic athletes are impossible to ignore and, for some, equally impossible to resist.

Olympic Scandals Post Salt Lake City

Recent Games have had a mixed record since 2002. IOC members have officially kept their noses clean after the organization's near-death experience in Salt Lake City; so far only Beijing has had organizing committee members caught pilfering. The number of athletes testing positive for banned substances has been about par for the course in Athens and Torino. Of course, the Beijing, Vancouver and London Games have yet to run, still being six months, two years, and four years in the future, respectively. There is still time for mischief to come to light. The lack of official scandal in the Vancouver Games so far has led at least one newspaper columnist to conclude that Vancouver's pre-Games period is thus somewhat boring.[18]

Olympic Scandals:
The Response of the Mainstream Media

It is certainly true that the media love to titillate their audiences, and the Olympics Games provide the ideal venue for voyeurism. After waves of purple prose building up the Olympic frame and extolling the sacrifices of the athletes, what could be more dramatic than to show that some of the heroes have feet of clay? It's sort of a media win-win situation: build the whole enterprise up, knock down the bad guys and gals, then rebuild the frame.

This pattern is so reliable as to be utterly predictable, and while it serves the corporate media's market share admirably, it also completely misses the point. The problem is not that a few bad apples fall off the tree and out of grace; it's that the entire Olympic industry is endemically corrupt, conceptually as well as practically. What else could one call an industry that knowingly puts cities and states into debt, promises social inclusion but directly penalizes the poor or labels itself as environmentally friendly while abetting outright destruction? As one very moderate Olympics critic puts it,

> I have no interest in being known as an Olympic wrecker. But I don't mind being known as someone who holds the Olympic Family to account when they try to mislead the public and politicians about the costs of holding the Olympics. If they can't bid and organize the Games openly and honestly, they lose all right to control the Olympic patrimony.[19]

The IOC and local organizing committees may have lost the "right," but not the means, to control the Games and, with it, our societies. This is the ultimate scandal, and it is insidious, much like a disease whose ultimate virulence is only noticed after it's far too late to save the victim. Consider again the progression of events in the selling of the Games and the early Games frame. It starts out all very Nigerian banking scam-like: Hosting the Olympics won't cost a penny and will advance world peace. By the time the citizens in any country awake to the reality of what's actually happening to their city, contracts have been signed and facts created on the ground by venue and infrastructure construction. The citizens of Colorado stopped the Denver Games two years after they were awarded, but it is far from clear that such a late decision would have stopped Vancouver's 2010 Olympics. The reasons are partially psychological, but mostly revolve around economics. Once the IOC gets the Host City Agreement signed, usually immediately after announcing the winner, the document locks cities and countries into a legal straightjacket. Denver had the *cajones* to break free of the 1976 Winter Games and wasn't penalized, but no city since has tried. For some, the threat of lawsuits from the IOC and the NOC is just too scary. Moreover, in the life of every host city there comes a point, a drop-dead moment when the bulk of the construction projects have been contracted and are underway. These projects — infrastructure and venues — form the core costs of every Games. Once the money has been paid and the work started, it's all over. That drop dead moment is clearly understood by organizing committees and the IOC alike as the point of no return. For this reason, they both seek to get to this point with all possible speed. Halting the Games after this point might be the honorable and socially just thing to do, but will not bring back the money spent or the trees and habitat destroyed. Yes, it will spare the city future security costs, but will also subtract future television revenues. Since both are of about the same magnitude, the net cancellation provides nearly nothing in the way of savings while underscoring the potential liabilities: infrastructure and venues already paid for and partially constructed, the possibility of legal action by the IOC/NOC and the embarrassment of bailing on the Games when there is no longer an economic reason to do so. Angry citizens can bray at the moon all they want about broken promises, but once here, the machine is unstoppable. Which is not to say invulnerable, as I will show in part 5.

Political writer George Monbiot recently nailed it when he wrote this about the IOC's connivance with organizing committees acting to defraud citizens of the host city and state:

> The International Olympic Committee raises no objection to any of this. It lays down rigid criteria for cities hosting the Games, but none of them include housing rights. How could they? City authorities want to run the Games for two reasons: to enhance their prestige and to permit them to carry out schemes that would never otherwise be approved. Democratic processes can be truncated, compulsory purchase orders slapped down, homes and amenities cleared. The Olympic bulldozer clears all objections out of the way. There can be no debate, no exceptions, no modifications. Everything must go.[20]

Are the above charges baseless? Hardly. Part 4 will show that for each of the above, Monbiot is absolutely correct. Before considering these, however, we need to explore the real context, the foundation that leads to all of these outcomes. As Monbiot recognized, it is this: the real estate developments that underpin each and every Olympic Games.

THE THIRD RING

It All Starts with Real Estate

· · · · ·

Well, real estate is always good, as far as I'm concerned.
ATTRIBUTED TO DONALD TRUMP

CHAPTER 7

VANOC: The Slick New Face of Vancouver's Games

*Mr. Furlong is a perfectly capable person and a nice person,
but he doesn't have the experience that you need for this
job.... I think it's very clear that the premier [Gordon
Campbell] and whoever else is in his circle wanted Jack Poole
as chairman and John Furlong as chief executive officer.*

RICHARD (DICK) POUND, IOC MEMBER

VANOC Stumbles out of the Gate

THE 2010 BID had been won by Vancouver in July 2003, yet it was well into 2004 before the new organization, VANOC, chose their CEO. Not only was the choice long in coming, the selection of John Furlong wrong-footed VANOC pretty much from the get-go. The most glaring fact was that Furlong simply lacked the experience to run an enterprise of the magnitude of the Olympics. This alone made it obvious to most neutral observers that Furlong was merely the front man for Jack Poole who had stayed on as Chairman of the Bid Corp to take on the same role for VANOC, all the while remaining Chairman of Concert Properties. The wearing of the two hats created, at the very least, a strong *prima facie* case for conflict of interest. Many in the media had expected that Furlong's name would be put forward as a sort of thank you for his work on the Bid Corp, but most expected that when the selection committee realized the enormity of the task, someone with more extensive business experience would be chosen. One name floated by the media was that of David Emerson, a man with abundant experience in both the private and public sectors. For example, Emerson had been CEO of Canfor, a major forestry company, as well as the federal Liberal Minister for International Trade, the Gateway project and the 2010 Olympics.[1] He looked like the man for the job, but that was never really in the cards.

The entire process by which Furlong wound up being chosen was shrouded in secrecy. The media were not only banned from the deliberations, they weren't even allowed to remain in the hotel, and the film clips of them being given the bum's rush by hotel security foretold VANOC's nonexistent commitment to public transparency. To this day, no one outside the selection committee knows what went on inside during the deliberations, but Dick Pound probably got it right: Those who planned to make hay on the Vancouver Olympics, Premier Gordon Campbell and Jack Poole, made the choice. And, as we'll see later, Campbell and Poole go way, way back.

VANOC's new board of directors was built from a combination of business types, retired politicians and former athletes.[2] It was a safe team, now minus the Bid Corp's developer-friendly board. All of the latter, aside from Jack Poole, had what they had wanted from the beginning and had gone off to reap the rewards. VANOC's executive management team similarly seemed competent, bland and unlikely to step into controversy by deeds of omission or commission.[3]

VANOC's fiscal transparency and accountability in regard to the Bid Corp records matched that of their CEO selection process. How the Bid Corp had spent $34 million given by the Province in 2002/2003, how much they had paid in salaries to top officers, what their exact operating costs were and, mostly, where precisely their money went remained secret items.

Not long after taking over, Furlong stunned the public with veiled hints that VANOC might be short of cash. These hints soon took on a more concrete tone when Furlong admitted that he would be going back to the provincial and federal governments for another $110 million, the amount to be split between the two. While no one in NO GAMES was surprised, the new cash grab came as a bitter surprise to those citizens and members of the media who had actually believed that the pre-Prague Bid Corp numbers were accurate. Furlong blamed the rising costs of construction for the increase, telling the media that VANOC couldn't have predicted, let alone be held accountable for, an overheated economy driving a development boom. It was an odd statement to make, and one that demanded collective amnesia from the intended audience. It was, after all, Furlong (and Poole) who had stressed during the bid period that getting the Games would benefit the building trades by spurring massive new construction across the city. Most reporters missed the obvious irony of this statement. When the media asked us, we at NO GAMES merely said, "We told you so," noting once again the obvious similarities between the corporate behaviors of wholly discredited multinational corporations, such as Enron and WorldCom, and corporate governance in VANOC. One key behavior that all shared was the tendency to claim financial benefits that were not their own while downloading costs to other entities. Another was the habit of making grandiose predictions of future outcomes then later denying knowledge that such future outcomes might have some negative riders attached.

The extra money eventually came through as it had to: The province was on the hook for any cost overruns so it was only a matter of time before they reached into their pockets and came up with the extra $55 million. The feds eventually followed suit.

Most of the rest of 2004/05 was pretty quiet. Construction started on some nearby venues, VANOC claimed that all was "on budget and on time" without providing details. In 2006 almost three years after winning the bid, VANOC began putting out semi-quarterly financial statements that were meant to demonstrate their commitment to financial transparency. These documents followed the same predictable pattern as before, each assuring the media and public that everything was still going great. Happy news indeed, but there was one problem: None of the financials were audited. In other words, we simply had to take VANOC's word that all was well. Secrecy about financial matters is one of the best-known hallmarks of organizing committees, bedeviling Summer as well as Winter Games, from cities that fail and from those that succeed.

VANOC's Media "Offensive"

In the spring of 2007, a flurry of reports starting flowing out of VANOC after years of relative silence. First came a series of supposedly independent reports on past Winter Games in North America. Freelance "reporter" Kate Zimmerman had looked at Lake Placid, Calgary and Salt Lake City.[4] All got glowing reviews for hosting the Olympics. A VANOC press release virtually chortled with glee:

> The report shows how these host communities continue to: increase tourism in their regions, remind the world of their attractions at subsequent international competitions hosted there, build sports participation, be national hubs for recreational and competitive sport, help the country's top high performance athletes achieve their full potential, attract major sports companies to locate there, and encourage local children to excel in sport and other areas of life.[5]

The first assertion that tourism goes up is simply not true, a fact well documented by those who study the impacts of mega-sporting events:[6] strike one. Did the Games turn a profit when *all* costs were considered? Not a word about it, just more intangible, illusory feel-good "legacies": strike two. And last of all, who is Kate Zimmerman and how independent is she? Well, it turns out that Ms Zimmerman was paid by VANOC for the reports and happens to make her living writing happy reports for various companies who need a bit of spin doctoring.[7] Did she talk to anyone who might have less than a laudatory opinion about the impact of the Games? Nope, she only talked to organizing committees and host city officials. Some in the press, notably Wendy Cox of Canadian Press, asked some of these questions, but Zimmerman was suddenly not feeling all that chatty: strike three. Apart from Cox, however, most of the media reported the joyous news as just that, more reassurance that all was going well for an increasingly wary Vancouver audience.

VANOC's next attempt to hit one out of the ballpark came with their first "sustainability report," covering the period from 2005 to 2006[8] and listing six areas where VANOC thought they'd done a really swell job. These included: "accountability, environmental stewardship and impact reduction, social inclusion and responsibility, aboriginal participation and collaboration, economic benefits from sustainable practices, and sport for sustainable living." The first thing to note was how often the new corporate-friendly buzzword "sustainability" cropped up. In fact, for the first section alone, the word was used six times in the backgrounder provided, two of these in context to internal committees that report to VANOC's board of directors. What "accountability" seems to mean to VANOC is not at all what I'd have assumed it would mean, that is, being accountable to the public for the money spent and the actions taken. No, instead the word meant "developing an integrated system for management of all aspects of sustainability." "Management" was clearly the key word here, and the public was the thing to be managed. The Environment Stewardship section was simply silly: lots of babbling about "green building criteria" and waste reduction, while virtually ignoring the vast carbon footprint created by the Games. The report extolled their efforts for protecting frogs in Whistler, neglecting to tell the readers about destroying other frog species at Eagleridge. No mention was made about the hundred thousand plus trees — much of it old growth — that were being cut down, but there was an amusing section on how VANOC was going to dispose of the "significant woody debris," which is the stuff left over from the same trees that used to be there. To show how "green" they were, VANOC was going to bury the debris rather than burn it. Hooray for sustainability! Social Inclusion consisted of passing the

homelessness hot potato to the city of Vancouver in the form of the 250 housing units in the future Athletes' Village that the City will own. As we will see
in chapter 13, the promises made about social housing for Vancouver's poor as
a "legacy" of the Games would rapidly evaporate from being promises in 2002
to "commitments" after Prague, then to "hopes," before being finally abandoned
altogether in 2007. Ah, but there might be jobs for "inner-city residents" to
provide services such as "recycling of beverage containers and janitorial services." Lucky them: They can clean up the trash left by the well-heeled tourists.
"Aboriginal participation and collaboration": Just as in the Sydney Games in
2000, aboriginals were going to be the unofficial Games mascots, doing their
quaint cultural dances for the tourists. As for collaboration, the very word says
it all, and in the most pejorative sense. "Economic benefits"? There was more
psychobabble without ever addressing the overall costs of the Games, conveniently ignoring infrastructure and security costs that form the bulk of the
final bill. Finally we come to "Sports for sustainable living." Ah, now we have
something really useful: VANOC was going to put some of our own money —
assuming any was left — into maintaining the white elephant sports facilities.
Did this mean that the facilities would be available at no cost to the public that
paid for them in the first place? Well, no, the $110 million trust fund was for
"operating and capital maintenance."

VANOC promised to release similar collections of unaudited reports in
each of the remaining years. But the really good news was that in 2009–2010,
the final report will be "evaluated by an outside source to ensure accuracy."[9]
Right, sure it will, after the Games are gone and no one is looking anymore.
Or maybe, as in Nagano (1998 Winter Olympics), the books will mysteriously
catch on fire?

VANOC's Sustainability Report came out shortly after its very own
"watchdog" organization, the IOCC, had released its own study. The IOCC
had known that VANOC's report was due out and wanted to get their licks in
first. Surprisingly, the watch-poodle had finally had enough nonsense from its
master and was going to take a nip out of John Furlong's leg, giving VANOC
a D– grade in all of the above areas.[10] At their press conference, an IOCC
spokesperson noted that VANOC and the government had simply failed
across the board and really deserved an F, but received the D– because there
was still three years in which to improve. All of this was par for the Olympic
course, rather perfectly fitting with past Olympic cities' performances. Most of
the media, however, reported the good news version without question, namely
that VANOC had received a "passing grade." One can only suppose that where
these journalists did their degrees a D– was considered a passing grade.

As outlandish as VANOC's Sustainability Report was, there was worse (or better, depending on your perspective) to come: VANOC's long-awaited business plan, almost four years after winning the 2010 Games in Prague, was about to be released. Real businesses put out such plans *before* launching into business, but then VANOC is not really a business in the true sense of the word. In the real business world, there are often shareholders who tend to ask pesky questions and want to know where the money is and what milestones are being met. In VANOC's corporate welfare world, the shareholders — the public — can go pound salt up their butts.

The release of the business plan itself was an odd event. VANOC sequestered reporters in its headquarters in East Vancouver, just as if the event were a government budget "lockup,"[11] gave them 20 minutes to digest the 196-page document, then gave a pep talk while highlighting the "good parts" version. VANOC noted the $1.68 billion operating costs and the venue construction costs of an additional $580 million, modestly admitting that a quarter of the former and all of the latter was taxpayer funded. Was the business plan, by any chance, audited independently? Um, well, no. "Audit, 'smaudit;' we don't need no filthy audits," has always been VANOC's motto, so why change now? There was also some unintended humor to the document: Nowhere in the lists of actual money spent were the billions for infrastructure, the key pieces of which had been crucial to getting the bid in the first place. As before with VANOC and the BC government, the convention center, RAV and the Sea to Sky highway upgrades were not Olympic debts at all since, according to both, the government "was going to build them anyway." Ah, but wait a minute, there in one appendix was a list of the "legacies" of the 2010 Games. How odd that these legacies included the very same convention center, RAV line and Sea to Sky highway upgrade. This is just wickedly cool, legacies that cost *absolutely nothing*. Also included in the legacies were the Athletes' Villages in Vancouver and Whistler, both slated to flow into the real estate market after the Games. Just as in VANOC's use of the word "sustainability," one has to wonder if they know what the word "legacy" actually means. We can, however, try to decipher what it is that VANOC means when they use the word "sustainability": the growing bank accounts of the developers; "legacy": the stuff (publicly funded real estate developments) that grows the bank accounts. No wonder they use these words so much.

VANOC had also ditched another of the perennial hot potatoes, the cost of security. Back in the days of the Bid Book, security had been pegged at a miniscule $175 million, far lower than any Olympic cities of the last dozen years, but now it was even better. Security expenses had now fallen to $10 million, the remainder presumably for private security for Olympic dignitaries and other "family" members. Gone were all the rest of the expenses, along with the nasty residual problem of having to account for the original lowball figure. This would now be the government's problem to deal with…and pay for, just one more freebie of the Olympic circus. (Just how un-free it will be we'll see in chapter 15). Another happy outcome of dropping $165 million from costs in such a cavalier manner was that now VANOC could crow that they might actually post a surplus in 2010. Thus, in a few keystrokes, a security bill that was absurdly low and a real embarrassment became instead a surplus of $100 million or so.

The rest of the document was a collection of what could only be called motherhood statements and platitudes. Amidst these were some frankly curious assumptions, such as this one: "The Canadian economy will remain relatively strong, with no recession, through Games time." How could they know this? They obviously couldn't since even the Bank of Canada and the US Federal Reserve seem to have gotten it wrong. As this book goes to press, the financial markets are in big trouble. What happens if there is a correction followed by a recession? VANOC's entire fiscal package falls apart is what.

This was not so much a business plan as a parody of Enron's accounting practices.[12] Did the press note any of this? Again, apart from Cox and a few other reporters, there was nothing. For many reporters, it may have been that they were pushing deadlines and couldn't take the time to sift through all the verbiage for anything resembling facts, let alone anomalies. Others were just as uncurious as they'd always been about all things Olympic, quite content to simply repackage VANOC's press releases for their presumably brain-dead audiences.

The IOC's Host City
Agreement for the 2010 Games

As part of the "candidature" package submitted to the IOC in 2002, the Bid Corp was required to answer a lengthy questionnaire covering 18 themes. From this arose an 81-page "Host City" document eventually signed by the Bid Corp, federal, provincial and municipal representatives (Vancouver and Whistler), the Canadian Olympic Committee and the Canadian Paralympic Committee.[13] The agreement opens with a series of 14 "whereas" clauses, one of which promises that the parties will "commit to sustainable economic, social and environmental practices as set out in Vancouver's bid to be awarded the Games" and "communicate openly with the public, the IOC and the host communities." Oho, we're in trouble already. We'll see later in part 4 that none of this happened, neither the "sustainable practices" nor the open communication with the public. Well, the glass is half full: At least they got through nine clauses before being in flagrant violation.

Next come 56 other clauses; number 4 under the "Operational" clauses calls for the development of a business plan. To be precise, the clause states: "Within *18 months* [italics mine] of the OCOG [Organizing Committee for the Olympic Games, i.e., VANOC] executing the Joinder Agreement as provided for in section 2.4(b), the OCOG will prepare a business plan that details, to the extent possible, the planning, organizing, financing and staging of the Games," specifically in regard to operating and capital costs. Let's see: this document was signed in November 2002...and the business plan was revealed to the media in May 2007, or, two and a half years late.

How about this clause: "6.2 (Financial and Other Reporting): The OCOG will provide the Parties with audited financial statements of the OCOG for each fiscal year of the OCOG, within 90 days of the fiscal year end. Final *audited* [italics mine] financial statements will be provided to the Parties within 180 days of the end of the Games." Didn't happen with any audits. As of 2008, nothing audited had been released. Violation number two.

Other notable clauses: 6. "Doping. OCOG will organize and implement a doping control program under the authority of the IOC Medical Commission or the World Anti-Doping Agency, whichever is applicable, and in consultation with the Canadian Centre for Ethics in Sport." Aha, one more expense for Vancouver taxpayers. Thanks IOC. Clause 14: "Intellectual Property. The cost of any protection or legal action taken to prevent any unauthorized use of intellectual property (e.g., copyright, industrial designs, trademarks, official marks) is borne by the OCOG." Moreover, the agreement calls on all levels of government to help them police the problem, as we will see below. Best of all, there is Clause 41: "Default by the OCOG: 'if the OCOG has submitted false or misleading information to the Parties or intentionally made a false or misleading representation' it is in default." I suppose this only applies if VANOC lies to its co-signatories, not to the public at large. If not, violation number three.

Now we come to the meat of the document: namely, who is responsible for doing what. In clause 17 we find "Canada's Contribution." Specifically, "$225 million for capital costs of sport and event venues [and] contribute $55 million to Legacy Endowment Fund; and provide all essential federal services "as they arise out of Canada's legislative obligations and prerogative." The latter presumably refers to security costs, conveniently not limited by amount. What else? "(Canada Agrees to) Import, use and export of Goods: to cooperate with the OCOG, the City, the COC and CPC, the IOC and IPC and other Games parties concerning the importation of goods required by the IOC, the IPC, delegations of participating National Olympic Committees and National Paralympic Committees, International Federations, as well as accredited media, sponsors and suppliers to carry out their obligations regarding the celebration of the Games. This has long been the practice for international athletic events. Consistent with this practice, relief would be provided from customs duties, excises taxes and GST on goods imported into Canada such as personal effects, gifts, awards, display goods and equipment." Nice. Translation: no customs duties for the Olympic Family.

There's more: "(Canada Agrees to) Peaceful holding of the Games: the Royal Canadian Mounted Police providing: (1) the lead in forming an integrated police planning group, (2) appropriate federal security measures which in the opinion of Canada are necessary, and (3) to cooperate with the OCOG, the City, the COC and CPC, the IOC and other Games parties on non-federal security matters; (Guarantee 18.27)." Whatever it takes to deliver the Games is what Canada will provide: cops, the military, you name it, and God help anyone who tries to protest.

Best of all: "(Canada Warrants that) Financial Guarantees: the IOC would qualify for an exemption from federal income tax, in which case the Goods and Services Tax (GST) paid by the IOC in its commercial activities would be fully recoverable through income tax credits." Sweet: no taxes to be paid by the IOC, as usual. No taxes in the host country, a non-profit tax-free status at home, and life is good.

Clause 18 lists British Columbia's contributions, and it's here that the financial rubber meets the road. First, the Province is on the hook for $255 million for capital costs of sport and event venues, $55 million for the Legacy Endowment Fund, "and [to] provide those services that would ordinarily be provided by the Province, as services that fall within its jurisdiction." Here's the best part: [the Province will] "guarantee the potential financial shortfall of the OCOG, subject to guarantee agreement(s) to be executed between the Province and the OCOG." Translated: The Province of British Columbia has signed a blank check. No matter what VANOC does or doesn't do, no matter how much over budget it goes, the Province can keep saying that there will be no more money, but at the end of the day, they signed the document that commits them to paying whatever the bill may turn out to be. British Columbians, by and large, remain unaware that the Bid Corp/VANOC, with the connivance of the government of BC, painted a very big S for sucker on the foreheads of every man, woman and child in the province.

We're still not done. The Provincial commitment also requires that, "legislation is in force that provides mechanisms, including the ability to prescribe regulations, for the purpose of reducing ambush marketing." The actual parts of this clause are worth quoting in their entirety:

5. a) i. the Land Act to control the use of Crown land within the vicinity of the 2010 Games venues,

    ii. the Highway Act and the Motor Vehicle Act to control the use of highways under the jurisdiction of the Province, and

    iii. the Trade Practice Act to control commercial representations which generate a false association with the 2010 Games; and

  b) additional legislation to reduce ambush marketing can be considered prior to December 31, 2007 if the Province concludes that the legal measures available to it today should be strengthened.

6. With respect to outdoor advertising spaces, the Province states its intention to:

  a) provide a binding option to the Bid Corporation to acquire, at market rates, any outdoor advertising space available on Crown land not leased or otherwise licensed to other parties as of January 1, 2003 in Vancouver, in Whistler, in the vicinity of the 2010 Games venues in the Callaghan Valley and in the vicinity of the 2010 Games venues at Cypress Mountain (collectively, the "Games Areas") and adjacent to Highway #1 through New Westminster, Burnaby, Vancouver, North Vancouver and West Vancouver and Highway 99 (the Sea to Sky Highway) from Horseshoe Bay to Pemberton, for the duration of the "2010 Games Advertising Period" (January 5, 2010 to March 16, 2010); and

  b) agree, with respect to any Crown land in the Games Areas which is newly leased or licensed, or for which a lease or license is renewed, to include a provision in such lease or license requiring that a binding option on any outdoor advertising space be granted to the OCOG for the duration of the 2010 Games Advertising Period.

8. The Province confirms that it will enter into agreements with the OCOG regarding Games-related venues that the Province owns and controls. These agreements will grant the OCOG control of all commercial rights (including in-stadium signage, catering and concessions signage and services, and venue naming rights) for the period of the 2010 Games, including the five days preceding the Opening Ceremony and the two days following the Closing Ceremony."

In short, everyone is really, really worried about "ambush marketing." Apart from television rights, the Olympic trinkets that can be sold, the profits shared between VANOC and the IOC are the heart of the revenue stream, and all levels of government are *required* to become the enforcement arms for the Olympic industry.

Now, finally, we come to Vancouver's contributions listed in the document that are also worth quoting:

> 20.1 If Vancouver is awarded the Games, Vancouver will:
> a) at its cost, provide those services that would normally be provided by Vancouver within its jurisdiction and within its normal financial framework, subject to any cost sharing agreements with other levels of government or the OCOG in respect of shared responsibility for services and subject to agreements specifying otherwise. These services may include normal levels of fire and rescue services; street cleaning, snow and ice removal and maintenance; parking operations and enforcement; garbage and recycling collection; traffic signal operation and maintenance; graffiti removal; water and sewer maintenance; street lighting; and by-law enforcement;
> b) *at its cost*, [italics mine] provide a level of police services that will organize schedules to accommodate the maximum allowable deployment to the Games under Vancouver's normal financial framework;
> c) *at its cost*, [italics mine] subject to the terms and conditions of the Vancouver's Athletes' Village Agreement and subject to the contribution of $30 million by the OCOG to Vancouver, provide the permanent facilities at the Vancouver Athletes' Village; and
> d) forego the revenue lost by Vancouver due to activities approved by Vancouver and related to the Games, including rent for Vancouver-owned facilities (including the Vancouver Athletes' Village, the Curling Venue, the Figure Skating/Speed Skating Venue and the Trout Lake/Kilarney Practice Facility) and parking revenues for Vancouver's parking lots and streets.

Recall Mayor Larry Campbell's promise of not one penny in costs? No wonder he skedaddled to the Senate before citizens could see how the fine print would play out.

Vancouver is expected to be very concerned about ambush marketing too. After all, we're talking big bucks here:

> 6. The City of Vancouver declares and confirms that:
>   a. the following by-laws are currently in force and would be effective in reducing Ambush Marketing:
>   the Street and Traffic Bylaw
>   the Street Vending Bylaw; and
>   the Sign Bylaw;
>   b. the City of Vancouver has the authority, within its lawful jurisdiction, to enact additional bylaws prior to December 31, 2007 to further reduce and sanction Ambush Marketing should it conclude the legal measures already available must be strengthened to ensure the Olympic sponsor advertising rights are well protected; and
>   c. the City of Vancouver is the owner of the streets located in Vancouver and has the rights and privileges of an owner as well as the regulatory authority of a municipal government.
> 7. With respect to outdoor advertising spaces, the City of Vancouver states its intention to provide a binding option to the Bid Corporation to acquire any outdoor advertising space on billboards located on land owned by the City of Vancouver in the vicinity of the 2010 Games Venues for the duration of the 2010 Games advertising period (January 5, 2010 to March 16, 2010).

Oh, and there is this small tidbit (see chapter 8): the City is responsible for constructing the Athletes' Village.

What does Whistler commit to? Pretty much the same shopping list of costs as Vancouver in terms of civic services, cops, venues, and — just like Vancouver — also to "forego the revenue lost by Whistler due to activities approved by Whistler and related to the Games including rent for Whistler-owned facilities (the lot one/nine Paralympic Sledge Hockey Venue, the Paralympic Curling Venue, Meadow Park Sports Centre and parking revenues for Whistler's parking lots and streets)."

Finally, the Host City Agreement worries about what to do with legacies, physical and financial, if any. Clause 30 states that VANOC will dispose of real or personal property, and any money received from the sale of assets will be added to its operating revenue as earned income. It *can* donate assets to sports organizations if its audited financial statements don't show a deficit. Clause 33 tidies up the potential but usually unrealized problem of what to do if the

Games show a surplus operating revenue, that is, a profit: "In the event of a surplus in the Operating Budget, the surplus will be divided as follows: 20% to the COC; 20% to the IOC; and 60% to the OCOG, the latter payable to a special fund called the Amateur Sport Legacy Fund, to be managed by the 2010 Games Operating Trust." So on top of everything else it gets, the lion's share of TV rights, the marketing cut, *et cetera* and *ad nauseum*, the IOC gets a further 20% of any surplus funds generated by Games funded by taxpayers. Oh, by the way, Clause 32, the "Intellectual Property Legacy" clause, advises that VANOC "will transfer all intellectual property that it develops or acquires to the 2010 Games Operating Trust, unless such property belongs to the IOC or COC." Translation: the IOC probably gets it.

On a scale of liabilities from zero to 100, the IOC gets off scot-free. The Canadian Olympic Committee has learned from its master and also skates away if necessary. Clause 38 is the "COC's Indemnification":

> The Parties acknowledge that under the Bid City Agreement, Vancouver and the OCOG have agreed to assume all commitments, liabilities, obligations or undertakings in relation to the Games, and shall indemnify the COC against any claim from, or liability to, a third party for all losses and expenses of whatever nature or kind which may be incurred in relation to the organization and staging of the Games.

And to remind us all that the Province owns the ultimate risk, Clause 38.2 notes that, "It is also agreed that the indemnity obligations of the Province in respect of Vancouver and Whistler under their respective Participation Agreements with the Province remain in full force and effect."

There is more, but by now you get the drift: In the special familial relationship between VANOC, the Province and the IOC, the IOC definitely gets to be the poppa.[14]

VANOC's Costs and Revenues and the Role of Commercial Partners

Chapter 13 will deal with the actual costs of hosting the Olympic Games and not only give the current and projected costs to Vancouver, but put these into the context of past Olympic host cities. Here I want only to touch on costs since these bear on the issue of revenues. Briefly, costs come in three main flavors: infrastructure, security and operating. The first two are wholly paid for by the various levels of government — read taxpayers — the last, some ratio of private and public funding. In VANOC's case for 2010, roughly 75%

of the operating costs are paid by private sponsors. These sponsors, like those of the IOC, are divided into categories: National partners include the telecommunications giant Bell Canada, the Hudson Bay Company (Canada's oldest company), the Royal Bank of Canada, General Motors, Petro-Canada and Rona, a supplier of household items and building supplies. Each partner pays VANOC a significant amount for the privilege of saying that they are official 2010 Olympic partners. Official supporters include Air Canada, the BC Lottery Corporation, Canadian Pacific (railways), the Insurance Corporation of BC, Jetset (an international travel agency based in Australia), Ricoh (a Japan-based IT company), the Royal Canadian Mint and Teck Cominco (a mining company). Again, sponsors pay to have to have their brands linked to the 2010 Games. Finally, there are the suppliers who provide specific services, including: 3M Corporation, Birks (a jewelry chain), Dow Chemical, Epcor (a Canada-based energy company), Haworth (Canadian-US based office furniture company), Nortel (telecommunications), TransCanada (another energy company), Vincor (a US-owned wine marketing company), Weston (a major Canadian Bakery) and Workopolis (a Canadian company providing services for employers and job seekers). Each of these can also link their names to 2010 by virtue of providing, *gratis*, work and matériel in their respective domains. And this just in: Millennium, the company building the Athletes' Village with so much taxpayer money, just found $3 million to give to VANOC as the newest local sponsor.

VANOC and the Commercialization of the 2010 Games

In addition to the revenues derived for operating costs by the various partners, sponsors and suppliers, VANOC clearly intends to make up some of their operating budget by selling Olympic souvenirs and trinkets. Hence, the same obsession that IOC shows for protecting their product line also worries VANOC, and they take aggressive measures to protect what they consider to be their commercial rights to the various Olympic products. VANOC also frets a lot about whether people are going to buy these products.

To find out about the latter, VANOC recently started conducting consumer "research." Of course they didn't call it that since it might sound too crude to be trolling for consumer information using the same consumers' tax dollars, and a lot of them too: up to $40,000 per poll, with an unknown number to be conducted between 2007 and 2010. Instead, VANOC pretended that they were merely trying to see if the public felt that they were "meeting their mission goals," whatever those might be. As their marketing director, Renee Smith-Valade, said in an interview: "Our [mission] is to touch the soul of the nation." Sceptics like me were wont to question whether it was really about "mission" and "soul" or product line and pocketbook. Ms. Smith-Valade neatly cleared up the question for us:

> If you take the concept, which I know is a bit lofty…that can be everything from "Do you want to buy a ticket?" to "How many hours of television do you think you'll watch?" to "Would you buy a mascot toy in a certain price range?"… *The research will also inform how we finalize programs like the launch of the ticket sales, how we structure the ticketing program, our upcoming consumer-merchandise program*, our advertising campaigns, the mascot program, the transportation program, the torch-relay program and the volunteer-recruitment program [italics mine].[15]

Does anyone still think this is about sports? If so, Ms. Valade-Smith has just proven otherwise.

Part of a general concern for VANOC's aggressiveness about ambush marketing is that it spills over to impact those who are not at all involved in commercializing real Games products. The VANOC/IOC need to keep unofficial folks (that is, non-VANOC or IOC or those who have paid the latter for the privilege) from making a buck on the Games may be legitimate: They do, after all, have products; it costs them (really us) a lot to host the Games, so their profitability, if any, may entirely depend on licensing. Olympic symbols and logos, not to mention product sales. However VANOC has copyrighted an absurd number of words that now can't be used in any commercial sense without paying them royalties. Such words include obvious choices, such as any variation of Olympics, but go far beyond this to include, for example, the year 2010.[16] In one case, a Vancouver restaurateur who has been in business for decades before Vancouver's bid has been threatened with legal action because his restaurant, the Olympic, not only has the name but also features the five interlocking rings.[17]

On behalf of VANOC, the federal government has passed copyright legislation to further guard against ambush marketing. Called C-47, the Olympic and Paralympics Marks Act, the legislation is so broad as to restrict the ability of artists and others to use any Olympic-related themes or symbols. As one artist noted:

> I first heard about Canada's new Bill C-47 when I was printing off my artwork for this year's graduation exhibition at the Emily Carr

Institute. My artwork, the Transit Shelter Project, focuses on the current debates around the Vancouver 2010 Olympics and homelessness. As my artwork ran off the printer, the technician asked, "You know that these are illegal?" I replied that I had used different pantone colors and computer fonts so I wasn't infringing upon any copyright laws. "What I mean is VANOC has copyrighted the number 2010," he added. I was completely floored and asked how anyone could copyright a number.[18]

The artist in question, Kimberly Baker, goes on to say: "In my opinion, Bill C-47 was a direct infringement of our freedom of expression under the Canadian Charter of Rights and Freedoms." Indeed it is, but this is perfectly in keeping with the entire thrust of the Games: It's all about them and their profits, and they can, and will, use any legislation or other method of intimidation required to secure their product line and make sure that no disruptions occur in the Games themselves. The book you hold in your hands is almost certainly subject to the same legislation, and my use of the terms "2010," "Olympics," "Games," "five rings," "Sea to Sky," etc. throughout may well be viewed as a violations in law and ambush marketing against the IOC and VANOC.

All of this goes far beyond copyright protection versus civil liberties. In part 4, I will touch on the impact of the Games on civil liberties in general, as well as the specific effects they have on the poor and homeless.

CHAPTER 8

Johnny Furlong's Privateers

We were told we'd cruise the slopes for Olympic gold
We'd spend no cash, shed no tears
Now I'm a broke(n) man on Vancouver pier
The last of Furlong's privateers

"FURLONG'S PRIVATEERS"[1]

After Torino, 2004:
Vancouver Steps into the Crosshairs

MARCH 2006 saw the end of Torino's Winter Olympic adventure and the handover of the Olympic flag to the next sucker, Vancouver. Actually, it was less a handover than a holdup, a transfer of IOC ownership. One could almost hear the IOC chortling, "Torino, we got what we wanted, now you get your city back; Vancouver, brace yourselves, your new owners are on the way." As the Games closed in Torino, Vancouver's new, paraplegic mayor, Sam Sullivan, wheeled up to take the IOC's emblem: five colored rings on a field of pure white, one ring for each continent (the IOC has never been good at counting), the white field intended to represent the purity of Olympic ideals. As we will see in the following, it's far less about "ideals" than "deals."

Flags are highly emotive symbols, striking many chords. Running a national flag up the flagpole stirs patriotic pride in the hearts of most, a fact that the IOC shamelessly exploits to full effect. When the cost overruns become too obvious to hide, local boosters and the IOC default to what Samuel Johnson once called "the last refuge of a scoundrel": patriotism.[2] Olympic organizing committees, the IOC and the media will all remark that no matter what else happens, what price can you put on seeing your athletes on the podium, modestly weeping as the Olympic medals are placed around their bowed necks, the national anthem blaring from loudspeakers as the crowd goes wild? Well actually, one *can* put a price on patriotism, but if packaged properly, patriotism for most people will trump fiscal, social or environmental realism each and every time. The IOC flag handover is a symbolic sleight of hand: Their flag over your city now, maybe your flag on the podium in four years time.

Sam Sullivan was the perfect choice for his assigned role as flag waver for the 2010 Games. Crippled in a ski accident years before, Sullivan had overcome adversity to become mayor after years of serving in the trenches of civic politics, the ever-loyal member of the NPA and a water carrier for the city's developers. In Torino he basked in his new stardom, taking the Olympic flag and spinning around in his wheelchair as he waved it for the crowds, a shining example of Olympic pluck and tenacity, our very own Citizen Sam. The cameras stayed focused on him, perhaps in part to avoid panning to the crowds reacting to the unbelievably cheesy pageant put on by VANOC to showcase Vancouver and Canada to the world. The pageant had featured a pseudo-modern Inuit-like creature driving out on stage in a snowmobile and pretending to ice fish. The spectacle may have been weirdly intriguing for the locals in Torino, perhaps serving to confirm the stereotypic suspicions that all Canadians live in igloos in a land of perpetual ice and snow. Back home the show received somewhat more scathing reviews, particularly in multicultural Vancouver where it may snow twice per year and then only briefly. The Canadian media dutifully cut away from Sullivan waving the flag for all he was worth to IOC *jefe* Jacques Rogge calling on the "youth of the world" to add to greenhouse gases by converging on Vancouver in 2010. The IOC had just cemented its conquest of yet another city. And the developers back home, already hard at work, were in absolute pig heaven.

The IOC's pass-the-flag spectacle in Torino had kicked off a series of VANOC-sponsored happy events back home in Vancouver. First, there would be a public Olympic flag-raising ceremony at Vancouver City Hall, complete with bagpipers and marching bands, Mayor Sam in his wheelchair and, of course, the IOC's flag of conquest. A few days later, VANOC and the City were going to have a ceremony at Sunset Beach in Vancouver's downtown West End at which they intended to kindle a pre-Olympics flame at a statue that had long graced that stretch of beach. Years earlier, the City had erected an Inuit stone monument overlooking the bay. It consisted of a number of stones roughly in the shape of a man, of which several of these formed the legs, a few made the torso, an elongated horizontal stone represented the arms and a final smaller stone on top served as the head. It was all very nice in principle, intended by earlier City fathers as a multicultural nod to Canada's far northern native peoples. Now VANOC had made this stone statue — or at least a stylized version of it — their logo for the 2010 Games.

The choice of this symbol called by VANOC an "inukshuk" and given the name of "Illaanaq," had, however, badly misfired. First, BC's aboriginal community had taken umbrage to the use of an Inuit symbol over one from their very own incredibly rich artistic legacy. "We've nothing against the Inuit people," they said, but what have the Inuit got to do with the Vancouver 2010 Olympics? Why didn't the organizers choose something symbolizing local native culture? A good question to which VANOC had only a lame reply: "Illaanaq" was to represent "friendship, hospitality, strength, teamwork and the vast Canadian landscape." It was "Canada's Games," VANOC said, the latter maybe not a bad public relations ploy considering that they had already gone back to the federal and provincial governments for an additional handout of 110 million taxpayer dollars. BC's First Nations, however, were not mollified, nor were those who knew something about the real meaning of Inuit symbols. Various commentators pointed out some rather glaring misconceptions surrounding the choice of the inukshuk as the logo for the 2010 Games. First, the correct term for such a statue is not "inukshuk," but "inunnguaq." While sometimes serving as signposts to help people find their way in the wilderness, the inunnguaq also has a somewhat darker purpose: They are placed along ridgelines in part to funnel migrating caribou into zones where they can be killed by hunters. For those of us in NO GAMES, the choice of an inunnguaq seemed perfectly appropriate as an inadvertent but subliminally accurate depiction of the future slaughter of taxpayers. Letters to the Editor of Vancouver's newspapers simply savaged the logo, one letter writer calling it a "Pac-man with a bazooka."

Regardless of what VANOC and Vancouver's Sam Sullivan intended with their post-Torino events, we had made our own plans to unveil what we thought was a more appropriate symbol of the 2010 Games: a pirate flag. I'd taken a skull-and-crossbones flag made years ago for my son when he was young and had a local seamstress add the Olympic rings above the grinning skull with dollar signs in the eye sockets. The numbers 2010 and 2040 were in one corner symbolizing the year of the Vancouver Games and the projected date when the debt from 2010 would be paid off.[3] Our goal was to take the flag to Sullivan's IOC flag-raising ceremony, then wave it at the "inukshuk" (sic) flame-lighting ceremony a few days later.

The flag-raising ceremony was scheduled for noon on a sunny spring day in 2006 just outside City Hall. The City had set up a stage with chairs for the dignitaries composed of civic, provincial and federal politicians, various high-profile boosters and the inevitable Jack Poole and his sidekick, the hapless

John Furlong. They'd also thrown up a police cordon around the stage and flagpole and were clearly braced for trouble. There had been some rumblings from anti-poverty groups, the protesters at Eagleridge had vowed to attend, and, of course, there was the potential that I would show up with NO GAMES "troublemakers." I had brought along the pirate flag and some lyrics to a modified version of an old Stan Rogers song, "Barrett's Privateers," that I planned to sing with local musician Andy Vine. Vine had taken an earlier version, spruced it up and was going to help me find some Eagleridge folks to help us sing it for the television cameras. He had also brought along paper pirate hats to get us in the mood.

As I approached the site, a beefy mustachioed police inspector approached me, addressed me by name, introduced himself and said that he really hoped I wasn't there to "cause trouble." I assured him I wasn't, merely intended to raise my flag. He was fine with that and quick to stress that he didn't want to interfere with my freedom of speech. These formalities past, I wandered past the wire fence that blocked off the stage and mingled with some of the Eagleridge folks who were standing silently with their picket signs, largely ignored by the media. Their "leader," Denis Perry, came over to politely ask if I would go stand somewhere else. My flag implied that there was something amiss about the Games and it would be a "public relations disaster" if the protest at Eagleridge was somehow associated with anything even vaguely anti-Olympic. This was a mantra that Perry would repeat until the Ridge was blown to dust, but at the time I respected their desire to have their own protest unsullied by my flag, so I wandered off to find Andy Vine. We put on our pirate hats, recruited a few of the younger and less squeamish Eagleridge protesters, waved the flag and sang "Furlong's Privateers." The media seemed to love it, and our point was made, while that of the Perry and the others was pretty much ignored.

In due course, a firefighter's marching band piped Sullivan to the podium, "O Canada" was sung, Sullivan and Furlong praised the Olympic spirit (all the while being jeered by some in the crowd), the pirate flag flapped in the breeze and then Sullivan wheeled himself to the flagpole to raise the five-ring banner. When he had finished, the pipe band marched him off again, and that was that. In the end, for all the hoopla and hype promoted by VANOC, protestors nearly equaled in number the boosters in attendance.

The Illaanaq flame-lighting a few days later was somewhat more successful for VANOC, which seemed to have gone all out to bring in supporters. Perhaps stung by the low attendance at the flag-raising ceremony, they had bussed in elementary school children to sing the national anthem for the crowd. It was a cute touch, not only patriotic, but using kids to sell the product. They'd also found some native drummers to prance around in front of the statue. I was there as well, Jolly Roger flying above my head as darkness fell and the flame was lit. I had taken a position just to the left of the stage, and it was amusing to watch Furlong look anywhere but toward the black flag. We had our own lighting ceremony: I lit up some play money to symbolize the costs of the Games.

The piracy angle was certainly a fun one for us to project and as apt an analogy for the Games as any. It also worked well for the media and those still not sure what the Olympics really meant for Vancouver. The skull and cross bones juxtaposed to the five Olympic rings certainly made a strong visual statement that was instantly understandable. We in NO GAMES had also worked up a culinary metaphor for food-conscious Vancouverites: escargot. What, after all, are escargot? Well, the obvious answer is that they are garden snails used as a vehicle for garlic butter. Indeed, apart from the latter, snails don't often make the culinary hit parade, at least outside of France. What they do offer is a suitably textured surface for garlic butter to stick to, one that won't get soggy (unlike bread or croutons). It's a far more discreet and Julia Childs-approved means of hoisting the garlic butter into your mouth than simply sticking your face on the plate. So what are the Olympic Games? Simply the fiscal equivalent of escargot: A superb means of taking taxpayer dollars and transferring them to the pet projects that local developers have been trying for years to fund. Such projects have usually failed before for two main reasons. First, the developers couldn't find the capital themselves. Or more likely, these same developers had in the past gone cap in hand to the government for corporate welfare in the form of public dollars, but failed here too. The latter, after all, can be a risky venture: Notionally, the various levels of government are responsive to citizens, citizens who might be able to do math and can ask nasty questions. When such capital projects are on the line, the uppity bourgeoisie are likely to be curious about business plans and bottom lines, about who ends up holding the bag if the project goes south, and what, *really*, are the benefits versus the costs, the actual risks versus the potential pie-in-the-sky rewards. Convincing skeptics, government and governed alike, is hard work. Often, as we will see in the examples below, it simply doesn't work at all if citizens get jumpy and politicians get nervous about what jumpy voters might do in the next election. If, say, you are Jack Poole or David Podmore or any of the others in Vancouver or their equivalents elsewhere, you need a vehicle to convey the money from my pocket into yours. What snails are to putting garlic butter down your throat, the Olympic "time to shine" is to real estate development. Poole and the rest understand this perfectly. Average citizens do not, hence the advantage is to the former. Politicians are sometimes in the loop, at least those parked in the back pockets of the developers. Other politicians are just too lazy to question the Olympic frame, or find the prospect of doing so too scary.

Jack Poole's Real Estate Dreams

To see the Olympic real estate frame in all of its glory, there is no better place to start than with our old friend Jack W. Poole. Poole is hardly unique, as the following examples will prove, but best typifies the phenomenon of how the Games are used by developers. It was Poole, after all, who chaired the Vancouver Bid Corp and who continues as Chairman of VANOC, who lobbied mightily for the 2010 Games with provincial and civic politicos, who offered up sidekick and Concert CEO David Podmore to ramrod through the vote for the Yes side in the plebiscite, and who recruited the excitable and out-of-his-depth former Arbutus Club manager, John Furlong, as CEO for the Bid Corp and VANOC. One way or the other, whether Poole wins more awards and honors, goes to the Canadian Senate like Larry Campbell or winds up in jail — or all of the above — the Games of 2010 are his baby.

The record of how Poole went from small-town prairie boy to kingpin of BC real estate makes for a remarkable story, one that has a number of parallels with the Olympic saga that emerged early in the new century. As we'll see later on, there are also remarkable similarities between Poole's early history and that of the group that later won the contract to build the 2010 Athletes' Village. Poole's Olympic saga also shows a number of similarities to Olympic developments in past and future host cities.

Poole, now in his early 70s, was born and raised in Mortlach, Saskatchewan. He had set his sights on an ice hockey career, but those rink dreams died in a freak car accident. Poole trained as an engineer, but seems to have had various other jobs before he moved to Vancouver in 1963 as a sales executive with a house building company. In 1964 Poole joined up with developer Graham Dawson and helped create Dawson Developments. Daon Developments arose from Dawson, also in 1964, by the simple expedient of dropping a "w" and an "s." Poole was the president and CEO, Dawson the chairman of the new company, and they did very well indeed in a burgeoning Vancouver real estate market. Between its start and the early 1980s, Daon became the second-largest real estate company in North America with properties in BC, Alberta, Ontario, California, Nebraska and Florida, amongst others. During these golden years, Daon's total assets increased thirty-six fold.[4] Alas, there was trouble brewing in the industry, and by 1982 Daon was in big trouble with a whopping debt of $2 billion.[5]

Poole and Dawson tried to face down the creditors and bankers, attempting time and time again to negotiate a restructuring deal to allow them to manage Daon's staggering debt. Things did not look promising, and the end of Daon seemed to be in sight. In 1985 Bell Canada tossed Poole a lifeline. Bell (Bell Canada Enterprises Inc.), initially a telephone/communications company, wanted to create a real estate arm, BCE Development Corporation (BCED), and saw that Daon might be the vehicle to allow them to do so. Bell offered Daon a one-to-one share trade; the outcome would be that Bell would own nearly 63% of Daon. Daon for all practical purposes would now be a subsidiary of BCED, but at least would still be alive; even better it would now be free of debt. Best of all, Poole and the other top Daon brass would stay and manage the new company. Dawson decided to retire, but Poole took the offer.

Various creditors objected and called for an Ontario Securities Commission investigation of the deal,[6] but the deal went ahead anyway. It was a new lease on life, but it was to prove a remarkably short one: BCED, with Poole at the helm, quickly lost another billion dollars and by 1989 was close to collapse. Poole resigned as chairman, selling off almost $6 million of his stock before the curtain came crashing down.

Daon and BCED, depending on one's perspective, were either glorious failures or unmitigated real estate disasters, ultimately costing shareholders somewhere in the $3 billion range. Blame either the higher interest rates of the 1980s or Poole's fiscal acumen, but by 1989 Poole's reputation was not stellar, one insider calling him, "a high-stakes Vancouver developer with a spotty record."[7] Still it could have been worse, and while Poole lost money, he still came out of the debacle far from poor.

One might have thought that future investors would be a bit wary of Poole's skills in the marketplace, and indeed he came in for his share of harsh commentary. Vancouver developer Larry Killiam noted that, "There's heavy boosterism with Mr. Poole on everything he does. He's of that old '70s school of thought and intimidation where if you're not positive about something you're some kind of a public villain."[8] These were curiously the same attitudes Poole would take with him in his bid for the 2010 Games, where opponents of all stripes were simply portrayed as simpletons, if not outright liars and knaves.

In 1989 it seemed that Poole was headed out to pasture, but actually he wasn't through with real estate, not by a long shot. Not long after BCED thundered in, a new chance — some might say the prime chance — appeared when an old friend came knocking on the door. The old friend was none other than Vancouver's NPA Mayor, Gordon Campbell, later to be the Liberal Party premier of BC. In both roles, Campbell neither was — nor is — a social democrat, nor is he unduly troubled by the woes of the middle class, let alone the poor. In 1989, however, he was supposedly quite worried about the availability of rental units in Vancouver's booming real estate market. His concern led him to approach Poole with the request that the latter start up a new company to provide "affordable" rental units in a city that was suffering from a severe housing shortage. Ironically, the very same housing crunch was in large measure created by the successful real estate boom driven by Expo 86.[9]

The scheme that Campbell, Poole and others put together behind the scenes was nothing short of brilliant: The new company, Vancouver Land Corporation (VLC) Properties, would fund itself as a sort of public-private partnership (P3) not only involving traditional private angel investors, but also including the City of Vancouver as a shareholder. To finish off the novel recipe, VLC would add on the unique notion of a massive capital tranche provided by 29 BC union pension funds.[10] If finding investor angels was the usual mechanism of Vancouver real estate funding, locking in the union pension funds was simply inspired as the means to a fiscal breakthrough. It not only ultimately provided all the initial capitalization needed, it also brought with it solid union support and, crucially, absorbed the "left-leaning" political parties allied to organized labor: COPE and the NDP. VLC's guarantee of union jobs and union pay rates pretty much ensured that the unions stayed on side as VLC grew through its future incarnations. When VLC's ultimate descendant, Concert Properties, pushed forward the 2010 Olympic bid, big labor was as firmly attached as a remora on a hammerhead. Union jobs are, after all, union jobs, was the ostensible rationale. As well, the pension funds were seeing big profits in real estate, just like everyone else. Did this mean big labor was turning its collective back on the poor and the environment? Well, not officially, but the political party of organized labor, the provincial NDP, would later show a remarkable callousness to both under their regime in the 1990s.

VLC's first board of directors combined union bosses and corporate bigwigs, a marriage that must have seemed odd to both sides. One can imagine the first few board meetings as traditional unionists broke bread with the Vancouver Board of Trade types and the developers, the latter who still used the old-fashioned methods for raising capital. The third leg of the company that Poole built was the City of Vancouver with its hands firmly into the mix. Vancouver was an early shareholder (in for $2 million), and Vancouver City Manager Ken Dobell became a member of VLC's Board of Directors. This was an obvious conflict of interest, a point not lost on some in the press and on City Council. Nonsense, just goodies for everyone, Poole may have replied. The same admixture of non-traditional allies and a something-for-everyone approach would be one that Poole would later use to good effect during the 2002/03 plebiscite campaign to get the 2010 Games. Along the way as the deals got bigger, Poole and his colleagues would further refine their methods with each reinvention of the VLC. All of this was practice for the mother of all deals: How to capitalize on the real estate boom that would follow a successful Olympic bid.

Mayor Gordon Campbell had been a real estate developer himself (Marathon Realty) and had once allegedly worked for Poole, who would later financially support his former protégé at each stage of his political career. For a future conservative premier who was relentlessly hostile to unions and who would make much of this reputation by union bashing, Campbell found it remarkably easy to work with VLC and its union pension funds and labor friends. It was so easy in fact that he didn't see any need to put the project for "affordable housing" out for tender.

The deal that Poole and Vancouver/Campbell negotiated was sweet: VLC would get $48 million of City land comprising 14 parcels, for a total of 81 hectares. Some of the parcels were in downtown Vancouver, others along the Fraser River. VLC would build 2,000 units per year with union labor and would hold an 80-year lease on the land for which they would pay just $10. The City would sweeten it more by investing $2 million in the company. One city councilor, Jonathan Baker, thought this all a bit rich when he noted that, "This is the best land deal for a developer since Manhattan Island was sold for $20 worth of junk jewelry. It's a steal for VLC. The company has tied up nearly $50 million of city land for 80 years, and the city is paying it $2 million."[11] Any potential COPE/NDP opposition was rendered impotent by the presence of the union dollars and VLC's promises of a strict union job policy.

The project by VLC to build "affordable" housing for lower-income Vancouver residents garnered an additional $15 million in 1993 from the NDP government of Premier Mike Harcourt, perhaps in part due to the lobbying of Ken Georgetti, the head of the BC Federation of Labour…and a member of the Board of Directors of VLC. In the end, VLC only built a total of 1,143 units, and they were not at all "affordable."[12] No worries, no one seemed to care; both civic and provincial governments had their hands in the trough and were hardly about to investigate.

Poole had found the real estate sweet spot: As a corporate player, VLC had ties to the business interests of the province and Vancouver's ruling party. With the unions onside, they could get the ear of the provincial opposition, the NDP. It was, thus, land and money from the right side of the spectrum and eventually more cash from a future provincial government of the left. How

Poole and Dobell had united right and left in a joint greed quest remains one of BC's great and largely untold success stories.

With the bottom line secured, VLC was up and running, and it soon had more ambitious projects in mind. VLC managed an Alberta offshoot called Prairie Land Corporation in the early 1990s, also built with union pension funds. VLC had also now split into two entities (real estate and properties), the better to separate land holdings versus construction projects. The entities had done well with the Vancouver deal and were now armed with significant capital and looking for bigger challenges. In due course, the next challenge hove in sight. In 1993 VLC actively went after the most lucrative thing going: an expanded Vancouver Convention Centre with an associated casino. VLC won the approval of the Vancouver Port Corporation.

By 1995 VLC was an entity called Greystone (actually two entities, just as with VLC: Greystone Real Estate Corp and Greystone Properties), "Greystone" was a friendlier, "more comforting" moniker according to CEO David Podmore, long-time Poole associate who had been VLC CEO since 1991.[13] Greystone was wholly owned by union pension funds. Greystone took on VLC's ambitious notion of the convention center/casino project, one that included a thousand-room hotel, an associated casino, a convention center and a cruise ship terminal. There would even be room for numerous theatres and shops. The project was initially called Seaport, and Greystone was to fund the construction itself, then lease it all to the City. The casino project would involve a Las Vegas company, Mirage Resorts Ltd., as a partner, obviously taking the view that Las Vegas certainly knows casinos, so who better to partner with than the owner of one.[14]

Financially, Greystone was doing well and had $300 million in assets by 1997. They'd even tried their hand at building a ski resort, Silver Star near Vernon. The convention center plan was coming along well, too, and Greystone seemed to be firmly locked into the inside track. Originally, three companies had been in the running: Greystone, Marathon Developments and Concord Pacific. The province's NDP government of the new premier, Glen Clark, appeared to favor Greystone with its union funding and jobs. The Vancouver Port Corporation, then under the control of Carole Taylor, future Canadian Broadcasting Corporation head and BC Liberal Minister of Finance, was firmly on their side as well. With godfathers like these riding shotgun, it was all a done deal. The other companies read the tea leaves and dropped out. The deal was better now too. Originally VLC had been solely responsible for financing, with the bill running in the $200 million range. Now the tab looked a lot higher, and suddenly Greystone really didn't want to have to pick up the bill on its own. Wouldn't it make sense, they wondered, if the provincial government would pick up the lion's share? Premier Glen Clark who had risen through the union ranks, notionally as staunch opponent of the corporate sector, seemed to agree that this was just a peachy idea. VLC's original pandering to the unions was paying off yet again.

By 1999, just as the Greystone twins were morphing into two other siblings, Concert Real Estate Corporation and Concert Properties Ltd., the project starting going south. The name change was not a particular worry indeed, according to Podmore, it was a more-fitting name, symbolizing the "working together — in concert — with contractors, suppliers and communities."[15] The real problems, however, were twofold: The escalating costs for the project were now so high that the NDP government was getting cold feet. In addition, there was growing public opposition to a casino. On the financial issue alone, the NDP was getting clobbered by the opposition Liberals. Gordon Campbell, now leader of the Liberals said, "We should not be pursuing any open-ended contracts. They [the NDP government] don't even know what the final cost will be, and if you can't guarantee the costs, I guarantee you it will go up."[16] It was a curious comment for a man who later as premier would provide the equivalent of an unsecured line of credit to VANOC and the 2010 Games in the total absence of a business plan.[17]

In regard to the proposed casino, Podmore explained the inclusion as a solution to the problem of finding sufficient capital funding. Not all the public saw it this way: A Las Vegas partner evoked the image of the big casinos, in turn raising the specter of possible mob connections, connections that just might have been quite real.[18] While not all Las Vegas casinos are extensions of the Mafia, there is little point denying that the latter used Las Vegas gambling and real estate in various places to create a legal identity untainted by gang wars, drugs and prostitution. This prospect alone seems to have spooked the NDP government that up until this time had been committed to the project. To add to their concerns, Concert was now demanding that the government underwrite all extra costs associated with the Convention Centre expansion. Oddly reminiscent of future Olympic cost escalations, the original $200 million price tag was rapidly approaching $900 million. By 1999, union buddies notwithstanding, Concert and the government couldn't strike a deal. It seems that Concert and the hotel partner, the Marriott chain, wanted still more from the public dole. The government balked and the project seemed doomed. It was, but Concert was actually doing pretty well: By now they were one of the biggest and richest real estate development companies in BC, if not in all of Western Canada.[19]

The NDP government's concerns had been legitimate, both in regard to the potential to introduce organized crime to BC (which, by the way, has been here for quite awhile) and for the almost inevitable cost overruns. But in politics a year is forever, and the government of Glen Clark was on shaky ground. He, for one, would soon be hounded from office for allegations that he was in bed with none other than a potential casino developer. Clark's eventual replacement, Ujjal Dosanjh, would soon take the NDP for a dive in the 2001 provincial election, and Jack Poole's former protégé, Gordon Campbell, would assume the premiership.

The Path to "Millennium Water"

Once Gordon Campbell and the BC Liberals were in power, the privatization floodgates opened. The reborn P3 fever matched up perfectly with Poole's now upfront campaign for the 2010 Winter Olympic Games that had started in 1998 with the shadowy Vancouver-Whistler 2010 Bid Society. And, to no great surprise, early in 2002 with the Bid Corp up and running full steam ahead, a revitalized convention center scheme had become an absolute necessity for capturing the Games. Strike my head and call me a carpet tack, Buffy, but does this stuff ever die? Nope, not as long as you've got the equivalent of escargot… or more precisely, the Olympics, and gullible rubes to sell it to.

And Jack Poole did. He had perfected the formula of co-opting labor for capital and support and melding it into the entrepreneurial class for projects to be built on public land at taxpayer expense. With the advent of the Games bid, the convention center, City land at Southeast False Creek, Eagleridge Bluffs, the Callaghan Valley and more were now up for grabs and, best of all, to be financed by the greatest suckers of all on behalf of Olympic glory: the taxpayers. Sprinkled with Olympic pixie dust, the dumbest capital projects suddenly seemed sensible, even sublime. It was, after all, "our time to shine," and what better way to shine than to build lots of infrastructure? No doubt Poole also considered that his sometimes acrimonious relationship with the developers he'd pissed off in his Daon days might vanish with all the goodies being showcased; maybe the disasters would be forgiven if not forgotten? For Poole, it must have been all he could do to suppress a belly laugh, let alone the famous smirk.

Even before Vancouver was shortlisted for the 2010 Games in the summer of 2002, the original Bid Society had dissolved to be replaced by the newer, slicker Bid Corp with Jack Poole as its Chairman and John Furlong as CEO. Podmore was left back at Concert's office until the unexpected happened, and some fools in the newly elected COPE-dominated City government called for a plebiscite. Well, this certainly wasn't good news, and Poole said so, threatening that, if the pro-Games side lost the plebiscite and Vancouver pulled out, the City might get sued by the Canadian Olympic Committee. Poole even managed to smirk as he made the threat. This did not go over well with some of the public and even some in COPE who didn't much like the attitude on display. Poole promptly put a sock in it, more wisely deciding perhaps that while he had to fight tooth and nail for the bid, making him the public face of the Yes side was not a clever move. Instead, it was time to bring over Concert's key apparatchik, David Podmore.

Podmore ran a smooth campaign, well greased by the Bid Corp's money, as well as financial and in-kind contributions of the City, the Province and the federal government. It seemed obvious to us in the NO GAMES Coalition that Concert was putting its resources and personnel behind the Games for one reason only: They hoped to skim off some of the eventual real estate and construction projects if Vancouver won the bid. Poole hotly denied it; Podmore, the better politician, basically agreed with Poole while leaving the door open, if only so slightly, for Concert to contribute in some small way. How small that might be, he didn't spell out.

By the fall of 2005, with the bid won and VANOC spending taxpayers' dollars like drunken sailors, the City of Vancouver put out a tender for the future Athletes' Village at the City's Southeast False Creek lands. Five companies submitted initial letters of intent: well-known Concord Pacific and Wall Financial were in, along with the smaller and less well-known corporate creature variously called Millennium Properties Ltd. or Millennium Development Corporation by the media. Another relative unknown was Windmill Development.[20] And, there was one other: Concert. Concert Properties? Jack Poole's Concert Properties? The very fellow, Chairman of the Bid Corp and VANOC, who said his company wouldn't bid on any Olympic venues? Yes, the one and the same, Jack W. Poole. No conflict, Jack Poole said of his own bid, we never said we wouldn't bid on Olympic things, not really. No conflict, said VANOC's Furlong, Poole's loyal lieutenant, as did the City of Vancouver. Did they all think the public was stupid? Well, yes, they did. The press, however, was for once not being their usually sycophantic selves, and even Jeff Lee of the *Vancouver Sun* was stunned. Lee, who had long ago written about VLC and its successors, had also covered the bid period and remembered quite well Poole saying that Concert had no intention on bidding on the Athletes' Village. Lee wrote a scathing column about it,[21] and other reporters began to take note.

At the time, I was on sabbatical in New Zealand, but CKNW and other media tracked me down there to get my comments. "We told you so," was my

typical reply. "Why else do you think Poole and Podmore and Concert backed
the bid?" Back home in Vancouver, the media scrutiny intensified to the point
where the Liberal's then finance minister, Colin Hansen, took the unusual step
of forcing Concert to back out. Sulking mightily, Concert did, and there were
four companies left, three of which would eventually submit full bids that included the plans for the future village and how much they would pay the City
for the land.

A Mysterious Company Called Millennium

In April 2006 the City of Vancouver announced the outcome: The winner was
— surprise — Millennium. Why? Mainly, said Jody Andrews, director of the
Southeast False Creek Project, because Millennium offered $20 million more
than the other companies, a total offer that had come in at a sweet $193 mil-
lion.

Reading the news reports, I realized I'd never heard of Millennium. Not
that I knew all the myriad real estate companies operating in the Lower Mainland, merely that with things Olympic, I had thought I knew the major players. So, I starting to do some digging to see who the corporate officers were,
what kinds of projects they'd done before, all the sorts of things one would
want to know in a multimillion dollar deal. None of these details seemed to
be in any of the media reports. Millennium's website talked about some past
projects and mentioned that they were part of something called the Armeco
Group of companies, but that was it. A quick survey of the corporate registry
revealed that the Armeco Group was not registered as a corporation in BC,
but Millennium had been around since 1988. The helpful receptionist did find
something resembling Armeco: Armeco Construction Ltd. What was interesting was that both Armeco Construction and Millennium Properties Ltd.
had their corporate offices at 198 West Hastings Street in Vancouver. This
made sense if they were both part of the overall Armeco Group. Figuring that
the latter would be registered federally, I tried the equivalent Government of
Canada registry office. Nope, no federal registry for Armeco or Millennium.
None of this excluded the possibility that the Armeco Group was registered
in another province, in the US or offshore. So who was Armeco Construction?
The sole director was one Paul S. O. Barbeau, a lawyer. The other listed official
was the secretary. The records revealed that Armeco Construction had been in
existence since 1981 and filed blank-page corporate yearly summaries. In other
words, they didn't actually do anything. Certainly they did no construction.
Digging back a bit more, I found that Armeco Construction had been previously called 596106 British Columbia Limited and had changed their name in

2003. Both Armeco and its predecessor were, in other words, "shell" companies. More Google searching told me that there were two brothers involved in Millennium, Peter and Shahram Malek (sometimes given as Malekyazdi), both originally from Iran.[22]

At this point, I didn't know what I was looking at so I called Charlie Smith of the *Georgia Straight* and told him what I knew so far. "Barbeau?" he asked. "I think he used to be the president of the NPA and left a few months ago."[23]

A few hours of digging — something the journalists at the *Sun* or *Province* had presumably not done — had turned up some rather glaring anomalies: The company that had just received the go-ahead for the high-profile and presumably extraordinarily lucrative Olympic Athletes' Village seemed to have a murky history in BC, and their only clear lineage linked them to a company presided over by a formerly high-ranking official of Vancouver's ruling party, the NPA. Nothing illegal yet to be sure, but just as surely a potential conflict of interest and one that citizens might just want to see the media explore a tad more aggressively. Since, however, the media had restricted themselves to official press releases, I realized that it would be up to us in 2010 Watch. I would have to do more digging into Millennium's background, but first I had to see the City's contract with them.

First, I asked politely with a letter to the City's information officer. When she responded that the information was proprietary, I put in a Freedom of Information (FOI) requesting to see the contract and any paperwork concerning how Millennium was chosen. The information officer logged in my request and suggested I speak to the City's director for the Southeast False Creek/Olympic Village project, Mr. Jody Andrews. I called the gentleman up and left a voice mail in which I introduced myself and my purpose. Andrews called back in a few days to tell me that I couldn't see the contract because "fine points" were still being negotiated. Not to worry, he told me, he'd let me know when the material was available. In fact, he'd just "put a yellow sticky" on his computer screen to remind him to give me a call when the contract was ready for outside viewing.

The City legally had 30 days to action my FOI request, and Andrews didn't know when the contract with Millennium would be finalized. There was little else to do on the file for now, so when stuck, it must be time for a beer. That night I went down to my neighborhood pub to mull over the odd features of Millennium's agreement with the City. The bartender, Justine, a tall redhead, had long kept abreast of my anti-Olympic activities and was eager for news. "Well, there's this odd deal with a mystery company and the City of Vancouver to build the Athletes' Village for the Games," I told her. As I described the bits and pieces of what I knew, her face told me she found it puzzling too. It was a quiet night in the pub, and our conversation must have drifted over to a nearby table where a large 30-ish dark-haired woman and several men were chatting. The woman kept looking our way. Justine called her over and introduced us. The woman, who will remain anonymous, turned out to be an accountant with a private firm in Vancouver. She was getting tipsy, and perhaps later she would regret what she told me, but after shaking hands she blurted out: "Yeah, I heard about it [the deal]. You aren't looking in the right direction; you have to find the 'mother ship'; think about Hastings Park." "What's that mean?" I asked. "I really shouldn't be talking to you about this," she said, taking the drinks back to her companions. Later, even tipsier than before, she passed me again en route to the bathroom, whispering, "Find the mother ship."

The "mother ship" comments seemed perfectly typical of the general weirdness of all we had learned about the Vancouver bid up to this point, and for an organization such as ours with little in the way of financial resources, difficult to act on. Obviously, the comment was meant to suggest that Millennium was a front for something else, a company or organization, perhaps an individual. But what or whom? Or maybe the woman had just been watching too many *Star Trek* reruns. The reference to Hastings Park suggested that the key might lie in either the racetrack or slot machines, or both. Did this suggest a connection to organized gambling operations? It all made for tantalizing clues, but no more. There was only one clear path: Find out the details of the contract between Millennium and the City of Vancouver.

The City's deadline for disclosure came and went. Their position now was that since the material involved a third party (Millennium) they didn't have to disclose details without the company's approval. I complained to the office of the provincial Freedom of Information commissioner who must have had a chat with Vancouver officials because the documents finally showed up in my mailbox, albeit six months after the initial request had gone in. There were some 500 pages, many irrelevant, but some of the material was very revealing. Even more revealing was what was cut out, notably the lender's agreement with Millennium, now called Millennium Southeast False Creek Properties Ltd.[24]

For starters, the contract specified the actual nuts and bolts of the deal. Millennium would pay the City $193 million for a 23-acre parcel of land along False Creek, called 2A by the City and part of an overall redevelopment plan of some 50 of a total of 80 acres aimed for the real estate market. Millennium would construct 1,100 housing units of differing sizes. Two hundred and fifty of these would belong to the City and provide the so-called affordable housing units that were some of the earliest promises the Bid Corp and City had made in 2002. Another term for "affordable" was "non-market." Both terms were used at various times in the documents, but the meaning seemed roughly the same. These units were aimed at the lower third of the income range in the City. The rest would be for Millennium to pre-sell at whatever price the market would bear. Fifteen percent of the $193 million, or about $29 million, would be paid by Millennium to the City up front, the balance in 2010 when the company took possession of the buildings after the Games were over. While future owners couldn't move in until after the Paralympic Games in 2010, nothing was stopping Millennium from raking in the dough now. As of this writing, Millennium Water is up for sale; indeed, the first phase is already sold out.[25]

As part of the overall deal, the City would pay Millennium a total of $82.2 million, with payments as the City's units were constructed. It is a fair assumption that these units will be built first. The City's payment would be made up of the invoiced costs for building the units along with a $10,000/month bonus. In addition, the City would be responsible for a raft of other expenses to help get the site ready for construction. These included: road excavation and backfill; construction of water pipes, sewers and storm water systems; provision of district heating systems and third-party utilities (including hydro, gas and telecommunications); and finished roads, sidewalks and bridges. Shoreline reconfiguration and construction and compensatory fish habitat were thrown in as well. Since the site was a former industrial area and massively contaminated with heavy metals and hydrocarbons, the City was to provide for soil removal. If the project was behind schedule for any reason, the City would pay for extra workers and heavy equipment to get it done on time for the Games. The shopping list went on: the City would pay for terrorism insurance ($1,474,000); all permits, licenses and approvals; the care and maintenance of the Village up to the Games; taxes on property and more. During the Games, the City would also toss in other services such as garbage collection, natural gas, ventilation and air conditioning. The total tab to the City of Vancouver for site remediation would come in near $153.4 million, above the $82.2 million for the 250 city units.

All one could do was say, "Wow," was this a sweetheart deal, or what? I sat down to do some back-of-the-envelope calculations. Not having upfront costs for site remediation or excavation is a great beginning for any company about to launch into a major project. Their first real cost would thus be the $29 million that they would have to cough up now; but they would get back $82.2 in installments as City parcels were built. In other words, after an initial cash outlay, Millennium would be building the Village with City money.

Putting the low-end cost per unit at $450,000 (the current price for a small condo in the area), and the upper at $6 million (Millennium's projected cost for the top-end units), we can safely assume that the bulk of the units will eventually be worth above $1 million each, so this number is a good average estimate. Here is where the numbers get really odd. The estimated building cost of the entire village of 1,100 units is about $362 million (Vancouver paying $82.2 million for the 250 smaller units; the other 850 units at the same ratio are almost $280 million more).[26] Hence for a total cost to the company in the ballpark of $473 million ($193 million for the land; $280 million for construction), Millennium's return will certainly vastly exceed its expenditures. While it's not clear what fraction of the units will go for the lower prices, it's safe to bet that most of those at $450,000 will be the same size as the City units and hence only a fraction of the total. If average prices come in over a million each, a profit margin of over 100% is not impossible. Indeed, it's likely and a pretty awesome deal in anybody's business. Given that Millennium can already sell the units in advance, they are going to be ahead of the game from the beginning. The profit spread could even be a lot more, depending on where the market goes in the next few years. In addition, Millennium might just end up inheriting some or all of the City's 250 units.[27]

Here is another odd thing: An earlier estimate put Millennium's construction costs at only $233 million for the 850 larger units. If true, the cost to the City is about $329,000 per unit, while the costs to Millennium are $274,000 per unit. It might look to an independent observer as if the city is overpaying for its share of the units. Why they would do so remains an open question, one more odd financial angle that Olympic real estate ventures seem to be so full of.

Tracking Vancouver's Millennium Deal

The magnitude of the housing deal brought me back to my initial question: Who or what is Millennium? This, in turn led to a related question: Who are the project lenders? The documents provided by the City included a project lender agreement with the name(s) of the lenders whited out. There was also the related question for the City: Precisely how much is all the site work going to cost Vancouver's taxpayers? I wrote to Andrews for the information, suggesting that I would do another FOI, if necessary. Instead, he suggested a face-to-face meeting with the City's director of financial planning and treasury, Ken Bayne.

After much e-mail discussion, the time for a meeting was set: early May 2007. I told Andrews that I would show up with Conrad Schmidt of the Work Less Party and Maureen Bader, the new director of the BC office of the

Canadian Taxpayers' Federation (CTF). The plan was that Andrews and Bayne would do a short presentation about the Southeast False Creek project then answer our questions.

Jody Andrews' office is in a shoebox shaped concrete two-story structure practically under the south end of the Cambie Street Bridge. The building sits plonked at right angles to a seawall walkway that runs from Granville Island and dead-ends at a chain-link fence a few feet to the east. If you put your nose to the fence, you can look down False Creek toward the future site of the Athletes' Village. On the day of the meeting, a crane in the distance marked the far boundary of the site. A metal staircase near where the seawall stops climbs upwards to a pedestrian overpass on the bridge deck. At the various landings, one can look out and gaze upon the massive project now underway: dump trucks coming and going with monotonous regularity, backhoes digging and bulldozers pushing the soil around.

The day of the meeting arrived. Jody Andrews came to great us at the reception, looking like the epitome of an up-and-coming city executive: 30s, fashionably long hair, nice suit. He even managed to project an earnest can-do attitude and candor as he ushered us into a small conference room to meet Ken Bayne, 50s, mustashioed and serious in a dark suit, looking like he was expecting an ambush, but friendly enough for all that.

The meeting began with an overview of the City's grand scheme for the entire parcel. When it came time to discuss the Village, Andrews and Bayne were at pains to emphasize that the City was not going to lose money, rather they planned to make bags of it, about $64 million by their count. Perhaps they stressed the financial windfall because Bader of the CTF was present and both she and the CTF have a well-deserved reputation for chastising those who waste taxpayers' money. We asked the question: With all the costs to the City, how were they going to make money? The answer: on the sale of the land to Millennium and the rental and maybe future sale of the City's units, units they were now calling "subsidized housing." Could they provide a breakdown of all their costs for the parcel to justify the notion that the City was going to get rich? They'd get back to us about that, they promised. Next question: Who was on the City panel that selected Millennium from the other competitors? "I don't remember," said Andrews, "but I'll find my notes and get back to you." He was as good as his word and later provided documents showing how the process was structured.

Now I wheeled out my big question: "Who are the project lenders?" "I won't give you their names…ask Millennium," Andrews replied. "If you won't tell me, why would they if they don't have to? Did you know about Millennium being connected through the Armeco Group to Barbeau?" Andrews did not seem particularly comfortable with the question and for the first time seemed annoyed. In regard to the Barbeau connection, Andrews had this to say: "After the 2010 Watch press release,[28] I asked Peter Malek if there was any conflict… and he said there wasn't; merely a case that their dad's Armeco Group had some dealings with Barbeau through Armeco Construction, and so to honor their dad, they kept the relationship."

There was silence in the room as Schmidt, Bader and I absorbed this last tidbit. What this meant, of course, was that he hadn't *known* about the connection and thus hadn't thought to ask the question until after it was pointed out to him by the press release. This, to me, was an amazing statement. "That was the extent of your due diligence?" I asked at last. "If you are suggesting that we did anything wrong…," he said, beginning to bristle, then changed to a softer note. "The explanation seemed sufficient." I let it go for the time. There would be more time to revisit the issue in the future, and I still wanted the two pieces of information Andrews had promised, namely those who sat on the selection committee and the full cost breakdowns for the City's expenses on the project.

The meeting ended on a cordial note. Weeks went by, but there was still no further information coming from Andrews or Bayne. In reply to an e-mail prompt, Andrews replied that there was a lot of work on the project going on, so thanks for being patient…we'll get back to you soon. Eventually, some six weeks later, some of the material showed up. The list of panel members gave their titles, but not their names, so we were forced to find these ourselves from staff lists on the City's website. The cost breakdowns for the various parts of the Southeast False Creek project only served to complicate matters. At the meeting, Andrews and Bayne had said the City would make more than $64 million net profit on the entire project. Now they showed figures suggesting that the Athletes' Village would return about $30 million. The problem was that they had calculated the fees from Millennium against the site remediation for the *entire* 80 acres, making figuring out the actual expenses versus revenues for the Village alone subject to a lot of guesswork.

The Continuing Hunt for the "Lenders"

On the subject of the project lenders, I still don't know who they are, but finding out could open the entire can of worms. Why, after all, would you want to hide being involved with the Games? VANOC usually crows that companies will reach deep into their pockets to be associated with the Olympic rings, so why the secrecy about the project lenders? One source suggested the tantalizing possibility that Millennium, like Concert, had tapped into the same mother lode of union pension funds.

There are many missing bits to this story, but here is what there is overall as this book goes to press: A very sweet deal for a relatively little-known company has been signed onto by the City of Vancouver. The company has a somewhat mysterious past, unknown investors and lenders and ties to individuals associated with Vancouver's ruling civic party. In my view, all of this seems more than enough to galvanize a curious investigative reporter into asking some hard questions. As of this writing, no one in the corporate media has. While I've shared the FOI material with a number of news organizations (three so far), there has been little follow-up. Those of the mainstream media profess interest but claim to be too busy to look into it in detail. The non-mainstream media with their limited resources are simply scared of being sued.

Whether or not we ever get to the bottom of it, there are some remarkable similarities to VLC back in 1989. Then, as now, City land was on the table. Then, as now, the City's terms were remarkably generous. VLC got rich off of their deal with Gordon Campbell and his governing NPA. Millennium will get fabulously rich in their dealings with Vancouver's current NPA mayor and council. Both projects slid through City Council as if on greased rails, with little or no scrutiny of the players involved. Given all of this, it's difficult to avoid the queasy feeling that the grand cookie-cutter scheme of 1989 that helped developers get filthy rich is still in play.

The main differences between 1989 and 2008 lie not in the minor details of the projects, but rather in their scale. VLC's original "social housing" deal was relatively big money in the late '80s...but peanuts compared to the money on the table after 2003, thanks to the magnifying effect of the Olympic Games.

Kevin Falcon's Two Trenches

*No one there ever questions the need to build infrastructure like
this. Now, granted, China has a bit of a different governance
structure. But, in many ways, it is the ideal governance structure.
China really has the ultimate Kevin Falcon government
structure...[emphasis added]. [The Chinese] don't have the
labor or environmental restrictions we do. It's not like they have
to do community consultations. They just say "We're building a
bridge," and they move everyone out of there and get going within
two weeks. Could you imagine if we could build like that?*

KEVIN FALCON[1]

Vancouver's Olympic Building Spree

OF THE FOUR massive projects associated with the 2010 Games,
two are pretty well-known to the media and public; two others
are sleepers, not well-known at all, but just as costly in the end. The
well-known ones are the Richmond Airport Vancouver (RAV)
connector, now called the Canada Line, and the Convention Centre. The first has been in the press a great deal of late, mostly for
annoying the public with the gaping holes in Cambie Street that
back up traffic in all directions, for destroying the livelihoods of
local merchants, by limiting public access to their businesses.[2] The
company building the line simply misrepresented the nature of the
project in a classical "bait and switch" manoeuvre. The Convention Centre
had been in the developers' spotlights for well over a decade. The sleepers are
the real estate bonanzas at Eagleridge in West Vancouver and the Callaghan
Valley west of Whistler. One of each has provincial minister of transportation
Kevin Falcon's fingerprints all over it. Both of these crucial parts of Vancouver's bid for the Games.

The RAV Line,
aka Falcon's Trench South

The mess created by the RAV project puts me in mind of the opening stanza of Robert Service's poem, "The Cremation of Sam McGee."

> There are strange things done in the midnight sun
> By the men who moil for gold;
> The Arctic trails have their secret tales
> That would make your blood run cold;
> The Northern Lights have seen queer sights,
> But the queerest they ever did see
> Was that night on the marge of Lake Lebarge
> I cremated Sam McGee.

Maybe it's the "moiling" part that always gets my attention because there's a powerful lot of moiling happening on what used to be Cambie Street. From the Cambie Street Bridge all the way to Richmond, huge gouges have been ripped in the street, the exposed sections resembling more a muddy open pit mine than anything else. Welcome to "cut and cover," SNC-Lavalin's cunning plan to build the RAV Line without tunneling. Men in hard hats scurry around, tractors and backhoes rumble and grind, and commuters who haven't figured out alternative routes are utterly screwed. Finding a way around the mess is not simple since Cambie runs north-south across the city and anyone going east-west way has to cross Cambie at some point. The cut-and-cover scheme makes it nearly impossible to figure out where the mess will be at any given time and those who miscalculate are in for a long wait. Double lanes shrink to single lanes on the east-west main routes, side streets are blocked off seemingly at random, and drivers have begun to wear looks of quiet desperation as they try to negotiate the bottleneck of what was once one of more pleasant routes in Vancouver. It's not easy being a pedestrian either: Sidewalks that at first appear open suddenly disappear behind chain-link fence, and you have to cross the street to continue walking. A few blocks later, it all reverses again. It makes getting to any given store an orienteering challenge, sort of like being an involuntary boy scout, something pedestrians and the shop owners need like a hole in the head. Around City Hall, pedestrians have to take a detour around the entire building or scoot down alleyways to avoid the barricades. There may be some justice in the turmoil around City Hall since it was former mayor Larry Campbell and his COPE "Lite" fraction that are largely to blame for this, but to extract vengeance on the innocent seems egregious.

There may not be gold down there in the Cambie street mine, but what's going on is sure a bonanza for a few of the chosen ones. In particular, Montreal's SNC-Lavalin Group Inc. has done quite well, thank you, landing the $1.64 billion contact to build the subway line from Vancouver International Airport to the downtown core.[3] The subway was called the RAV Line at first, back when it was supposed to be about bringing Olympic visitors from the airport to downtown hotels. It's the Canada Line now, the latter name a nod to the massive infusion of federal funds that made it all possible. SNC-Lavalin is required to pony up $200 million, but that's OK since they get to operate the line, too, getting an annual operating payment from government for 35 years, more than offsetting their upfront costs. What we have here is a perfect P3 arrangement, a public-private partnership of the type so beloved by the provincial government in general and even more so if five Olympic rings are attached.

The notion of a RAV Line had been under discussion for years and moved forcefully to the front burner when the Olympic machine passed the torch to Vancouver in July 2003. Our old acquaintance Ken Dobell had been busy behind the scenes to line things up and get all the parties to the table. Just over a month later, the federal and provincial governments, the Vancouver Airport Authority and the Region's transportation authority, TransLink, whose board was composed of the mayors of the municipalities of the Lower Mainland, had each committed to $300 million. The private sector was also expected to ante up its own $300 million.

With $1.5 billion ready to go, there was only one problem, but it was a big one: most of the TransLink board didn't want the project as proposed…and neither did their constituents. A few months later, the BC government coincidentally introduced Bill 75, the Significant Projects Streamlining Act. The new legislation gave the provincial cabinet the authority to overrule provincial or municipal laws or rules deemed a "constraint" on projects that the government considers "provincially significant" such as RAV or the Sea to Sky Highway upgrade.

The first vote on RAV by TransLink members was held in May 2004. Five of seven members voted against the project for reasons that spanned a number of their concerns: It was very expensive, there was a lack of transparency, it was to be a P3, and mostly it wasn't clear at all that it was the right solution to Vancouver's transportation woes. Some of the board members just didn't like Gordon Campbell's interference in what they saw as a local transportation issue. Kevin Falcon, the diminutive and hungry-looking provincial transportation minister, didn't take this first rejection well. He was clearly furious, and in the media interviews that followed the vote, his face had taken on a feral intensity: It wasn't over he said, offering TransLink cost overrun protection, an extra $50 million from the provincial government and a bonus $170 million funding top-up for other transportation projects. Uncharitable folk were wont to call the last a bribe. Falcon also proposed that the Province own the line but with a long-term contract allowing someone else to operate it. All of Falcon's bluster and bribery were to no avail: TransLink's board turned him down and again voted against the project. At a press conference, Falcon was red faced and shrill, in fact he looked moments away from an infarct. His response was to announce his grandiose plans for a "Gateway" project, an eight-lane highway aimed straight for Vancouver's heart.

A month went by, and to quote again Robert Service's poem, "The Arctic trails have their secret tales; That would make your blood run cold…." We may never know the details of RAV's secret tales, but something damned odd had been afoot, since on the third vote TransLink board members had reversed themselves and voted 8-4 *in favor* of the project. The belated approval came with a cap of $1.35 billion of public money. The private sector was expected to make up the difference of the newly projected cost of $1.7 billion.

Two companies were in the bidding to get the contract: SNC-Lavalin and Bombardier, the latter the same company we've met before when their chairman sat as a director of Vancouver's Bid Corp. SNC-Lavalin won, merely proving that Olympic alliances of convenience are made to be broken. Another odd thing was that SNC-Lavalin's bid was $343 million over the cap previously imposed by TransLink. No matter, it was only taxpayers' money. By December TransLink had given final approval to RAV, triggered by land rush along the Cambie corridor as developers tried to anticipate where the train stations would be.

Two surprises awaited Vancouverites and British Columbians in August of 2005. First, the distribution of costs to taxpayers had been revealed for a project now topping $1.9 billion and still rising. The federal government was in for $419 million; the BC government, $235 million; TransLink came in at $245 million; the Vancouver Airport Authority and the City of Vancouver tagged for $321 million each. The public was now on the hook for over $1.2 billion ($1.247 billion to be exact). SNC-Lavalin and its partners graciously agreed to pick up the difference, but it's easy to see why. Their final contract for construction was pegged at $1.64 billion and they get to operate and maintain the line with guarantees from government for minimal monthly revenues for the next 35 years. Second, everyone thought that the company was going to bore a tunnel, minimally disrupting traffic and local businesses. Nope, it was now going to be a cut-and-cover operation in which some blocks are torn up, a segment of the line built, then covered over again, only to have the process repeated time and time again. Local merchants were furious as they began to see future disaster for their businesses. Motorists were soon to discover their own level of frustration in the change of plans.

Oh, by the way, Kevin Falcon never forgets: in March 2007, he proposed scraping the TransLink board and replacing it with more controllable government appointees.

Not all businesses were dismayed, however. Great Canadian Casino got some land for another casino along the RAV and a stop right at the door. Imagine: get off a plane, onto a train and, shazzam, you're at a casino. And, businesses going out of business can't be all bad. Someone is sure to snap up the property on a corridor now just screaming for condo development. It seems there was indeed gold in Falcon's Trench.

Eagleridge, aka Falcon's Trench North

One of the "stronger" suggestions the IOC allegedly made to the Vancouver Bid Corp was that it would have to do something about the road from West Vancouver to Whistler. This 120-kilometre stretch of road — formally named Highway 99, less formally called the Sea to Sky — is one of BC's scenic wonders. After passing Horseshoe Bay and the ferry terminal en route to Whistler, it begins to traverse the east side of Howe Sound. To the left, steep cliffs reveal dramatic ocean vistas while tree-covered bluffs tower on the right. The highway traverses ritzy enclaves such as Lions Bay and picturesque, if run down, villages like Britannia Beach, and then newer, upscale condo developments. About midpoint it passes through Squamish, a blue-collar logging town rapidly being transformed into a suburb of Vancouver. From Squamish, the road heads straight inland through mountain valleys and over roaring streams until finally arriving at the outskirts of North America's premier ski resorts Whistler Valley and the Resort Municipality of Whistler.

The Sea to Sky is generally well maintained and certainly safe enough for all but the most careless drivers. Much of it is two-lane only; those in a hurry have to be content to wait for the passing lanes that crop up every few kilometers. Some of those who can't manage to be patient have found that speeding and passing on the route's curves, especially in poor weather, is not wise. While the number of fatal accidents has not been large, they provided more than excuse enough for the BC government to declare that "fixing" the Sea to Sky was a number one priority. It is hard not to suspect, however, that speed was less a factor in terms of accidents than in enabling the well-to-do to get to their condos in the shortest possible time.

The idea of widening the Sea to Sky had surfaced from time to time, but in the past it was usually put on the back burner because some really awful roads elsewhere were in vastly greater need of attention. With the bid up and running, however, "fixing" the Sea to Sky became *crucial* to clinching the Games. This notion was strongly reinforced by some of the IOC's top brass during an early visit to Vancouver in 2002. The IOC crew had taken the two-hour-plus drive between Vancouver and Whistler, shook their heads in shock and declared it much too long. Usually when the IOC doesn't like something, bid cities and their countries genuflect and scramble to obey. The Bid Corp and the government promised serious action, action that, as we will see, fit perfectly into existing plans for the highway, or, more precisely, for the land along the route. Once again, a real estate agenda was driving the bid.

The first of the supposed "problems" to be fixed was actually just before the start of the Sea to Sky Highway. About a kilometer from the junction, Highway 1 passes by Eagleridge Bluffs, a unique ridgeline with some of the last arbutus forest in the Lower Mainland, thought to be 500 years old. Other old-growth cedars in the area had been culturally modified by native inhabitants centuries before, the old scars where bark had been removed a silent testament to another age.

Back before construction started, Eagleridge was a world unto itself. Just meters off the parking lot, an old trail ascended so quickly into forest that the road below was quickly lost from view and the rush of traffic silenced by the whir of insects and the chirps and whistles of the various migratory birds that made the area home. The old trail continued up over a ridge then down toward a swampy area, the Larson Creek wetlands, one of the last such wetlands on the North Shore and home to the endangered red-legged frog. Numerous bird species were common to the area, some also on the endangered list. Bear and deer and other wildlife were also frequently sighted, including the eagles that gave the bluffs its name. Majestic bald eagles could frequently be seen soaring above the ridgeline, riding the updrafts effortlessly, magically. Eagleridge is — or was — a mystical area, one much loved by many for its uniqueness and solitude, near the city, yet apart from it. Many West Vancouver residents considered it to be the very gem of their district, a place to go for solitude and respite from the bustle of modern life, a transient sojourn from the "normal" world.

Soon after Vancouver won the 2010 Games, the BC Ministry of Transportation began considering plans to move the highway past or over Eagleridge as part of the now-"essential" Sea to Sky highway upgrade. How to do so was the question, or, at least, the official question. The answer was that there were basically three options and a few variants on these options. The first option was

simply to do some local Highway 1 widening and readjustments to the Sea to
Sky interchange at Horseshoe Bay. The second option was to blast over Eagleridge and put in a four-lane highway. The third option was to tunnel under the
ridge. The Ministry of Transportation simply rejected the first option out of
hand, although no particularly cogent reasons were ever provided. Based on
their assessment, the best option was the overland route, the tunnel rapidly dismissed as more expensive and less safe. To come to this conclusion, the ministry had to manipulate the facts and numbers considerably, ignoring those that
simply couldn't be shoehorned into what seemed to be a pre-set plan. At least,
this is the way it looked to a lot of West Vancouverites who had started coming
together to oppose the overland route that would destroy Eagleridge Bluffs.

A group calling itself the Coalition to Save Eagleridge Bluffs had formed
after Vancouver won the bid. It began by lobbying the Municipality of West
Vancouver and the provincial government to reconsider the Ministry's plans
and replace the overland option with a tunnel. Initially, the West Vancouver
city government was on their side, declaring Eagleridge Bluffs a unique environmental treasure that needed to be preserved for future generations. La-
boriously, the Coalition and municipal government laid out their arguments
about cost and safety, showing that the Ministry was simply wrong on all
counts. Stubbornly, passionately, they talked "truth to power," and for West
Vancouverites and many others, their arguments made a lot of sense. Here
was a group that was not anti-Olympics by any stretch of the imagination, indeed the opposite: both the city and the Coalition simply loved the Games and
wanted them to be the promised "greenest ever." Blowing up Eagleridge was
not a green solution, and it would look terrible in the eyes of the world. So,
pretty please, wouldn't the Ministry reconsider? Nope. Minister Falcon, dug
in his heels, declared the Coalition and its supporters troublemakers and announced that the decision was made and that was that. West Vancouver lost
a civil suit against the Province and promptly bailed, declaring the battle lost.
The Coalition vowed to fight on and do whatever it would take to stop the
overland route.

By the spring of 2006, with legal challenges behind them and the Minister's hired bulldozers ready to begin leveling the Bluffs, the Coalition found
itself in a bind, with really only two options left on the table. They could give
up, perhaps consoling themselves with the thought that they'd fought the good
fight against an obstinate provincial government; or they could turn to civil
disobedience. Surprisingly, it was the latter to which most now cast their eyes.

Dennis Perry, the outspoken leader of the Coalition, knew me from the
provincial Green Party. Perry, a former investment banker, had gone green a

few years earlier, had joined the provincial Green Party to run in the 2005 provincial election and had been more or less instantly catapulted into the role of deputy leader by party leader Adriane Carr. Carr was hoping that an electoral breakthrough might come about in 2005 if only the party could capture the squishy political center. The insider thinking was that Perry with his background as banker-capitalist mixed with his new green persona would convince skeptical voters that the Greens had matured from tree-hugging hippies into a serious middle-of-the-road political party.

Perry knew I came from a far more-radical perspective; indeed he and I had been engaged in a running e-mail battle about the nature of the party both going into and coming out of the 2005 election. That was now all in the past, and what he wanted from me was information: The Coalition was planning civil disobedience, and its members were willing to get arrested to protect the Bluffs. Did I know anyone who could train them in civil disobedience, someone who knew what it was like to break the law and take the consequences? I did.

A few years earlier, I had got to know Betty Krawczyk, the legendary grandmother of the woods who had stared down logging trucks and angry fallers from Clayoquot Sound to the Elaho River. Krawczyk was now living in the Lower Mainland and still more than feisty at 78. Her short white hair framed a weathered, angular face, the features capable of shifting in a heartbeat from a sweet granny giving you milk and cookies to the fixed deadly stare of a Rebel hellion. The drawl she still carried from her youth in the American South could fit either persona. Still unbowed by company injunctions and government connivance in the rape of the forests, unbroken by the many months she had spent in prison for her actions, Krawczyk was legendary in environmental activist circles. I had run into her a few months earlier at a weekend retreat in the Fraser Valley near Chilliwack. It had been organized by a local First Nations band trying to save part of Mount Cheam, a sacred mountain within their traditional territory, from being developed as yet another ski resort. Krawczyk was there with a feminist environmental group called Women of the Woods. I was there to speak about the impact of the Olympics and the spillover of the main real estate deals to opportunistic ventures like the one at Cheam.

I told Perry I would get back to him. I called Krawczyk, reintroduced myself, then told her why I was calling. She seemed quite skeptical at first: "Sounds like a NIMBY issue to me." I'd had the same reaction at first, too. After all, the Coalition was hardly anti-Olympic, in fact quite the opposite. Still they were trying to preserve something unique, and they needed Betty's help to put on a day-long civil disobedience workshop. Krawczyk said she'd think about it and said I could give Perry her number.

In a lifetime of political activism, I'd never seen an event as cognitively dis-sonant as that which greeted me the following weekend. I'd met up with Conrad Schmidt and David Maidman from the Work Less Party[4] early on a Saturday morning outside an old clapboard church high up on the hillside above Horse-shoe Bay. We were going to film the day's events for our future documentary about the 2010 Games.[5] Inside the church, over 50 of West Van's most upstand-ing and normally law-abiding citizens were going to get a crash course on radical environmental activism from Betty Krawczyk. Unlike at most political activ-ist training events I'd attended, the crowd was more inclined to have grey hair than multi-coloured locks, more likely to be sporting ties than piercings. Still, if the age of most participants marked them as boomers, there were a number of 30-something types, often with young children sitting on their laps or scam-pering about. And, as the press would later note sarcastically, many of them *had* shown up clutching soy lattes after parking their BMWs. Anyway, having served as a go-between to set up the event, I wasn't going to judge if the folks in-side were really future environmental activists or merely radical wannabes. My job was to film the event, even if I had to suppress the odd chuckle to do so.

Perry gave the introduction, highlighting Krawczyk's years as an environ-mental crusader. One had to wonder what many in the audience must have been thinking as Perry heaped praise on a woman who had served serious jail time and had once been declared an "enemy of BC" by a former premier.[6] Still, she was here to get them ready for what was to come, and so they listened in-tently as she described the actions she had been on, what happens when you get arrested and what the consequences are thereafter. Krawczyk told them that the most likely and most dangerous legal challenge they'd face would be an insidious one: the injunction. She had seen it used time and time again in the logging wars of the 1990s and knew the tactic inside and out. Basically, it worked like this: Rather than have protesters arrested for trespassing, a com-pany would seek a court injunction barring protesters from the site. To violate an injunction carried a far harsher criminal penalty than mere trespass. The re-ality of it all was beginning to sink in. This was not just an idle twilight discus-sion, a glass of French Chardonnay in hand while watching the sun go down over English Bay; this was the real world of social activism where bucking the political establishment had real-world consequences. Most of the good folks in the Coalition had believed for a lifetime that they *were* the establishment. Now they were beginning to understand that if they blocked the construction, that privileged status could come to an abrupt end: They could be arrested, could go to jail and could be fined by the court, not to mention get sued by Kie-wit and Sons, the company hired by Falcon to do the Sea to Sky upgrade, for lost construction time. These new activists were getting a reality check on the nature of blockades and their consequences. To be in their shoes must have seemed scary and frankly overwhelming. In spite of whatever terrors the future held, most of those in the church stayed all morning as Krawczyk walked them through some role-playing to depict the likely scenarios when the police would execute the arrests. Younger couples turned to each other to discuss who would pick up the kids if one of them were arrested, boomers considered how they'd get their medications in prison, who would walk the dog and all the minutiae that follows a life-shifting decision to take on the machine.

I came away frankly impressed, any residual cynicism about rich West Van NIMBY protesters dispelled. No, these folks hadn't been born as "pink-diaper babies," but what they planned to set in motion at Eagleridge would soon put to shame the "official" social activists on Vancouver's left. At least, that is, until the East Vancouver-based Anti-Poverty Committee (APC) began their actions months later.

But the APC events were still in the future, and the here and now was a damp parking lot at the Eagleridge off-ramp with a cold drizzle coming down as the Coalition and their supporters pitched their tents later that week. That next weekend was just as damp and windy, but spirits were high as more tents went up all over the parking lot and on the Bluffs above. Someone had put up some giant protest banners along the cliff face. Others had erected large tents to serve as media centers and food stations. The protest site rapidly took on a carnival air, and as the sun came out, brightly colored helium balloons were filled, kids and dogs romped, and there was a real feeling of cautious optimism that the outcome just might be the preservation of Eagleridge Bluffs. The media were there in force for this was big news: West Vancouver, Canada's most affluent postal code was going toe-to-toe with Kevin Falcon…and only one could win. The media had fun zeroing in on the fancy cheese platters inside the food tent and the frequent latte runs by supporters, and while I don't think they intended the "spoiled rich NIMBY protesters" angle to dominate the coverage, it invariably did. Oddly, this perspective spilled over onto social activist circles in East Vancouver and elsewhere, and people who normally didn't trust the media very much began to parrot the NIMBY line.

Dennis Perry had convinced most of the Coalition members that anything resembling an anti-Olympic stance would be a public relations "disaster." He even asked, politely, if I'd keep my anti-Games pirate flag away from the site. Most members of the Coalition toed the line of "we love the Olympics, we just want them to be the greenest ever," many because they actually believed it, others because Perry had told them it was the only way to go. All in all, the position of the Coalition seemed so eminently reasonable: The tunnel option would accomplish the same aim of upgrading this part of the Sea to Sky highway, it was actually cost effective and quite probably safer than the four-lane highway option, and, best of all, it was green…sort of. Eagleridge could be saved for future generations, and the province could have the Olympics too.

It was a win-win, right? Well, not actually, because the protesters didn't know one crucial piece of information: Eagleridge had been doomed since before the 2010 bid was won. Getting the Games merely changed the pace of what was to come, namely the complete development of Eagleridge to accommodate some 1,800 houses, villas and condos sprawled up the Ridge.[7] The Coalition had forgotten, if most of its members ever knew it, that the land they wanted to protect for their grandchildren mostly belonged to British Pacific Properties (BPP), one of BC's oldest real estate development companies. BPP had no intention whatsoever in leaving the eagles in charge of Eagleridge Bluffs.

BPP had owned much of what was to become West Vancouver from early in the 20th century and had been gradually moving westward. The last major patch of their holdings was the undeveloped land stretching kilometers east and west of the Eagleridge off-ramp, up over the Bluffs toward Larson Creek. BPP could measure their progress by the addition of some 30 to 40 houses per year, the speed of development largely determined by the need for roads and other servicing. It was too expensive to build roads for all the holdings at once, hence the gradual pace. The Olympics offered something new, a chance to pick up the pace dramatically, especially if taxpayers could be convinced to spend the money for a highway, and not just any highway, but one with off-ramps leading to new developments. When the issue of the Sea to Sky expansion first was floated in 2002, BPP had expressed a preference for a tunnel, and thus they, like the Municipality, were initially on the same side as the Coalition. The reasoning was simple: A tunnel did not prevent them from building on top of the Bluffs, but a four lane certainly cut into the available land considerably. BPP had floated the idea of compensation if a four lane were to be built. What they got it from the government in the end was a substantial $13,656,300, and their early opposition to the overland route vanished. West Vancouver was not at all averse to more development in the area, as a series of memos released after a Freedom of Information (FOI) request revealed, it just wanted to avoid the eyesore that a cut over the Bluffs would bring.[8]

The FOI story could be a chapter in its own right, but I'll simply summarize it here: Not long after the protest camp went up at Eagleridge, I launched a Freedom of Information request with both the District of West Vancouver and the Ministry of Transportation. I was seeking confirmation that both levels of government had long had plans to develop Eagleridge and that the highway was meant to accelerate the process. Delay followed delay, and both levels of government tried to bill me excessive amounts for "staff time" needed to gather the documents. I complained to the Freedom of Information commissioner for the province and after some more back and forth with the two governments, bulky packages eventually showed up at my office. It had taken over 10 months, but at least I hadn't had to pay for anything. This was just as well since the West Vancouver documents, about 70 pages, were mostly blank. West Vancouver had "severed" material they considered confidential. The Ministry of Transportation was more open and, given that the FOI requests had overlapped considerably, some of the Ministry documents were likely the same as those deleted from the pages sent by the City.

All in all, it made for a revealing read: Both levels of government had been warned that the area was a sensitive and unique environmental zone that would be lost if the overland route went through. The author of one environmental report even wrote to the provincial and federal environmental protection offices for their help.[9] It didn't matter. Eighteen hundred homes were going up on Eagleridge, frogs and arbutus trees be damned. What West Vancouver was hiding with their blank pages was the extent to which they connived with this plan and only gave lip service to environmental protection. For the municipality, the tunnel was merely a cosmetic detail, the real issue of actually preserving Eagleridge Bluffs never entering the picture. Once West Vancouver lost the lawsuit against the Province, the highway was a done deal and, in their view, maybe not such a bad thing, considering the property tax revenues they saw flowing down from the new homes on the Bluffs.

The Coalition had seen BPP and the Municipality of West Vancouver bail on them. Now they were alone and facing an irate Kiewit and Sons, the latter losing money every day that they couldn't start work. Kiewit did what Krawczyk had predicted and got their injunction on May 15. Some protesters went home, but most stayed. Eight days later, as the sun came up, the West Vancouver police rolled paddy wagons into view and set up a processing tent on the overpass near the off-ramp. At first they tried to keep the media back, but when Conrad Schmidt, his girlfriend Chantal Morin and I crossed the police lines with our camera to get footage, the media took notice. As we passed the police line, a constable warned us that we risked arrest. "Thanks for telling us," we said as we walked across the overpass toward the camp. Media crews began to follow us, and soon there was a virtual scrum at the campsite with reporters madly doing interviews and filming as protesters sang and police got ready to do theirwork.

It was late morning when Staff Sergeant Jim Almas of the West Vancouver police arrived. He came to plead with the protesters, many of whom he knew personally. These were not scruffy radicals from East Vancouver, but neighbors, and the last thing he wanted to do was haul them off to the paddy wagons. Still, he had an injunction to enforce. Almas pointed out that lots of media attention had focused on the Coalition and their goal of stopping the highway, but now it was time to move on. No good could come from getting arrested. Wouldn't they now, please, leave? No one took him up on the offer. He then read the injunction to the crowd of protesters, supporters and media. Those determined to get arrested refused to budge. Squamish Band elder Harriett Nahanee,[10] who had joined the camp a week or so earlier, began singing "We Shall Overcome" with Betty Krawczyk. Most of the crowd joined in. In twos, the West Vancouver police moved forward toward individual protesters. The Staff Sergeant repeated his request that the injunction be obeyed. When each refused, the police took them away to be booked. Many had to be carried off the site, including Krawczyk, who was placed on a sort of blanket then lifted by four constables each holding a corner. It was a West Vancouver moment, the police acting with the utmost formality and being as gentle as possible, the protesters saying "no thank you" solemnly but politely when given their chance to leave. One by one they were led away, Dennis Perry one of the last. In the end, 23 people were arrested and charged with violating Kiewit's injunction.

By the next day, all the protesters had been released after being booked. I went back to the site to see if the work had started. Sure enough, Kiewit crews were already clearcutting the ridgeline above where the camp had been. I watched for as long as I could bear it as workers with their chainsaws mowed down 500-year-old arbutus trees. Then, sickened, I left.

Those arrested would eventually plead guilty, apologize to Kiewit and be given fines ranging from $250 to $5,000, some in the later category ordered to pay an additional $1,000 to Kiewit. Betty Krawczyk had not only refused to apologize, but had gone back to the campsite to set up her tent again. She was rearrested. For this, the 78-year-old grandmother received ten months in jail. Harriett Nahanee also refused to apologize and received 14 days in the Surrey Pre-Trial Detention Centre. She would contract pneumonia there and die a few days after her release, the first martyr of the 2010 Olympic real estate wars.

If you drive past Eagleridge now, all you see is a huge, ugly 50-meter-wide scar in the earth that starts where the protest camp once was and goes up and over the bluffs, a total distance of almost two and a half kilometers. The Bluffs

are gone, along with the arbutus forest that used to shroud it. Old growth along
the cut has been chopped down — some 4,800 trees in all — and a kilometer
of wetlands pulverized. When Peter Kiewit and Sons[11] are done, there will be
a four-lane highway over the ridge, bypassing Horseshoe Bay completely. In
place of solitude, there will be the endless swoosh of speeding cars, the drivers presumably judging it worthwhile to have built the bypass — if they think
upon it at all — to save two minutes on their journey to and from Whistler
and the chi-chi condos and sprawling mansions along the route. Most will
never know the full cost, the trees cut, the species endangered and the life of
Hariett Nahanee lost. Any memory of what was on the ridge will have faded
from public memory, just another forgotten real estate deal that crept in on the
coattails of the Olympics.

Oh, and one footnote: the Ministry of Transportation papers I got under
FOI revealed that Concert Properties had purchased a sizeable chunk of BPP
property on Eagleridge. In the end, there was even something extra for Jack
Poole.

The Callaghan Valley or, How to Get
Crown Land for Free: Just Bring on the Games

The Callaghan Valley lies just to the west of Whistler, the road entrance off
Highway 99 is about six kilometers south of the Village. The valley, about 13
or so kilometers north to south, is surrounded by mountains on three sides
and contains several lakes, the largest, Callaghan Lake, and a provincial park.
Much of the lowlands have been logged over the years, but quite a lot of the
valley still retains old growth. It is Crown land and, apart from the logging
licenses, had only one full-time resident business, a resort called Callaghan
Country Wilderness Adventures, which had wangled a license to operate in
the valley some years earlier.

The notion that there could be a resort in the making on Whistler's left
flank hadn't escaped the notice of various potential developers over the years.
Nan and Diane Hartwick made up a mother-and-daughter team who had developed plans to build a new international destination alpine resort in the Callaghan. The Hartwicks' company, Powder Mountain Resorts Ltd. (PMR), had
won three public government proposal calls put out by the ruling Socred government of Premier Bill Bennett. In 1985 PMR, with the sole proposal, was
selected by the government as the winning submission. The Hartwicks' lawyers were in the process of finalizing legal documents with the Attorney General's lawyer, Colin McIver, who had been seconded to the BC Lands Ministry.
Days after new Premier Bill Vander Zalm took office, the Hartwick deal fell

apart. The Hartwicks allege that Vander Zalm personally intervened to block the agreement and that the Victoria bureaucrats directly involved were Land and Water British Columbia (LWBC) vice-president Jack Hall and his associate George McKay, the alpine ski development project manager. Forests and Lands Minister Jack Kempf would later testify under oath that Premier Bill Vander Zalm told him in 1987 to "cease and desist" with the Hartwicks' application and proceed in favor of Callaghan Resorts Inc., an enterprise started by former Social Credit Attorney General Les Peterson. The land bureaucrats had other favorites as well: Brad Sills, who had started Callaghan Country was given a license to operate by Hall while the Hartwicks' case was still contested.

Years of litigation followed. In the 1990s, the Hartwicks took their complaints to the new NDP provincial government and received sympathetic hearings from ministers Glen Clark and Moe Sihota. In spite of the interest by members of this government, the bureaucrats in Victoria sidestepped around the complaints. A "breach of contract and abuse of office" suit brought by the Hartwicks was dismissed by the BC Supreme Court in 1999, and later the BC Court of Appeal refused to overturn that verdict. The Hartwicks, however, have never given up the fight for their project, one they strongly believe they can document was stolen from them.

With Vancouver's Olympic bid in the works in 2002, the Callaghan had suddenly resurfaced as the potential site for the Nordic events including biathlon, ski jump and cross-country skiing. Other, likely better-suited venues, could have sufficed, but that wasn't the point of the exercise. The Callaghan was now firmly in the crosshairs of the developers who once again saw a way to get the land courtesy of the Games. The Bid Corp wasn't even shy about the eventual goals for the valley. The Bid Book had gone on at some length about the future, even going so far as to suggest development into a full four-season resort complete with golf courses.

LWBC bureaucrat Jack Hall was now, conveniently, the director of Property Assessment Appeal Board and Real Estate Foundation of BC, and he happily led the way for Jack Poole and the Bid Corp to get access to the valley. In 2002 the Liberal provincial government seconded George McKay to become the director of the Callaghan Valley Master Plan for the Bid Corp. McKay later stayed on to become VANOC's director of environmental approvals while remaining on the government books as the Ministry of Tourism's manager of special projects.

Other players in the cabal that took down the Powder Mountain Resorts winning proposal also had ongoing ties to the bid. One was Colin McIver, the

Attorney General's ministry's lawyer in the 1980s, now a partner with Fraser Milner Casgrain, a law firm that represents VANOC in Callaghan Valley Nordic venue development schemes (and in what is likely not a coincidence, Millennium Southeast False Creek Properties Ltd., as well). Last, but not least, was David Emerson, then a deputy minister to Vander Zalm, now the federal minister responsible for the 2010 Games. All just another nice, tight circle of friends…and interests.

Just as the Bid Corp had blocked the Hartwicks' access to the IOC Technical Team, something further seems to have been afoot as the IOC's decision in Prague approached. The potential for the ongoing criminal investigations brought by the Hartwicks to derail the bid were still very problematic for the Bid Corp, which didn't need a blowout over the Nordic venue sites. If the RCMP found wrongdoing in the past concerning the Hartwicks' complaint or funny business with the Bid Corp in the present, there could be trouble with the IOC. Just weeks before the IOC's decision in Prague, an RCMP Commercial Crime investigation was halted without charges being laid, thus ending a potential embarrassment to Vancouver's bid. It was all very convenient for the Bid Corp and may have actually saved the bid.[12]

Once the Games were won by Vancouver in 2003, plans for the Callaghan began to take on tangible form. The value of the Callaghan had been estimated at $100 million, and Whistler had long coveted it as a spillover community to house the service personnel who worked the bars, restaurants and ski lifts of Whistler Village. Whether the Callaghan will remain Crown land is uncertain, but there are lots of folks who have their eyes fixed on the valley. Two First Nations saw clear opportunities: the Squamish and Lil'wat, whose band councils would each get $10 million to put the Games on their traditional but overlapping territories. Later the BC government and Whistler would get the bands to accept various smaller parcels outside the Callaghan in exchange for dropping claims in the valley.[13] They wouldn't lose it all, however: There was room for a golf course in the southern part of the valley that they would be allowed to build and operate.

The RCMP widened the existing road into the valley for "security" purposes, creating an alternate road as well. VANOC hired First Nations members to log the areas needed for the Games, including 23 kilometers of cross-country and biathlon trails. One of the "legacies" that VANOC promised to leave was a further 50 to 100 kilometers of trails. All of this activity would have a dramatic environmental impact on the valley (see chapter 15), but in spite of promises to be "the greenest games ever," this didn't really matter to VANOC, the provincial government or to Whistler. An artist's drawing of the Callaghan's Nordic venues prepared for the Vancouver Sun showed readers just how massively the valley would be changed by 2010.[14]

The goal, remember, was to build a new four-season resort and community, to basically duplicate — if not exceed — Whistler. Carving the Callaghan into chunks via the legacy trails neatly accomplished this purpose. Who would get rich? Whistler for one, along with all the developers who could get their hands on the real estate now up for grabs. It looked like the bunch who had bumped the Hartwicks aside in the late 1980s were finally going to get the land they had coveted for so long.

Nothing about any of the Callaghan shenanigans was unique in Olympic Games history. The Salt Lake City Games in 2002 had spawned a similar expansion of a resort called Snowbasin. As Andrew Jennings documented in his book, *The Great Olympic Swindle*,[15] a large part of Snowbasin had been part of a national forest prior to Salt Lake's bid. Then, just as in the Callaghan, the developers saw land free for the taking. Jennings describes how resort mogul R. Earl Holding managed to score 1,370 acres of prime land and add it to his burgeoning ski resort empire. What used to be public forest is now a complete four-season resort featuring "golf, tennis, swimming, winter sports, shops, hotels, 600 luxury homes and 800 condominiums.[16] All it took was some grease for a federal senator, some congressmen and Utah's state governor, all of whom got generous campaign contributions from an appreciative Mr. Holding.

If the Callaghan deal sounds suspiciously like early Snowbasin so far, the perception is bang on. When it's all done, the similarities will be even more striking, and the outcomes will be virtually identical. Certainly the Bid Corp plans made it abundantly clear that the Callaghan Nordic project was headed in this direction. All it took was the stroke of a pen, magically making Crown land part of the Olympics…and from there into the pockets of the developers waiting in the wings. Was there financial "grease" involved in the capture of the Callaghan? Whether this will ever come out in the mainstream press remains far from certain, but it's pretty clear that the Callaghan, just like Snowbasin, is a case of SSDD: same shit, different day. The precise same scenario is already playing out in the mountains above Sochi, Russia, the venue for the 2014 Winter Games.

The Callaghan Valley remains the Achilles' heel of VANOC and has the capacity to blow up into a major scandal linking government, developers and VANOC insiders. Not that much additional linkage is required, given the open revolving-door relationships between these organizations. As of this writing, the BC Criminal Justice Branch has recently submitted material to

RCMP Commercial Crime investigators who have reopened their files on the Hartwicks' complaint, now for the third time.[17]

When, or if, it all comes out in the media, it will put VANOC squarely in the headlights. What happens after that is anyone's guess.[18]

The Convention Centre: Bigger, Better, More Expensive

With the bid gathering steam in 2003, the plans for an expanded convention center leapt back into view. Indeed, the plans had never really gone away, merely been put on a back burner while the players figured out how to get taxpayers to finance it. The Olympics provided the magic; the three levels of government just had to ante up the dollars.

Shortly after Concert's former proposal failed in 1999, Tourism Vancouver, the Vancouver Hotel Association, the Vancouver Board of Trade and the Pavillion Corporation (PavCo), a Crown corporation, created the new Vancouver Convention Expansion Task Force chaired by none other than the ubiquitous Ken Dobell. By 2001 the BC Liberals were in power in Victoria and the Olympic machine was up and running. The federal government would put up $202.5 million to match the Province's contribution to the capital costs. The Bid Corporation was in there, too, in 2002 signing a deal with PavCo to host the international media who would be covering the 2010 Winter Games.

This time around it wasn't the cost or a casino that were deal breakers; in fact, there was no way this deal could go awry with the Olympics possibly coming. The potential hiccup for taxpayers was clearly laid out by Charlie Smith of the *Georgia Straight*: "What," he wrote, "if hosting the Olympics has no effect on attracting business to the expanded center? The biggest North American trade shows are shrinking, according to industry data." Smith noted what Phil LeGood of NO GAMES had already said back in 2003: The number of convention delegates at the existing convention center had already peaked in 1997–1998 with 314,553 attendees. By 2003–2004, overall numbers had dropped by 43 percent. Smith went on to quote Professor Heywood Sanders of the University of Texas on the status of convention centers across North America. It wasn't only Vancouver's convention center attendance that was in a decline, it was an across-the-board phenomenon. Sanders had concluded that the driving force for convention center expansion was not the people you'd expect, that is, the tourism industry. Rather, the driving force was often provided by "major downtown property owners seeking massive public subsidies to their areas of the city.... It has nothing to do with conventions. It has to do with land." Once again, the Olympic project was revealing itself to be primarily about real estate.

Sanders went on to say, "As in Atlanta, part of the logic of having an Olympics is all of a sudden you get a higher level of government involved spending lots of public capital dollars for buildings. I mean, the Olympics ceased being about sports a long time ago. If you look at Athens, for example, or you look at Sydney or you look at Atlanta, these are about large-scale building projects."[19] Sanders was completely right, of course, but the notion that the entire project was a scam just as in 1999 was largely ignored by the media.

Smith went on to name names of those who had driven the project, observing that one of the most fervent boosters of the new center was Graeme Stamp, who just happened to be chairman of the Vancouver Board of Trade and executive vice-president of Fairmont Developments Inc., the latter a subsidiary incarnation of Marathon Developments Inc., Premier Gordon Campbell's old company. Stamp's company had already sold the land to the provincial government for $27.5 million.

From 2002 onward, costs just kept going up, again in the grand tradition of all things Olympics-related. In 2003 the minister in charge pegged the absolute top at $495 million. Within months, this had ballooned to $565 million. As this book goes to press, the cost to taxpayers alone is over $883 million with no end in sight. Not only were taxpayer dollars heavily tied up in the project, but the province slapped on a "voluntary" levy for the tourism industry in order to raise $90 million of the overall costs. The latter was certainly not what the tourism industry was hoping for when they whored themselves to VANOC for the Games. It was to be a boon to tourism, not an endless surcharge for future tourists and residents. Sure they had planned to make a killing during the Games, they just didn't think it would ricochet back on them.

Does it matter to VANOC that the prices have gone up? Not at all. They used the notion of an expanded convention center to bring the Board of Trade and the tourism crowd onside with the Olympic bid (not that they needed much convincing), and now it's just one more taxpayer-paid cost of doing business. The business of the developers, that is. Oh, and by the way, David Podmore of Concert Properties is now running the show, so it appears that Concert got their convention center in the end, just like they wanted back in the 1990s.

Camp Followers of the Olympic Gravy Train

The above are the five prime real estate drivers and beneficiaries of the 2010 Olympics (including the Athletes' Village discussed in the last chapter), but by no means the only projects that will do well. Starting from Vancouver and working up toward Whistler are a number of smaller projects whose impact on people and/or the environment is likely to be profound. The greatest negative impact on people will occur in Vancouver's scruffiest section, the Downtown Eastside, home to legions of the homeless, drug dealers and users, sex trade workers and thousands of those who simply have the misfortune to be amongst the working poor. I'll come back to the Downtown Eastside in context to the "gentrification" of Vancouver in chapter 13.

Moving across English Bay and up along the Sea to Sky Highway, it's less economic cleansing than suburban sprawl. The patch of road after Horseshoe Bay now has huge developments of some 1,400 homes at Porteau Cove courtesy of Concord Pacific Developments, two of whose former chairmen were on Jack Poole's Bid Corp and connected to Hong Kong billionaire Li Ka Shing. Britannia Beach has also blossomed under the development plans of Rob Macdonald, a major contributor to the BC Liberal party, whose 202 hectares are expected to sprout 1,000 housing units. Furry Creek is the creation of Caleb Chan, once a prime member of the Bid Corp board of directors. Squamish has numerous developments, all capitalizing on the Games hype. One of the largest is that of former University of British Columbia President David Strangway and his project leader, Peter Ufford, in a housing development associated with the creation of a private university. Ufford was also on the Bid Corp board of directors. All of these projects should do enormously well in the booming real estate market.

In contrast to the developments considered earlier, the latter ones along the Sea to Sky at least involved private rather than public money…that is if you don't count the nearly $775 million price tag for the highway. Entrepreneurs risking their own money on what the future will bring is the way it's supposed to work. Gambling on real estate, however, is made vastly easier by insider information and friends in high places pushing hard for both the Olympics and the linked Sea to Sky Highway upgrade. Once these were in place, making a killing on real estate in the corridor was not rocket science.[20]

Ski resort developers throughout the province have also seen opportunities come knocking. To name just those in the Vancouver/Whistler areas: former Olympic ski champion Nancy Greene Raine and developer husband Al Raine still have high hopes for their proposed ski hill at Cayoosh/Melvin Creek, a project now happily stalled by the determination of Rosalin Sam and others of the St'at'imc Nation. Other resorts have been planned for Broome Ridge above Squamish and near Mt. Cheam above Chilliwack. Still other existing or proposed resorts in the Kootenays are hoping for spillover from the hordes of tourists expected in 2010. Many of these have drawn the ire of First Nations and may, blessedly, fail.

The Mr. Fix-It Guys

Some of the characters we've met before during the bid remain key players in the rapidly developing mega-projects associated with the 2010 Games. Concert Properties' President and CEO, David Podmore, chairs VANOC's capital works advisory committee, while at the same time having a major role on the Convention Centre Expansion board of directors.

And, of course, there is the ubiquitous Mr. Fix-it. If Jack Poole is the visionary, the man who overcame serial failed real estate ventures to bounce back and thrust Concert and the Olympics upon Vancouver and British Columbia, it's worthwhile to consider the man who really made it all possible. Political journalists knew him as did the captains of industry and politicos in Victoria and Vancouver, but most of the public had never heard his name. He was, and remains, the ultimate insider, the master fixer, the liaison for any deal big or small, the man whose name rarely showed up in print: Ken Dobell. His fingerprints are on all the major files that have led Vancouver to 2010. But first scroll back in time, and you find him as Vancouver's city manager at the same time he was on VLC's board of directors, an obvious conflict of interest as noted by City councilors of the day. Even today, he is adept at wearing several hats at the same time, lobbying on behalf of both Vancouver and the Province while representing each...to each other.[21] Could it have been Jack Poole who came up with the plan to put union pension funds in bed with real estate development? Not likely, not given that Poole then was only famous for the Daon and BCED disasters, hardly the mark of a master fiscal wizard. Someone other than Poole or Campbell was the key tactician. Dobell fits the picture to a "T," as the projects now in the Olympic pipeline prove.

Dobell followed Gordon Campbell to Victoria in 2001 as deputy minister. From there he's had a role in the nearly every major project that has come down the pike, those associated with the 2010 Games first and foremost.[22] The renewed convention center project? Dobell was in there as the Chairman of the Convention Centre Expansion board, along with David Podmore. The RAV line? Yup, Dobell's been there too and is all over the planning for Kevin Falcon's latest scheme, the Gateway project.[23] The Callaghan? Once again, Dobell has ties with the land bureaucrats in Victoria and VANOC. What about the Athletes' Village? His ongoing links to Vancouver's ruling party, the NPA, join him directly into the project since, conveniently, Dobell sits on VANOC's Board of Directors with John Furlong and Jack Poole, at the same time he advises Vancouver Mayor Sam Sullivan. Conflicts of interest? Nonsense, just as he said way back in 1989 and just this year when the accusation rose yet again. Is it merely coincidence that Dobell has his hands on all of the projects that have spilled out of the 2010 piñata? Possibly, or maybe it's just remarkably cozy in the insider world of Vancouver politics where deals are done, where it helps to have the willing and able assistance of a Mr. Fix-it.

Like Poole, Dobell has been waiting for the main score, the culmination of the P3 scheme he dreamt up back in 1989 when VLC was formed. And the ultimate P3 is, of course, the 2010 Olympics. When all is said and done about the 2010 Games, if Jack Poole is the father, Dobell is the midwife.

As we've seen in the chapters in this part of the book, the Olympic deal all hinges on real estate, and the very stench of it permeates every aspect from the early bid phase to final delivery of the Games. All of this comes with a bill, not only for taxpayers, but for the poor and the environment, topics to which we now turn.

THE FOURTH RING

Olympic Myths and Realities

·　·　·　·　·

In every city it examined, the Olympic Games — accidentally or deliberately — have become a catalyst for mass evictions and impoverishment. Since 1988, over 2 million people have been driven from their homes to make way for the Olympics. The Games have become a license for land grabs.

GEORGE MONBIOT,
"THE OLYMPIC GAMES MYTHS BUSTED,"
MONBIOT.COM, JULY 5, 2007:
ALTERNET.ORG/RIGHTS/55928/

Selling the Olympics with Journalism "Lite"

I know what you're telling me about the powers behind the bid is right, but I can't report that…I like getting a paycheck.

ANONYMOUS CBC REPORTER[1]

The Mainstream Media and the Olympic Frame

WATCHING THE mainstream media approach the subject of the Olympic Games offered me some rather startling insights into the very nature of the beast. Like most Canadians, I had started out with a number of well-conditioned assumptions, many of which were to prove wildly incorrect. For example, the notion that the Canadian Broadcasting Corporation (CBC/Radio Canada) is a public entity that is truly independent, apolitical and above being manipulated by corporate interests is simply wrong. Later in this chapter, I will provide examples proving that the CBC was, in far too many cases, vastly worse at reporting real news than the private news organizations. It was, for me, a real awakening to find that CBC could usually be counted on to toe the party line and uncritically parrot pro-Olympics hype. In contrast, private radio, TV and print media sometimes offered up some truly unbiased reporting. This is not to say that the private entities wouldn't ride the Olympic bandwagon most of the time, merely that occasionally they defied their own vested interests when they thought they could gain a larger viewer share/readership by so doing.

As discussed in a previous chapter, the so-called Olympic movement, which includes the IOC, the national Olympic organizing committees, and the various organizing committees for each Games, has successfully framed almost every Olympic debate by the constantly reinforced message that the Games are purely about elite sports in peaceful competition as the best vehicle to service a goal of world harmony. It's a simple message, and the fact that it may once have been even vaguely true adds credence to the official frame. The official frame is reinforced with the running of every Games, Winter and Summer, as the world's media audience is treated to a 17-day sports orgy, a virtual saturation overload of "the thrill of victory, the agony of defeat." It is pure soap opera in all respects: Beautiful young bodies in Spandex or Gortex (weather depending), new champions standing proudly at attention while national anthems are played to wildly cheering throngs, medals and flowers, tears of joy and sorrow, pomp and ceremony. The winners high-five and gambol, the losers appear tear-stained and heartbroken…but still plucky. The odd scandal of whatever sort only "sexes" things up. Yes, indeed, "soap" of the sort that daytime television can only dream of. And it's clearly a formula that the IOC recognizes as one of the most successful advertising campaigns ever invented.

Against such a dynamic machine, the media are simply dazzled and overwhelmed. Partly this is because their owners are of the same class as those who stand behind the national bids, that is, by the corporate elite who stand to gain by getting their pet projects funded. Even for those journalists inclined to be skeptical, the notion of critiquing the Games themselves seems the equivalent of farting loudly during High Mass in the Vatican: It's simply not done, it's unbecoming and is frankly disloyal to the dedicated young athletes whose whole lives have brought them to this moment in time. And it's just downright unpatriotic as well.

While most of this is particularly obvious during the Games themselves, the same frame is on display in the pre-bid process, during the awarding of the Games to the target city, and throughout the years of preparations before the actual Olympics. Skepticism declines in direct relation to phase: Earlier in the process, general skepticism is greater, the closer to the actual events less so, declining to near zero by the Opening Ceremony. Skepticism recurs after the Games have passed by, but this is a local phenomenon as citizens start to ask questions about what was actually achieved and where all the money went. Any hard-hitting investigative journalism done at this latter point is pretty much irrelevant since the money has vanished and the white elephant venues now mar the landscape. Other than bemoaning the facts, it's far too late to do much about it but complain.

Journalists often claim that they are unbiased because they provide damning critiques after the Games, conveniently ignoring the fact that the same information was available early in the process when it might have served to educate the public and might actually have made a difference in the outcome. For example, had Vancouver-based journalists done a solid exposé of the Salt Lake Winter Olympics and provided this information during their pre-plebiscite period, Vancouverites could have made a far more informed choice. Providing essentially the same information as a post-mortem in 2010 will do nothing for the audience, merely for the journalists themselves, making them feel that they have done an honest job. That they haven't is part of their own frame of reference and one that is easily lost within the context of the general Olympic frame.

The failure to challenge the existing Olympic frame, or even to know that it exists, is thus the first failing of many journalists. Add to that the obvious fact that the owners of the media outlets are solidly on side with the Olympic industry and always have been makes moving away from received wisdom about the Games potentially a career ender.

Journalists, pretty much like anyone else, are not oblivious to who pays their salaries and innately know where the boundaries lie. During the course of my media work with NO GAMES, I had dozens of journalists record my answers to their "official within-the-frame" questions, then turn off their microphones and say that, off the record, they completely agreed with me…but liked getting their paychecks. Sadly I realized that most journalists are pretty smart people, relatively knowledgeable about the way all things associated with the Olympics really work, but in the end not really independent and able to tell the whole story. For a certainty, they are not able to try to shift the carefully constructed and guarded Olympic frame. All of this is understandable as human nature, but reflects a failure in some real sense of journalistic integrity.

Before the Plebiscite

Our focus at NO GAMES in 2002/2003 had begun to be on exposing the moneymen and developers behind the Bid Corp. Getting the information about the who's who in the Bid Corp wasn't particularly hard. Much could be found online, mostly culled from the business sections of local and national papers. It was merely a matter of sifting through mounds of material and drawing the lines that connected the various players. It was time-consuming to be sure but not particularly onerous. The real problem lay in getting the media to pay attention long enough to see that Vancouver's bid, like that of any Olympic city, was driven by the pet projects of real estate developers. The developers knew that they could count on the politicians they had bankrolled into office, or the business types who sat on their boards of directors. The relationships between developers, politicians and board members, although not always in plain sight, were there nevertheless for anyone willing to do some modest digging. And nowhere was this in plainer view than with the CBC.

CBC had long held the Canadian rights to broadcast the Games, paying serious gelt for the privilege over the years, and doing so for the obvious reason that they've thought it would generate advertising income in excess of the costs. Alas, for CBC, the 2008 Beijing Summer Games will be their last, but they didn't anticipate this going into the planning for 2010. Before getting the 2010 Games scooped out from under them by Canadian TV (CTV) and Rogers Broadcasting in 2005, CBC thought they had the Canadian broadcasting rights and acted accordingly. When the NO GAMES organization began in 2002, we were constantly amazed how little outright curiosity CBC showed about the emerging opposition. In fact their coverage of anything that smacked of anti-Olympic sentiment hovered firmly near zero. What made this particularly odd at the time was that the other press and media outlets, all private, were starting to cover us and dealing, at least in passing, with our concerns about Vancouver's bid. Had one only watched or listened to CBC, it would have seemed that there was no opposition whatsoever. This made little sense at the time, but slowly the pieces fell into place. First was the obvious television rights, but this was only one part of the puzzle. It should be noted that French CBC, both radio and TV, was a far more curious entity and had begun to cover the growing opposition to the Games, especially once the plebiscite was announced.

Gradually English CBC woke up and even offered to host some "debates" between the pro-bid side and the anti-Games forces in the weeks prior to the plebiscite. Two in particular stand out in my memory, one televised on national television and hosted by CBC correspondent Ian Hanomansing. On the pro-bid side sat Bid Corp CEO John Furlong, Vancouver Mayor Larry Campbell and the federal and provincial ministers responsible for the Games. CBC had brought in researcher Kevin Walmsley from the Olympics Research Institute of Western University in London, Ontario. Walmsley was supposed to be "neutral," but his institute received IOC funding. The opposition consisted of…me. CBC thought this eminently fair and said so over my protests. It was clearly a case of "show up if you want your voice to be heard; don't if you don't." Since I did, I showed up, and the 5:1 ratio did not go unnoticed by many viewers who wondered why CBC felt the need for such overkill.

The second CBC "debate" was hosted in downtown Vancouver at the Wosk Centre for Dialogue. The moderator for this was the host of CBC Radio's *Early Edition*, Rick Cluff, whose upfront bias in favor of the Games was — and remains — remarkable in a city chock full of media Games boosters. Cluff's idea of fair play consisted of putting me alongside BC Green Party leader Adriane Carr as the No side, and pitting us against Concert Property's CEO David Podmore, as head of the Yes side sitting next to Vancouver's Mayor Larry Campbell. Officially neutral was Kevin Shoesmith of the IOCC, the brainchild of Vancouver City councilor Jim Green, a staunch bid backer. Shoesmith would soon drop all pretence to neutrality and often wound up at later events sitting directly next to Podmore and other pro-Games types. Admittedly, this lineup had more balance than the TV debate, but this reflected less CBC's conversion to the notion of fair play than the fact that Carr and I had threatened to pull out if they went forward with their original lineup. The latter had included supposedly neutral observers representing First Nations and poverty organizations. What was wrong with this? Everything — the proposed representatives sat on the Board of Directors of the Bid Corp. "How," we asked, "could they be neutral under the circumstances?" We had a bit of negotiation around this point, CBC not giving in until I told them to have their debate without us.

The Media After the Plebiscite

In the plebiscite the Yes side prevailed after weeks of saturation advertising by the Bid Corp and three levels of government. CBC gleefully reported the outcome, cutting away to the downtown hotel where the pro-bid gang was holding their election vigil and later celebration. Close-ups followed a joyous Premier Gordon Campbell hugging Mayor Larry Campbell and Councilor Jim Green and backslapping Concert's David Podmore and Jack Poole. It all made for surreal television to watch ostensible political enemies coming together to hoot and holler and prance around the stage to celebrate their bought and paid for "victory."

In the weeks following the plebiscite, English language CBC went back to sleep about any anti-Olympics opposition, viewing the issue as basically over and done with. There was a flurry of interest when the IOC Technical Team visited in March 2003, virtual silence in the months that followed, then again growing interest as the Prague decision loomed in July of that year.

Media Frame, Media "Balance"

Any group trying to go up against the Olympic machine is faced with formidable challenges, the largest being access to the public. The gatekeepers of this access are the journalists and their editors who decide what is or isn't news. And, quite simply, if it is not selling air time or newspapers, being against the Games on principle is not particularly newsworthy. This became clear to us in NO GAMES after the Vancouver plebiscite was over and again after the IOC's

Technical Team had completed their inspection of Vancouver, the Bid Corp and the proposed Olympic venues and skittered out of town.

We started to dig into CBC's corporate structure more strenuously, focusing in particular on Carole Taylor. Taylor had ridden a somewhat unlikely path to chair the board of directors of the premier news organization in Canada. Before settling in Vancouver, she had been a radio and TV reporter and talk-show host. Along the way, she married Art Phillips who would become mayor of Vancouver. Taylor's career was one of rapid upward mobility, first as Vancouver City councilor (1986–1990) then Chair of the Vancouver Port Corporation (1995–1997), presiding over the port's privatization. Taylor even had time for a stint as Chair of Canada Ports and the Vancouver Board of Trade. She also served on the Vancouver Whistler 2010 Bid Society and as a board member of HSBC Bank and some of its subsidiaries. The latter two caught our attention: the Bid Society was directly involved in getting the Olympics for Vancouver; HSBC Bank's chief shareholder was none other than Hong Kong billionaire Li Ka Shing whose colleagues in the Vancouver real estate world were firmly entrenched on the Bid Corporation. By the time Vancouver's Olympic bid came around, Taylor was still Chair of CBC and very much in charge.[2]

NO GAMES held that Taylor — and hence CBC —potentially had a conflict of interest in regard to the Vancouver's bid. Not only would CBC profit handsomely if they controlled the TV rights in 2010, Taylor's business associates were joined at the hip with the Bid Corp. How, we asked, could CBC be expected to be impartial? And, indeed, we stressed, perhaps these relationships went a long way toward explaining the dismal coverage CBC had generally given to the opposition. CBC officially ignored these suggestions, although individual reporters would often acknowledge, off the record, that there might be something to it. Comments such as the quote that opens this chapter were not uncommon.

If we needed further evidence that CBC's attention to Olympic opposition or scandal was highly selective, it was provided in a big way just before the vote in Prague. We had been following the links between IOC Technical Team leader Gerhard Heiberg and a company where he had long served on the board of directors, Norway's Aker Kvaener as described in chapter 4. Was the resulting contract between Aker and Power Corp's TotalFinalELF just good luck? A coincidence? If so, it was a very odd coincidence, indeed.

We put the information out as a press release and soon had European and American reporters asking the same questions. Heiberg was in close competition with his nearest rival, South Korea's Un Yong Kim. Kim had been accused of corruption during the Salt Lake Games of 2002 and would soon be charged with further misconduct in his role in the International Taekwondo Federation and ultimately be heading for jail. That was all in the future. What counted now was that he and Heiberg were going head to head, and Kim's supporters wanted anything they could get their hands on to discredit Heiberg. Our material was gleefully released by persons unknown to the European media that then contacted us for details. The outcome was a series of headlines throughout Europe and elsewhere.[3] The Canadian press and TV picked up on it too, but curiously it was never on the CBC nightly news. It wasn't simply a case that the Olympics were not making news — they were— but anything hinting of any impropriety in any part of Vancouver's bid was not going to come out of news anchor Peter Mansbridge's mouth.[4]

I watched in shock, not for the last time, as CBC ignored the events transpiring in Prague. A few days before the IOC's vote, a CBC Radio producer from the national morning show, *The Current*, called to ask if I would be on the show the day after the vote. Whether Vancouver succeeded or failed, they wanted my reaction and planned a five- to ten-minute segment. I agreed and the producer scheduled a call-in by me for 5 AM. I would be interviewed by correspondent Laura Lynch, sitting in for the regular host, Anna Maria Tremonti.[5] Was there anything besides the Prague outcome I would like to talk about? Yes, I told him, I'd like to talk about Carole Taylor and CBC's apparent conflict of interest concerning the Olympics. Sure, he agreed, that would be fine.

CBC Exacts Its Punishment

As detailed in other chapters, the Prague vote was held, curious and curiouser events occurred and Vancouver's bid prevailed. The next morning before dawn, I was on the phone to Lynch. Before we went on air, she laid out the plan. She'd mention that I represented a group that had opposed the Games and would ask me what we would do now. Would we now get behind the event and join the joyous throng, or continue to oppose? "Great, fine," I replied, "but what about my questions concerning Taylor?" Lynch's reply was to the point: "We're not going there." That wasn't the agreement, I started to reply, but then we were on-air. The preordained question was asked, I answered and before I could go further, it was "thank you" and click. I was on and off the air in less than two minutes, Carole Taylor's reputation safe for another day. My day with the powers at CBC was not over, however, as I would soon find out.

I hung up the phone, kissed my newborn daughter goodbye and got ready to go to my laboratory. A few hours later, I was sitting at my desk when there was a knock at the door. It was the Vice President of Research at the Vancouver General Hospital (VGH). He had a "touchy" issue to discuss with me. It seemed that the Public Affairs Office at VGH had been getting "complaints" about me using my office to "run" the No campaign. Who was complaining exactly? Well, he couldn't say, but it was worrying to the hospital administration. "Actually," I told him, "the phone is paid for by me, I work my university hours and then some, and this is just where the press can find me during my working day." "I know that," the VP said, "We don't want to interfere with your political activities, freedom of speech and all that, but we have to be sure that you don't give the impression that the university or hospital share your views." I pointed out that I'd never implied that either organization did. "We'd be grateful if you'd make sure that the contact address for NO GAMES on your website is not in any way related to VGH." I agreed to change the website address. He thanked me for being so cooperative, then departed.

Minutes later the phone rang. It was a CBC reporter whose name I didn't catch at first, in fact never did because he wanted to ask me about conflicts of interest, namely mine. It seemed that someone had told CBC I was using University property to promote my anti-Olympics views. Coming within minutes of my conversation with the VP Research, this was more than passing strange and a weird coincidence to boot, if coincidence at all. How, the reporter wanted to know, could I be accusing anyone on the Yes side of conflicts when I was clearly guilty myself. My explanation that I was using a phone I paid for myself, on my free time, was simply ignored. "How could I be talking to you now if I didn't make myself available at my work?" I asked. It didn't matter, the reporter replied, "conflict of interest was conflict of interest." He'd also heard that the University was considering disciplining me for the unauthorized use of University facilities. "Simply not true," I told him. "In fact, the VP Research was just here, and we had a very cordial conversation." "That's not what I heard," he said as he hung up.

That weekend's *Vancouver Sun* featured an article about how Gerhard Heiberg had lost the vice-presidency of the IOC due to allegations originating with the NO GAMES group (among others). CBC's radio and Web coverage focused all weekend on my "conflicts of interest."[6] The message couldn't have been clearer: "We'll decide what is and isn't news. And there is a price to pay for accusations we don't like." Illusions die hard, and my pre-Games respect and trust in an independent CBC has never recovered, nor do I expect it ever will.

The Good and the Bad
in Media Coverage of Vancouver 2010

Some may think I have unduly slammed the CBC for its lopsided coverage of the Vancouver Games bid and the events thereafter. I haven't, but I should also note that, in fact, some CBC reporters eventually did some decent reports, or least as good as the corporate powers at CBC would allow. Much of the more critical coverage of things Olympic came long after the Prague decision.[7]

As mentioned, the private TV stations were often far better than CBC. CTV was not bad considering they eventually scooped the Canadian TV rights to 2010–2012 broadcasting. Global TV did a decent enough job. The ethnic station Fairchild TV was actually very solid, always there and anxious for interviews.

Radio coverage of the Games debate was a totally mixed bag: CBC Radio (English) remained routinely awful and misinformed; under the control of Rick Cluff and others, it even began to sound more like outright Games boosters than independent journalists. CKNW was variable, especially after Rafe Mair got fired for saying controversial things about salmon farms, and their Olympic coverage and commentary lay largely in the hands of the hosts of the various shows where routinely Michael Smyth and Bill Goode could be counted on to boost the Games, regardless of the facts. News 1130 did neutral, "just the facts Ma'am" coverage, usually reporting events at face value.

The print media offered the greatest range in terms of quality of reportage. The national paper, the *Globe and Mail*, quickly defaulted into a "hear no evil, speak no evil" position on the Games. This view would eventually be set in concrete. After the tardy release of VANOC's business plan in 2007, columnist Gary Mason claimed to be "shocked," not by VANOC's perennial failure to keep promises or keep to the initial budget, but because he could *not* find any really decent scandal associated with VANOC or the Games. How hard he may have looked remained an open question.

Closer to home, *Province* reporter Damien Inwood at least had the honesty to seek opposition opinions while still writing glowing reports about the Olympics in general and VANOC's progress in particular. His colleague at the *Province*, Kent Spencer, had joined the paper's Olympic file after the bid succeeded. He first crossed my path in early 2006 when he was tracking the funny business deals behind the rental of the ice rink at GM Place to VANOC for highly inflated prices. VANOC had gotten hosed, Spencer realized, but why? He called me for my take on the situation, one that was pretty obvious: GM Place was owned by the Aqualini family, who just also happened to own Orca Bay, the company behind Vancouver's hockey team, the Canucks. VANOC wanted to rent the space for the 2010 Olympic ice hockey events. Fine, said the Aqualinis, it will cost you $18 million.[8] The normal rent was $100,000 a day for any other organization. The Aqualinis were going to pocket a windfall of over 500% additional profit because of the Games. Oddly, they had seconded one of their own at Orca Bay, Dave Cobb, to be on VANOC's board of directors. Spencer wanted to know what was going on. I recounted the facts and noted that the Aqualinis were just doing what came naturally to businessmen, that is, going with what the market would bear. After all, there were no other ice rinks of the right size in Vancouver, so what could VANOC do about it? The answer was nothing. VANOC had to pay the going rate and that was that.

I had liked that Spencer stayed with the story and got a decent version of it in print.[9] So when the Athletes' Village story later emerged, he seemed the fellow to take it to. He showed up at my university office one afternoon along with a photographer from the *Province*. Spencer is soft-spoken, bearded, casual and non-threatening, not at all your typical type-A investigative reporter. Dressed in blue jeans and a long-sleeved shirt open at the collar, Spencer seemed about as laid back as one could get. Slowly, carefully, I walked him through the City's agreement with Millennium, pointed out the stuff that should have been there but wasn't, then talked him through the financial aspects of the deal. During the meeting, I was sure that he saw the overall picture and understood what it meant, namely that something smelled very wrong about the whole package.

Indeed he did (as did the photographer), but the story that finally hit the newsstands was weighted heavily toward the pro-Games camp. The day before it came out, Spencer was quick to inform me that his editors had wanted "balance" and that he hoped I wouldn't be disappointed in the outcome. The outcome was a surprise, even for someone as media-jaded as I sometimes tended to be: Yes, Spencer had reported on the costs to the city and how sweet the deal was for Millennium. The facts were all there...in the bottom two inches of an inside page. And directly above this, lay a huge story about the Village itself, illustrated by an artist's full-color drawing showing what the Village was supposed to look like. Spencer had taken the initial story of the unusual deal involving Millennium and "balanced" it with fluff. The "news" had been about a potential insider deal. Now it was about what the athletes would have for supper.[10] This was one of the more egregious examples of media "balance," but not the first and just as surely not the last.

The efforts of the other print media reporters covering the 2010 Games were also a mixed bag. The *Vancouver Sun*'s columnists Vaughn Palmer and Daphne Bramham continued to do the math and told British Columbians what it would likely cost. Their columns were consistently insightful and accurate.

In contrast, the *Sun*'s Jeff Lee, one of the reporters busiest on the Olympic beat, was a mystery. (To be fair, he says the same about me). Lee is a smallish, compact man with a shock of dark hair and a rakish goatee. A perpetual scowl completes the picture, a scowl that hints of a gravitas borne of deep cynicism about human nature. I first got to know Lee during the plebiscite period. During this time, he did an in-depth interview with me for the *Sun*, trying to put a human face on the opposition. I was, by then, fairly well-known to the public and media, well into my 15 minutes of fame, and the *Sun*'s editors clearly judged it time to find out who exactly this Shaw character was. As we chatted about my history, it turned out that we had rather a lot in common, at least in ancestry. Some of my grandparents had come over from the "Pale of Settlement" in the borderlands between Russia and Ukraine, then in the midst of the Russian Civil War of the early 1920s. They had endured hardships galore before making it to the US and a new life. The family name was anglicized to fit in, and fit in they did. It turned out that Lee's family had come from the same general area but had chosen Canada, shortened their name to Lee to fit in and so on.

Lee's articles in that early period had been consistent in the media definition of balance, that is, writing one negative thing about the Games could be equaled by writing ten good things. Since, at the time, the alternative was no coverage at all, we in NO GAMES could hardly turn it down. Lee's articles were actually more than balanced, and while he asked me hard questions, he turned the same scrutiny on the Bid Corp and later VANOC. There was no doubt that he saw through the façade of the Olympic spectacle and knew what the real driving force was. In particular, he helped expose Jack Poole's attempted sleight of hand when the latter claimed during the plebiscite that Concert Properties had no interest whatsoever in bidding on any of the construction projects for Olympic venues, then later flip-flopped and tried to sneak a bid on the Athletes' Village into the mix. Lee had clearly remembered what Poole had said, obviously didn't like being lied to, and called VANOC and Poole on it. His article may have been the stimulus that forced BC Finance Minister Colin Hansen to kick Concert out of the competition. When the article came out in September of 2005, I was in Dunedin, New Zealand, at the University of Otago during my sabbatical from UBC. Nevertheless, I heard about Lee's story and was decidedly impressed. Here was a reporter who didn't like getting screwed around and was going to hold VANOC to account. Maybe, just maybe, we at NO GAMES had educated a few of the Fourth Estate? Something then happened: Lee and his articles went from healthy skepticism and balance to more and more laudatory depictions of the emerging Olympic venture. Perhaps he had finally become convinced that the Games were all that VANOC and the IOC said they were. Perhaps he just got tired of digging and scrambling to find the hidden history and real frame, knowing that most of the audience didn't really care. I wasn't the only one who noted the transition. Many of my colleagues in NO GAMES commented on it; even some in the media mentioned it.

In marked contrast to Lee, there was Wendy Cox of the Canadian Press. She had also begun as one of our toughest critics, then started to do some of her own homework rather than just regurgitate VANOC's happy-face press releases. Cox, a tall pretty brunette with an alarmingly direct manner, had become the countervailing example of what the media could do if it wanted to. Just like Spencer, Cox had come into the Olympics file, at least to my end of it, in 2006. She had started showing up at press conferences put on by 2010 Watch and the Work Less Party. There was no doubt, she was tough. Conrad Schmidt and I found this out during one press conference when hard pressed by her for facts and figures. We provided these and then turned the tables and asked that she apply the same scrutiny to VANOC and things Olympic. She did. Her reports, especially the one examining VANOC's tardy business plan managed to cover off a number of issues and succeeded to find true balance beyond the fluff that VANOC was sending out. Not only was Cox increasingly critical, she made her staff do the same, with one staffer, Stephanie Levitz, writing some really accurate pieces about VANOC and the Games preparations.

Another increasingly tenacious reporter, Bob Mackin writing for *Business in Vancouver*, did some serious digging to get out the story about the Callaghan and the Hartwicks,[11] only to see a more detailed story get shut down by his editors at 24 *Hours*, a local metro paper.[12] The latter illustrated another response of the mainstream media: when no amount of "balancing" will suffice, pretend the news didn't happen. This was what CBC had done with the Heiberg material and what the *Province* and *Sun* would soon do when we released the hard numbers about the actual damage done to the environment by Olympic preparations.[13] Mackin's later stories about the Olympics in 24 *Hours* began to provide the investigative reporting so long neglected by most journalists.

What all of the above highlights is that there are some very good journalists out there, more than capable of getting to the roots of a story. They struggle against a corporate media mindset that is often paralyzed in its coverage of the Olympics (and one suspects much else) by conflicting currents: trying to get the story right versus appeasing corporate managers who are there to make sure the spin comes out the way the owners want. Some of the stuff the public needs to know gets out; much gets buried and forgotten, either completely or by the ten-to-one ratio of good to bad. Time and time again, when the microphones are switched off, journalists tell me that they understand that the Olympics are a scam and that BC's citizens are getting screwed. When the story hits the papers or TV, the "happy" version is the one the public sees.[14]

The sad reality is that most of the mainstream media is not independent and serves in most cases as an active agent to promote Olympic bids and the Games themselves. This outright promotion of the Games by media is one of more powerful ways that organizing committees have to sell the Games to an often uncertain public. In the following chapters we will see how this has worked in Vancouver as well as in past Olympic host cities.

CHAPTER 11

"Owning the Podium," or What's in It for Me?

A lot of the athletes thought that winning medals would supercede or protect them from racism. But even if you won the medal it ain't going to save your momma. It ain't going to save your sister or children. It might give you 15 minutes of fame, but what about the rest of your life? I'm not saying they didn't have the right to follow their dreams, but to me the medal was nothing but the carrot on the stick.

JOHN CARLOS[1]

Jock Sniffing as an Olympic Sport

IT'S HARD TO overestimate the respect many people have for professional athletes. When it comes to the stars of any major sport, this respect turns to an adoration that borders on idolatry. Academics certainly don't enjoy any such prestige, nor do those involved in most other professions, including the politicians who often feed off sports hero worship. Maybe the hero worship arises from the oft-made comparison of organized sports to a form of choreographed warfare, the worshiper expressing a kind of wannabe-ism for athletic/martial prowess. Whatever the reason, the phenomenon — colorfully and aptly known as "jock sniffing" — seems mostly to reach its apogee in middle-aged men. One has only to scan the list of those members of the IOC or look at VANOC's directors to see this demographic in full force.

The Olympic Games are every bit as much about professional sports as are pro baseball or World Cup soccer. Long gone are the days when Olympic athletes had to be amateurs, that is, holding mundane real day jobs just like the rest of us. The major difference is that Olympic athletes don't make the same amount of money. Jock sniffing remains the same, however, most obviously with the star Olympic athletes — those who win medals — who become national and often international heroes. The IOC and Olympic family, the bid boosters, the politicians and Olympic sports writers are all jock sniffers of the first water, indeed have taken the whole phenomenon to a cult level that gets mercilessly flogged for the full 17 days of the Games. Olympic boosters ensure that this occurs by stressing the need to "own the podium," hyping every medal into a collective national jock-sniffing frenzy. None of this is to suggest that individuals shouldn't enjoy sports or cherish their sports heroes on their own dime. It's just that when the phenomenon becomes a national, publicly funded sports orgy, that it becomes obscene.

Sports writer Dave Zirin is not particularly charitable when discussing the powers behind the mega sporting events or the omnipresent white noise that the events disperse across the airwaves. He is even less kind to the powerbrokers behind the perennial and peripatetic financial scourge of the modern Olympic Games. In our consumer culture, mega events, Olympics included, use sports as a platform to sell stuff. Advertisers extol their products, often adding to the allure by having star athletes wear their shoes or drink their power cola. Politicians, in turn, use sports and athletes to connect to the public, to bask in the reflected adoration which fans have for their sports heroes. As Zirin writes:

> There is so much inspired joy on the playing field that it's easy to forget how people in power use sports to advance their own narrow agendas. Sports has always held a tremendous sway over public imagination. Politicians from the days of Teddy Roosevelt have successfully used the games to manipulate public sentiment. This is not to say sports are some kind of Jonestown Kool-Aid with the power to lead us like lemmings off a cliff. It's merely a tool — a tool both political parties [in the US] are quite adept at using to their advantage. Our bipartisan emperors drape themselves in sports as a way to connect with the workaday reality of ordinary people.[2]

All of this is equally if not more true of the Olympics where the five rings become the vehicle of choice to peddle junk food, credit cards, telephones and whatever else that corporate sponsors hope to link to Olympic magic. And, just like professional sports, the Olympics specialize in fostering lemming-like behaviors, an almost messianic fervor for the Games that for many sweeps away all doubt.

That Olympic athletes would go along with the greed and hype of the Games is not surprising in the slightest. Why shouldn't they get what they can while at the peak of their athletic prowess? Do they and the Olympic movement really need to be purer than the corporate sporting world? In a society where everything is viewed as a commodity, a "What's in it for me" attitude is perfectly understandable, even rational. The Canadian Olympic Committee apparently completely agrees, deciding in 2007 to give medal winners cash bonuses: $20,000 for a gold; $15,000 for silver; $10,000 for bronze.[3] The only problem with adopting such an ethos is that the Olympics were conceived as something quite different.[4] The Paralympics seem to have kept the original spirit, but for the IOC and the organizing committees, the "purity of athletics" is as dead as the dodo. The ongoing pretense that Olympic sports are somehow purer than their professional siblings simply adds the sin of hypocrisy to that of greed. As this book goes to press, riots in Tibet have led to widespread killings of protesters by the Chinese military and police. In spite of calls for a boycott of Beijing's Games, the IOC, the NOCs and most athletes refuse to countenance the idea. The pious rationales for participating in the Games while such overt repression is ongoing merely serve to highlight, once again, the triumph of self-interest over any concern for human rights.

Olympians and the general public know all of this at some level of consciousness. There have been too many Olympic scandals over the years to not know, but somehow the five-ring-circus-like spectacle of the Olympics, the high drama of "the thrill of victory, the agony of defeat" makes all the dirt and eventual societal debt seem somehow inconsequential, at least for a time.

While the outcomes may not be in doubt, the official Olympic frame that the Games are really about the athletes competing for world peace creates a huge obstacle for Games opponents when faced with an argument that goes something like this: "Sure, there may be problems, maybe the IOC should be reformed, but how can you be against the dreams of people who have trained their entire lives to get to the Olympics? You are not against the athletes are you?" It is certainly true that Olympic athletes are dedicated people and few opponents of the Olympic Games would argue the point. Viewing it solely from the perspective of the athletes, however, is also to miss the main point. What the Olympic Games may have been at their inception and for perhaps some of the 20th century is not what they are now. Not only is this true for the IOC and the host cities, but also for the athletes themselves for whom coming home with gold, in the West and elsewhere, is the entire focus and the pathway to years of lucrative contracts endorsing various product lines. Silver is also pretty good, bronze OK, but a gold medal is best. All Olympic athletes clearly know this, as does the television audience. If you doubt this for a second, consider: In many events, the difference between first and fourth place can often be measured in milliseconds, a difference so small that an absolutely opposite outcome could just as easily occur if the race was run a second time and the wind changed ever so slightly. If it were really about sports, we'd all be celebrating the amazing achievement of *anyone* able to perform at such a high level at all. But we don't. Who, after all, remembers anyone who came in fourth? Outside of the athletes' friends and families, no one does. Will a fourth-place contender get products to endorse? No. It's all about winning: gold, silver and bronze medals which make their owners household celebrities at home and abroad. Everyone else is just a forgotten number.

Not only can the results be capricious due to a bad break — an "off" start — the quality and honesty of the judges can also make a world of difference. As Andrew Jennings documents in his books, judges can and have been bribed with cash or other rewards to skew the results toward a particular athlete or nation.[5] Every Olympic Games has one or more questionable outcomes. For Canadians one of the more glaring occurred to their own athletes in the ice-skating freestyle event in Salt Lake City in 2002. Canadians Jamie Sale and David Pelletier were initially robbed of a gold medal by a French judge who seemed to have taken a bribe to toss victory to the Russian skaters. This was certainly a bad enough outcome, but what made it worse was the response of the IOC when the theft was revealed. The IOC instantly did what it does best: It denied that anything was wrong at all and, absurdly, continued to hold this position even as they issued a second set of gold medals to the Canadians. How could two teams both win gold? Only in the bizarre doublespeak world of the IOC could this make sense. But it made all the difference in the world to Sale and Pelletier who could now come home as champions and slide directly into lucrative contracts.[6] Would they have been as marketable without their gold? It's highly doubtful.

If gold is what drives the athletes, what advantage accrues to a country when it tries to "own the podium" by bringing home as many medals as possible? It's a question worth exploring since enhancing any nation's medal count becomes the rationale used to sell the Olympics to a gullible public. We are routinely asked to believe that putting our athletes on the podium with our flag rising behind them and the national anthem ringing out somehow makes us superior as a people. It is, in fact, a deliberately fostered sports nationalism that suits the IOC perfectly, regardless of whether Baron de Coubertin might now be spinning in his grave. The Nazis used the Games for overtly political purposes in 1936. The Chinese will do the same in 2008.

The "owning the podium" notion also figures strongly into the organizing committee's messaging about why any host city needs to construct the sports venues at public expense. The basic idea here is that our athletes will train on these facilities before the Games and thus have a home-court advantage when the real Games roll in. In other words, taxpayers are being asked for a massive subsidy to train Olympic athletes. This might be a reasonable enough proposition if presented honestly as such, with the public able to vote on it. This doesn't usually happen. The outcome is that the venues are constructed with taxpayers' money, may be used by local athletes pre-Games (*if* ready in advance), are used intensively during the Games, then wind up in the private sector after everyone has gone home. Unlike the benefits that might flow to everyone from building a hospital or school, the benefits are for the select few: the athletes, the developers and the eventual owners.

One follow-up rationale for "owning" podiums is that beyond what it does for the athletes, it actually helps the nation. Really? If an athlete wins gold and gets a Nike contract afterwards, will he/she share the profits with society? Not likely. So what's in it for the rest of us that makes this direct subsidy worthwhile? Answer: We get to sniff their jocks.

As further proof of what "owning the podium" really means, countries that score poorly in the medal count get a stern lecture from the IOC. In 2004, after a "disappointing" collection of trinkets followed the Canadian team home from Athens, IOC President Jacques Rogge was quick to point out to the Canadian government that "more funding" was needed to make Canada more "competitive." Or, loosely translated from IOC corporate speak, Rogge's message really was this: "Your part of the product line sucks and is hurting our television sales, so fix it." It was an obvious message, yet its true meaning was lost on the politicians who promptly kowtowed and promised more cash to train Canadian athletes to a more saleable IOC standard. No one in Ottawa, after all, wanted to be the one to let down the company, the brand or the product. This incident reinforced yet again the nature of commercialization of Olympic sports for a television audience. If jock-sniffing nationalism is used to build the audience, how many in TV-land will tune in if none of their countrymen are in the running? The answer is obvious: relatively few.

Athletes, the Media and "Manufacturing Consent"

Most of what the average person knows about the Olympics in general, and any local bid in particular, comes from one primary source: the corporate media. The IOC has its tame coterie of reporters in television, radio and the press who repackage IOC press releases virtually verbatim. Each bid city's mainstream media has, at the very least, significantly interlocking financial and social interests with the developers who form the shock troops for the local organizing committee. Having public relations firms ready and able to provide instant copy for the IOC or organizing committee, and being able to place such copy directly into the hands of the media, doesn't hurt either.[7]

In the last chapter, I discussed my own media experiences, both good and bad. The good part was that many reporters turn out to be sincere professionals who genuinely want to get the facts and background right. The bad part is that most of them labor under a structure that often doesn't let them do so, or, if it does, imposes the leg irons of "balance." Balance, as we've seen, often means acknowledging one negative — for example, environmental damage — and "balancing" it with some larger number of supposed positives. In many cases, the corporate media simply abandons any pretext of seeking balance, rolling out lopsided pro-Olympics purple prose that can set your teeth on edge.

For the most part, the corporate media collaborates with the bid boosters and city fathers/mothers to create an image of their city that differs radically from reality. The term "imagineering" was coined to describe the process by which Atlanta's Committee for the Olympic Games (ACOC) invented a positive image of Atlanta as a caring, inclusive, responsible "world-class" city. ACOC needed the IOC and the world to see a city truly worthy of the great privilege of hosting the Games, not one plagued by crime and homelessness. Imagineering as a marketing concept may have originated with Atlanta, but it was hardly unique. Vancouver, like many other candidate cities, is no different.

Imagineering is not only aimed at sweet-talking the IOC, but is designed in part to convince a city's own citizens that theirs can be "world-class" too, save but for a vehicle like the Olympics to make it so. To put this into perspective, let's do definitions first. What does it mean to be a "world-class" city? According to Lenskyj, citing an earlier work, a world-class city has "a critical mass of visitor attractions and facilities, hallmark events, urban tourism strategies, leisure and cultural services to support tourism."[8] In other words, a world-class city has to have the sorts of amenities and entertainment that the world's traveling rich have a right to expect when they visit. A world-class city is a "bourgeois playground."[9] Hosting the Olympics can help give your city this brand, a very good thing if you're in the real estate or tourism business. Alas, it's not such a good thing if you are middle class or poor, certainly not if you're one of the homeless. For those who have the misfortune to be in the latter groupings, your only utility to the process is not to enjoy your "world-class city" status but to pay for the means — the Olympics — to make it one. And, for this to happen, you need to believe in the Olympic dream, and no one is better prepared to make this happen than the mainstream media.

It is the media's job to ensure that your dreams mirror those of the developers, and they accomplish this feat by unleashing wave after wave of Olympic coverage, all designed to reinforce Olympic frames. Toronto's two failed bids, just like Vancouver's successful one, were completely supported by media far too close to the organizers to be objective in the slightest degree. In Toronto, both CBC (radio and television) and CTV television were official partners of the bid, as was the *Globe and Mail* newspaper.[10] As Varda Burstyn writes, "the myth that the Games are an unalloyed good for host communities, a plum to be had for the most worthy and deserving, remained firmly in place in the public imagination and *mass media* [italics mine]."[11]

Burstyn leaves little doubt who she thinks owns the bulk of the blame for fixing the myth so firmly into public consciousness:

> The main culprit in maintaining public ignorance about both Olympic corruption and the Games' negative impacts are the mass media. It is impossible to escape the conclusion that the structural integration of the media into the Olympic industry has turned them into promoters — not journalists or critics — of all things Olympic. In all the cases explored in this book [Helen Lenskyj's *Inside the Olympic Industry: Power, Politics and Activism*], an integration of media, politicians', IOC, NOC and local Olympic committees' interests was strongly in evidence during both bid and preparation processes. This elite integration resulted in systematic media censorship of opposition to the Games and of analyses of their problems and negative consequences. This has taken place largely through the powerful act of pure omission, with a strong dose of distortion, ridicule and minimization thrown in for good measure. The Olympic industry is a large component of what Sut Jhally has termed the "sport-media complex." One of the great lessons of the past decades is that when the media's economic interests in a sporting event or institution are significant, journalists turn, in their majority, from reporters to impresarios.[12]

Mega sports events, in particular the Olympics, are the ideal tools for transforming cities, but the tools can't be used — at least in notional democracies — without a compliant public. The media's job is to create this compliance, and it does so by setting the frame of the debate, the context within which all discussion about the Olympics and the overall agenda turns. Or, as Len-skyj writes, "The pseudo-religious allure of the Olympic spirit rhetoric distinguishes the Olympics from more mundane hallmark events such as world fairs or historical commemorations, and from other urban mega projects such as downtown revitalization or waterfront regeneration."[13]

Building the Olympic Frame: The Three Pillars Approach, Part 1, Pennies from Heaven

Just as the Olympic movement has three official pillars (sports, culture, environmental sustainability), the frame the Olympic industry seeks to create has three distinct moving parts. The one trotted out first when local boosters start peddling the notion of their city as host is that the Olympics are a money-making machine par excellence. Boosters and much of the press will focus selectively on past Olympic success stories, for example, the profits made by Los Angeles during the 1984 Summer Games, but tell only part of the story: Yes, the LA Games did turn an operating profit, but virtually all of the infrastructure was already in place. In addition, LA had the financial boost from burgeoning television broadcast rights. Other times the boosters and the media will focus an even more selective lens on particular host cities by simply omitting crucial details that might stand in the way of the emerging frame. A case in point for this, particularly for Vancouver's bid, was the alleged financial windfall from Calgary's 1988 Winter Olympics. Again, yes, the operating revenues may have exceeded the operating costs, so technically Calgary made some money. Most of the press held to this story even in the face of investigative journalism by Thomas Walkom of the *Toronto Star* who looked at all the numbers and reported that any operating profits were swamped by the infrastructure ($451 million) and security costs, the total being nearly a $1 billion net loss.[14] In spite of Walkom's work, the notion that Calgary's Games had proven that *any* Games would be profitable remained firmly fixed in the public mind. In Vancouver's bid, this incorrect "factoid" led many citizens to vote yes in the plebiscite. The message of financial goodies awaiting Vancouver and the lack of any possible downside was reinforced virtually daily during the plebiscite campaign. The Bid Corp, the provincial government (usually the premier), city councilors and Vancouver Mayor Larry Campbell all stayed on message, Campbell even issuing his famous quote that the Games wouldn't cost Vancouverites "one penny."

NO GAMES tried with some success to bring reality to the debate by a historical analysis of past host cities, notably the Calgary example cited above and Montreal's own fiscally disastrous Summer Games of 1976. The debt from the latter — close to $2 billion with interest payments — was finally retired in 2006, 30 years after the event, making a mockery of the infamous statement by Montreal's then Mayor Jean Drapeau, "The Montreal Olympics can no more have a deficit, than a man can have a baby." Some of the media noted the irony in passing, others simply ignored it or dealt with it as an anomaly, pretending the problem wasn't that the Olympics generally generate debt, rather it was the *way* the Olympics were run. The attempt to blame the outcome on practice rather than theory has clear historical and current precedence: The near meltdown of the energy sector in California in the late 1990s followed an orgy of deregulation leading to complete privatization. California had followed the advice of various "think tanks" who had advocated that a wholly private, unregulated industry would provide consumers with greater choice and, ultimately, lower prices. That none of these predictions came to pass was blamed by the same think tanks not on their own flawed theory, but on faulty implementation. The same "blame the tools, not the blueprint" mentality permeates current political posturing in the United States about the implosion of Iraqi society. Commentators from both political parties routinely lay the blame squarely on none other than the victims, the Iraqis themselves. Formulated in various guises, the message is that the collapse of Iraq is certainly not due to the military invasion and the deaths of some 600,000 people, but rather the inability of the Iraqis to move forward with the great gift of democracy bestowed on them by a benevolent America. In the same way, the Olympic frame is so firmly entrenched that any failure to provide profits or keep promises is seen as a failed application of a generally sound model.

As we will see in the next chapter, the fiscal picture that emerges from virtually all Games — LA, for the reasons cited above, being a notable exception — is uniformly dismal. This history rarely matters to bid boosters or the media in the run up to the IOC's decision. The reason for this is that, even when their financial projections are shown to be patently false, the bid-boosting organizations have several other cleverly constructed arguments ready and waiting in the wings.

The Three Pillars of the Olympic Frame, Part 2, Civic and National Pride

Once the "Olympics equals manna from heaven" mantra gets kicked out of the park by those who actually know economics and can do math, Olympic boosters neatly segue into the patriotism angle. "Maybe it will cost us something, but what price can you put on pride?" The notion of making the potential host city world-class gets blended into this approach.

The "pride" approach is made while still stressing that while costs will be minimal, pride — civic or national — is going to be immense. At first glance, especially for journalists for some reason, this is considered a killer argument. Like others, I've fallen for it before, because after all, what price can you put on pride? You've *got* to be joking? People have been putting a price tag on pride and patriotism for as long as there have been people, at least if the Old Testament and other religious texts are to be trusted on this account. Oddly, the types who try to pretend that pride is not a commodity are quite often the same folks in the neo-liberal press and think-tanks who urge us all to put a dollar sign on every rock, every tree, the air we breathe and the very water we drink. What about selling your kids or your gods? Well, there are certainly enough who have done precisely that over the span of human history, again as various holy books teach us quite clearly. Not to say any of this is admirable, merely that, for those choosing to view the world in a one-dimensional way, pride has its dollar value just like any other commodity.

When the Vancouver bid started, the majority of the public was onside, at least in some measure because they were told by the Campbell twins that it wouldn't cost a penny and, even better than that, we'd all make oodles of money. It may be only coincidence, but this is precisely the pitch of the now infamous Nigerian "banking scam." Originally from Nigeria and other countries in West Africa, variant forms of this scam now arise from countries all around the world: Someone who claims to be a reliable bank manager in country X has obtained your address (e-mail or snail mail) from a disinterested third party. It seems that a foreign national, call him John Smith, has died suddenly and tragically, leaving his vast bank account of tens of millions of dollars unclaimed. Such accounts must now accrue to the government of X who will use it to pursue evil deeds. The manager wants to offer you a deal you can hardly afford to turn down. If you will claim to be Smith's relative, he can transfer the funds to your bank account back in Canada. If you agree, the manager will split the funds with you (the percentages vary). It is all risk-free. All you have to do is send your banking details. And, oh yes, there are some minor transaction fees. He might just need your account PIN also. However, in case this causes you some concern, in the words of a recent letter I received, "you should not entertain any atom of fear" about any of this. It's always good to know that no atoms need be perturbed. The scam is oddly reminiscent of Mayor Larry Campbell's assurances that the Games wouldn't cost a penny.

It's really quite remarkable how closely the Olympic hype and the banking scam coincide, so much so that it is difficult not to conclude that both sets of scam artists are pretty adept at reading human nature. Think about this: You are doing a good deed (keeping funds out of the hands of an evil government, helping elite athletes be their best/fostering brotherhood through sports/promoting your city and country), *and* it will make you a bag of money, *and* it's all risk free. The scam has the elegance of simultaneously appealing to both altruism and greed, the fusion so neatly done that it's hard to see where one leaves off and the other begins. The sole difference is that while the banking scam targets one individual at a time, the Olympics go after whole cities, if not countries, at the same time.

Back to the question: "What price can you put on pride". In spite of saturation advertising, the backing of three levels of government and a nearly complete media blitz, over 36% of Vancouverites still voted no in the plebiscite. So if you were in the "I'm backing the Bid" camp, this example is for you: It's now five years later, and you've maybe developed the queasy feeling that Larry Campbell and John Furlong and the rest were not quite as candid as you'd thought back in 2003. Now harsh reality may be setting in as you realize that the chance for Vancouver to shine in the eyes of the world is going to cost you some of your paycheck. But what price can you put on pride, right? Well, for starters, let's say something like $1,000 for every man, woman and child (this was in 2003; it's worse now). You've got a family of four, so this is getting pricey, but what can you really do now that we're into it? Oh, I forgot to mention that the hypothetical deal is that those who don't want to pay can opt out if their pride is feeling a bit strained. Remember that it's not the lives of your kids, or the freedom to practice your religion, or the sovereignty of your country that's up for grabs; this is about a 17-day party. OK, here we go, round two. You now discover that nine of ten of your fellow citizens have decided they can definitely put a price tag on their pride when it comes to the Olympics in their city and would prefer to use the $4,000 for a vacation. OK, Captain Vancouver, the bill to you is now $40,000. Are you still in? If so, I admire your spirit and abiding commitment to seeing Vancouver on TV, but I'm beginning to doubt your sanity, because the next round will cost you your house. Still think that no one can't put a price tag on pride? If you had any doubts, you now know differently. The pride "argument" was always a non sequitur wrapped up in the flag, as insipid and stupid then as it is now. Sadly, our usually ingrained loyalty to home and nation was skillfully manipulated to hell and gone by those who had an Olympic agenda to sell.

The pride part of the frame worked quite well, indeed still does for much of the public. But the boosters and the media had one more card yet to play: the myth of the "pure athlete."

The Three Pillars of the Olympic Frame,
Part 3, It's All for the Athletes

This argument is one the IOC and local organizing committees like a lot, largely because it forms the core of the official Olympic industry frame and because it provides an escape hatch when scandals boil to the surface and risk upsetting the IOC's (and local organizing committees') reputation and, especially, profits. Here is one shining example pulled from the files of Canada's leading national newspaper:

> The Games are the free trade of sport — they invite athletes everywhere to leap the walls of parochialism and reach the highest expression of grace and beauty…they invite humanity into a cauldron of competition and hope that its glow will displace the darkness of the age. For a fortnight, people everywhere are transfixed. Touched by the spirit of goodwill, inspired by the majesty of the human form, they refuse to think ill of these Olympic Games.[15]

Well prose certainly doesn't get much more purple than that. The message is clear: No matter what else happens, no matter what the costs overruns or deceit, regardless of the lack of transparency or process, irrespective of who gets caught stealing or doping, it's all about the purity of Olympic ideals as typified by the athletes. Athletes caught cheating are merely the bad apples who can never really tarnish the purity of the others.

Fighting the Olympic Frame

In the next chapters, I'll discuss in detail how to deconstruct the Olympic industry frame, crucially what works and what, most definitely, doesn't. For the moment, however, I want to focus on some of the problems NO GAMES and other anti-Olympics groups faced in dealing with the moving targets of the three pillars discussed above.

First, whether you are against the Olympics altogether — initially a very challenging position to take — or just against some part of what it will do to your city, you are faced with the uphill task of trying to promote a negative message. Human psychology being what it is, people prefer happy, positive messages and the Olympic industry provides these in abundance. It's Disneyland and Santa Claus and puppies and all the good things that can be yours if only you believe. They have a vision and want to throw themselves a fabulous 17-day party and invite the world. The opposition has an anti-vision, is against fun, full of naysayers who probably hate kittens and Christmas presents. The naysayer image is hard to overcome in the public mind, especially as it gets reinforced by the media. In my own case, I was given various sobriquets, amongst them "sourpuss" (Rafe Mair) or "Dr. No" (radio station CKNW after Mair had departed).

Aside from having a negative, seemingly anti-fun message, NO GAMES and other opponents had qualified success in dealing with the financial part of the Olympic frame, so much so that the bid boosters eventually downplayed this angle, shifting instead to the patriotism/pride pillar. This, being an intangible, was harder to fight. Not that it can't be done, as in the above example, but it does require that your audience be willing to follow you through a *reductio ad absurdum* argument that takes time to present. And, even if this barricade can be breached, and it was by NO GAMES eventually, the target had moved on to the last pillar: Seeming to be against the athletes and their dreams was simply viewed as selfish, even cruel. Indeed this part of the official frame is doubtlessly the strongest, the redoubt to which boosters and the IOC fall back when the inevitable cost overruns or scandals emerge.

It's important to realize that the pillars of the frame have a different resonance with the public at various phases of the process. In the bid phase, all three pillars are used in the sequence described. In the post-bid phase, the financial pillar is downplayed as it becomes crystal clear that it simply isn't true. Even the mainstream press has woken up to the falsity of the economic projections by this stage, a situation that only grows as the Games approach. This should matter to the public at large, and it does for an interregnum of several years post-bid, but fades away as the Opening Ceremony draws closer. Most people naturally are caught up in the excitement that a mega event generates, most opponents have grown weary of the fight and have moved on in the face of the inevitable, and the media hype grows with each passing day. There is also an insidious message put out by organizing committees, boosters large and small, and the media. It shows up while the bid is still up for grabs, fades after the bid is won, then rebounds in the year or so before the Olympic circus arrives. It goes like this: If we don't get the bid or if something goes wrong with the Games, it's all because of the naysayers and malcontents. In the first instance, it attempts to shift the burden for the IOC choosing some other city away from any faults that the bid might have had onto the backs of the opposition, basically stating that "we lost this because of you and your negative anti-our city/country attitude." This was the message the Toronto Bid laid on the doorstep of the opposition group Bread Not Circuses. During the pre-bid stage, this tactic forces some opposition groups to become defensive, to soft-peddle their own arguments. Inevitably, it leads to the fatal, "We're not against the Olympics, but…" position.

During Games preparations and the actual running of the Games, the "blame the opposition" message takes on more ominous overtones and leads to outright calls in the media and by some in the public for the outright suppression of any form of dissent about any part of the Olympic industry. Naysayers are now termed "activists" and "radicals." The hint is that you could even wind up being labeled a terrorist, not a trivial concern in this age of perpetual war. "Anti-terrorism" legislation passed in the US (Patriot Acts 1 and 2), in Canada (C-37) and elsewhere in the West defined terrorism in such broad strokes that the label could be made to fit anyone or any activity, including those that might be directed against any aspect of the economy. Indeed, in the months after September 11, numerous commentators in the mainstream press went out of their way to link Al Qaeda with the anti-globalization movement, in spirit, if not in deed.[16] Companion legislation in both countries added economic disruption to the list of defined terrorist acts.

The status of the Olympics and IOC neatly finds protection under this legal umbrella. Governments routinely evoke the first pillar of the Olympic frame, that is, that the Games bring wealth; hence to interfere with them in any way could be viewed not only as an embarrassing annoyance, but outright economic terrorism. The officers of the IOC also enjoy the equivalent of diplomatic status; interfering with diplomats is also a crime. Governments in Canada and elsewhere thus have more than enough tools in place to crush Olympic opponents at will. Whether they choose to employ these powers will depend on the type and level of threat they perceive. There may, in fact, be no threat whatsoever from demonstrators, but the potential of government to use draconian anti-terrorism legislation against those "blamed" for any Olympic hiccup cannot help but cast a chill. With this, all but the most ardent Olympic opponents will likely realize that they have to watch their step and that maybe it's best to retire into resentful silence than risk a confrontation that they are not likely to win.

All of the frames used by organizing committees and boosters have their origins in the IOC's headquarters in Lausanne. Indeed, Olympic opponents often have the eerie feeling that the local bid boosters have significant advice coming from higher up. Historically the IOC has dealt with opposition before and knows how to diffuse it. Some of the ways it has perfected will be discussed in the concluding chapters. But, before going there, we need to apply the *coup de grâce* to the first pillar of the Olympic frame. To do so we only need look at the history of the Games and their financial numbers.

Selling Snow to Eskimos, or
Cookie Cutters Make Cookies

*Yes, Red Ken [Livingstone, the Mayor of London] has turned
the Olympics into a social-welfare program. But in between
the cheers, Livingstone has also announced that each London
Council taxpayer will have to pay £20 a year for twelve years
(i.e., £240), even if the Games do not make a loss, which is
about as likely as seeing the Queen wear leather pants.*

DAVE ZIRIN,
WELCOME TO THE TERRORDOME: THE PAIN, POLITICS,
AND PROMISE OF SPORTS, HAYMARKET PRESS, 2007, P. 133

*I think if people expect the Olympics to be a money-
making enterprise, they will be disappointed. If they
are looking for economic development to follow the
Olympics, most likely they will be disappointed.*

MITT ROMNEY, FROM AN INTERVIEW IN THE *VANCOUVER SUN*,
JEFF LEE, "2010 GAMES WILL BE 'UNIFYING FORCE,'" FEB. 13, 2006[1]

The Power of the Olympic "Brand"

I VIVIDLY RECALL one radio interview I did with Rafe Mair at
CKNW early in the plebiscite campaign. Rafe, as usual, was
waxing eloquent about the thing that had him most riled up about
the bid: If successful, the Sea to Sky Highway was going to be
upgraded and, with it, a piece of road that Rafe cared about near
where he lived at Lions Bay. Sure, the uncertain costs of the Games
bothered him as well, somewhat. Mair knew enough Olympic history to know that costs rarely met the bid boosters' initial claims and that
the promises of manna from heaven were bogus. But on this day, it wasn't the

money that got his goat, rather the fact that he was going to be seriously inconvenienced by construction noise and turmoil. As usual, I let Mair rant on, biding my time and organizing my notes in order to be ready to take on my rival, the Bid Corp's own highly excitable John Furlong. Rafe finally sputtered to the end of his diatribe then started posing questions, first to me about why I was against the bid. My first point had been the hidden and always deliberately underestimated costs. When Furlong's chance came, he jumped right back with what he clearly hoped was his strongest financial card: Didn't the No side realize the power of the Olympic brand? Moreover, what that brand could do for business in BC if used correctly? "Why," Furlong exclaimed, "the five Olympic rings could be used to sell snow to Eskimos." By implication, Vancouver and British Columbia were going to get very rich by hosting the 2010 Games. (Furlong seems to have a thing for Eskimos as the later choice of Illaanaq as the 2010 symbol was to show.) My main thought listening to this statement was that, lousy political correctness aside, perhaps, for the first and last time, Furlong was quite right: The Olympic brand is a very powerful devise designed to suck cash out of the wallets of consumers and taxpayers.

In the ever weird world of things Olympic, Furlong couldn't know that five years on the socialist mayor of London would agree with him, offering up London for the 2012 Summer Games. Nor could he have foreseen that a very conservative Mormon politician who ran the Salt Lake Games would flatly contradict the Bid Corp's, and later VANOC's, rosy economic projections. Having to make a wager on whether Queen Elizabeth would be wearing leather pants or if British Columbians would be disappointed in 2010 plus one, I'd put my money on the latter.

Shell Game:
Assessing the True Costs of the Olympic Games

The basic economic argument in favor of hosting the Olympic Games is that it is a massive wealth generator for any city, region and country entrepreneurial and lucky enough to win them. Business confidence will boom, investors will see your city in a new light and buy in, real estate will blossom and the tourist industry will get a 17-day free advertising blitz, care of the media, to an audience of six billion eager future visitors. Not only will these goodies flow, but other levels of government will want a piece of the action, and the host city can leverage money from them to help make your city "world-class." The latter will take the form of larger convention centers that will draw ever more business, new transportation facilities, and fancy sports facilities as "legacies." Best of all, the record number of tourists visiting your city will leave behind significant amounts of cash, goose the hell out of the service sector with this infusion of paper gold, and the outflow will send massive numbers of tax dollars to the treasury. These additional tax dollars can now be recycled into more schools and hospitals by a caring government. The idea that money will flow from the Games into all aspects of the host city's/region's economy is very much like the old Milton Friedman-esque notion of trickle-down economics: If you put enough oats into your horse's feedbag, eventually enough of it will come out the back end for the sparrows.

The IOC firmly endorses this happy-face picture since it is part of the official, and sellable, Olympic frame used to suck cities into their maw. A recent book by a German Olympic academic, Holger Preuss, *The Economics of Staging the Olympics*, reinforces this frame with numerous equations, charts and graphs all designed to prove the thesis.[2] It even has a preface written by IOC President Jacques Rogge. Other than the fact that the direct linkage to the IOC creates some skepticism about the author's independence, there are still many useful and surprisingly honest numbers to be found within. For example, some of the actual costs of the various games, especially their deficits, from 1972 onwards are listed. These numbers can be remarkably hard to find since the IOC's and host city Olympic organizing committee's commitments to full fiscal transparency are often amongst the first promises to be broken.

When trying to get a grip on real Olympic expenditures, the first issue to resolve is this: What constitutes an "Olympic cost" and for whom? The first part of this question hinges on the various line items that make up the Olympic budget of any Games. These include: the operating costs of the 17-day Olympic Games followed by the 10 days of Paralympics; venue construction; infrastructure needed for the Games (upgrades and new) and security. Organizing committees have no choice but to accept the fact that the operating costs and the venues are part of the bill. However, to determine how much of such costs are public versus private, it is essential to know how these costs are distributed between the two sectors. This is not always known with any certainty. For Vancouver's 2010 Games, sponsors are picking up about 75 percent of the operating costs (approximately $580 million), taxpayers the remainder plus all the venue construction costs (estimated at $1.68 billion). It is important to note that some venue costs are largely hidden, that is, those that involve "rentals" rather than new construction. In Vancouver's Games, such rentals include over $18 million for the GM Place ice hockey rink and from $18 million to $30 million for access to the company that owns the Whistler-Blackcomb ski runs during the Games.[3]

Both Games organizers and governments try to download infrastructure costs from the final Olympic tally as "projects we were going to do anyway." While such assertions are sometimes true, more often they are not. The extent to which they are not and/or the urgency that the Olympic deadline forces on such projects *should* put them firmly into the category of Olympic expenses to be borne by the taxpaying public. Finally, security is often overlooked by organizing committees, but clearly shouldn't be since without security there could be no modern Games. Security costs are fully borne by the public. In Vancouver's case, the provincial and the federal governments are picking up the lion's share of security costs, but those that will fall solely on Vancouver taxpayers will also be considerable. Hence, Vancouverites are paying three tax bills for Olympic security.

Olympic Games profits are usually calculated as the difference between operating costs and revenues. For reasons cited above, this is a false measure of the overall "profitability" of hosting the Games. With all of these caveats in mind, we can nevertheless attempt to get the dimension of the problem using some of the numbers supplied by Preuss in context with other sources.[4] Figure 12.1 shows some comparisons to past Summer and Winter Olympic host cities in millions of dollars (all converted to $US and rounded up to the next highest million). Preuss's numbers are shown in bold.

As the numbers show, the notion that the Olympics is a money-making machine is all lovely...and almost always a myth. Based on the 13 Summer Games between 1964 in Tokyo and London in 2012, the overall costs have exceeded a billion dollars *ten times*, with a net profit only *once*. Most of the Summer Games cities claimed operating profits that, however, were much smaller than the known overall expenses.[5] The last Summer Games in Athens cost at least $14 billion; Beijing in 2008 is now predicted to top $60 billion.[6] The fiscal consequence for Greece was that it got its national credit rating lowered, not a trivial economic outcome for a country of modest means. The consequences for China are unknown, but are likely to prove significant, certainly in the long-term. The exception to this carnage was for Los Angeles that had no infrastructure costs to speak of. Munich's overall costs are unknown, but it posted a huge net deficit. The Winter Games show a similar pattern. Of the eight Games listed after 1980, four or five show costs exceeding $1 billion; for three cities, costs are not known. No Winter Games city has posted a "profit" that can't be contested based on infrastructure and security costs.

The notion that the Olympics make money can thus be shown to be a myth, but one that the business community loves. Boards of Trade always support Olympic bids because they see future goodies for themselves. More goodies give them confidence that their future (not yours) will be rosy.

Figure 12.1. Reported costs of Games, 1964 to 2006 (in millions)

City Summer Games	Overall costs (public and private): in millions	Known costs to public	Operating profits (operating revenues minus expenses)	Overall debt
Tokyo (1964)	$6,000*	Unk.	Unk.	Unk.
Mexico City (1968)	$175	Unk.	Unk.	Unk.
Munich (1972)	Unk.	Unk.	$654	-$893
Montreal (1976)	$2,729	Unk.	$641	-$2,192
Moscow (1980)	$2,000?	Unk.	Unk.	Unk.
Los Angeles (1984)	$1,276 (plus minor infrastructure)	Unk.	$745	—
Seoul (1988)	$4,000	Unk.	$1,047; claimed $193 overall	Unk.
Barcelona (1992)	$6,950	Unk.	$266; claimed $3.3	—
Atlanta (1996)	$2,220	Unk, but may be as high as $1,400	$542	—
Sydney (2000)	$4,788	$3,956	$326	-$45
Athens (2004)	$10,000 to $20,000 (best guess about $14,000)	Unk.	$57	—
Beijing 2008	$60,000 (60 billion); their Bid Book had said $1.6 billion.	Unk.	Projected: $12	?
London (2008)	Projected $10,000*	?	?	?
Winter Games				
Lake Placid (1980)	$242	Unk.	Unk.	Unk.
Sarajevo (1984)	Unk.	Unk.	Unk.	—
Calgary (1988)	$1,000	$451 infrastructure; security unk.	Unk.	
Albertville (1992)	Unk.	Unk.	Unk.	Unk.
Lillehammer (1994)	Unk.	Unk.	Unk.	Unk.
Nagano (1998)	$10,000 (some estimates go as high as $12.5 billion)	Unk.	Unk.	—
Salt Lake (2002)	Unk. (even the US GAO was stumped)	Unk.	Nil	Uncertain
Torino (2006)	$2,207	Unk.	Nil	Uncertain

*In millions: For example, $6000 million = $6 billion. See also Mathew Beard, "Cost of Olympics Rises by £900M as Jowell Is Forced to Rework Sums," *The Independent*, London, Nov. 22, 2006; also, George Monbiot noting that the original budget of £2.375 billion was up by 900 million more since the 2010 Games were awarded to London in 2005.

Next, real estate prices do go up — in fact, skyrocket — obviously fabulous if you are a realtor or developer. If you own your home, it's a happy time to be you, and you can sell it and pocket the equity. If you don't but want to, you will find that the prices have pushed you outside a city that is now beyond your means. The impact falls most heavily on middle- and lower-class workers trying to keep their heads above the waves or on young couples just starting out.

A second myth bid boosters/Boards of Trade claim is that hosting the Olympics will drive tourism up. Actually, according to mega-sports economist Professor Philip Porter, it rises during the run-up to the Games, shows a sharp spike during the Games, drops like a rock to below pre-Games levels and eventually levels out to almost exactly where it was before the Games were awarded.[7] Even Preuss is forced to admit that the outcomes of any Olympic city are variable, with any increases in tourism not necessarily associated with the Games at all.[8] The notion that tourism increases are an economic legacy of the Olympics yet again seems to be simply another Board of Trade-driven urban myth. Are there more jobs? Well, while Preuss tries hard to make it sound like there may be, his own graphs give away the fact that most Olympic jobs are transitory.[9]

The "legacy" infrastructure is usually another key Olympic selling point in most candidate cities, not least in Vancouver's case where the word "legacy" crops up in VANOC's vocabulary with offensive frequency. Vancouver's supposed legacies include the sporting venues that aren't cheap in the first place and, just as in past Olympic cities, risk turning into white elephants. Not only that, but to use them at all, the public will pay a fee. In other words, you pay for them to be built, then pay again to use something that is supposed to belong to you. Next, Vancouver's claim that a larger convention center was needed for more business was also a key facet of the bid. Alas, it wasn't true at all: Occupancy rates had been falling, not rising, even before the bid. Was a cut-and-cover semi-subway the answer to Vancouver's transportation woes? Not likely.

Finally, there was the tax angle: that all the jobs and tourists would pour money into the provincial treasury. Yes, the construction workforce in the years before the Games and the increased tourism during the Games will generate tax dollars. The only problem is that they don't generate as many dollars as those spent by government for the Games in the first place. The contributions to the massive infrastructure projects and the onerous security costs see to that. In fact, all expenses versus all returns laid out shows that the various levels of government — that is the taxpayer — take a serious hit.

This has been the trend for all of the Olympic Games back to Los Ange-les.[10] It is the Los Angeles Summer Games, however, that are used by the IOC and organizing committees as the model system, the one to be emulated. But as Figure 12.1 makes clear, LA wasn't a long-range trend, it was a fluke, one that hopeful bid cities have been trying to duplicate ever since. Even Calgary's Olympic economic "miracle" was nothing of the sort once all the costs were fac-tored in. In a 1993 Calgary audit, the 1988 Games operating profit was pegged at $38 million; then again, it might have shown a deficit of $14 million, depend-ing on what was being counted. Thomas Walkom showed that various levels of government paid $461 million for the Olympic Village and the sports venues. The province of Alberta and the federal government paid hundreds of mil-lions more for security. The final tab was nearly a billion dollars to taxpayers.[11] Sure there were some tax dollars that flowed from tourists back into govern-ment coffers, and yes, the University of Calgary did get some student hous-ing and sports facilities. Temporary jobs were created with more taxes paid on salaries, but how much of this was purely due to the Olympics remains always an open question. The costs, however, as always, exceeded the modest benefits that could just as easily have been achieved for far less money.

The outcome in other cities mirrors that of Calgary: huge capital costs borne by taxpayers; some trinkets that the Olympic organizers would contin-ually trumpet as Games "legacies" — Atlanta (university student housing and sports facilities) and Sydney (former industrial sites converted to sports ven-ues, housing and parkland).

As Vancouver approaches 2010, the costs are becoming clearer by the day and the story they are telling is the same one told by other host cities: over-runs and eventual debt. Vancouver is paying $82.5 million for its share of units in the Athletes' Village and all the additional site remediation costs (see chap-ter 8) for which it may or may not realize a final profit. A $35 million bill for Vancouver venues in 2005 had risen to $46.1 million by the fall of 2006. All of this has meant an increase in property taxes that could reach a 10% increase in 2007 alone.[12] Richmond's speed-skating oval was initially priced at $95 million but has since risen to $178 million and will likely increase further. Whistler's Athletes' Centre, originally budgeted at $16 million, approaches $41 million, requiring a bailout from VANOC of $25 million. Consequently, VANOC's contingency budget is rapidly shrinking.[13] Maureen Bader, the local director for the Canadian Taxpayers' Federation observed, "We only need to look at the cost overruns with the Vancouver convention center to see where we are go-ing with the Olympic venues. The taxpayer will be left with a legacy of debt."[14] Across the board, costs are going up, and there is no end in sight.

What about provincial costs? The initial commitment from the government was $330 million before Vancouver was awarded the Games, later topped up with $55 million when VANOC's John Furlong went back to them, cap in hand, in 2004. Considerable indirect costs include undeclared in-kind contributions from using government staff on Olympic projects, and at least half of the final security budget, whatever the latter turns out to be (see chapter 14). And, never forget that according to the Host City agreement with the IOC, the Province is on the hook for *whatever* cost overruns may occur. What about federal costs — the same $385 million as the Province, at least half the security costs (actually, likely more because of all the federal agencies involved; again see chapter 14).

Finally, none of this addresses the massive infrastructure costs associated with the major Games "legacies" claimed by VANOC: the convention center, the RAV line and the Sea to Sky Highway upgrades, all of which involve massive amounts of provincial and federal monies.

The total real cost of the Games from all levels of government is thus somewhere around $6 billion if the Games were held today. Breakdown for these costs is as follows (in millions of Canadian dollars):

Games venues and other 2010 taxpayer-funded expenses (money VANOC gets from different levels of government, not sponsors' money) (in millions)

• Provincial and federal funding	$770
• Additional federal costs (Olympic "party parks"[15])	$10
• Costs to Vancouver (includes sports venues and the "Olympic parks" as above at $5 million)	$110*
• Athletes' Village	$82.2
• Athletes' Village site remediation	$153.4
• Costs to the City of Richmond	$115.6*
• Costs to the Municipality of Whistler	$38.2*
• Costs to the University of British Columbia	$10.2*
• Infrastructure costs (less private sector contributions)	
Sea to Sky:	$775
Convention center:	$883.2
RAV line:	$1,247
• Security (federal, provincial and municipal) estimate based on Torino (see chapter 14):	$1,400

(*These costs are above the contributions of VANOC, which uses parts of its $770 million budget of provincial and federal funding to supplement venue construction in each of these locations.)

The total is about $5.604 billion, representing minimum costs at all levels. This total includes part, but not all, of the 25% of Games operating costs ($1.168 billion) funded by taxpayers. More recent federal contributions to the opening and closing ceremonies and to the Torch Relay put the magic number closer to $5.7 billion. It does not include potential interest charges on financing, which can be considerable. Nor does it count in-kind contributions, which usually remain hidden but can also be enormous. Even without these last numbers, the calculated numbers are those calculated in 2002 by *Vancouver Sun* columnist Vaughn Palmer who pegged the number at about $6 billion;[16] Daphne Bramham, another *Sun* columnist, came out with numbers in 2003 closer to $4.1 billion.[17] Not only did the newspaper columnists get it about right, but several organizations from opposite ends of the political spectrum (the left-leaning Canadian Center for Policy Alternatives, the libertarian Canadian Taxpayers' Federation and the neo-conservative Fraser Institute) were joined by the office of the Auditor General of British Columbia in predicting a 2010 financial hangover. The estimated costs varied, but there was remarkable consensus that the Games would cost taxpayers a bundle.[18] Even with all of these vast expenditures of public monies, VANOC, like past organizing committees, still needs sponsorship income just to make the operating budget work at all.

Finally, it is important to note that these are the costs as of 2008, almost two years prior to the Games. If history is our guide, just as in Sydney, Athens and Torino, costs can be expected to jump sharply higher as the Games grow closer. What the final tally for taxpayers will be in 2010 is anyone's guess.

Sorting out Direct from Indirect Costs

Bid cities like Vancouver, past ones like Sydney and future ones like London all calculate costs in a manner that would make a Mafia Don or the late Ken Lay of Enron infamy blush. They do the fiscal sleight of hand in three primary ways. The first is by low-balling all the numbers so deliberately that such manipulation can only be considered a fraud against the public who will wind up paying the bills. The second is a shell game in which Games costs are cleverly divided into manageable — and disposable — bits. The third is by concealing or downplaying indirect or in-kind contributions.

The first is easy if you are ready to lie and can hope for a public that doesn't know what previous cities have done. Basically, the method is to identify a figure for the various bid items (venues, security, etc.) that you think the public will accept, then stick with this number through thick and thin, no matter what happens, at least until your initial valuation is shown to be a sham. VANOC tried this stunt with 2010 sport venues until their massive low-balling became obvious when they went back to the provincial and federal government for more handouts as construction costs skyrocketed. John Furlong whined that neither the Bid Corp nor anyone else could have predicted construction cost increases, yet a large part of the Bid Corp's Olympic frame was precisely that winning the 2010 Games would accelerate the real estate market. The latter would certainly have predicted the former.

Deception number two is equally easy: Separate operating from infrastructure and security costs. For example, the Vancouver Bid Corp, like that of all Olympic cities, attempted to portray the Games as revenue generators by the expedient of subtracting the operating costs of the 17 days of the Olympics and 10 days of the Paralympics (public funds plus sponsorship contributions) from the revenues generated during the same periods (tickets, Olympic merchandise, television rights, etc.). If things go well, the outcome can appear to show a Games profit as they did for Los Angeles and some other Olympic cities as cited above. This is the number all bid cities trot out when trying to convince the citizenry of the financial "wisdom" of hosting the Olympics. In Canada, Calgary's 1988 Winter Games are often falsely used for this purpose. Montreal's disastrous 1976 Summer Games, in contrast, are written off as anomalous. What the bid organizers don't want is for the public or any inquisitive reporters (and there are some) to note that Olympic expenses are quite a bit more extensive and include the roads, convention centers and all other infrastructure projects that along with real estate development are the raison d'être of the Games bid in the first place. In Vancouver's case, the success of the bid was said to hinge on three main projects: the convention center to be used for the world's media, the RAV line to get the tourists from the airport to downtown hotels faster and the Sea to Sky Highway upgrade so that the Olympic Family could get from Vancouver to Whistler more quickly. At every opportunity, the IOC reinforced the message that these were absolutely crucial projects to have in the bid if Vancouver wanted to be successful. In spite of their supposed necessity, these projects kept vanishing from either the Bid Corp's or the BC government's acknowledged Olympic expenses. Both the government and the Bid Corp, and later VANOC, would claim that these were not really Olympic expenses since the various levels of government were "going to build them anyway." Maybe so, but it neatly sidestepped the reality that these projects had been driven to the top of the heap by Olympic considerations and were therefore Games-related expenses.

The third trick is to try to bury as many costs as possible in the "indirect" costs list. These tend to be the hardest to uncover since they are rarely reported and hard to track through the maze of government bureaucracy. For example, during Vancouver's bid, all levels of government contributed hundreds if not thousands of hours of staff time to promoting it. Afterwards, thousands of additional hours were put into the various preparations. Do these count as Olympic expenses? Yes, they do. To confirm this, I asked the director of my university's Financial Services department how he would view indirect costs in the following hypothetical example. What if the University lent some staff to work on a project at the associated Vancouver General Hospital? Who pays for it? His response was immediate: The University would send the hospital a bill for the hours its employees spent working there. It would therefore be an expense to the receiving organization. What about other indirect labor such as university students being asked to serve as Olympic Games volunteers? Once again, it's an expense. What about private firms contributing time and resources? To answer this, I'll go back to what a reporter told me when I was tallying up how much NO GAMES had spent on the plebiscite. One union had contributed some posters they had designed and printed. "Yep," he said, "it's an expense," and duly added it to the column of cash expenditures that NO GAMES had run up.[19] The value of student volunteers is not going to affect the public purse, but an honest accounting of the overall expenses would have to add it in.

The direct versus indirect cost issue surfaces in another form when the obvious contribution of personnel is impossible to hide. For example, the RCMP and the Canadian military will have a massive presence in 2010, but you can be sure that VANOC and the various levels of government will try to pretend that it's not part of the Olympic bill since "they get paid anyway" whether working on Olympic projects in Vancouver or anywhere else. Again, maybe so, but having them here for this particular purpose is an Olympic expense since the work they do here comes at the expense of potential work elsewhere. Work has a monetary value: If it's for the Games, it is an Olympics expense.

Olympic Priorities and Lost Opportunities

One unstated and dramatic cost of the Olympics is that of lost opportunities. That is, what might society have done instead with all the money lavished on a 17-day party? Olympic boosters dismiss this as unknowable and even naïve, as if somehow the very notion that money spent on the Games could be better employed elsewhere was an absurd utopian ideal. Intangible as it may be, the concept of lost opportunities is no more intangible than the second pillar of the Olympic frame, patriotism. In fact, the question of what things society might need more than a party is one of those "red pill"[20] questions that arose during the bid period in 2002–03 that directly linked the Olympics to the subject of social priorities and how our money gets spent and for whose benefit.

Over 20 years of government cuts to services and the under-funding of health care and education are typically blamed on debt loads that all levels of government typically carry. "What can we do? We have to live within our means" becomes the official mantra. The Olympic machine exposes this as a lie since for projects the government *wants* to fund on behalf of their friends in the private sector, even at enormous expense, it can. The glaring reality is that money exists, just not for purposes of ordinary people. An illuminating example of this — one could say an epiphany — is unfolding as these words are written: North American and other Western markets are falling into panic due to the sub-prime lending schemes of the last dozen years. Western governments and their national banks moved within days to inject almost a trillion dollars into the market to ensure "liquidity," the same governments and banks that have for years made the argument that any timely and equivalent funding to combat climate change is impossible.[21] Clearly the problem isn't money; it's priorities, with theirs completely trumping ours.

From the cost accounting cited above, I've projected a reasonably accurate cost of the Vancouver's Olympic Games, so it may be worthwhile to do a thought experiment to see just what $6 billion could provide instead. The same will apply, of course, to whatever billions have been spent on previous Olympics or the untold billions still to go for Beijing ($60 billion), London (upwards of $10 billion) or Sochi (whatever the Russian mob wants the government to spend). Could we, for example, eliminate poverty in British Columbia, if not Canada, for $6 billion dollars? No, but this amount would certainly put the problems plaguing Vancouver's Downtown Eastside into an entirely different perspective. For well under this amount, all of the 3,200 housing units needed could be provided,[22] with lots of money left over for new enterprises aimed at job creation for the local residents, drug addiction services and basic healthcare. On a larger scale, $6 billion would certainly have a profound impact on BC's healthcare provision, could be used to find solutions to the rapidly emerging pine beetle crisis, provide aid to save the wild salmon fishery, retrain workers in forestry communities now in dire straits as the lumber industry fails and encourage alternative energy ventures to combat global warming. Arts and culture? Imagine the flowering of creativity that would spring forth from even a fraction of the dollars spent on the 2010 Games. How about providing this money to universities to allow kids from aboriginal communities to attend? Might this not be one path out of dependency and despair for native youth?

In my own field of neurological disease research, $5.4 billion is the equivalent of over ten years worth of funding for the national health research establishment (Canadian Institutes for Health Research). Focused funding of this amount could supply the basic and applied research that in the same period would make most cancers, diabetes and the neurological diseases Alzheimer's, Parkinson's and Lou Gehrig's only distant memories. The overall societal cost of these neurodegenerative diseases alone is *half a trillion dollars per year* in North America. What if the money spent on the Olympics reduced these diseases by only 10 percent? We'd still save billions per year. The same is true for all the listed diseases. If the percentage of success was higher, the societal savings would increase in lockstep. Pipe dreams? Not at all. Any one of these outcomes, individually, or large parts of each in combination, are do-able with $6 billion. There are dozens more.

The money spent on the Olympic scam forces us to realize that these alternatives simply aren't priorities for our politicians. Why? The simple reason is that our politicians would prefer to put our tax dollars into the private sector as corporate welfare. Even if we were to accept the Olympic frame that hosting the Olympics brings billions of dollars in economic returns — and we've seen that it rarely does — the magnitude of the difference between imaginary Olympic outcomes and very realizable medical ones is simply staggering. The failure of our politicians to see across this gulf speaks to a truism that has become starkly obvious to millions in North America and many more around the world: The world's economy is not run for the benefit of the majority of those on the planet.

The impact of the Olympics goes beyond lost "intangible" opportunities, such as those cited above, to extremely tangible ones. Hosting the Games is promoted as a boon to businesses big and small, but this rarely materializes. Certainly some companies get lucrative contracts, and just as surely, parts of the tourism sector and businesses close to Olympic venues can do very well during the actual Games period. However, transportation headaches created by construction during the pre-Games period, or traffic jams or security perimeters during the Games often make the access of tourists and locals alike to parts of the city nearly impossible. Chapter 9 described how construction of the RAV line has negatively impacted local businesses along Cambie Street. This disruption even led BC's Finance Minister Carole Taylor to admit the obvious, without, however, offering anything in the way of compensation to those going under.

Even the very pace of construction in Vancouver for Olympic and non-Olympic projects alike is likely to have long-term negative consequences. Construction of the RAV line in 2007 slipped behind schedule, and to pick up the pace, workers began pouring poorly mixed concrete. The result was concrete full of air bubbles — the "honeycomb" effect — structurally much weaker than properly prepared concrete. A long-time friend of mine who works as a safety inspector in Vancouver not only accepted that this was likely at the RAV line construction, but mentioned that it was happening all over the city's numerous building sites due to time pressures and the lack of experienced site managers.

Corporatization of Universities under the Olympic Rings

Helen Lenskyj's incisive book, *The Best Olympics Ever: Social Impacts of Sydney 2000*, addresses the impact that the Sydney Games had on universities in that city.[23] One major aspect of the 2000 Games was that it helped speed up the "corporatization" of the universities, a process that had been unfolding for years. Much the same happened at the University of British Columbia where links between members of the Board of Governors and the Bid Corp and later to VANOC put the University's administration completely under the spell of the Games. Former Board of Governors member Robert Lee was an early bid booster and, as noted earlier, is a likely future beneficiary of the real estate explosion that would soon sweep up the Sea to Sky corridor. The late Chancellor Allen McEachern was appointed to the Bid Corp and served as "Ethics Commissioner" for VANOC. The University was part of early discussions with the Bid Corp about the ice rinks for the 2010 hockey events, seeing in this relationship the potential for new sports facilities. Consultations about the wisdom of joining the bid process never went outside the Board of Governors, and their meetings were held *in camera*. NO GAMES Freedom of Information requests for records of these meetings with Bid Corp members were unsuccessful: Some records UBC flatly refused to disclose; others came with a price tag too costly for us to afford. What the University had understood were going to be free goodies for them, in the end cost them over $10 million as construction costs escalated after 2003. This was, incidentally, during a time when infrastructure on the main campus was literally crumbling. The building where my laboratory used to be was housed in the former Department of Anatomy of the Medical School. The front steps had literally fallen off, forcing the future physicians of the province to enter the building by the loading dock.

As 2010 approaches, UBC is contemplating how they will make student schedules compliant with VANOC and the IOC's needs rather than the other way around. Current plans call for the rescheduling of much of the winter term and if this is hard for the students, tough. As in Calgary and Sydney, students will likely have their accommodations subjugated to the needs of Olympic tourists, and students and staff will be encouraged to use the time off to work as unpaid Olympic volunteers. The needs of the Olympics clearly come first, those of the students, second, if at all.

Societal Impacts
of Hosting the Olympic Games

The next chapter will deal at length with the impact of the Olympic Games on housing, both in regard to overall costs as well as the result of the usually dramatic outcomes for homebuyers, renters and the poor, outcomes that can be summarized by two words: displacement and homelessness. The remainder of this chapter will look at the "other" multiple and usually damaging impacts on society, impacts that in Vancouver, as elsewhere, begin with real estate.

The Real Estate Deals
Behind Every Olympic Bid

The real estate basis for Vancouver's bid was presented in the first part of this book. Before discussing those of other bid and host cities, it's worthwhile putting the entire real estate craze in North American into its correct context as a social and economic pathology. To introduce this, the following example, which ran as a full page ad in the *Los Angeles Times*, will suffice:

> Everyone wants a nice home. And with the many interest-only and adjustable loans available today, it's possible for people to afford that nice home for a little while.... But sooner or later a day will come when they can't make that payment...they've put themselves and their families in a horrible situation, and they need help. That's where you come in. As a Foreclosure Specialist, you can step in BEFORE the homeowner ruins their credit and score on a great deal. It's the ideal win-win situation! Hundreds of foreclosures happen every month in your town... find out how you can help your neighbors and find great deals at the same time.[24]

As someone who has followed with some interest the often bizarre and self-destructive nature of what passes for free enterprise in 21st century North America, I confess to actually being amazed by the above ad. Actually, the amazement came in waves between bursts of laughter: After nearly a decade of insane real estate speculation in which the banks dropped down-payment requirements for homebuyers to near zero and allowed people with horrible credit ratings to mortgage and remortgage endlessly to buy more property, it was only a matter of time before the bubble burst. Anyone who has followed the market could have predicted this outcome. Now with the market dipping across North America, some of those who bought houses at the high end of the boom found that they were in way over their heads. With interest rates rising, many began going under; the lenders who had purchased all the sub-prime loans were in very big trouble too. The "genius" of such an ad and the mentality it reveals reflects on an economy of disaster.[25]

This ad — and believe me, I could not have made it up — is about encouraging people to become foreclosure experts. The idea is that, as their neighbors thunder in financially and begin to default on their mortgages, those in the know can step in and buy the properties for under market prices, then flip them for a profit. Win-win for everyone, the suckers as well as those savvy enough to see the opportunities...or so the ad would have us believe.

Vancouver's real estate market rose with the general boom in North America, but really took off in 2002, and the speculation that it was at least partially fueled by the 2010 Games is likely justified. Although the market has since slowed, the prospects still seem bright for Vancouver real estate in the near term, but this notion sort of presupposes that we are somehow uniquely different from everyone else in the North American economy and that our interest rates won't eventually rise again or the market go soft.[26] The question no one here seems to ask is this: Can we avoid the downturn as the North American market bubble collapses, a collapse that may occur regardless of tinkering with interest rates by the US Federal Reserve or Bank of Canada? In particular, what becomes of all the over-priced real estate and all the boom-time construction jobs once the Olympic party is over? To this the financial gurus of the business sections of the mainstream newspapers have no clear answers, apart from the usual generic nostrum that "over the long term, stock and real estate prices always go up." In general, they do not seem to have considered the question as if, somehow, to challenge the fundamental assumptions of a market economy, even an obviously terminal one, would be somehow unpatriotic... as unpatriotic as, say, criticizing the Games themselves. At least in the above ad, eager "foreclosure experts" can step in to bail out those foolish enough to have tasted the poisoned real estate fruit. What happens, however, to the taxpayers who find themselves holding gargantuan Olympic debts? The answer is that they pay it off themselves, or far more likely, their children or grandchildren do.

With this context in mind, we can examine the real estate realities of other host and bid cities. The reason for including bid cities is that, while their bids and hence overall outcomes may not be the same as the successful host cities, their initiating impulse is identical. Additionally, the real estate prizes that they sought to obtain often remain on the table until another opportunity, another bid for example, comes along.

The Sydney bid and run-up to the Olympics in 2000 show remarkable similarities to Vancouver's and the progression of real estate developments in Vancouver after 2003. First, Sydney had its own "Olympic corridor," remarkably like that of Vancouver. Vancouver's Olympic corridor starts in the Downtown Eastside, crosses several bridges, then runs along the 120 kilometers Sea to Sky Highway to Whistler and the Callaghan. Sydney's corridor was initially smaller, just a 12-kilometer strip running westwards from the city's central business district to the main Olympic Village site. Overall, there were 31 sites for potential development, 13 in planning or actual construction stages.[27] In Sydney, the term "Olympic corridor" was coined by real estate developer L. J. Hooker, apparently Australia's Jack Poole clone. Before the Games came in 2000, the corridor had expanded from the suburb of Bondi all the way to the town of Penrith, 55 kilometers away. Many of the suburbs in the corridor were formerly occupied by low-income tenants. Of these, many were aboriginal, much the same way that Vancouver's Downtown Eastside population contains many Native inhabitants. Sydney, it seemed, also absolutely needed a new harbor tunnel, a ferry service up the Parramatta River and a third runway for their international airport. Vancouver's bid needed a convention center, a RAV line and a wider, faster Sea to Sky Highway.

Just as in downtown Vancouver, landlords in Sydney's Olympic corridor failed to do necessary repairs in order to get tenants out, raised rents and generally adopted tactics that Lenskyj characterizes as "evict and renovate, or evict, demolish and redevelop."[28] One consequence of Sydney's Olympic preparations was a dramatic increase in homelessness, tripling from 1992 during the bid to 1999, the year before the Games. Vancouver's homeless population has also increased to about 2,500 in 2007, over two times higher since Vancouver won the Games and double again the number during the bid period in 2002.

Sydney had promised housing legacies during the bid period. Eventually, however, all the permanent housing at Homebush Bay was sold or rented at market prices. Vancouver's Athlete's Village was initially to have held a solid core of "non-market"/social housing, but the promised 30% has been falling steadily ever since 2002 and may well hit zero by 2010. Sydney faced a student housing crisis as housing rentals fled to the Olympic tourist market. A betting person would wager on the same occurring in Vancouver. In Sydney, as in Vancouver recently, protesters were forced out of squats by police riot squads.

Just as in Vancouver's bid, all of the major Sydney Olympic infrastructure was to be a "legacy" gift of the Games, but miraculously didn't show up as an Olympic expense to taxpayers. Once again, the government was "going to do it anyway." As Helen Lenskyj writes:

Of course, politicians and Olympic boosters could well claim that such mega-projects were in the planning stages long before work began on an Olympic bid, and/or that it was advantageous for the city if the Olympic bid served to accelerate projects that might otherwise take years to complete. However, what is sinister about all of these scenarios is that when such infrastructure items are excluded from Olympic budgets, citizens do not have complete and accurate information on the real costs of mounting an Olympic Games.[29]

In Sydney, as in Vancouver, "legacy sports facilities" cost projections failed to include indirect or capital costs. When, predictably, budgets were found to be inadequate, additional funds had to be provided by government. In Sydney's case, one consequence was that core spending in health, education, welfare and transportation went down; the same outcome is another sure bet for Vancouver 2010.

Finally, what happens to the legacy infrastructure projects once the Olympics have gone? Can the taxpayers who built them use them for free? The answer is no. In most cases, some level of privatization occurs, with costs, often significant, for the public to access their own "legacies."

Toronto failed to win either the 1996 or 2008 Summer Games, but the proposal of the organizing committee, TOBid, contained familiar infrastructure ingredients. These included a train to Toronto's Pearson International Airport, a bridge to the regional airport, expansion of both airports, sewage treatment plant and a new route for the Gardiner Expressway, one of the city's main freeways. Toronto's bid, by the way, was headed by yet another Jack Poole clone, David Crombie, who also happened to be Chairman of the Waterfront Regeneration Trust, an organization that played a leading role in developing waterfront property on Lake Ontario.

Promises, Legacies and Other Goodies

A prime characteristic of all bids, successful or not, is an absolute Christmas stocking of promises. These promises serve various purposes. Those already locked into "the Olympics are going to bring wealth to us all" frame are already onside and don't need a sweetener, but those still on the fence might. For this reason, "social inclusivity" (that is, "the poor get something too") and "environmental sustainability" (these will be the "greenest Games ever") promises make the Olympic venture seem to be socially and environmentally responsible. If these promises are also mouthed by local politicians who have reputations for being progressive so much the better. Such political support tends to dampen rational skepticism, and many people who should smell a rat never do. For other folks, the promises are simply bribes by any other name: jobs for unionized workers on Olympic venues, land and cash for First Nations and "Cultural Olympics" and arts legacies for the arts community.

The most common use by organizing committees of the term legacy refers to infrastructure, but, as Lenskyj notes,

> A legacy, according to dictionary definitions, is something "material or immaterial": that is "bequeathed or handed down by predecessors." In Olympic industry rhetoric, *legacy* refers to infrastructure, housing and sporting facilities that are represented as some kind of windfall profit for the host city, with the significant contribution of public money to Olympic projects — usually totaling at least 50% of the budget — often overlooked in this kind of calculation.[30]

Such legacies are not really intended for the average person either in the specific case of the Olympics or in other mega-projects. Again, from Lenskyj:

> As was the case pattern with other hallmark events and other subsidized public sport arenas, the Olympics left behind limited benefits — "the bourgeois playground" legacy — to be enjoyed, for the most part, by the more privileged sectors of society, while the powerless disproportionately bore the burden.[31]

Aboriginals and Other "Cute Critters"

Having an aboriginal or First Nations community handy works well in selling a city's bid to the IOC. Not all bid cities are so blessed of course, but Sydney's bid once again bore remarkable resemblances to Vancouver's. Not only did both possess native people "discovered" by the same Englishman, Captain James Cook, but both populations had also suffered years of outright oppression that was nothing less than cultural genocide. British Columbian First Nations (and those across Canada as well) and the aboriginal population of Australia had seen white governments sequester native children in residential schools in order to extinguish what was considered to be an inferior culture. Both groups lived in general poverty and substance abuse on and off reservations; both had waited generations for full rights and for the just settlement of long-overdue treaties. All of the above might have been considered a serious liability to an Olympic Bid, but actually, for the organizing committees of both cities and the IOC, this was actually a decided plus: The IOC considered both groups of aboriginal people to be cute...and marketable. In VANOC's case, it actively promoted aboriginal themes, including the ill-chosen "Inuk-shuk" (sic) as its symbol for the 2010 Games. If only they could use aboriginals as their mascot too....[32] In the end, VANOC came up with no less than three mascots, all imaginary creatures. One was a combination of killer whale and bear, another the sasquatch, the third a thunderbird/eagle-like beast. To ensure maximum market coverage, they added an additional "companion," a Vancouver Island marmot.

For Sydney, as later for Vancouver, the glass was half full and there was indeed a use for natives after all. First, some of their leaders could be co-opted into going along with the bids, serving as "representatives" of their communities and sometimes even persuaded to give up land for Olympic venues and future development projects. Next, their children could be used at Olympic opening ceremonies to add local color with native music and dancing for the international television audience. None of this, however, was meant to address the glaring disparity in wealth between aboriginal and non-aboriginal communities. Nor was it designed to remedy the appalling levels of poverty, the lack of basic health care, educational opportunities or future prospects of native people. Nor was any amount of dancing for foreign tourists going to get long-stalled treaties signed. But none of this was the real point: Once again, native people were being exploited for the commodity that they've been forced to relinquish since Captain Cook came ashore: real estate.

So Much Hot Air:
The Promises of "Green Games"

All Olympic bids and host cities claim to be green. They sort of have to: The IOC has made "environmental sustainability" (whatever that is supposed to mean) a pillar of Olympism. And, with the emerging global concerns about climate change, most citizens of Western nations want the Olympics to be green, or at least, greenish. The latter better describes a form of what Lenskyj terms "corporate environmentalism."

The greenness of Vancouver's Games will be the subject of a later chapter. For now, it will serve to see just how green the Sydney Games were. Sydney claimed the title of "the Green Games" thanks to the Australian wing of Greenpeace that allowed itself, at least initially, to be thoroughly hoodwinked by the organizing committee. One environmental group, Green Games Watch 2000, had funding from both the government of New South Wales and the federal government. Independent watchdogs? Hardly. We'll look at some other Olympic city histories in chapter 13, but before finishing this part, let's consider the most glaring environmental event of the Sydney Games because, once again, the similarity to Vancouver is remarkable.

Bondi Beach in the Sydney municipality of Waverley is one of the most famous beaches in the world. Certainly when most people think of Australian beaches, Bondi comes to mind. Bondi was to be the site of Olympic beach volleyball according to the Sydney organizing committee. The only problem was a bit of a sticky wicket: It turned out the locals didn't want it, certainly didn't want the stadium that they thought (correctly) would spoil the beach. Olympic organizers were quick to slap a NIMBY label on opponents, and the press took up the charge, much as they were later to do at Eagleridge in West Vancouver. But there was more than a stadium at stake: The Bondi Beach opponents, organized as Bondi Olympic Watch, feared that the stadium would shut off nearly half the beach's 5.9 hectares and further wanted no part of the proposed tunnel or heavy rail line and station slated to be built on parkland. There were also lurking fears that developers had secret plans for the area. To solve the problem of the opposition, the Sydney organizing committee chose the simple expedient of pretending that it didn't exist…then it sent in the tractors. At Eagleridge, the local community was consulted for its opinion. When this didn't match what the Minister of Transportation wanted to hear, the tractors rolled there too. As with West Vancouver, Bondi's mayor flip-flopped, and political deals were suspected. At Bondi 21 protestors of the project were arrested. The toll at Eagleridge was 23, one ultimately a fatality.

Promises of Accountability: More Hot Air

VANOC, like the Bid Corp before them, seems almost pathologically adverse to public accountability, notwithstanding numerous promises at various stages of the bid and a constant stream of platitudes since it was won. None of this is remarkable in the slightest: All bid organizations and organizing committees share the same culture of secrecy, the same tendency to be close-lipped and circle the wagons against potential raids on their inner workings. Toronto's bid was shrouded in secrecy and, like VANOC and the Vancouver Bid Corp, was exempt from Freedom of Information/Access to Information Legislation as a private company. In precisely the same spirit, Sydney's organizers hid infrastructure costs and failed to file independent annual audited reports from 1993 to 1999 in spite of being advised to do so by the Auditor General of New South Wales. In the end, the Auditor General did it himself, but was unable to figure out where all the money went.[33]

Security and the Games:
Canada's Past and Future and the Legacy of Sydney

The true costs of security in treasure and civil rights will be addressed in chapter 14. Here I will merely note some of the more obvious aspects from other Games. Canadian Olympic Games have, in general, been extremely security conscious and expensive. Montreal's Summer Games in 1976 put approximately 16,000 soldiers, police and other security personnel on the streets at a cost of over $200 million (VANOC 34 years later thinks it will only cost $175 million). Calgary's security costs remain unknown but surely exceeded $175 million.

Again, a comparison with Sydney is relevant to plausible future security crackdowns for the Vancouver Games in 2010. As summarized by Lenskyj, the total cost was enormous (see chapter 14), of which $34.7 million went for new equipment for the New South Wales police forces. Thousands of security personnel were deployed including 4,000 from the military. Some of these were "special operations" troops, that is, commandos. Legislation was passed enabling the Australian military to deal with any potential protests. Military personnel were also present from other countries, notably from the United States and Israel. Security cameras were everywhere, watching everyone and everything. In advance of the 2000 Games, various levels of government passed special laws that in effect criminalized dissent and poverty. The Olympic Arrangements Act (2000), for example, prohibited "banners, flags of non-participating countries, signs, and items with corporate branding," basically anything that the authorities, or the IOC, might not like for any reason. The IOC's Charter, Bylaw 61, requires that each host city guarantee that "no political meetings or demonstration will take place in the stadium or on any other sports ground or in or near Olympic village(s) during the Games." Sydney complied, duly suspending freedom of assembly as a civil right during the Games.[34]

Watchdogging the Games
with "Watch Poodles"

As noted in chapter 2, Vancouver's bid initially spawned a "watchdog" group called the Impact of Olympics on Community (IOCC), founded by Vancouver city councilor Jim Green, one of the bid's most ardent supporters. The IOCC would never say it was against the Games, even when it later realized that it had been lied to by the Bid Corp from the start. The IOCC would later grow some courage and use its baby teeth, but the eventual response was reactive rather than proactive and hence went largely unnoticed, especially by VANOC. But in the beginning, it had neither courage nor teeth, and despite some truly sincere members, was not, in truth, watching anything. Its real purpose was to depoliticize the Olympics, to obscure the IOC's true agenda and that of the developers behind the bid and to give a false sense of security to those who might harbor reservations. Mainly it was there to prevent any real opposition from forming and, failing that, to dilute any message that such an opposition might send. In the end, it failed in this last task as surely as it failed to be an Olympic watchdog.

Sydney, too, had a pseudo watchdog group called the Social Impact Advisory Committee. The Committee's chairman would comment that, "members of the committee are *not opponents of the Olympics. They have never argued that the money spent on the Olympics would be better spent on other things*" [italics, mine]. Their goal was, instead, to "maximize the good and minimize the bad."[35] All of this has to lead to speculation that the IOC and hence bid cities clearly recognize the need to create or support false opposition groups who will in turn serve as social safety valves, bleeding off any potential serious opposition to any city's bid.

The costs of the Olympic Games to society and the social and environmental outcomes in various cities show remarkable similarities, so much so that it is difficult to not believe that some master plan, some giant cookie cutter, is at work designed to produce identical outcomes. The following chapters will explore some of these outcomes in more detail.

Olympic "Economic Cleansing" and Gentrification

The law in its majesty prohibits rich and poor alike from sleeping under bridges.

ANATOLE FRANCE

I'm watching things speed up in my own city, Vancouver, as legislators tighten the noose around society's most defenceless members. In the lead-up to 2010's Olympic orgasm for developers, the city council has passed laws to keep street people from sitting on park benches or reclining in parks. Behind this crazy-making effort to create a "civil city" is a conception of humans as rubbish.

GEOFF OLSON,
"THE FUTURE ISN'T WHAT IT USED TO BE,"
COMMON GROUND, JULY 2007

Citizen Sam

IN THE RUN UP to the municipal election of 2005, COPE was in big trouble and knew it. Larry Campbell had seen greener pastures, bugged out of Vancouver and was now a Liberal Senator in Ottawa. COPE itself, a patchwork quilt of a party of the supposed left at the best of times, was now coming apart at the seams, divided into fractions jocularly known as COPE "Classic" and COPE "Lite." The latter, more developer friendly and pro-Olympics from the beginning, bolted the party and formed a new entity called Vision Vancouver. After some feverish negotiations, COPE and Vision decided to share a mayoral candidate, Jim Green, one of those who had gone over to Vision, but to run separate council slates. In the ensuing debacle, COPE was knocked back to one seat. Vision landed four seats, and a triumphant NPA with five councilors swept back into power with a vengeance. The NPA had chosen long-time NPA councilor Sam Sullivan as their mayoral candidate, an odd choice as it would turn out. At the time, however, he seemed a rising star and a politically correct choice, a plucky paraplegic who had overcome some long odds and made good. Sullivan's somewhat less illustrious attributes would later enter the public domain when a documentary about him, *Citizen Sam*, was released a year or so later. In the film, Sullivan was to boast that he enjoyed it when people underestimated him because of his disability as it gave him the opportunity "rip their throats out."[1] Sullivan would also later reveal that he'd engaged in the rather quirky pastime of buying crystal methamphetamine for drug users, after which he'd take them to his apartment and watch while they'd shoot up. What else might have transpired was not revealed…as if supplying illegal drugs to desperate addicts alone wasn't enough. South of the border, such admissions would have brought swift closure to his political career, but in Vancouver a largely unruffled citizenry exhibited a general tolerance for Citizen Sam's eccentric ways. The absence of rancor toward the errant mayor by Vancouverites, in many ways resembled the charitable response of British Columbians to their Premier, Gordon Campbell, when some years earlier he had been arrested driving drunk while on vacation on Maui. Campbell's police mug shot had made the front page of every paper in the country. What made it particularly amusing was that Campbell, soused to the gills, still remained above all else a politician: A cop aimed a camera in his face and he instinctively smiled, or tried to, the resulting photo showing an obviously inebriated, disheveled, middle-aged white guy with a loopy grin plastered on his face. On his return to British Columbia, his fellow citizens largely accepted his groveling apology, and both he and they moved on.

The level of charity Campbell, and later Sullivan, received was by no means indicative of their own for others, especially for the less fortunate. Sullivan would in fact show none at all for Vancouver's street people, many of whom found themselves in their predicament as a direct consequence of the social policies of both the NPA and provincial Liberals. As the Olympic machine marched on, Sullivan demonstrated time and again that the plight of the poor and homeless was pretty much their own problem. Sullivan eventually translated this egregious disregard into Project Civil City, an aggressive piece of legislation designed in no small measure to sweep away the unsightly poor and unhygienic homeless in advance of all the hoped-for Olympic tourists of 2010.

Canada's Poorest Urban Postal Code

The Downtown Eastside is home to legions of the homeless, drug dealers and users, sex trade workers and thousands of those who are simply the working poor. Overall, it comprises an area of some 15 blocks long, 8 blocks wide, with boundaries loosely defined by Clark Drive on the east, Cambie to the west, Venables/Prior Streets on the south, the waterfront and port to the north. Hastings Street runs right down the middle. The Downtown Eastside may well be the poorest postal code in Canada outside of aboriginal reserves; in fact, a huge number of its residents are native. It combines levels of disease that are comparable to the worst found in the Third World and crime rates on persons and property that exceed all of the rest of Vancouver. A sense of defeat hovers over much of Hastings Street like a fog. But in defiance to circumstance, there is pride here, too, and community. It's more than possible to imagine that the Downtown Eastside with its vibrant history would blossom in thousands of ways if only the various levels of government cared enough to help. That government doesn't care speaks volumes to social priorities in Vancouver's headlong rush to be a "world-class" city.

Those who only drive through the Downtown Eastside en route to somewhere else see only the long lines at the soup kitchens, the addicts congregating in alley ways, the hookers on their stroll and the homeless sleeping on benches and in doorways. Ground zero is Pigeon Park at the corner of Carrall and Hastings. I've been driving past this intersection for most of the 20 years I've lived in Vancouver, and at least once a week, usually more often, I have to slam on my brakes to avoid hitting someone who has wandered into traffic. Most don't even look up as my car stops only feet from them; those who do, stare at me from eyes without hope, eyes that seem to say, "Run me over, I don't care."

Others drive through the Downtown Eastside but don't see Third World misery, rather opportunity and a brighter future — for themselves, the developers. What others view as a vast urban wasteland filled with the homeless lining up for food, they see as a different kind of lineup — yuppies ready to live on the edge, as they move into upscale $500,000 one-bedroom condos overlooking the squalor in the streets below. If only they could "invent something," to use Jack Poole's apt phrase. In 2003 the miracle happened, and dreams became reality. The Olympic machine was coming to town, and with it, the power to transform the Downtown Eastside looked like an unstoppable tsunami of gentrification.

Before the 2010 Games were Vancouver's, the fleabag hotels in the Downtown Eastside were fairly strictly regulated; City inspectors routinely cited the owners for safety and hygiene violations. To avoid fines, the owners had to comply with what were really the most minimal of regulations. After the 2005 civic election, with the NPA triumphant, the City's attitude abruptly seemed to change. Now rather than fine the owners, the City began closing the offending hotels. Often, with only hours' notice, residents were dumped onto the streets to join the thousands of others who wander the alleys by day and sleep on the sidewalk by night. Anti-poverty groups such as the Pivot Legal Society, the Anti-Poverty Committee (APC) and the Downtown Eastside Residents Association (DERA) estimate that a number of hotels have closed in this manner, adding many more people to the legions of the homeless.[2] The time frame of the increase alone tells the tale. In 2002 the City itself put the number at 628. When Vancouver won the 2010 Games in 2003, homelessness in the city stood at around 1,300. By 2005 the numbers had risen to over 2,000. It's now (2008) estimated at 2,500 to 2,800…and still rising.[3] Many more are homeless throughout the suburbs that make up the so-called Lower Mainland.

The City claims that the hotel closures are the simple result of enforcing bylaws for the safety of the residents of the closed hotels, but Pivot, the APC and the DERA see a more likely explanation: The City is helping landlords close the hotels deliberately because they want to flip the property so that it can be sold to developers. The developers, in turn, plan to tear the old buildings down and put up hotels to fill with Olympic tourists in 2010. After the Games have gone, the new condos will be for the urban upwardly mobile. Urban gentrification accompanied Vancouver's fabled Expo 86, so the basic idea has been in circulation for a long time just waiting for the right stimulus. The Olympics was that stimulus.

"Economic cleansing" is the ticket, and Mayor Sam Sullivan has the plan. If the Downtown Eastside is ugly and drug infested, he can sweep it all away courtesy of Project Civil City, Sullivan's less than subtle manoeuvre to rid Vancouver of the relics of years of institutional neglect. Or, maybe the City could ship the homeless out to other parts of the province "for treatment," as the Province's Liberal Forests Minister recently suggested,[4] the idea eerily reminiscent of the wholesale urban clearances of the poor in the run-up to Atlanta's Olympics in 1996. The statement seemed likely to be a trial balloon, sent up to gauge public reaction.

Mayor Sullivan, the NPA, the provincial government and their real estate developer backers can see a new Kitsilano[5] arising out of the drug dens of the Eastside. Did the Olympics and VANOC do this? Not directly, but those involved knew it would come to pass. Indeed the Bid Corp knew, too, even as it and the City made their now useless promises that no one would get left out of the Olympic legacies.[6] The promise of "inclusivity" was not really meant for the city's poorest and most vulnerable.

"Red-zoning" and Other Economic Cleansing Practices

Cameron Bishop lives on the street near the center of the Broadway corridor, a corridor that runs east to west across the city. Bishop is in his early forties, slim, bearded, with a ball cap covering longish receding hair.[7] He's been on Vancouver's harsh downtown streets for over a decade, pretty much from the time he came out of the Canadian Army where he served in the infantry. Bishop knows guns; he's certainly seen his share of them in his life, many recently. Vancouver police officers have taken to placing their revolvers up against his head at night while he lies sleeping on the ground. During one such incident, the officer told him: "It's the Olympics or you, and it ain't you, so you'd better move on." Bishop has been threatened with beatings and worse if he stays in the area, threats that suddenly became reality when he was set upon by unknown assailants and severely mauled. He's also been handed court summonses for loitering, for begging, for whatever the police want to charge him with. One officer told him that he was banned from the entire Broadway corridor, "red zoned," from the boundary with the neighboring city of Burnaby in the east, nearly all the way to the University of British Columbia in the west. He faces fines that he cannot possibly pay, or jail time, if he doesn't move on. But move to where? Like the homeless across the city, Bishop has his own local community of fellow homeless. He is also afraid of the far more hostile streets of the Downtown Eastside.

The area where Bishop "lives" didn't have a homelessness "problem" before the 1990s. The Fairview district of the city has historically been an upscale district with high-end condos and restaurants, all within a long stone's throw of Vancouver's City Hall and General Hospital. The urban poor and the homeless then were across False Creek, pretty much segregated in the Downtown Eastside. This all changed in the 1990s as government cutbacks spilled hundreds then thousands more onto the streets across the city. No one knows how many of the homeless live in and around Fairview, but the scale of the problem can well be estimated from the dozen or more who congregate in the few short blocks between City Hall and the hospital. And it's not just in Fairview, but in districts across Vancouver, even in the surrounding municipalities. Poverty in the Lower Mainland didn't originate with the Olympics, but there was a remarkable coincidence in the extent of it. As cited above, the rate of change makes it difficult not to conclude that there was some sort of cause and effect relationship.

Red-zoning, itself, was definitely a by-product of the Olympics coming to Vancouver, as were the various punitive pieces of provincial and municipal legislation. Such legislation serves to highlight the utter failure of the different levels of government to actually address the gnawing poverty that affects so many, in the process demonstrating to anyone with an ounce of social conscience the chasm between a world in which the Olympics are the party of a lifetime and another where the Games are yet another kick in the teeth to those already battered to their knees.

The implications of red-zoning for civil liberties are not trivial either, not for the homeless, not for Olympic opponents, ultimately not for anyone.

Criminalizing Poverty

Sam Sullivan came back from his great big Torino flag-waving adventure, determined to "clean up" the city before 2010. He could have, for example, actually chosen to keep promises to the poor and provide the 3,200 housing units that would end the current wave of homelessness in the city. Instead, he and the NPA decided to legislate the problem away. Thus was born Project Civil City, Sullivan's path to ending the poverty problem by making its victims criminals...and treating them as such.

The City's Project Civil City, as launched in 2006, set four main targets by 2010.[8] First, it aimed to eliminate homelessness, with at least a 50 percent reduction, the "how" not specified, and at absolute variance with the lack of funding for the housing that would be required to meet this goal. Second, the plan called for eliminating the open drug market with at least a 50 percent reduction. How to do so? More cops, obviously. Third, Civil City planned to eliminate the incidence of "aggressive panhandling" by 50 percent. Reducing panhandling so as not to inconvenience rich Olympic tourists was nothing new; in fact, it followed by several years some earlier provincial legislation, notably the "Safe Streets" Act, that saved the good citizens of the province from "aggressive squeegie kids." Finally, Civil City called for a 50 percent increase in "the level of public satisfaction" with the City's handling of public nuisance and annoyance complaints. What this might mean seemed very open to interpretation, but at the least, it suggested that the "public" in question was more the Vancouver Board of Trade type than average citizens, the latter including many who wanted real solutions that actually helped rather than punished the poor.

Overall, there were some 54 sub-recommendations, 10 of which Sullivan wanted undertaken immediately by city council, while a more comprehensive implementation plan was being activated. Key amongst these recommendations was to let Sullivan raid the City's Olympic "Legacy" Fund of at least $1 million. The fund had been part of the 2007 City budget. A lot of the million was to go to hire more police and to increase the street presence of those already on the payroll. More than $300,000 more was to come from the 2006 municipal contingency reserve fund in order to hire a Project Civil City commissioner; this would turn out to be BC's former Attorney General, Geoff Plant. One controversial item that had emerged from public "stakeholder" meetings was the "eyes on the street" recommendation. In brief, it proposed using "City employees such as parking enforcement and sanitation engineers to become new eyes and ears on the street [and] have these employees become part of a new public order enforcement continuum." In other words, use City employees as spies, mirroring a practice that had already been used by Sydney in the run-up to their 2000 Olympics. Asked about this recommendation by the press, Helen Lenskyj noted, "These [the city staff members] are thinly disguised, un-credentialled, untrained security guards." As she also observed, "That's exactly what Sydney did. They gave thousands of people 12 hours of training and empowered them to enforce all kinds of bylaws that were put in place before the Olympics to criminalize homelessness. Calling them ambassadors or sanitation engineers with special training, or parking enforcement guys with special training, is offensive, to say the least."[9]

Some other notable recommendations included: "Re-institutionalize the severely mentally ill. Use existing facilities such as Riverview [a mental health facility located outside of Vancouver] to provide treatment and housing for some of the most severely mentally ill people living on Vancouver's streets." Aha, moving the pesky homeless away from Olympic tourists. Also, the City was suggesting to "introduce dumpster-free alleys," or, in other words, take away one of the few sources of income for homeless people by removing their access to dumpsters, again a proposal that had previously surfaced in other Olympic host cities. The City also proposed to "conduct a public awareness campaign on the negative impacts of providing money to panhandlers," just to ensure that they really had no possible source of income short of crime. There were multiple recommendations about more police, police auxiliaries, bylaw enforcement officers, prosecutors and the presence of security cameras everywhere, the latter earning a pointed comment from civil liberties groups that called that recommendation "a serious erosion of a citizen's right to appear in public spaces without being monitored."[10] There was also a raft of proposals for a Community Court, ticketing and fines, etc. And, amongst all the punitive measures, the City proposed to "conduct a study of our homeless population." Hence, first penalize those you've put on the streets, then figure out why they are there, as if you don't already know. And all under the banner of the five colored rings, supposedly the symbol of peace and brotherhood.

Olympic Promises: Just More Carbon Emissions

The promises as touted by the Bid Corp and the City of Vancouver seemed, for many, to guarantee that the Olympic Games would be for everyone. Although the environment didn't really score a promise as such, Vancouver's poor and homeless sure did. But, just as surely as Vancouver's temperamental weather can shift from brilliant sunshine in an azure sky to torrential downpours 15 minutes later, so too, the promise to the poor began to degrade. What had been an officially unbreakable "promise" in the bid period became a "commitment" post-bid, drifting to a "goal," then a "hope," before being finally abandoned altogether. Even late in the process, VANOC's sub-boss John Furlong had said:

> Our housing commitments are quite specific. They fall into three categories. We have committed $30 million to the direction of the village in Vancouver, with that commitment we will of course be assured of 250 units of housing that fall into the category of non-market social housing.[11]

Alas, the City of Vancouver was soon to bail on the 250 units, the number dropping by 90 percent not long after Furlong's quote. According to a report prepared by City staff for Vancouver's City Council, "It's not clear whether any more than 10 percent of the 250 units of social housing at the site can be reserved for the poor." Then the number fell to a guarantee of...zero. The same report noted that of the 3,200 units promised overall, it was "questionable" if the units could be built by 2010. In fact, it was clear that if construction of the units didn't start by a drop-dead date of October 2007, it simply couldn't happen by 2010 at all. As this book goes to press, the drop-dead date has come and gone, and *no* construction has started. All in all, the report suggested that a total of 25 recommendations made by various stakeholders in what was termed the Inner City Inclusiveness (ICI) Tables, were not going to be met.[12] There had never been any real plan to do so. The exercise from the onset had not really been to "include" the poor, it had been to hoodwink the public with the idea that they would. All that anti-poverty advocates could do was complain and try to raise the issue to the international level. While such publicity might have been embarrassing for Vancouver, nothing changed in the realities on the streets.[13]

Furlong went on to say:

> In Whistler we have committed approximately the same amount of money, the legacy after the Games will be housing that will be used to take care of a particular challenge that they have in Whistler which is that people who work in Whistler can't afford to live there. That housing has been committed, it is non-market.

Um, actually not: The entire Village was going into the market after the Games.[14]

Finally, there was this from VANOC's CEO: "Also there is a $6.5 million commitment to aboriginal housing as well for a total of about $67.5 million."

Funny, no one told the thousands of poor Native people in the Downtown Eastside. Furlong concluded with a final blast of hot air: "Those legacies will be achieved, those are our only obligations. All the other housing discussions and housing initiatives that are going on are in the hands of our partners. Although we work with them, that's their area and not ours."

Yup, VANOC did its part; it was just the "partners" who had screwed up the plan.

The Homeless as a Marketing Obstacle

The homeless are an obstacle to the happy face that the Olympics tries to impose on the cities where the Games are held. The frame, remember, is all about athletes for peace. Having poor people stick their beggars' bowls in the faces of the tourists is definitely not going to encourage them to buy Olympic trinkets. Seeing the homeless huddled up in doorways against the winter rain and snow can spoil a carefree dinner after the gold medal hockey game, especially if the nasty buggers try to hit you up for some spare change. Rather than trying to deal with the underlying reasons for homelessness, Olympic (and other) cities deal with the problem by not dealing directly with the problem at all. Worse, before the media and tourism glare of the Olympics, the problem is best dealt with not only by ignoring it, but by actively hiding it.

The Impact of the Olympics
on Housing and Homelessness: Past Histories

After any Olympic bid has been won, the urgency to keep the homeless and tourists miles apart becomes paramount. As Helen Lenskyj writes, "A key part of the host city's image-building process involves the 'disappearing' of homeless people and slum housing, lest potential tourists and investors be deterred by sights and sounds that are incompatible with the 'world-class city' image."[15] "Civil City" legislation thus becomes the norm rather than the exception. Atlanta in 1996 found that it was best to move the homeless somewhere else.[16] Atlanta also went out of its way in the "criminalization of poverty," passing legislation targeting "aggressive panhandling, loitering, camping in public, remaining in parking lots without having a car parked there, being in abandoned buildings, washing a car windshield, urinating in public," and generally acting "in a manner not worthy of a law abiding citizen."[17] The cookie-cutter-like legislation of Project Civil City was already fully test driven in Atlanta fourteen years before Vancouver would follow the same path. Toronto, New York and Paris had been prepared to do the same, but the homeless in these cities were "saved," not from poverty, but from outright expulsion by failed Olympic bids. Those in Beijing and London are not going to be so lucky.

As in other Olympic host cities, there are two key outcomes, neither one positive for average citizens. First, with the focus on the host city and its required Olympic projects, public and private projects in other cities and regions are neglected. In Vancouver, the billions spent on the RAV line and on the Sea to Sky upgrade, as the top priorities dictated by the artificial needs of the Games, meant that significant highways and transportation problems in the rest of the province were left dangling. In many cases, the road conditions elsewhere were far worse than those on any part of the Sea to Sky highway, the need for alternatives to automobiles just as pressing.

The second typical outcome is that the Olympics real estate boom, bubble though it may be, begins to push people out of the city. As rents and home prices escalate, thousands of middle- and lower-income earners in Vancouver and the Lower Mainland have been finding that they can't afford to live there anymore.[18] The gentrified market created by the Olympics simply displaces a whole class of society.

Such a displacement effect has been a feature of Olympic host cities going back at least to the 1980s. As Helen Lenskyj noted:

> In the last two decades, the vast majority of bid and host cities have shared a common problem: a housing and homeless crisis. Examples include Seoul, Barcelona, Atlanta, Amsterdam, Sydney, Beijing, Toronto, Athens, Turin, New York and Vancouver...the actual post-Olympic situation in recent host cities suggests that an affordable housing legacy is unlikely to materialize, and that, in fact, conditions for homeless and inadequately housed people are exacerbated by the hosting of the Olympics.[19]

Lenskyj's conclusion is supported by the Centre on Housing Rights and Evictions (COHRE), which has documented displacements that range from those caused by market price increases to outright evictions. The numbers compiled for the last 20 years suggest that the overall figure for displacements due to the Olympics is well over 2 million people.[20] Until Beijing began its building spree, the worst case was Seoul where 720,000 people were forcibly evicted as slums were torn down to improve the city's image for Olympic tourists. As documented by Anita Beatty of the Atlanta Task Force for the Homeless, Atlanta's efforts to sweep the poor away was wildly successful: 9,000 people arrested or given a one-way bus ticket out of town, some 15,000 evicted outright from their homes, the final tally of those displaced in one way or another topping 30,000. Lesser known examples of Olympic displacement include: the jailing of thousands of black men by Los Angeles Police Chief Daryl Gates during the "Olympic Gang Sweeps" before the 1984 Summer Games; in Calgary, 2,000 people were temporarily or permanently displaced by the 1988 Games; in the run-up to the 2000 Athens Games, psychiatric hospitals were forced to lock up the homeless, the mentally ill and drug addicts, and some 40 Roma families were moved out of an area they had lived in for a generation in order to build a parking lot for the Games.

Beijing's Games aim to be the biggest and best in most things, including costs that are now approaching $60 billion and an overall displacement of people that now stands at 1.25 million, the total expected to rise by another quarter million or higher by August 2008.[21]

Vancouver fits the Olympic displacement model perfectly with hotel closures in the Downtown Eastside.[22] Displacement does not always lead to people relocating to cheaper accommodations outside the city; sometimes, in fact far too often, it generates more homeless people. As political columnist Reed Eurchuk wrote in an article on displacement in Vancouver, "The homeless are the evicted who do not have the means (financial, social, familial) to reenter the housing market."[23] And, as noted above, the government was already thinking ahead about shipping the homeless out of the region entirely.

The promises of social housing in Olympic host cities are typically illusory: In Barcelona all but 76 of 6,000 units in the Athletes' Village were sold into the market, and overall house prices rose by 250 percent in the period from 1986 to 1992, the year of the Games. As cited above, the same future outcome is now becoming clear for the Athletes' Villages in Vancouver and Whistler.

In many Olympic host cities, the impact can go far beyond mere displacement: Mexican students protesting the transfer of $200 million from Mexico City's social services budget to city improvement projects designed to "re-image" the city for the Olympics were massacred. Moscow in 1980 featured the arrests of dissidents, and Los Angeles in 1984 targeted young blacks. Barcelona in 1992 conducted street sweeps of the homeless, arrests of their own dissidents; a further 400 homeless people were subjected to "control and supervision" during the Games.[24]

If the Olympic Family
Really Believed in "Inclusivity"

After the 2010 Games were given to Vancouver, the ICI working group was established. It comprised a number of groups working on issues of poverty in Vancouver alongside some in the real estate/development sector.[25] VANOC was there too. The different levels of government didn't sit at the table but notionally signed on to the report's recommendations. These included:

+ 800 units of new housing constructed per year for four years, giving a total of 3,200 new units of housing for the city's homeless. These numbers were based on the City of Vancouver's projected housing needs;
+ 200 units of single-room occupancy (SRO) to be bought or leased for each of four years, with the goal of improving and protecting 800 units of existing housing;
+ 200 units of Olympic worker housing to be converted into low-income housing after the Games;
+ increasing all social assistance rates by 50% above March 2007 levels; and
+ eliminating barriers to access to income assistance of various types.[26]

The City of Vancouver's response was that the ICI's recommendations were in line with Council's policies, but simply couldn't be funded without provincial assistance. The City also refused to make any guarantees about *any* number of units in the Athletes' Village for social housing: It seemed they'd first have to see how much money they made on selling the bulk of them.

At the council session where City staff presented these conclusions, David Eby of the Pivot Legal Society offered them a lifeline: The City didn't have to break its housing promises; instead it could find fiscally creative ways to make these a reality. They could, for example, take their profits from the sale of the False Creek lands to Millennium, estimated by the City to be over $64 million, ask VANOC to take funds from their employee bonus package, add on money now slated for more police, etc., and *voilà*, the money to build the 3,200 units would be available.[27] It was simply a matter of being willing to do it. City Council had signed off on the promise to protect the homeless back in 2002 when the Games were still just a twinkle in Jack Poole's eye, so it all seemed a no-brainer. How about it? Some councilors found Eby's ideas "interesting." Would they do it? Well, no, they wouldn't.

In its failure to keep promises of inclusivity, the City of Vancouver is no more guilty than the IOC itself, which had become pretty adept at the politically correct rhetoric as long as no actual binding commitment needs to be made. One could envision that the IOC would one day adopt a fourth pillar of Olympism, "social responsibility," for example. Doing so, however, would be precisely the wrong thing from the IOC's corporate perspective. As Lenskyj wrote, "Realistically, however, the profit-making motives of multinational corporate sponsors of the Olympics would not be well-served by any requirement that, to their eyes, smacked of socialism, or even one that took social responsibility seriously." [28]

The IOC is also fond of saying that it doesn't like to "interfere" in social issues, while interfering in every way possible with local social priorities. Whether pillars get added or not, "as long as the Olympics remain a source of enormous profit for the major sponsors and television networks, and as long as Olympic-spirit and world-class-city discourse continues to disguise the real costs to taxpayers and the real impact on already disadvantaged populations, the [IOC's] proposed reforms pose no threat to the status quo and hold no promise of significant change." [29]

Broadcasting Misery

The problem posed by having the homeless still wandering around when throngs of tourists descend on the Olympic host city is potentially manageable: The numbers of the former are not that great and are containable; moreover, many tourists, especially those from North American cities, have homeless problems back home, so the shock factor is not extreme. It becomes a more urgent problem of management, however, due to one key factor: television. The broadcast companies will be sending trillions of pixels around the globe to an audience estimated at well over three billion. For their sponsors, trying to sell stuff when sick, hungry, ragged people wander in and out of the frame can be definitely off-putting to those watching from the comforts of a warm home. The magnifying effect of the television cameras makes a semimanageable problem into a really embarrassing headache for the IOC and the host city organizers alike. The solution, as always, is to move the problem.

Resistance and Hope

By 2006 it had become obvious to the various anti-poverty groups in Vancouver that not only was poverty worse and homeless rates increasing, but the City of Vancouver was not going to do anything about it. The most radical of these groups, the APC, staged a series of protests and actions that served to make government and VANOC nervous. Each time VANOC would hold a special event, the APC was there. At the unveiling of VANOC's "Olympic clock," one activist grabbed the microphone and shouted obscenities against the Olympics. Native activists drummed and sang, drowning out the songs of the "cute" natives that VANOC had brought out for the event. The APC began to get media coverage, and while the latter tended to be very negative, the genie was out of the bottle; many British Columbians were forced to face the fact that poverty in Vancouver had increased, as a consequence of the 2010 Olympic developments. The City struck back: APC members were arrested and charged, and another anti-poverty group allied to them, the DERA, had their City funding cut off. Punishing DERA in the end simply wound up punishing some senior citizens of Chinese ancestry that DERA had been helping.

Vancouver City Council had meanwhile dug in its heels, and Mayor Sullivan declared that the City was not going to "surrender to hooligans." They weren't going to do anything serious about the underlying poverty issues either. The promises to the poor, promises that had led many social progressives to vote yes in the plebiscite, were simply abandoned. Although many Vancouverites noted the broken promises, a large number didn't really seemed to care, at least if the mainstream media were to be believed. In this regard, Vancouver also mimicked Sydney where, "Sydney Olympic organizers relied on 'Olympic spirit' discourse to diffuse public outrage on the numerous occasions when Olympic officials failed to live up to the lofty standards touted in pseudo-religious rhetoric."[30]

And just in case anyone in APC or any other organization had thoughts of doing anything even more radical, the Olympic security machine was beginning to sputter to life. As we will see, the 2010 security forces might not be able to do much against a real external threat, but perhaps that wasn't to be their main purpose: Maybe their raison d'être would be to contain domestic Olympic opponents.

"Imagineering" Security

Canada is certainly going to be hit by al-Qaeda sooner
or later. So we can anticipate that Vancouver might be
a venue where they would try to do something.

PETER ST. JOHN, SECURITY EXPERT,
QUOTED BY CHARLIE SMITH IN
"2010: IT'S THE TERROR, STUPID,"
GEORGIA STRAIGHT, AUGUST 11, 2005

Initial Security Cost Projections:
Ignorance or Lies?

WHEN THE Vancouver Bid Corp's bid book came out in 2002, it contained various unsupportable items, but none more so than the projected costs for 2010 Olympic security. The bid book listed this as $175 million, an odd sort of number given that Salt Lake City had just racked up an impressive overall security bill between $330 million[1] and $350 million.[2] Well, the argument went, the costs were high in Salt Lake City because it was just after 9/11. OK, but 2010 is also in the uncertain post-9/11 world, and Canada is fighting a nasty insurgency in Afghanistan, so why the lowball number?

Those of us in NO GAMES who had been in Kananaskis earlier that summer remembered reading that security for the three-day event had cost the various levels of government over $300 million, so how could a 17-day Olympics, followed by a 10-day Paralympics come in almost 40 percent lower? How even could the Games in 2010 be cheaper than Montreal's 1976 Summer Olympics that came in with a robust cost of $244.6 million?[3] Those reporters who noted the discrepancy and bothered to ask received a snooty reply from the Bid Corp that basically said: "We've got our own security experts, we've talked to the RCMP, and this is the number they gave us." Who were these experts? The Bid Corp wasn't giving names. These nameless experts, however, were really the very best, most senior people in the security field so the media and the public were just going to have to trust them. The Bid Corp stayed with this number through thick and thin, insisting repeatedly that their projections were bang on and that it was only the naysayers — NO GAMES for example — full of hatred for all things Olympic, who were questioning the final security tab.

Even after the bid was won, the newly formed VANOC stuck religiously by the $175 million figure. The Summer Games in Athens in 2004 came and went with security costs totally out of control, topping out somewhere near $1.5 billion. Officially unperturbed, VANOC still wasn't budging from their magic $175 million projection. "Summer Games are more expensive than Winter Games," they sniffed. The Torino Winter Games of 2004 arrived, and security there was a whopping $1.4 billion.[4] VANOC was unmoved, even annoyed, as some in the media began asking those pesky questions again.

I had been talking with Stefano Bertone, the lead spokesperson for No-limpiadi!, the Torino opposition. During one exchange, Bertone had mentioned that Torino's original bid book had listed security at $146 million... and of course it had gone much higher. The original Torino number kept floating around in my head for days. Torino had obviously been absurdly wrong, had clearly low-balled their original estimate back before they won their bid. Other than the obvious deception of the original number, there was something damned odd about Torino's $146 million and Vancouver's projected $175 million. I looked up the currency exchange rate between the US and Canada back in the summer of 2002; CAN$1 was worth about US$0.65. What if you multiplied the exchange rate by $146 million? It came out to be about CAN$225 million. In other words, VANOC hadn't even kept to the same absurdly lowball figures of Torino, but had lowered the bar even further. Maybe it was a psychological thing, like stores that try to pretend that their products are cheaper than they really are by listing them as $19.99 rather than $20. Maybe $175 million was easier to sell to the public than something over $200 million?

Figure 14.1 shows security costs for Summer and Winter Olympics going back to Montreal in 1976. There are several necessary caveats to the information in this graph. First, it is virtually impossible to obtain accurate numbers (all except for 2010 in US$) that include all the probable players, that is, all levels of government that provide the various security services and costs. In many cases, records don't exist or were destroyed. Before the 1980s, with the exception of Montreal, accurate numbers are hard to find for all cities and are remarkably variable; therefore, they have not been included. Also, some Winter Olympics numbers are simply not available — Albertville, Lillehammer and

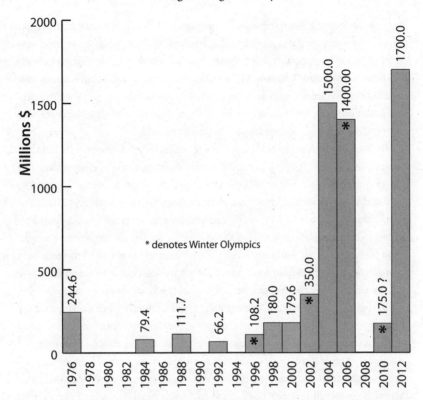

Figure 14.1. Summer and Winter Olympic security costs (US$) from 1976 to 2010 [5]

Calgary. The second is that the numbers shown may not include the intrinsic security costs to the organizing committees in addition to those of the security services. Therefore, these numbers should be taken as *underestimates*. Finally, as difficult as it is to obtain accurate Olympic security costs in democratic countries, doing so for authoritarian regimes such as those in China and Russia makes any potential accounting virtually impossible.

Nevertheless, the data show a clear trend, and for the most part the Summer and Winter Games track each other quite closely. For most of the reporting period, security costs gradually rose to about $200 million before 2001. If one plots the curves that the graph indicates for both Summer and Winter Games, what one sees is termed a "power law" function, in which the rate of increase in costs goes up as a multiple (in this case by a factor of over four) against a linear rate for the succeeding years. Such a function is typical of any process undergoing explosive growth. In the aftermath of September 11, 2001, both curves begin a sharp upward deflection with both Summer and Winter Games again showing the same trends, although those for Beijing in 2008 may never be known. Arguably, the Winter curve is more reliable since it reflects two post-9/11 Winter Olympics (Salt Lake City, 2002, and Torino, 2006) versus only one Summer Games (Athens, 2000). The latest estimate for the Summer 2012 Games in London is now $1.7 billion, so it appears that the costs here are trending upwards for the Summer Games as well.[6]

In marked contrast to these curves, the projected security budget for Vancouver 2010 at $175 million is clearly an anomaly, pushing the costs down to a level not seen since the 1998 Winter Games in Nagano, Japan. It's hard to look at the curves derived from numbers available on the Web and in various publications compared to VANOC's projections and not sense a profound ignorance of historical trends. The alternative to ignorance would be outright fraud if the Bid Corp, and later VANOC deliberately low-balled the numbers in order to keep the public from appreciating the exact cost to taxpayers.[7] We will see later in this chapter that this is precisely what these organizations did.

VANOC continued to hold to the $175 million figure from 2003 until they finally got around to releasing their long-overdue business plan in the spring of 2007. There, miraculously, the security costs that were "theirs" had plummeted to a measly $10 million, most of this for site security, presumably involving private security agencies guarding IOC family members and other foreign dignitaries.[8] The overall security hot potato had been neatly passed to the various agencies of three levels of government and was now off VANOC's plate for good. It was a timely pass, since a memorandum of agreement signed between different federal and provincial agencies in December 2006 had described the $175 million figure as an "interim" budget only.[9] Not only had VANOC offloaded a potentially embarrassing cost over-run, but in so doing had trimmed their overall operating costs by $165 million. Amazingly, in the same business plan, they then had the gall to claim that they were $100 million in the black. It was more "fun with numbers," VANOC style.

The Security Picture for the 2010 Games

The security costs derived by the Bid Corp and VANOC are an example of fraudulent manipulation not only to get the public onside, but that actually put that same public at risk, particularly in the case where security agencies actually try to stay within the imaginary budget. It is, therefore, worthwhile examining the players in the security picture for 2010. At the federal level, they are numerous, the big ones being the Royal Canadian Mounted Police (RCMP), supposedly the "lead" agency for the overall security umbrella under a new organization called Vancouver 2010 Integrated Security Unit, or V2010-ISU, and the Department of National Defense (DND), which plans to provide a "robust" backup of lots of essential equipment, not to mention "boots on the ground."[10] Smaller but still important agencies include the Canadian Security Intelligence Service (CSIS), Canada's spy agency; the Coast Guard (under the Department of Fisheries and Oceans); and Transport Canada, the Canadian Border Service, and Public Safety and Emergency Preparedness (PSEPC). Health Canada will even be involved.

CSIS will provide intelligence on various real or imagined threats.[11] The other agencies will have equally specialized roles to play. It should be stressed that these are only the agencies we know about at present: There may well be others. At the provincial level, there really isn't something operating under the Province's direct authority, although British Columbia as signatory to the December 2006 memorandum of agreement is in for half the overall costs. At the municipal level there are the Vancouver Police Department (VPD), the West Vancouver Police Department and the Vancouver Port Authority, the latter an essentially private entity operating under the federal umbrella of Transport Canada.

Officially, all of the above players will be part of V2010-ISU whose command post for the Vancouver area will likely be the provincial emergency communications center (E-Comm) in East Vancouver.[12] There are, however, some plans afoot for a separate command center. As lead agency, the RCMP is supposed to coordinate all of this. However, there are problems within the ranks of the Mounties, having just come through one of the most painful and embarrassing years since the force was created in 1873. In the last year alone they had suffered a string of disasters and revelations that left the public disenchanted and the force itself demoralized. For example, an inquiry into the Air India bombing in 1985 has revealed just how badly the RCMP and CSIS botched the screening of terrorist suspects before the disaster, and how each agency covered up their ineptitude in the years that followed. The RCMP was also outed for complicity in sending an innocent Canadian citizen, Maher Arar, to be tortured in Syria, and then lying about it. A pension fund fraud within the organization pretty much convinced Canadians that their national police force was not only incompetent, but on the take as well. The top cop, Commissioner Giuliano Zacardelli, was forced to resign in disgrace to be replaced for the first time in RCMP history by a civilian, William Elliott, a senior bureaucrat. Elliott quickly had a lot on his plate and little time to get up to speed. This lack of experience showed up in spades during October 2007 when RCMP officers at Vancouver's International Airport took down a hapless Polish immigrant named Robert Dziekański who died after being repeatedly hit by Taser blasts. Elliott hid from the media for days after the event, leaving the media and public wondering if anyone was in charge of the shop. It would be safe to say that, at the moment, the RCMP is in considerable disarray. To prepare, rehearse and coordinate the massive security operations that the 2010 Olympics will demand and desperately need is a whole different matter, and they certainly won't do it on a budget of $175 million. In fact, whether they can do it at all in the time remaining before the opening ceremony in February 2010 remains in question, no matter how much money gets put on the table. It's worth noting that the RCMP's Chief Superintendent Bob Harriman, the head of the 2010 security detail, was recently reassigned to "other" tasks. Harriman's sudden move to "pursue other opportunities" came on the heels of media reports citing internal RCMP documents obtained under Access to Information Legislation that revealed that the Mounties clearly knew the costs for 2010 would go higher than $175 million.[13] The RMCP appointed a new Chief Superintendent, Bud Mercer, to take over from Harriman. Mercer was due to announce a revised security budget in November 2007, but if he did it was never made public.

The Canadian military (officially the Canadian Forces, or CF) is also in disarray, albeit for a very different reason: They are now up to their butts in their first war in 50 years, fighting a vicious and unpredictable insurgency in southern Afghanistan. At present there is one battle group of about 2,500 soldiers in Kandahar Province. More senior and planning staff are headquartered in the Afghan capital, Kabul. What this means is that the Forces — Regulars (Regs) as well as reservists — are thinly spread, barely able to cover off on minor UN missions and virtually unable to undertake a second major assignment of any sort, certainly not as a long-term commitment. In spite of significant losses in killed and wounded in the last year alone, the Regs genuinely like the Afghan mission with the challenges it brings and the new toys the CF enjoys, care of a grateful government. Simply put, the Regs haven't been bloodied enough yet for morale to drop significantly or for the top brass or government to want to bring the troops home. Not only don't they want the combat mission to end, the military has gone outside the traditional boundaries separating the military and its civilian masters and are now actively agitating both in private and public to extend their current combat role beyond February 2009. Before then, however, most of the major infantry, artillery and armored regiments of the CF will have rotated through Afghanistan at least once, and the pool of reservists ready to risk life and limb for the flag will shrink as the novelty wears off and the body bags and the maimed continue to come home. Those not deployed at any given time are practicing to deploy in the future. Parliament has now extended Canada's mission to December 2011, leaving a depleted military to sort itself out for a role at the 2010 Olympics. If the Regs can't do so, then the bulk of the task could fall to the Army Reserves. Generally highly competent, the Reserves are increasingly sapped by backfilling the Regs in Afghanistan and simply lack the time, organization and experience to undertake a lead role in 2010 security. It might come to this, but betting the safety of hundreds of thousands of people on an unknown is more than a bit unnerving. Also, the costs associated with putting the bulk of Olympic military security in the hands of the military would cost taxpayers a whack of money beyond DND's regular budget, since Reservists are normally only paid for the actual time they serve.

This is not to suggest that the Canadian Forces or the various police forces come for free, which they most decidedly do not. It is important to address this last point here since we may be certain that both the federal government and their provincial counterparts will try to pretend that there is no "real" cost associated with personnel for either the Regs or police during the Olympics since "they're already employed and we pay them anyway." Really? OK, let's look at it another way: When the Regs deploy for Afghanistan, does the mission there have a price tag or not? Clearly the former. When Defense Minister Peter MacKay or Prime Minister Steven Harper get up in front of NATO, they continually stress how much Canada had been contributing in blood *and dollars*. They most emphatically do *not* state that Canada's participation is free, since "the soldiers are employed anyway." Bottom line: the Regs are already employed, but if not for the Olympics, would be doing very different tasks, so tasking them to provide Olympic security is as real a Games-related expense as building a ski run. They might, for example, be deployed to Darfur were it not for the Games, but surely won't be, at least in part because of them. The entire issue of direct and indirect costs plagues any and all attempts to put a realistic number to anything Olympics-related and pretty much guarantees that true costs will remain unreported. It's as true for military spending on the Games as it is when Vancouver city staff devote their working hours to Olympic issues instead of dealing with conventional municipal matters.

Doing the Math:
The True Low End Cost of 2010 Security

Getting a precise dollar figure is thus likely to be difficult if not impossible, not only for me and other Olympic watchdogs, but also, I suspect, for the government itself, particularly if they don't really want anyone to see the final figures.

Accepting these limitations, however, there is still value in trying to get an estimate of the 2010 security costs. To do so requires knowledge of a number of factors, for example, which organizations exactly will be involved and with how many people, using which resources and employed for how long. Although I now have multiple Freedom of Information and Access to Information (the former is provincial, the latter federal) requests pending on behalf of 2010 Watch and the Work Less Party, it will certainly take many months if not years to source out this information from each organization. Indeed, I may never receive much of the necessary information at all.[14]

Even in the absence of the official information, making some minimal assumptions, it is possible to undertake a rough calculation to get a sense for the likely *low-end* dimensions of Olympic security costs in relation to VANOC's stated figure of $175 million. The upper-end number, that is, the real number, is unlikely to ever be known for certain.

A good place to start is with the 2004 Winter Olympics in Torino, Italy. We know that security was provided by some 15,000 police and soldiers and cost about $1.4 billion, or eight times more than VANOC has budgeted for Vancouver's Games. Vancouver's 2010 situation is assumed to be generally similar, and a total personnel number of 15,000 is thus likely realistic.[15] As discussed above, the CF commitment in Afghanistan past 2009 limits the number of Regulars available for the Olympics. The entire full-time CF (Army, Navy, Air Force) total about 62,000, as of this writing, 19,500 of these in the Army.[16] At a guess, 5,000 — the equivalent of two battle groups — would be the upper limit for what the Regs could contribute. The RCMP have about 16,000 personnel in the ranks from constable to staff sergeant who are potentially available for Olympic duty.[17] As in Kananaskis and Quebec City, the RCMP will likely have to draw on police forces from across Canada to fill their levy. Whatever they do to make up the numbers, they might bring on about 5,000 personnel. This leaves the only other official source of manpower, the CF Reserves of approximately 25,000. Of these, about 15,500 are in the Army Reserve and are the likely source for the last 5,000 personnel needed for 2010. In British Columbia, Army Reserves total just under 1,500, so at a bare minimum, 3,500 others will have to be recruited from across Canada.

We now have the 15,000-strong security force needed, so what will it cost? A good place to start is with the Reservists. Although all ranks will be involved, we'll assume for simplicity that all 5,000 are brand new privates. This assumption will lower the overall cost and thus serve to lowball the final figure. A Reservist serving for a set continuous time on contract, and most Olympics-related service would qualify, goes on "Class C" status, basically at the same salary as a Regular Soldier at the same rank. The lowest rank, Private 1, makes about $82 per day or $2,484 per month. A Private 3 makes $3,649 per month. Higher ranks obviously come with more pay. The overall period of the Games, Olympic and Paralympic, is about 30 days.[18] Taking the very safe assumption that all Reservists involved will start their service a month before the Games begin and finish a month afterwards, we have 5,000 soldiers serving for 90 days minimum. Salary alone is thus close to $37 million, assuming each is a Private 1. Soldiers have to be fed, and the current food per diem is close to $100, or $45 million more. Lodging and transportation? Easily another $100 a day for another $45 million. Even if a number of these were housed in the former CF base at Chilliwack, the costs don't change appreciably since the base has to be made ready for winter usage after years of virtual abandonment. How about flying the 3,500 reservists from other parts of Canada to BC? Assuming $1,000 per round trip ticket on commercial airlines adds another $3.5 million.

Thus, even at an unrealistic low-end pay scale, without the additional costs of other allowances, *and* the vast expenses associated with equipment, we are at over $130 million and this is *only* the Reserves! In other words, most of the budget that the Bid Corp put together has been spent on the military alone. How much will the Regs cost? The same general conditions apply in terms of salaries, food and lodging, so this doubles these numbers. Transportation becomes a larger issue here since the Regs move with all of their equipment, and as there is no Regular Force Army contingent in BC, all the assumed 5,000 personnel have to come from elsewhere. However, let's keep it simple and assume that the cost merely doubles at this point. Now we have over $260 million.

What about the police? An RCMP constable starts at $44,500 per annum, rising to $72,000 in three years. For the Vancouver Police Department (VPD), it's $45,500, rising to $63,000 in three years. Taking the lower salary gives us a cost per cop of approximately $11,000 for the three months of Olympic duty. To be even more conservative, let's say all the police, unlike most in the CF, can simply go home after the Games are over, so the period drops to two months, at $7,400. With 5,000 so employed, our total salary comes in near $37 million. The thousand VPD members and local RCMP won't have to be housed and fed three meals a day, but all the others will. Hence, the overall police costs of salary, food, lodging and transportation will come in with roughly the same ratio as that of the military, that is double, putting it at $74 million, and overtime has not even been factored in. There is likely to be considerable overtime costs in all of this, but for simplicity, I'll ignore these. Combined with the military costs, we are now at $334 million.

So far, I've only dealt with the Army part of the CF. The Regular Navy and/or Naval Reserve will be patrolling up and down the coast (in addition to screening the ports and all shipping), in particular around Vancouver and up Howe Sound. The Air Force will have to provide air coverage using manned and unmanned aircraft, etc…and the costs go up further. Per person costs may be the same as for the Army and there will be fewer of them, but ships and planes are expensive to maintain and operate; say for each separate part of the CF (that is, Army versus Navy or Air Force), another $100 million as a conservative assumption. This puts the magic number close to $534 million, and still climbing.

I also haven't touched on equipment costs yet, but these are certain to be extensive. The Army doesn't plan to walk once they get here; it will require trucks, Jeeps and whatever light armoured vehicles (LAVs) aren't tied down in Afghanistan. The Air Force is now talking about using unmanned aerial vehicles (UAVs), which are not cheap.[19] If they don't have enough ground vehicles, the military will rent vans and SUVs as troop carriers and for officers and senior staff. Army Engineers will require their specialized vehicles and bridging resources, Signals units their equally specialized radio equipment, and Air Defense units will be present with their anti-aircraft missile-launching low-level air defense anti-tank system (ADATs) mounted on armored personnel carriers. The specialized units that monitor for chemical, biological and nuclear threats will be in Vancouver as well, with more specialized equipment, and there will be a role for Canada's commandos of Joint Task Force 2. The Air Force will have F-18s in the air, along with various types of helicopters for transport, surveillance and reconnaissance, and the UAVs mentioned above. The Navy will have its frigates and other patrol craft along the coast and as far up Howe Sound as Squamish. Both police and military will require computers and other sophisticated electronic equipment.

Not only will existing equipment and other resources have to be transported to the Lower Mainland from all across Canada, shortfalls will have to be filled with new purchases. The Games in Torino had some police and military patrolling on skis, so add on ski and outdoor kit to Vancouver's security costs. "March madness," that fiscal free-for-all that happens in government agencies near the end of the fiscal year, is certain to arrive in 2009, as all military and police units involved order as much new kit as possible.[20] What will all this cost? In the absence of information from the DND and the lead police agencies at present, all one can do is guess, but adding on a very conservative $100 million more is probably fair. The grand total is now close to $634 million, still far short of Torino's tally, but almost four times higher than VANOC claims.

Remember, the above are the minimal best-guess figures only for the military and police, and only for the period of the Games. If we now add on all the other agencies involved and their costs from now until after the Games in 2010, the capacity of the costs to skyrocket becomes obvious. If we also replace the minimal salary and resource estimates with a more realistic range, the costs bounce even higher. As cited above, Torino's eventual bill of $1.4 billion for security is probably the best predictor of Vancouver's ultimate bill.[21]

All of this leads to one of two inescapable conclusions: Either the Bid Corp, and later VANOC, along with different levels of government, have been lying to us since 2002 or — and I'm not sure if this is not more disturbing — they are all in denial about the true costs for protecting the Olympics and still hope to provide security on the cheap. The latter possibility seems to have rattled the IOC as well.[22]

Guarding a Hundred Sites and a Very Long Defile

To understand just how scary the latter prospect is, consider the complexity of the security picture and hence the enormity of the task facing the various agencies involved in 2010 security planning. To make the comparison, remember the situation facing the security people preparing for the G8 meeting in Kananaskis in 2002. There the police had to deal with potential anti-globalization "threats" at various sites in Calgary and at one lodge in the middle of the Kananaskis Valley. Police intelligence likely told them that, hysterical newspaper headlines aside, the demonstrators posed no real physical threat to the G8 leaders or to anyone else. The potential embarrassment to the government could hardly have been considered a real threat. Given this, the city venues could easily be covered by cops on mountain bikes. The Kananaskis resort was simplicity itself: No one but the top politicians was supposed to be there, so the police and military simply sealed the valley off at both ends with layers of chain-link fencing, and that was that.

Security for Vancouver in 2010 presents a vastly different picture. For one thing, there are more than 100 venues scattered across the Lower Mainland, including those in Vancouver, Richmond, and the North Shore mountains, all needing to be secured against a Munich-style attack. To add to the mix, the Vancouver sites need to connect to those in Whistler and the Callaghan, over 120 kilometers away along what the military terms a "defile," a geographical feature that limits movement. All the bridges in Vancouver and the entire Sea to Sky Highway form a series of continuous defiles, each absurdly easy to block for anyone contemplating doing so. The Sea to Sky also passes through some of the densest forests in the world.

Imagine the following scenario: One day during the Games, very early in the morning, the lead vehicle driving the route comes under fire from someone with a rifle hidden in the treeline. With luck, bad aim or non-murderous intent, no one is hurt, but the police and army are surely not going to allow the convoy of athletes, dignitaries, journalists and spectators to proceed until the route is secure. They now do what the security forces are trained to do: deploy on foot to try to find the shooter. In this terrain, this takes hundreds of security personnel many hours to find…absolutely nothing. Long before they arrive at the suspected site, the shooter has moved to another location. The shooter remains in control and can play cat and mouse with the security forces as long as his interest and stamina last. Or, say that someone deliberately stalls a car on the Lion's Gate or Second Narrows bridge and walks away. Police suspect a bomb, so the police bomb squad and maybe the military engineers show up… hours more pass while the bomb, real or imagined, is dealt with. All of this means that, with relatively little effort and without actually killing anyone, a minimally determined opponent could impose delays that could utterly jam up the workings of the Games.

A more bloody-minded operative could put a bomb on a bus or in a trash bin, with the resulting carnage and pandemonium bringing the city to a standstill. Or, terrorism could be specific, targeting, for example, any of the 10,000 journalists or the thousands of volunteers or the hundreds of thousands of spectators. Working against the security forces is the simple equation that, unlike in Kananaskis where security measures were designed to keep people *out*, at the Olympics, the IOC and VANOC need as many people as possible *in* so that they can put the maximum number of behinds on seats. It's a dilemma to which there is no correct answer except to spend the cash, flood the city with cops and soldiers and hope like hell for the best. The best of all outcomes might turn out to be like Athens where $1.5 billion couldn't stop a man in a tutu from jumping into the Olympic pool or another fellow in a clown suit from tackling the lead marathoner. Both incidents were silly rather than fatal, but just as easily could have been the latter. If $1.5 billion can't stop clowns, what will it do against a really determined foe? The answer: nothing.

Gone are the days when Canada had no enemies. The war in Afghanistan has seen to that, and if anyone wanted to make a political point, there would be no better place to do it than on prime-time television before the eyes of the world at the 2010 Games. The Palestinian group Black September patented the method of harvesting the Olympic audience for propaganda back in 1972. Since then, the Olympics have been lucky; 2010 might well be the year the luck finally runs out. In regard to this last point, think of the message that the low-ball $175 million sends to the world: Vancouver 2010 is a soft target.

Freedom of Information and Its Discontents

I don't have my Freedom of Information and Access to Information requests back from all of the various agencies but, sometime before 2010, hope that I will be able to provide a more accurate accounting of Olympic security costs. Realistically, with all the procedural and legal loopholes that government agencies toss in the path, I will not likely find all the necessary numbers. Nor, I suspect, will I even know if I have missed key agencies.

Some material may simply go missing, as in the following example. One of my Access to Information requests went to Fisheries and Oceans Canada to get the 2010 budget for the Canadian Coast Guard. My original letter had been posted to Ottawa with my return address clearly listed. In due course, I received a letter back from a third party in Halifax. It seems that Fisheries and Oceans had typed out a reply to me, complete with my correct North Vancouver mailing address, and then inexplicably sent it to another Chris Shaw of Binnacle Yachting Equipment and Accessories Ltd. — in Bedford, Nova Scotia. The latter was kind enough to repackage the letter and send it to me. How could this happen? Is the Coast Guard confused about which coast they are supposed to be defending in 2010? I hope not, but am far from reassured by this incident.

Misdirected mail is only one problem. A far greater one will be trying to read between the lines to see actual dollars spent versus in-kind contributions, both Olympic costs. A case in point concerns the Vancouver Port Authority, which initially said it hadn't spent anything as of late May 2007 but later noted that it had invested some 70 "man-days" or a sum of about $2,800.[23] The amount here is not the key take-home message. Rather, it's this: Without specifying everything that could contribute as an Olympic expense, accurate numbers will likely never be known. To get real numbers would take a full investigation by the offices of the Auditors General of Victoria and Ottawa, an unlikely outcome to be sure.

Social Impacts of 2010 Olympic Security Measures

The cost of Olympic security is, as we've seen, likely to be astronomical; the ability to prevent terrorism or disruption, based on a combination of dollars and luck where the latter may have a much greater impact than most of us would like to believe. Still unaddressed is the social cost of militarizing a city, in other words, the impact on civil liberties. Given real or perceived threats, civil liberties often take a hit. We don't have to delve far into Canadian history to see that similar events have had wide-ranging impacts. In Vancouver, the event that comes most readily to mind was the Asia Pacific Economic Cooperation (APEC) conference in 1997. In the course of a one-day event, much of the city was gridlocked by police barricades, and the civil liberties of Canadians were shown to be held in utter contempt by the police and politicians. Not many lessons were learned from APEC because, in the summer of 2000, different cops but the same politicians trashed human rights all over again in Quebec City. Legislation in place since 9/11 makes it all the easier for security forces to monitor potential opponents, and the very real capacity for preventative detention exists, not only for anti-Olympic activists and the poor, but for anyone else that the police simply want swept up for any reason. It's hard to imagine Canadian police and troops using the brutal tactics seen in Mexico City in 1968, in Korea in 1988 or in China today, but not impossible by any means. No one died in Quebec City, but not from an obvious lack of effort by the police.

It's not even clear that the security folks have a particularly acute view of the threats that the 2010 Games may face. Just before starting this book in 2006, I ran into a fellow officer from the Army Reserves. He had just finished the Militia Staff course, a course I had taken a few years back. Part of his homework, he told me, had been to evaluate the security threat to the 2010 Olympics posed by different organizations. These were Al Qaeda or other terrorists, native protesters, and…NO GAMES 2010. I stared at him in disbelief. Did the military really see NO GAMES as a threat to the Games worthy of military scrutiny? Well, not like the others, perhaps, but one to think about regardless, was the answer.

Finally, most of the agencies involved in 2010 security haven't really done much to date. The Israel Defense Forces used to have a saying, similar to other armies, "hard in training, easy in battle." This well-tested aphorism seems to be getting short shrift from the security forces in charge of 2010. With the RCMP in disarray and the CF preoccupied in Central Asia, the various subordinate agencies seem content to sit back and wait for someone to tell them what to do. Eventually, the RCMP and CF will wake up, but by then, with time growing short, panic will start to gain purchase on the collective 2010 security community. Considering the sorts of "so what" questions that lead to contingency planning and figuring out sequels to these actions and those of potential adversaries takes time.[24] To test these ideas against realistic best- and worst-case scenarios in rehearsals — war gaming — takes more time, time that the 2010 Olympic security team is now unlikely to have. Given this, Olympic security forces will start late off the blocks, spend money like madmen to catch up and, in the end, focus on the easily defined "threats." Such easy threats may not, of course, be the ones that the 2010 Games will actually face. Vancouver 2010 might thus take gold, silver and bronze in how *not* to do security, as they spend hundreds of millions, if not billions, of dollars and sweep the streets of those the authorities deem annoying, all the while missing the real threats that could cost lives. As it now stands, a protester from the APC is probably in more danger from the police and army than an Al Qaeda operative with a bomb.

Vancouver's Olympic message to visitors on Opening Day may well read: "Welcome to Vancouver, enjoy the Games…and good luck." We as a country will have a lot to answer for if things go sideways and people get hurt or killed. Right now all that stands in the way of this happening is just that, luck.

The Real Costs Start to Emerge

By the summer of 2007, the RCMP was finally waking up to reality and noting that the $175 million price tag was insufficient. Someone seems to have leaked to the media serious concerns about the RCMP's operating budget. Questioned about the discrepancy by reporters, an RCMP spokesperson said, "We were initially told there would be 20 venues, and as time has evolved, there are now more than 100 venues we will be responsible for." Also quoted in the media was a 2005 security document which noted, "At first blush, numerous financial funding gaps and risks have been identified which will negatively impact security operations…. While a comprehensive review of resource requirements has not been completed due to the non-availability of venue-specific information, it is anticipated total cost of games security will exceed the cost-sharing agreement budget allocation by a significant amount."[25] Gaps and risks, all right, and still "lacking a comprehensive review." Somehow, I'm not feeling too reassured. The RCMP spokesperson also acknowledged that Canada's involvement in Afghanistan would figure into the final costs.

Some in the press were starting to emerge from their five-year long slumber. Jeff Lee and Miro Cernetig wrote an article entitled "Fortress British Columbia" for the *Vancouver Sun*. Buried amidst shopping lists of equipment and military and police units and a generally upbeat "it's all gonna be fine, you're protected" message was a small paragraph with the real meat: Former soldier and current editor of *Esprit de Corps* magazine, Scott Taylor, was quoted as saying, "I'd be looking more in the half-billion dollar range — just for the military." Taylor has obviously done the same math that I have — indeed that anyone could have. Lee and Cernetig hide this tidbit so well one almost has to wonder if they are more worried about scaring the public with the final bill rather than the potential threats. One other item screams out from the article:

Get ready for really, truly, amazingly awful security lockdowns, traffic snarls and delays…and violations of anything approaching privacy and civil liberties, but all in a very nice Canadian way.[26] Gosh, if Lee and Cernetig could get it partly right at long last, the lies and obfuscations by VANOC and government are really getting obvious.

Updates on My Information Requests

CSIS took about two months to respond to my initial request, eventually sending me a cost spreadsheet for 2003/04 to 2010. There were no numbers attached, and the project code listed at the top of the table was still to be determined. Did this mean that there were no numbers or that they simply didn't want to reveal them? Probably the latter since the table had broken down expenses into salaries, employment benefits and premiums, "O and M" (whatever that is), operating expenditures, capital expenditures and a 13 percent accommodation cost. An accompanying photocopy of a letter dated December 7, 2006, from "DG, BC Region" to "DG, HQ" (Director General BC Region to Director General, Headquarters?) seemed to support the notion that considerable money had already been spent, at least on staff time. The letter noted that BC Region was actively working on Olympic security:

> It should be noted that BCR has already incurred some expenses in this regard. Specifically, we are in the process [whited out] in order to enhance Regional readiness for the 2010 Games. As such, BCR will be seeking to recoup this expenditure from federal funds designated for the security of the games [very long white out that goes on for a paragraph].

The letter goes on to note:

> Specifically, BCR anticipates a total of [white out of numbers] for the 2010 Games. BCR has devoted much time and energy to compiling these figures, and it is felt that these identified resources will be required in order to ensure that BCR can operate effectively during the games. We would also ask that FIN [financial department of CSIS?] assist in translating FTE [full-time equivalent] hours into dollar equivalencies.

Translating between the gaps and acronyms, it seems that CSIS in British Columbia has been working on the security aspect of 2010, has put in staff time, needs an unknown amount of funding overall and wants to be reimbursed from the federal government for monies spent so far.

The request to Public Safety and Emergency Preparedness Canada (PSEPC) filed in May 2007 elicited a reply at the end of July. It seemed they would need an additional six months to "consult with other federal government institutions." Another request to Transport Canada on the same date has also come back, this one dated August 3, 2007. They also need an additional six months since they have to have a chat with different agencies too. The same holds for the Department of National Defense. Fisheries and Oceans need only another three months.

The Vancouver Police Department (VPD) decided not to pussyfoot around with delays or excuses, telling me outright that they were withholding all records concerning current or projected costs: "It is our position that information pertaining to current and projected costs by sub-department, personnel and material [sic] expense is properly withhold [sic] per the aforementioned sections." VPD's motto of "To serve and protect" seems to have undergone some modest revisions, perhaps now reading: To Serve (Sam Sullivan and the NPA) and Protect (our lack of accountability to anyone).

The Canada Border Services Agency (CBSA) came up with a completely novel twist: "Any funding CBSA receives related to the Olympics is not for 'security' and does not come out of the Federal government's identified security envelope for budgeting." Ah, so if we don't call it officially "security," it's not a cost, right?

The response of CSIS thus appears to mirror what we are seeing from the different agencies involved in 2010 security: Agencies are behind the eight ball and spending money to catch up and clearly knowing that the original Bid Corp security estimates were garbage. Mix this with an utter lack of fiscal transparency due to ingrained institutional secrecy and it becomes obvious that to find out the true costs of 2010 security will be nearly impossible. Whether it ever happens at all is far from certain at this point. It seems more likely that, as in previous Games, the true numbers will never be known.

Hold the Phone: It's the RCMP on the Line

Just as this book was about to go to press, a large package from the RCMP arrived in the mail. To my considerable surprise, their information commissioner had clearly decided that it was indeed in the public's interest for the RCMP to disclose the true picture. Here is some of the information they provided:

+ Their slogan is "Safe and secure Games through an integrated security model."

+ The threat level, at least as of now, is still considered as medium, that is, an individual or organization might do something, or might not.
+ The $175 million was mostly for them and did not include separate VPD or military 2010 budgets; of this, their actual and projected spending through 2008 was $84,972,575.
+ They didn't really know what their security operations in 2008/09 or 2009/10, the big years of spending, would cost. Robert Jorssen, Executive Director, Corporate Management Branch, Pacific Region in a letter to Kevin Begg, Assistant Deputy Minister and Director of Public Safety for the government of British Columbia said: "We are unable to project costs beyond 2007/08, as we are just now entering the operational planning phase, and there are many unkowns (sic) and variables that cannot be costed at this time" and "V2010 ISU anticipates to incur the balance of expenditures near Games time. However, if additional costs are to be incurred in 2007/08, V2010 ISU will seek additional funding from both Federal and Provincial governments."
+ They had figured out the likely accommodation costs for their members for the period from January 4 to March 23, 2010: $34,450,000. (My estimates above for per diem and transport are close to their own at "$100 per diem, $500 transport for 21 days.")
+ They acknowledge they don't know the threat level or how to estimate it in advance.
+ They state that security clearances will be required for all Olympic site workers multiple times for a minimum of 216,000 such checks.
+ They accept that there will be severe shortages of security personnel available from within the province and that, therefore, most will have to come from outside at unknown cost.
+ The Torch Relay of the Olympic flame that is supposed to crisscross the country from "coast to coast to coast," some 35,000 km over 100 days, has to be protected as well. The RCMP documents advise, "A security team must accompany the torch: the bearers and a contingent of support, media and medical staff. There is no allotment of funds for this venture. The cost of providing safe transit (i.e., police escort) across the country is expected to be borne by the individual cities and communities that it passes through." Does anyone want to bet that this exercise will cost a bundle...and that no one will ever be able to determine what the real costs were?

The RCMP clearly knows that it's been handed a political hot potato and that media "management" will be required. One e-mail contained in my Access to

Information package was dated June 1, 2006, sent by one Jeni Sandeman to Inspector Pierre Leblanc, and speaks about managing the media to avoid embarrassment. The need for such "management" is confirmed in others of the obtained documents, specifically, in briefing notes to the BC Secretariat Annual Report: "While the security budget has been published in the bid book, it is not necessarily in anyone's best interest to continue sharing that number publically (sic). If anything, we are seeing more and more media reports ridiculing the budget when compared to other host cities."

All in all, it seems that the RCMP is due to consume the vast bulk of the $175 million themselves...and likely have to go back for more. Did they know this? Did VANOC? Actually, yes. From briefing notes to the RCMP Commissioner before the visit of the IOC's Technical Team (March 1 to 6, 2003), we learn that:

+ Gerhard Heiberg had said that the budget was "not enough."
+ Jack Poole responded: "I believe the RCMP continues to be comfortable that [$175 million] is an adequate number.... The evaluation commission was left with no uncertainty in the fact that was ever [sic] the cost of providing security, *the provincial and federal government will supply that cost*" (quoting from a Canadian Press report). [italics mine]

From the briefing notes come more revelations: "At this early stage, the estimated security budget strictly represents a commitment of funds *for the purpose of the bid process. It is impossible at this point to anticipate the threat levels or the international security environment that will be in effect in 2010. Therefore, details on equipment and personnel is (sic) impossible to forecast.*"[italics mine]

And: "*The original security bid budget of $175 million was compiled without input from the RCMP for the purposes of the bid book submission to the IOC* (International Olympic Committee). There were a number of gaps in the original budget such as provisions for a Command Centre and Planning Office." [italics mine]

And a letter from then-Chief Superintendent Robert Harriman to Annette Antoniak (BC Olympic and Paralympic Winter Games Secretariat) dated November 25, 2005, calls the $175 million security budget "conceptual."

We've already done the math and seen that the projected costs are nonsense, as the RCMP top brass and VANOC have long known. Inside the organization, there are likely many dedicated members trying to do the best with the mess that they've been handed. They know that they were lied to outright by the Bid Corp and VANOC, that the politicians went along to help get the bid, and now they've been left to sort out the mess. As an organization loyal to the chain of command, the RCMP will suck up its discontent at being made the fall guy and try to do what it has to do to make security work.

It's a crappy way to protect the world you've invited to Vancouver, but then no crappier than any of the endless broken promises made since 2002. The lack of transparency for the true costs of securing the Games thus joins the burgeoning list of broken promises to the poor and the environment.

One final note: Documents just received from PSEPC consider at some length how 2010 Olympic security is an important matter for the Security and Prosperity Partnership (SPP) of Canada, the US and Mexico. Canada recently signed a military cooperation agreement with the US that allows the military forces of either nation to deploy into each others' territory during various potential "emergencies." Reporter Bob Mackin of 24 *Hours* dug up a Department of Homeland Security document showing their own planned training for the 2010 Olympics. All of this leads to a crucial question: Will US military and police be part of the Olympic security picture? The answer is likely yes. And if they do deploy on Canadian soil, they will operate outside a Canadian chain of command (as they always do in foreign countries)…and they will likely send Canada a bill for their services too.

The Desolate Realities
of the "Greenest Games Ever"

What if government and big business can operate irrespective of public opinion and without having to fairly obtain legitimacy for their projects, while those who protest go into the slammer?

RAFE MAIR, "LET'S LEARN FROM EAGLERIDGE BLUFFS PROTEST," *THE TYEE, MARCH 5, 2007*

Greenwashing the Olympics

THE OLYMPICS always pretends to be green. Like many governments in the West that nowadays try to adopt a greenish hue, the IOC knows that citizens of the same countries are increasingly vocal in stating that environmental concerns outweigh all others. In response, the IOC and local bid organizers have become quite slick in producing "greenwash" to make the Olympics appear to be not only environmentally friendly, but even a leader in preserving the natural world. Nearly four years after winning the bid, VANOC produced a "Sustainability Report" in 2007 that was long on public relations platitudes but remarkably short on true means to protect the environment.

The very notion of environmental sustainability was given official Olympic status in 1998 when the IOC passed Olympic Movement Agenda 21, thus officially joining sports and art as the newest pillar of Olympism. To put it into the proper frame, or more precisely the one the IOC would like you to remember, a recent example from the City of Richmond admirably serves the purpose.

Richmond is the suburb of Vancouver that scored the dubious honor of obtaining the right to construct the Olympic ice skating oval, having snatched it from the neighboring city of Burnaby after a particularly nasty squabble. To put the theft in a somewhat loftier light, Richmond City staff came up with a vision statement that they presented to their city council. The opening paragraph reads:

> Olympism is a state of mind. It envisions a world of peace, international brotherhood and a manifestation of the highest ideals of human achievement. For many around the world, the Olympic Games are seen as a sporting event, but the Olympics are a worldwide cultural festival. Art and athletes are the cornerstone of the Olympic movement. Sport, Culture, Sustainability. These are the "three pillars" of the Olympic movement.[1]

There you have it, it's official, at least in Lausanne, Switzerland, and Richmond, British Columbia: *The environment is important to the IOC and to host cities as well*. Well that is certainly comforting to know, since some of the more jaded of us on the receiving end of the Olympic machine keep pointing to the uniformly failed promises of the past, noting, perhaps uncharitably, that reality doesn't quite match the soaring rhetoric. In fact, vision statements such as that above are like the constitution of the old Soviet Union or George Bush's fervently expressed desire to see democracy bloom in Iraq: words, even uplifting words, but merely that and nothing more. Or, to be even less charitable, rhetorical gymnastics that obfuscate the real agendas being played out behind the scenes. We can know what the founders of the Soviet Union truly intended much in the same way we can peer into the dim recesses of Dubya's brain by surveying the emergent havoc in the world. In the same way, we can actually hold up the IOC's sound bites, amplify them with the lovely prose from Richmond and ask ourselves if the Olympic reality matches Olympic dreams in any honest accounting. The failure to do so, which we will see as the utterly predictable outcome, does not suggest evil intent by the authors who penned the words, merely blind subservience to the official Olympic frame. In some measure, however, when words so totally fail to match reality, when words are used to hide the opposite of what they pretend, one has to also query if at least a casual negligence of the truth, if not outright deception, hasn't been the goal all along.

The Extinction of Eagleridge Bluffs

To examine how green the Olympics really are, no place is more fitting to start at than Eagleridge Bluffs. The history of the "battle for the Bluffs" has already been covered (chapter 9), so it will suffice here to cover the outcomes. On May 2006, 23 protesters were arrested by the West Vancouver Police Department, the officers being as gentle and scrupulous as possible in the face of dozens of watching television cameras. Of those arrested, all but two got monetary fines of varying degrees of severity. All of those so sentenced apologized to the court and to Peter Kiewit and Sons for messing with their construction schedule. The two who refused to apologize, veteran forest activist Betty Krawczyk (aged 78) and native activist Harriet Nahanee (aged 71) got jail time of 10 months and 14 days, respectively. Krawczyk's sentence in part reflected the fact that, several days after her initial arrest, she had returned to the former campsite and blocked Kiewit's machinery once again. She was promptly re-arrested. Nahanee spend her jail time in the Surrey Pretrial Detention Centre, contracted pneumonia while there and died shortly after her release. Krawczyk was released from prison at the end of September 2007.

Rafe Mair, former talk show host at CKNW, had this to say about the Eagleridge Bluffs protest and outcome:

> Of much more serious consequence was the death of native elder Harriet Nahanee, aged 71, after being sent to jail for refusing to apologize for her contempt of court. I don't believe it's a stretch to conclude that Ms. Nahanee, not well at the time, died because she was sent to Surrey Pretrial Centre, a prison for men and a noted hellhole for women in poor health. Another woman, a veteran environmentalist, 78-year-old Betty Krawczyk, will be sentenced today for contempt of court for her non-violent passive resistance at the construction site. We idolize Mahatma Ghandi and jail Betty Krawczyk and Harriet Nahanee. Some democracy.[2]

That was the part of the human toll. The toll on nature was dramatic and utterly betrayed the various green promises made by VANOC and all levels of government. The day after the arrests, I went back to the Bluffs with a camera and filmed as workmen strode along the Bluff, cutting down 500-year-old arbutus trees with chain saws. After a few moments of filming, I became nauseous watching the wanton destruction, shut off the camera and drove away. Over the next few months, Kiewit logged a 50-plus meter-wide swath through various species of old growth on the top of the Bluffs, down through the Larson Creek wetlands and up again over the next rise, a total of 2.4 kilometers hacked through the forest. The loss of the arbutus trees, already endangered in British Columbia, wiped out one of the few such forests in the Lower Mainland. For this road alone, the estimate was that over 12 hectares were destroyed and, at approximately 400 trees per hectare, this represents a loss of some

4,800 trees.[3] Added to this "greenest Olympic Games ever" butcher's bill was the loss of a kilometer of one of the last wetlands in the Lower Mainland, home to the endangered red-legged frog. When done, the highway will have very little setback from what remains of the wetlands, virtually ensuring that this last precious remnant also won't survive the pollutants spewing from the thousands of cars expected to use the route daily. What was once a pristine forest overlooking a highway far below is now an angry gash in the earth. By 2010 it will be a four-lane highway, neatly dividing the new housing units that will eventually straddle it.

The Environmental Impact on the Callaghan Valley

Moving northwards from Eagleridge toward Squamish, the extent of the environmental impacts become ever more obvious. In the 40 or so kilometers of highway undergoing widening, a simple count I conducted revealed over 1,000 more trees down, entire bluffs and cliff faces blown apart and creeks contaminated by slash from felled trees and rocks pulverized by explosives. The damage done along the rest of the route from Squamish to Whistler was not measured, but it is expected to be even greater, given that it accounts for the bulk of the total 120 kilometers from Vancouver to Whistler.

All of this seems bad enough, but once in the Callaghan Valley, the numbers really begin to mushroom. According to the Western Canada Wilderness Committee (WC²) and Whistler municipal Councilor Eckhart Zeidler, over 600 truck loads of old-growth forest will be cut to provide the trails for 23 kilometers of Olympic Nordic events. An average truckload would be 30 cubic meters of wood, somewhere between 20 and 30 trees according to Joe Foy, one of WC²'s directors. From this, we get a low estimate of the amount of mostly old-growth forest cut, almost 19,000 trees.[4]

The number of destroyed trees is already enormous for an event that prides itself on being green, but we haven't really begun to see the enormity of the problem, considering that VANOC and the RCMP have created a new secondary road into the area. Making a minimal assumption that it will duplicate the two-lane existing route (approximately 9 kilometers long and 25 meters wide), 9,000 more trees will be downed. The proposed Nordic Centre is going to be built on previously logged areas according to VANOC, so the number of trees involved here may not be extensive, but won't be zero.

We're still not finished, since VANOC will also construct other sites in the Callaghan, including: "parking areas, three permanent stadiums, two ski jumps, a biathlon facility and servicing areas for sewage, water and power, a

Nordic day lodge, sport operations buildings and maintenance facilities."[5] If we make a bare *minimum* assumption that each of these separate items will be roughly a hectare in size (100 meters by 100 meters) you have 11 hectares or 4,400 more trees that will fall. Parking alone is not going to take only one hectare. A best guess can be made from a ski site such as Mount Seymour in North Vancouver that probably comes in more with something like a five-hectare lot. This puts us at 16 hectares total and 2,000 more trees.

Based on these known items, the total tree loss directly attributable to the Olympics are, at a bare minimum, 39,200, much of it old growth. This is bad enough, not only *not* the greenest games ever, but likely the opposite — and that's saying quite a lot in the context of the Olympics. The only problem is that our calculations are not finished. Native bands will develop a golf course in the south end of the valley as part of a deal with VANOC and the BC government, by which they will cede any overall land claims to the valley. An average-sized golf course is about 75 acres (4,047 square meters per acre) for a total of 30.35 hectares, or 12,140 trees. Many golf courses are easily twice this size.

There's still more. VANOC's plans call for the construction of "legacy trails" throughout the valley, more of the vast developer-driven scheme to put the entire valley into private hands. How many kilometers? Fifty to one hundred. Based on the above calculations, this would add 37,499 to 75,000 trees to the butchery of what had been a relatively untouched alpine valley.

Sure, there had been logging in the past, and yes, there were a few roads, but the absolute scale of what's now happening means the Callaghan is being utterly transformed as it was always planned to be from even before Jack Poole and his colleagues first cooked up the notion of holding the Olympics in Vancouver. The grand total of trees cut down? Somewhere around 89,000 to 126,000, and these are only for the immediate projects, Olympic infrastructure, venues, legacy and behind-the-scenes native deals that we know about. I haven't even added up the tree loss for the skiing venues on the North Shore mountains. As this book goes to press, the Municipality of Whistler is preparing to clearcut a forested area in the village for the Olympic awards stadium. That's all sure a lot of "woody debris," to use VANOC's newly minted politically correct phrase.[6]

Did anyone who wanted the Games think this was going to happen to the Callaghan? The developers did. The rest of the public simply trusted the Bid Corp and government and their green promises, promises that have turned out to be as ephemeral as their promises about the poor, fiscal accountability and all the rest. The 2007 windstorm that slammed into Vancouver Island and the Lower Mainland caused massive damage, including knocking down some

10,000 trees in Vancouver's beloved Stanley Park. Many in the city mourned the devastation in the park, yet few likely had any idea that what had been happening in the Callaghan, let alone what was still to come, was going to be infinitely worse.

The Impact on Endangered Species' Habitat

The Vancouver Olympic preparations were already greatly exceeding the environmental damage of previous Olympics, but there was far more. The first was the loss of habitat for endangered species. One of these was at Larson Creek at Eagleridge Bluffs where a red-legged frog population fought for survival. Ripping out a kilometer of the wetlands seemed appropriate to the Ministry of Transportation and the contractors doing the logging and blasting. To those who worried about such "trivial" concerns as endangered species, Transportation Minister Kevin Falcon replied with a straight face that they had worked out a cunning plan: Kiewit would construct tunnels under the new highway through which the frogs could hop from side to side. What about rare migratory birds that used the bluffs? Nonsense, said Falcon's ministry, "we don't see any birds." In spite of pleas from citizens and West Vancouver's environmental officer, provincial and federal environmental ministries remained utterly silent, even when the former noted that there seemed to be plans afoot for 1,800 new homes on the Ridge.[7]

In the Callaghan Valley, similar habitat loss for the resident grizzly bear and caribou was about to be made worse by the almost 200 kilometers of planned Olympic and legacy trails. Environmental groups such as the WC[2] asked if the provincial Ministry of the Environment would be willing to provide the funds for a study of the issue. No study was needed was the reply, end of story.

The Carbon Footprint
of the 2010 Games

Aside from the trees, frogs, grizzlies and migratory birds, another not so tiny concern was greenhouse gas emissions. Those who've spent the last ten years living in a cave in the desert might be excused for not being aware of the impact of greenhouse gases on global warming and the near consensus in the scientific community that climate change is one of the greatest current threats to human civilization. In poll after poll, Canadians tell their politicians that climate change is the issue most on their minds. Could it be that the frenzied road building, venue construction and tree hacking for a 17-day party might not be such a clever idea from the perspective of the carbon dioxide debt it would generate? It could indeed, but it seemed that the politicians, the Bid Corp and the IOC never gave it a moment's thought as they made their plans for 2010. Did they crunch the numbers to see just how much greenhouse gas would be produced? Nope. So we in 2010 Watch and the Work Less Party did.

The easiest way to calculate carbon debt for the Games is to multiply total government expenditure on the Olympics by the average emissions intensity of the BC economy. A more accurate method would be based on a detailed breakdown of the expenditures and the emissions intensity of each expenditure type, for example in relation to the amounts of cement, steel, chemicals, energy production and other manufacturing associated with any project. In the following, we will take the simplest case and use a calculation based on dollars spent. Greenhouse gas (GHG) release can be estimated based on gross domestic product (GDP). Based on the latest numbers available (2004), BC had an average of 0.52 kilotons (520 tons) per million dollars GDP.[8]

The major construction costs for the Olympics' infrastructure and venues are as follows (in millions of dollars):

Sea to Sky highway upgrade:	$775 million[9]
Convention centre:	$883.2[10]
RAV:	$2050[11]
Vancouver area venues:	$580[12]
City of Vancouver:	$105[13]
Richmond skating oval:	$115.6[14]
Whistler venues:	$38.2[15]
Athletes' Village:	$515.08[16]
UBC (hockey rinks):	$10.2[17]

The total of over $5.077 billion is somewhat higher than the construction costs cited in chapter 12 since these numbers include the total construction costs, not only those borne by the taxpayers. Translating the construction cost into carbon emissions gives us 2,893,890 tons (2.89 megatons) of carbon dioxide.

Commercial air travel is increasingly being seen as a major contributing factor to the planet's carbon debt. Optimistic VANOC and City of Vancouver estimates of travel to Vancouver in 2010 include 250,000 visitors; 10,000 accredited media; 4,000 non-credentialed media; 5,000 athletes, their managers, and assorted hangers on; and 2,000 members of the Olympic family.[18] In addition, security personnel, perhaps 12,000 of the 15,000 who will be coming from somewhere else,[19] brings the total to 283,000 visitors.

Air travel can divided into short-haul (3,540 kilometers round trip), cross-country (10,460 kilometers) and international (20,920 kilometers).[20]

Assuming that roughly a third of all the people coming to the 2010 Games will fall into each category, we end up with 90,333 short-haul, 102,333 cross-country (including security personnel from across Canada) and 90,333 international trips.

To put these numbers into carbon emissions, we can convert from established values of approximately 110 grams of carbon per kilometer flight[21] and calculate that the 283,000 visitors will generate 360,794 tons of CO_2.

Our total carbon emissions for the combined construction and air alone are now over 3 megatons. There is more. Because carbon numbers from various human activities during the Games period are difficult to come by, rough values are based on the Torino Winter Games in 2006, which produced 300,000 tons of carbon emissions. Athens' Summer Games produced 500,000 tons, the equivalent of a city of a million people for the same time period.[22] These numbers excluded construction or air flight values, solely reflecting the carbon footprint of the running of the Games themselves. Nor have we added on the carbon dioxide emissions due to increased traffic along the Sea to Sky highway or all the driving by security personnel. To keep it simple, we'll assume that Vancouver's total for its 17-day Olympic party approximates Torino's 300,000 tons, adding on the Paralympics, another 10 days or 177,000 tons. Their entire Olympic carbon debt will be over 3.7 million tons, or the equivalent of a city of over ten million for a year. Or viewed another way, based on 2003 carbon emission measurements, Vancouver's Olympic Games will emit more carbon than the annual amount of over 77 of 191 countries on the planet, basically more than the Republic of Armenia at 3.43 megatons.[23] Viewed in terms of British Columbia alone, whose emissions in 2004 totaled 66.8 megatons of CO_2,[24] the 2010 Games will be responsible for more than 5 percent of one year's worth of emissions, or 70 percent of BC's total in the same 17-day period.

Putting out the equivalent of Armenia's one year total or 5 percent of BC's just to host a party for Jack Poole and his developer friends seems particularly obscene. This is so far from "sustainable," especially given the current public sentiment on the issue, that the third pillar of Olympism is just like all the other promises — so much hot air.

Five months after 2010 Watch and the Work Less Party finished the assessment of the environmental impact of the 2010 Games, the world-renowned David Suzuki Foundation waded into the fray with their own calculations about carbon dioxide emissions for 2010 and how to remediate them.[25] The report had been commissioned by VANOC, and the Foundation was paid $10,000 for what could only be charitably described as a shoddy piece of work. Not only had the Foundation violated their own previous stance about not getting involved in politics — for example, they had not taken a position on Eagleridge Bluffs for just this reason — they were also now taking money from one side of the debate. The report itself not only ignored the impact on habitat, trees and at-risk species, but completely ignored some 90 percent of the sources of carbon dioxide emissions, namely that of the massive infrastructure projects linked to the Games. The Foundation had, in brief, put their environmental stamp of approval on the 2010 Games and, indeed, on the Olympics in general. For many in the environmental movement in BC, this was a betrayal of the worst sort. VANOC, needless to say, was delighted by what they saw as a major propaganda coup.

Artificial Snow:
Let's Poison the Watershed

Finally, there is the sticky problem posed by the use of artificial snow. In the winter of 2005, IOC President Jacques Rogge was in town and noted the absence of snow on Vancouver's North Shore mountains, the site of many of the 2010 events. Not to worry, "they [VANOC] can make artificial snow," Rogge grandly announced. What Rogge doesn't know, or perhaps just forgot, is that there are only two primary ways to make artificial snow. The first involves using wastewater. Aside from the fact that the water is not necessarily suitable for the environment, there is the problem that the ambient temperature needs to be −5°C or lower to make snow. As this is rarely the case on the North Shore mountains in February, there is only Plan B, the use of various chemicals. Currently the most common, Snomax©, is made from the protein of the bacterium *Pseudomonas syringae* . Other methods use soaps, detergents, fungi, lichens and other compounds. A relative newcomer to the market uses a class of chemicals called trisiloxanes, which are organosilicone polymers. In snow-making, their utility comes from their properties as surfactants, that is they reduce the surface tension of water to allow the water molecules to freeze at higher temperatures. The trisiloxane product is marketed under the name of Drift©. Trisiloxane, however, is not only used to make artificial snow; it's also used as a pesticide.[26]

So imagine this — the winter of 2010 comes, and there is no snow. Out come the snow machines, and soon Drift covers large parts of the North Shore mountains and maybe the Callaghan, too. Maybe it's perfectly safe for the environment, but then again, maybe it's not. Maybe it's a concentration issue, or safe for some species but not others? Now as we get into late March, the masses of trisiloxane snow begin to melt, and where does the molecule go? It goes into the watershed and from there into the rivers and eventually into

Howe Sound, right into the path of migratory species such as salmon. For those not from BC who might not know, the salmon fishery is already in big trouble. A good strong shot of pesticide is unlikely to make it better. But once again, there is only thunderous silence from VANOC and all levels of government who may not even be aware there is a problem.

VANOC's Approach to "Sustainability"

VANOC's 2006 Sustainability Report,[27] on the issue of carbon emissions, noted piously that it would be great to do something about paying off the carbon debt, then blithely sidestepped any responsibility. This was understandable given that it's hard to maintain the illusion of greenness when you are responsible for more carbon dioxide than Armenia in a year. We at 2010 Watch and the Work Less Party asked if they were going to try to address the problem by buying carbon credits. Nope. Would the government? Nope. In any event, what would they buy the credits with? More of our tax dollars, of course. What about either VANOC or the government producing environmental impact assessments before, during and after the Games, as suggested by one environmental group?[28] Nope, too late for the first, which would have highlighted the complete idiocy of calling the Games green in advance; no interest in exposing the level of destruction during the preparations; and absolutely, certainly no chance of evaluating the impact after the Games when the mess will be obvious for anyone to see.

VANOC continues to crow about their environmental stewardship, noting proudly the various green building standards that the Vancouver and Whistler Athletes' Villages are supposed to achieve and the fact that they are burying in landfill the "woody debris" from their construction activities. Woody debris? Do they perhaps mean the remains of the 100,000 plus trees that have or will be cut down for the Games. Cute; perhaps the BC forestry industry should adopt the same euphemism: "That's not a clearcut, folks, that's a future meadow…those piles of 'woody debris' are just the leftover scraps from the stuff that used to be in the meadow." VANOC and the BC government have also violated the IOC's stated requirement for the host city to carry out environmental impact studies before starting work. Obviously, VANOC knew the IOC was really kidding and didn't give a fig about true sustainability.

This would be laughable if the outcome weren't so tragic for both humans and their environment. Amazingly, in the face of all of this, most environmental groups have remained silent, except for the Suzuki Foundation as cited above. WC[2] had tried to address some of these issues, but from the rest there was nothing. Just why this is so remains a mystery.

Environmental Impacts of Past Olympic Games

Were past Olympics any different? While Vancouver's may be the most destructive yet, no Games in memory have been environmentally friendly. Winter Games tend to be worse than Summer Games since they occur outside of cities and thus have greater impacts on wildlife and habitat, which is not to say that Summer Olympics are impact free. The Sydney and Athens Olympics both destroyed marine habitat, and both had massive carbon footprints. Winter Games, as we've seen, do this in spades. Although numbers are hard to come by for the older Olympics, some key findings are available for the more recent Games. Salt Lake City failed to meet their transportation goals for bussing visitors to Olympic sites; instead, they mowed down forests and constructed parking lots for private cars. Torino's Olympics included the loss of 4,000 old-growth trees in sensitive alpine forests, diversion of streams and the loss of habitat.[29] Lillehammer's Olympics (1994), also touted as "green," resulted in a loss of wetlands, forest and public green space and damage to lynx and bird habitat.[30]

What the Third Pillar Really Represents

The above information provides the definitive answer to the question of whether the Olympics are environmentally friendly or sustainable. They never have been in the past. Vancouver's track record to date is so grotesquely not green, so flagrantly at odds with reality that anyone who claims otherwise is simply in denial. It's either that or that boosters are part of the cabal creating the environmental havoc for their own profit. To call the Olympics, Vancouver's in particular, environmental disasters would not be in the slightest incorrect. To call them criminal would not be wrong either.

All of this perfectly illustrates the old adage, "Go big or go home." For example, compare the circumstances of Order of Canada winner Poole with fellow member, ex-media baron, Conrad Black. Lord Black of Cross Harbour, as he was known after he'd been elevated to the peerage by Queen Elizabeth, defrauded shareholders of his former company of millions of dollars. By the time these words are printed, Black will be serving the jail time he richly deserves. Poole, in contrast, "invented" the Vancouver Olympics, in the process defrauding British Columbians (and other Canadians) of billions of dollars and is far less likely to find jail time than to follow former Vancouver mayor Larry Campbell into the Senate.[31] For me, what he deserves and what he gets don't quite match.

I have this fantasy in which I sit down with the VANOC bigwigs over a pint or two, just us lads here, so we can all be as candid as we like. I can imagine

Jack Poole loosening up after a few drinks; it's harder to imagine John Furlong as anything besides uptight, but let's just try for a moment to picture the scene. Poole, made loquacious by the booze, characteristic smirk firmly fixed on his face, leans across the table while Furlong fidgets, and says, "You think this is bad? Wait for it...when we're done it's going to be wall-to-wall condos as far as the eye can see up the Sea to Sky corridor and a four-season resort in the Callaghan. We'll show you carbon debts!" And, indeed, I suspect he would.

Still, I can dream...dream that some of the real estate landmines strewn about and covered over by Poole in his haste to grab Olympic goodies could still, in the days before 2010, go off under the Olympic machine. Some of these may be slowly rising to the surface in the Callaghan...or so one can still hope.[32]

OOOOO

THE FIFTH RING

Resistance to the Olympics

• • • • •

The patronizing "people will forget" theme was central to Olympic supporters' attempts to downplay the seriousness of the bribery scandal [in Salt Lake City]. It portrayed potential Olympic spectators and television viewers as unreflective dupes with short attention spans and no critical powers, while at the same time exploiting the pure athlete and Olympic spirit rhetoric.

HELEN LENSKYJ,
INSIDE THE OLYMPIC INDUSTRY, POWER, POLITICS, AND ACTIVISM

CHAPTER 16

Breaking the Rings

*The successes of some anti-Olympic and Olympic watchdog
organizations, while limited, provide hope for future
interventions aimed at stopping the seemingly inexorable
progress of the Olympic machine. However, with the huge
public relations budgets at the disposal of Olympic boosters,
the challenge to grassroots protesters is formidable.*

HELEN J. LENSKYJ,
INSIDE THE OLYMPIC INDUSTRY: POWER, POLITICS, AND ACTIVISM,
STATE UNIVERSITY OF NEW YORK PRESS, ALBANY, 2000, P. 131

Understanding Community

JULY 22, 2007. It's an unusually cold and rainy day in Vancouver, and it's been like this for well over a week. Someone remarks that it seems more like November than July. For whatever reason, summer just hasn't really come this year, not yet at least. Elsewhere in the city, spirits may be as damp as the weather, but here on Commercial Drive in East Vancouver, people are outside having fun. Thousands have turned out for a car-free street festival organized by local volunteers. This is the third such festival this summer; in turn this is the second year the festival has been run. With no cars allowed along a stretch from 1st Avenue to Venables Street, some eight blocks of normally busy street are for one day a pedestrian mall. Musicians perform, jugglers juggle and kids scamper or are pushed in strollers as young and old, locals and visitors, activists and the merely curious alike wander past the impromptu food stalls, artisan tents and the information tables set up by various social and political advocacy groups that now fill the streets and sidewalks. The Green Party (BC) is here next to the Work Less Party; a few feet away, a woman's support group has set up shop next to the Anti-Poverty Committee, the Sierra Club and many others. The overall message of the organizers is about the intrusion of cars in our lives, and for one day, the purpose is to take back the streets for people. There is a more specific reason as well: The Ministry of Transportation under Kevin Falcon, of Eagleridge Bluffs notoriety, is pushing hard for the Gateway project, the plan to massively expand the various highways linking the Fraser Valley and Vancouver. In some sense, it's a spillover of the rapidly expanding infrastructure construction nightmare that has slopped over from the Olympics. If Falcon has his way, Gateway will also expand the Trans Canada Highway right into East Vancouver, dumping thousands of additional cars into the neighborhood each day. Opposition to the project is strong in East Vancouver and elsewhere in the Lower Mainland. Falcon is no more likely to listen to the opponents of Gateway than he was to those who stood in his way at Eagleridge, but this time the opposition is stronger, more vocal and remarkably united. There is also no nonsense in this part of town about loving the Olympics and wanting them to be green. Falcon is going to need all the riot cops he can muster if he is serious about slamming the highway into East Vancouver.

Taking it all in, it's hard not to be struck with the real sense of community on exhibit here on the "Drive," even the notion that this is how a liberated, grassroots society can and should function. It's revolutionary *and* it's fun. The anarchist writer Emma Goldman once said, "If I can't dance, I don't want to be part of your revolution," and she would have loved it.[1]

While both Commercial Drive and the Olympic "movement" call themselves communities, the first one clearly is, the second just as clearly is not. The Commercial Drive community and the vision it inspires typifies everything that the Olympics claims to be but fails to deliver: Commercial Drive's is open, egalitarian and creative. The Olympic organizations at all levels are elite, authoritarian and corporate. And, to add one more term describing the Olympics, "artificial." This is what the late novelist Kurt Vonnegut once called a "noyau," an artificial collection of people based on a trivial commonality, like all the people born in a particular place regardless of the meaning of that place, as if some sterile fact of geography alone could convey true affinity. The Olympics is a true noyau; it's a collection of cult fanatics, athletes and other adherents linked only by the brand of the five rings. Well, there is one exception to this, one real "community" within the Olympic family: the developers.

Resistance in Other Cities to the Olympics

As we've seen in previous chapters, some form of resistance to the powers behind the Olympic machine — those both inside and outside the IOC — has been in existence since the "people's" Olympics of the early 20th century. These counter-Olympics represented an effort to replace the IOC's Olympic Games with those truly belonging to ordinary people and the athletes. This effort died in the years leading up to World War II. In the late 1990s, the short-lived Olympic Athletes Together Honorably (OATH) movement from athletes within the Olympic movement tried to establish the precedence of the athletes themselves. I say establish, rather than reestablish, since it is not clear to me that the Olympics was ever truly about the athletes rather than the nobility who fed on them and on their fantasies of ancient Greece.

The first protest movement of modern times that linked the Olympic Games to local and national issues occurred in Mexico City in 1968, leaving hundreds of protesters dead or wounded in its wake. The IOC remained unmoved and unreformed. Other bid and host cities since then have experienced protests that, while not of the severity of Mexico's, nevertheless showed that opposition to the Olympics existed. In general, cities where opponents were able to field a strong, vocal and united coalition were able to derail bids early in the game. Examples include Finland's bid for the 2006 Winter Games, Amsterdam's No Olympics Amsterdam (1992), Melbourne with its Bread Not Circuses (1996), Berlin's Nolympic group (2000), Toronto's Bread Not Circuses (1996, 2008) and New York's Hell's Kitchen group, the Clinton Special District Coalition (2012). Tactics varied from large-scale street protests timed to IOC visits (Berlin, Toronto), to sabotage and vandalism against bid organizers or the IOC (Berlin, Amsterdam) and general education campaigns (all). In Berlin, the anti-Olympic groups had the help of the German Green Party. Vancouver opponents had the support of the provincial Green Party, but it alone was unable to overcome the power of the Olympic boosters in both governing and official opposition civic and provincial parties.

Where the opposition failed to achieve solidarity and any unity of effort due to internal squabbling or other divisions during the bid period (Atlanta, Sydney), they were ineffective at stopping the bids in their cities. Salt Lake City's organized resistance was minor, and the group Utahns for Responsible Public Spending was not an effective force. Vancouver, with its endless doctrinal infighting amongst progressives, not to mention the active co-option of potential opposition by the Bid Corp, joins this list and typified the phenomenon already cited by Lenskyj:

> The limited capacity of progressive individuals and groups to work together in coalition on Olympic-related issues — a challenge for both the fragmented non-Indigenous groups that constituted the

Australian left, and for the politically diverse Indigenous community
— was further undermined by police, government and Olympic industry officials.[2]

Opposition groups continued to be active in some host cities, although the impact of such groups was limited, and their efforts focused on education. These
included First Nations protests in Calgary (1988), Nagano's (1998) Anti-Olympic People's Network protests, and Torino's (2006) Nolimpiadi! Committee.
While Nagano's opposition was focused and had been in existence from the
1980s, it was unable to overcome the corporations and different levels of government that lined up behind the bid. Sydney's anti-Olympics groups failed
to stop the Games, but did have some limited local impact. A group called
the Anti-Olympic Alliance (AOA) engaged in educational efforts, as well as
some direct action. AOA spokesperson Vicki Sentas summed up what it took
to form an effective opposition, writing in the student paper *Vertigo*, "What
brings these groups together under a common umbrella…is that the Olympics
is the cause and the effect of mass social and urban change and the shrinking
of public space…there is an increase in social divisions, with the rich getting
richer and the poor getting poorer."[3]

One thing that becomes crystal clear is this: Opposition groups able to
convince the IOC that there was some risk associated with holding the Games
in their city succeeded; those who did not seem a threat to the IOC's Olympic
frame or profits failed.

In general, once the IOC has decided on a host city, it is all over. There was,
however, one success story where a city stopped the Games *after* they were
awarded. Denver, slated to hold the 1976 Winter Games, became the only city
to reject the IOC after the fact. Pushing the no side was Citizens for Colorado's
Future, a group of environmentalists and others who based their opposition
on the tax burden that the Games would impose on Coloradans and on the
inevitably negative environmental impacts. This last concern married up with
worries about uncontrolled urban and regional growth. State and city referen-
dums in 1972 said no to the Games. Ironically, Coloradans may have successfully stopped the Olympics but got the growth anyway, testament to the power
of the developers.

The Opposition to Vancouver's 2010 Games

NO GAMES 2010 and its eventual Coalition formed the first true opposition
to Vancouver's bid and remained active up until the IOC's decision to award
the Games to Vancouver in July 2003. Following this, NO GAMES gave way

to a watchdog group, 2010 Watch, that continued the battle using a website (2010watch.com), press releases and public critiques of the emerging Games preparations.[4] While much of this did reach the public and doubtlessly had some impact, they did not appreciably stop Games preparations from going ahead.

The Eagleridge protesters, as we've seen, were not anti-Olympics. As a consequence, once the members of this group were arrested and the work on the Ridge begun, they had nowhere to go with their opposition. Some First Nations groups, notably the St'at'imc, opposed the Games on their territories but had to face the fact that senior members of some of the affected bands had been brought onside with payments of cash and/or land. Nevertheless, at least some native groups began to be militant: The Native Warrior Society stole the Olympic flag from outside Vancouver City Hall in protest over the death of Squamish elder Harriet Nahanee,[5] and native anti-Olympic resistance began to emerge as a force in 2007. Various anti-poverty groups in Vancouver's Downtown Eastside became active relatively late in the game. The Anti-Poverty Committee conducted small-scale but vocal protests that caught the media's and public's attention for a time. The Downtown Eastside Residents Association and the Pivot Legal Society also used the Olympics to highlight the plight of the poor and homeless. The efforts of all three groups were not without effect on public opinion but remained unable to alter Vancouver's official neglect of those so marginalized. Indeed, the City rushed forward with plans to further criminalize poverty with Mayor Sam Sullivan's Project Civil City.

On the education front, 2010 Watch attracted the support of a new political party, the Work Less Party (WLP), founded by social activist Conrad Schmidt.[6] The WLP became an active source of media releases; promoted press conferences about the emerging social, environmental and economic costs of the 2010 Games; promulgated a more accurate mascot for the Games ("Ollie, the 2010 Olympic skunk") and further attempted to open up the frame on the Olympics themselves with the release of Schmidt's documentary film, *Five Ring Circus*. Each of these efforts met with some success as part of an ongoing education campaign really directed at future bid cities. This effort continues with the current book.

So what can really be done to stop the Olympic machine? This is the topic of the next chapter.

CHAPTER 17

No Games! A Citizen's Manual of Resistance to the Olympics

In any case, these Games are going ahead whether they cost $580 million or $2.5 billion...over the protests of the vocal minority that opposes them. These critics contend that the money spent on the Games should have been diverted to more worthwhile causes. And now they are demanding a referendum on hosting the Games. But Vancouver voters have been there, done that.... Opponents should give up on obstruction and work instead towards ensuring that governments and Games organizers commit to practices of accountability and full disclosure in all their Olympic undertakings.

VANCOUVER SUN EDITORIAL[1]

In consensus reality (the blue pill perspective) "left" and "right" are the two ends of the political spectrum.... This perspective on the political process, and on the roles of left and right, is very far from reality. It is a fabricated collective illusion. Morpheus tells Neo that the Matrix is "the world that was pulled over your eyes to hide you from the truth.... As long as the Matrix exists, humanity cannot be free." Consensus political reality is precisely such a matrix.

RICHARD K. MOORE, "ESCAPING THE MATRIX,"
WHOLE EARTH, SUMMER 2000

"Red Pill" Moments

VANOC had been promising to provide quarterly financial and progress reports for years, but had only begun to do so in the spring of 2006. These releases were the happy "everything is on time and on budget" mantra that had become their trademark. One problem was that all the financials were unaudited and, hence, unverifiable. Not only that, but rather than releasing it at a conventional press conference with CEO John Furlong taking questions, VANOC had come up with a new scheme: a press conference by teleconference. Many journalists I knew were increasingly pissed off by this, noting that VANOC had become remarkably skittish with the press in general. When VANOC missed their first deadline, Conrad Schmidt of the Work Less Party and I, representing 2010 Watch, decided to mix it up and put VANOC on the spot: If Furlong wouldn't show up and do a real press conference, we would hold a "shadow press conference," the one that VANOC didn't want to give. Each time we did, we highlighted more of the broken promises to the poor, the environment, fiscal transparency and cost overruns, the now familiar litany.

In the summer of 2006, we decided that VANOC's deceptions and broken promises constituted a breach of contract with the people of British Columbia. If the promises they had made to get the Games were bogus, then the contract was broken. Hence, there was a need for a real referendum to ask British Columbians a simple question: Do you still want the Games to go on? We knew that neither VANOC nor the government would entertain the notion of holding one, and indeed they didn't, but the referendum call got reported widely and drew considerable public support. So much so, in fact, that it warranted the editorial quoted above. We had clearly touched a nerve, a sign that we were doing our jobs right. The editorial also further exposed the lie about democratic institutions in British Columbia and elsewhere. To further understand this, it's time to bring on Richard K. Moore.

Moore, an American expatriate author living in Ireland, uses the "red pill" scene from the movie *The Matrix* as a metonymy for modern political illusion and reality. In this scene, the hero, Neo (Keanu Reeves), is offered the choice of two pills, blue and red, by resistance leader Morpheus (Laurence Fishburne). If Neo takes the blue pill, he will return to his dream world, one in which he has a humdrum job and events go on in a predictable manner. If he takes the red pill, he will be launched into the real world in which a tiny group of rebels battle a machine culture that has enslaved most of humanity. Neo takes the red pill, his eyes are opened and he more-or-less willingly joins the resistance. Moore uses this story to explain how most of us are taught to perceive the political structures surrounding us, our perceptions not based on the way the world actually is, but as a construct directly arising from years of parental and social conditioning and heavily reinforced by media saturation advertising. Much of what we think we know about human affairs and history, Moore argues, is simply wrong. Rather, our "knowledge" is the sanitized version told to us by the elite who really rule. As long as we remain locked into the official frame about how the world works, we can't make any but the most superficial changes. In other words, you can't really fix something if you don't know it's broken. In context to economic globalization, Moore writes:

> In matrix reality, globalization is not a project but rather the inevitable result of beneficial market forces; genocide in Africa is no fault of the West's, but is due to ancient tribal rivalries; every measure demanded by globalization is referred to as "reform" (the word is never used with irony). "Democracy" and "reform" are frequently used together, always leaving the subtle impression that one has something to do with the other. The illusion is presented that all economic boats are rising, and if yours isn't, it must be your own fault: you aren't "competitive" enough. Economic failures are explained away as "temporary adjustments," or else the victim (as in South Korea or Russia) is blamed for not being sufficiently neoliberal. "Investor confidence" is referred to with the same awe and reverence that earlier societies might have expressed toward the "will of the gods."[2]

Sometimes, however, events are so startling that they present us with an unexpected choice: to accept the "official" political reality and go back to sleep, or to take the red pill and break free of our conditioning. Moore calls these "red pill moments" when the chance to escape is ours.

The Vancouver bid, like those of past Olympic cities, presented the public with a number of red pill moments, many of which played into the hands of NO GAMES 2010 in our attempts to deconstruct the official Olympic frame. Invariably, these arose out of Bid Corp attempts to bolster their arguments in favor of Vancouver hosting the Games. One of my favorites concerned the issue of leverage. Basically, the argument went as follows: We need the Games in order to get money from the federal or provincial government to build the new convention center (or whatever other mega project was being touted); without the Olympics, the project will never succeed on its own because the different levels of government won't want to fund it. For many, the leverage argument was a concrete example of how Olympic pixie dust could help pry money loose from Victoria or Ottawa. Buried inside the argument, however, was a pair of red pills. First, who says that *we, Joe and Jane Citizen,* want to leverage money for a convention center at all? Maybe the Vancouver Board of Trade wants this, but do we? Second, in a small "l" liberal democracy, the people are supposed to create and control the government. If this is true, and we've been taught all along that it is, what's all this crap about leverage? Why do *we* have to leverage *our* own money back at all?

Those who began to have such doubts were reassured by every major party that all was well and that the bid really represented the coming together across the political spectrum to bring the benefits of the Games to all British Columbians. Again, Moore's essay helps to understand what the game was all about:

> In consensus reality (the blue-pill perspective) "left" and "right" are the two ends of the political spectrum. Politics is a tug-of-war between competing factions, carried out by political parties and elected representatives. Society gets pulled this way and that within the political spectrum, reflecting the interests of whichever party won the last election. The left and right are therefore political enemies. Each side is convinced that it knows how to make society better; each believes the other enjoys undue influence; and each blames the other for the political stalemate that apparently prevents society from dealing effectively with its problems.[3]

Moore's essay exposes what many already know: There is more to political reality than a neatly divided two-dimensional spectrum of left versus right, separated by some sort of squishy center. There are numerous examples of just how silly the notion is today, but none more glaring than that of former British Prime Minister Tony Blair. After all, what else can one make of the spectacle of a notionally "Labour" prime minister acting as George Bush's pet poodle, privatizing services in Britain, singing the praises of a globalized economy run by corporations and following Dubya to imperial wars around the globe? There is nothing in any of this that is even vaguely left-leaning, let alone pro-labor or socialist. So what is Blair? The answer is that Blair represents powerful interests for whom the Labour Party was, for a time, merely a flag of convenience.

In Vancouver, the Olympic political lineup proved the same principle at the local level. Vancouver and British Columbia have historically been a battleground of leftist unions, COPE and the NDP slugging it out with the official right wing composed of the NPA, BC Liberals and their provincial predecessors, the Socreds. Once upon a time it might have been as simple as left and right, but that was then, and in 2003 none of it was simple, especially when it came to the Olympics. If looked at from the correct angle, the Vancouver Olympic Bid and aftermath revealed the truth: left, right, up, down; it was all about special interests that were equally at home at NDP picnics as they were having cocktails with the Fraser Institute.[4] These same special interests controlled provincial parties, civic parties, federal parties and, behind the scenes, were all in lockstep about how the Olympics could be manipulated to divert taxpayer dollars into dormant megaprojects and real estate developments. Many average citizens, including the rank and file of the various official parties, were bewildered by the strange alliances that seemed to form around the Olympic flag, by the backslaps and high-fives between official political rivals. The Olympic bid and its aftermath are thus clear red pill moments for those who chose to accept them. Once swallowed, each red pill gives a peek behind the curtain to see who the great and mighty Oz might really be. Certainly, no one I know who has taken the Olympic red pill has ever been the same politically as they were before. Active resistance begins with awareness.

A lot of people who were undecided about how to vote in the plebiscite never faced a red pill moment, but enough did to coerce from VANOC and the provincial governing party jaded retorts along the lines of "Don't be naïve, this is how the system works." Depending on political experience and level of cynicism, the public's response varied. Most of the founders of NO GAMES had no illusions about the political process, so the fact that the other side brought it up simply reinforced a message we had been trying to deliver: "You, the citizen-taxpayer, are not really in control, no matter what you've been told." Those who had always believed the myths of popular control were initially shocked and dispirited by just how openly the pro-bid forces revealed the truth. Eventually, the bid side realized that this argument was a potential minefield and quickly abandoned it for the safer territory of patriotism.[5]

Breaking the Olympic Frame

A crucial concept in military planning is "center of gravity," that key characteristic, capability or locality from which any force derives its freedom of action, physical strength or will to fight. If you protect your own center of gravity while knocking out the other side's, you will win the battle; lose it and you are very likely to get clobbered. Although normally considered in a military context, it equally well describes any set of opponents, including those for and against the Olympics.

The center of gravity for the IOC is their ability to successfully deliver a sports spectacle to a world television market. To ensure that they can do so, they have to carefully pick the host city. One obvious consideration is the expected television audience and what it wants to see. The received wisdom in IOC circles is that viewers—especially those in the North American market—

don't want to see the Olympics on the same continent twice in a row. Whether or not geography plays a significant role, it is abundantly clear that the prime factor appears to be how slavishly the bid city kowtows to the IOC during the months leading to the decision. To the IOC hierarchy, serious bowing and scraping tells them that a candidate city will do whatever it takes to make them happy…and delivering the spectacle is going to make them far richer than they are now, which in turn will make them very happy indeed.

For the local bid organizers of any city, their center of gravity in the months before the IOC's decision is the ability to protect the frame of the debate: elite sports for peaceful cooperation amongst the nations; goodies for the host city. After the bid, their center of gravity becomes the same as that of the IOC. For any opposition, the center of gravity is their ability to get their countervailing message out to the public, not an easy task when the bulk of the mainstream media are already supporting the bid. The pro-Games folks get endless free publicity, not to mention always being bankrolled by the different levels of government. Opposition groups can't usually afford to advertise; instead, they have to make news in order to have their voices heard. One solution to this comes from Helen Lenskyj who suggests running municipal slates of anti-Olympic candidates for local office in candidate cities, using the resulting campaign to force a full discussion of the Olympic frame and the potential impact of the Games on that city.

The maintenance or destruction of the Olympic frame is thus the key to who is going to win. In the pre-decision days, if an Olympics opposition gets locked into the pro-Olympic frame, that is, that the Games are about the use of elite sports for peaceful competition, they are already doomed. Accept the Olympic frame, and everything else unravels. All the fiscal disasters that happen, all the environmental destruction, everything that has gone wrong in previous Games gets blamed on failures of performance, not on the reality that such things never mattered to the Olympic organizers or the IOC in the first place.

Early on, when the opposition is still young, the media will seek to put it on the spot: "Yes, we know you are against the Games coming here to Vancouver (or wherever), but you're not anti-Olympics, are you?" This is the absolutely crucial question. To flinch now, to answer, "No, we're not against the Olympics, but…", you're done like dinner. The media just parked you firmly in the frame, and you will not likely get out. The correct answer is this: "Yes, we *are* against the Olympics." The media rep will react with a combination of shock and titillation, and ask, "But wouldn't you agree that the Olympics have fostered peaceful competition between nations?" The answer, "Maybe, but they've also encouraged sports nationalism, fiscal irresponsibility, environmental destruction and the marginalization of the poor. We're not in favor of any of that. Are you?" If the opposition answers this way, it has started to shift the frame. At this point the opposition can offer the alternative — and real — frame. The IOC is in the business of marketing sport for television by showing cute young athletes in Spandex/Gortex; the local bid corp is composed of real estate developers who likely don't give a tinker's damn about sports but see in the Olympics a way to advance their pet projects with public money under the smoke and mirrors of the IOC's big circus tent. The press will be shocked at first — but this makes good copy. Remember that the center of gravity for the opposition is the ability to get their message out there into the world. If it makes news, future access to the media will grow rather than shrink. Just like any successful advertising — and the IOC is a master of this — the more times the opposition can get the media to describe its frame on the Games, the greater the damage it does to the pro-Games center of gravity as cognitive dissonance about the Olympics grows.

Some people in any broad coalition may be uncomfortable being anti-Olympic as they will consider this to be too radical a position. It will be a challenge to more-aware members to bring them around. Fortunately, this is becoming ever easier due to the Web and the emergence of opposition groups in virtually all Olympic bid cities. The latter groups are now starting to coalesce, sharing information and tactics. And one absolutely crucial piece of information is that cited above: no group that claims to be pro-Olympics ever got *any* concessions from the IOC or the local Games organizers. Acting pro-Games, with the "but we just want" clause tagged on, and any opposition gets steamrollered by the machine just like the sincere folks at Eagleridge.

If all of this goes well, if the opposition does succeed in shifting the frame, it might just convince enough of its fellow citizens that they want no part of the Olympic circus at all. Keep in mind also that the IOC will be monitoring events in the bid city. If they see the veil starting to slip and the real frame about to become public knowledge, they may ditch a particular city early on and save the opposition the trouble of a long fight.

Various Olympic opposition groups in the past had hoped to force the IOC and the local bid organizations and government into accepting reforms and some contractual conditions as the price of staging the Olympics. The proposed reforms put forward by groups in Toronto, Sydney and elsewhere were merely common sense. Toronto's Bread Not Circuses proposed a number of main items in their list, including full and democratic participation of the public, full accountability (including financial guarantees), proactive measures to

ensure social equity and the protection of the environment.[6] There was nothing radical here at all, merely a call for the organizing committee to live up to
the most basic of such standards if it wanted to host the Olympic Games. Such
conditions should also not have been seen as scary or contentious by the IOC.
After all, both the IOC and all local bid committees claim to believe in precisely the same things that Bread Not Circuses was proposing. The problem,
again, was the frame: The only people who really believe the official version are
its victims. The developers behind the bid and the IOC know the game. Living up to their professed ideals would only ruin what they have set out to do.
What, after all, is the point of staging the Olympics if no goodies are going to
fall off the taxpayer tree? Needless to say, such conditions were not accepted by
Toronto or other bid cities.

Revisiting the Frame
after the IOC Picks the Target City

In Vancouver's bid, as in so many others, the opposition did not succeed in
shifting the frame before the IOC awarded ("sold" would be the more apt
word) the Games to the city. We in NO GAMES were faced with a question that we had no ready answer to then: Can an opposition still win? As
we discovered in the ensuing years, the answer was this: locally, no; globally,
yes. Locally, we had lost the battle to keep the Games from coming and were
left fighting a rear guard action. The projects that the Bid Corp really wanted
were already on track, the money would soon be pulled from public coffers,
the areas slated for destruction were just waiting for the chain saws and backhoes. Short of massive protests — and if we could have organized these at all,
the time to do so was before the decision — we couldn't stop the Olympic machine afterwards.

What we began to realize, however, was that we could take steps to minimize the negative impacts: Our constant attention helped force at least lip
service to fiscal transparency, to protecting the poor and to minimizing environmental damage. Not that anything was done about any of these. Other
groups seeing the obvious deception began staging street protests and threatening a boycott of the Games. These actions are in their early days but may yet
serve to moderate the eagerness of government and the bid organization to ignore all the promises they made before the Games were awarded.

There is a larger role that an Olympic opposition can play after the IOC's
choice of the target city: It can help save future Olympic cities by making the
Games so unsuccessful that only a fool would want to bid on them. It can also
perfect tactics that opposition groups in other countries may be able to use to

effect. In other words, the opposition's efforts now have to shift to attacking the IOC's center of gravity, that is, their ability to pull off a successful spectacle. If it does, while its own city may be Olympic road kill, it can still help to win the long-term goal of defeating the machine itself. Below I'll consider some possible ways to do this.

The utility of shifting the frame locally, however, ends the day the IOC leaves town. Those who were against the Games understand what just happened; those who were undecided may have enjoyed the party or are waking up to the financial hangover that they'd just as soon forget. The booster crowd will be in the midst of an "amnesia and euphoria phenomenon" to use Lenskyj's term. The media may start picking up on any negative outcomes, but it is all irrelevant now to the local population: The IOC is gone, the party is over, the damage is done. All of this might be relevant to citizens in future bid cities, but their own corporate media will do their level best to make sure that they don't hear any of the complaints and bitterness emanating from Vancouver.

Olympic Reform:
From Forlorn Hope to Active Resistance

The question is often asked, "What would it take for the Olympics to be about sports, about what the IOC and others claim is the true motivation of the Olympic movement?" Here are some of the solutions put forward over the last dozen years.

Making the IOC and Bid Organizations
Honor Their Contracts with the Public

Just as various organizations have tried to set contractual conditions for bid organizations, lists of similar essential items — in essence, reforms — have been proposed to make the IOC into that thing it already claims to be. None of this is going to happen, of course, but it is worthwhile to know what an IOC that truly reflected "Olympic ideals" would actually look like. Many of these reforms overlap with those cited above for the bid organizations, including cleaning up the IOC's structure and function, removing the institutional resistance to public accountability and ending the IOC's public relations campaigns to push the Games.[7] None of this is impossible or even all that hard to achieve, not unless the Olympic Games are not really about what the frame says they are about. The failure of the IOC to institute meaningful reform or the bid committees to accept the most reasonable of conditions proves beyond doubt that the true Olympic frame of television rights and real estate holds sway over all things Olympic.

Stop Moving the Circus Tents Around

Andrew Jennings, George Monbiot and others have an absurdly simple suggestion that doesn't even require the IOC to reform at all: If the Olympic Games
are really about sports, they don't have to be continually on the go, an endless
traveling five-ring circus. Monbiot points out that there are more than enough
world venues for both Summer and Winter Games for the next 100 years, so,
really, why do they have to go anywhere? Just pick a Summer venue, say Athens since the ancient Games were in Greece; pick a Winter venue in Europe
or North America…. Now, we're done with the endless costly bids, the fiscal
overruns that bankrupt cities, the attendant social and environmental destruction. Simple, right? Well, actually no. The IOC and local bid organization re-
buttal to this is usually the refrain, "But if the Games don't move, it *deprives
other cities of the honor* of hosting the Olympics." This comment is one pulled
out of the drawer when the Olympic industry feels threatened by the obvious
fact that there really is no honest reason at all why the Games need to move
every four years. It's an attempt to reestablish the Olympic frame in the hope
that no one out there can do simultaneous translation to, "But if we don't move
them, *it deprives us of real estate and TV rights and the developer-owned politicians the honor of putting their citizens into debt.*" As Lenskyj writes,

> Obviously more complex than a mere sixteen-day sporting event, the
> Olympics are systematically organized to maximize private sector in-
> vestment, to generate multi-billion-dollar television revenues, and to
> capitalize on the competition between transnational corporations for
> exclusive Olympic sponsorship status.[8]

Athlete Control

Another thing that could be done to make the Olympics match its mythical
origins would be to put the organization and running of the Games firmly under the control of the actual athletes. Attempts have been made at this before,[9]
but the very notion is anathema to the "Olympic Family" who would lose their
carefully cultivated privileges, wealth and influence. To no one's great surprise
— maybe except for the athletes who still believe the official history of the
Olympics — a structural adjustment of this nature seems unlikely to come to
pass. There is simply too much money at stake at all levels, too much politics
and, sadly, too much overall greed of the "I want my piece of the pie, too" kind
to ever have the Olympics be just about sports.

Is it worth trying again? Could star athletes working together bring IOC
reform to pass? According to Dave Zirin, the answer is maybe. The world's top

athletes command the attention and affection of the public to a level that transcends that of virtually every other profession. Movie stars and rock idols have perhaps the same level of acclaim, but nowhere near the same level of respect. What would happen if significant numbers of high-profile athletes — Olympic and otherwise — started to speak out? What if Olympic athletes refused to participate in Games where the core promises had all been broken?

Do such reform-minded Olympians exist? Undoubtedly they do, just as reformers exist in professional basketball, football, soccer and baseball. It's no different than for some other professions dominated by money, such as medicine, law and business to name just a few. As Zirin writes in his remarkably cogent book, *Welcome to the Terrordome*, media coverage of sports allows athletes a "unique and underutilized bully pulpit" to promote change in sports and in society at large:

> Socially aware athletes could use this platform if they just stopped operating in isolation from one another. If the people I cited called a joint press conference to announce a new organization called — what the hell — Jocks for Justice, it would electrify the cultural landscape.[10]

Zirin notes that no such organization has yet come into existence, citing pessimism and the fear of being ostracized by their fellow athletes as the reasons. It hasn't happened yet, but it needs to, and urgently. Turning the athletes may thus be key to restructuring the Olympics, restructuring that really cannot be done by anyone else. The IOC is not going to change itself, nor will politicians or corporations, developers or the Olympic booster squad. Those of us opposed to the Olympics can embarrass the machine, certainly disrupt it and as we'll see below, maybe even destroy it. But we cannot be the vehicle used to reform it. If athletes want the Olympics to truly be about the stated goals of peaceful competition and our common humanity, they are going to have to do it themselves. And they are going to have to do it soon.

Make the Sponsors Nervous

A potential weak spot for the IOC and the local organizing committee consists of the Olympic sponsors. Threats of boycotts of Coca Cola, GE, Visa and the various others might work wonders, forcing the corporations that feed on Games advertising and publicity to put pressure on the IOC and local organizing committee to deliver on their promises. Once again, delivering on these promises forces the Olympics to become what they've long said they are. Another potentially credible threat could arise from an elaboration of sponsor boycotts, that is, a boycott of the Games themselves. Some opponents of the Sydney Games advised a multiphase approach, including a boycott of Olympic sponsors and the Games, getting people to refuse to watch the Games or show any interest in them, and matching all of these efforts by putting people in the streets in protest.[11]

Resistance

Any realistic hope of changing an institution as wealthy and as well connected as the IOC seems simply a forlorn hope. It's not going to happen by chance, certainly not through the actions of small groups of anti-Olympic activists alone nor will it arise because of internal apostasy of the athletes themselves.

Like other such ossified structures, the event that could bring down the IOC and replace it with a true Olympic movement would be a cataclysm. Such a cataclysm might be a scandal of such gargantuan proportion that the entire fabric of the IOC's carefully crafted frame unraveled. Or even a series of less dramatic scandals that culminated in a slower-motion loss of the frame might do the trick. Either could happen of course, but the IOC is well buffered by the corporate media, so much so that the scandals would really have to be too egregious to ignore. And there is the fact that Jacques Rogge remains too much the gray man, too careful an apparatchik, to let things go sour on his watch.[12]

If internal reform driven either from within or without the IOC is not going to happen, what is the solution? The solution is the same as that acted on by the anti-globalization movement that began in the late 1990s. Globalization's opponents discovered that one way to fight the assault of a globalized economic agenda was to create an international anti-globalization response. Each time the World Trade Organization, the International Monetary Fund or the G8 showed up, protesters were there too, never allowing globalization's proponents to pretend that all of the world's peoples were solidly onside. Each meeting became a protest; each protest was met with varying degrees of police repression that, in turn, made many otherwise uninvolved people take the red pill. After the lull created by 9/11, long-overdue anti-globalization protests are back.

How does anti-globalization tie in to the IOC? The IOC is an organization that clothes itself in platitudes as it conspires with local developers to convert public land to private use, all the while encouraging or bribing local politicians to raid the treasuries of the cities and countries that bid on the Games. Its "family" lives like royalty, exploits its employees — athletes and volunteers — shamelessly, and pays no taxes to anyone. It enjoys legal immunity in Switzerland. It even has the power to dictate public policy on transportation, the environment and poverty to those cities too foolish to resist its siren song. The IOC is, in short, the ultimate megacorporation, the very model of a corporate parasite.

The response to the IOC and to the local franchisers has to be the same as that of the anti-globalization movement. Oppose it wherever it goes, use the public awareness created by any bid to educate people and break the frame. Opposition needs to be both local and international to exploit the center of gravity of any bid. Unlike the G8 or other economic forums whose organizers would increasingly hide from protest and public scrutiny by choosing ever more inaccessible places, the IOC has no such luxury. It has to be public; television broadcasting demands it. It has to have an audience; ticket sales demand it. They cannot market their product in isolation. The fact that they must provide a public spectacle becomes their Achilles' heel, but only if those opposed to the IOC and the Olympics as they now exist begin to use the methods learned the hard way, running through the choking clouds of tear gas and the hail of plastic bullets in Seattle, Quebec City and Genoa. The very threat of action directed against the Games themselves, or even better, against the IOC or bid boosters in the lead-up to the choice of the next sucker city can do wonders. It did in Berlin's case in the early 1990s when activists deliberately targeted IOC vehicles and officials. Monkeywrenching and the threat of disruptions can clearly work, if applied early.

However, it's more than showing up and exhibiting a willingness to get pepper sprayed that will defeat the Olympic machine. The machine, remember, has two critical working parts: the IOC *and* the local bid boosters. Each has a center of gravity, a critical vulnerability that needs to be targeted. For the IOC, it's the need for an endless stream of positive publicity through television used to spur other cities to bid on Games in the future. Angry citizens in the streets, gas canisters exploding in public places and truncheon swinging riot cops on horseback don't make for happy Olympic publicity and are more than likely to scare future bidders away. There is a reason why the G8 has to meet in out-of-the-way places. If Olympic opponents made each Olympic city a protest "red zone," the IOC would be in a serious bind. In effect, protestors would have forced them into a Gandhian choice: Really become what the Olympics are supposed to be, an option they hate like poison, or vanish.

Mahatma Gandhi's "march to the sea" is the classical case, and it is worth considering it briefly. During the Raj, the British had imposed a salt tax on India and made it illegal for Indians to obtain salt outside of the official British monopoly. Gandhi recognized the opportunity the salt tax presented for his struggle for Indian independence. In March 1930 Gandhi organized a march from Ahmedabad to Dandi on the Arabian Sea, a journey of 400 kilometers. He would, he announced, take salt from the sea, in the process breaking colonial law. As he marched, the number of followers grew. Arriving at Dandi, Gandhi gathered salt. He now had placed the British in a dilemma. If he was arrested, he became a martyr to an unjust law and, by extension, an unjust regime. If the British did not arrest him, he would have successfully defied the Raj, thus undermining British authority. The British were trapped. In the end they arrested him, setting in motion a chain of events that would result in independence for India and Pakistan.

There is only one Ghandian paradox now in sight that could serve to derail Vancouver's 2010 Olympics: Indigenous peoples from across the Americas recently (October 2007) came together in Vicam, Sonora, Mexico for a four-day conference about the fight for native rights.[13] Regardless of nation, the stories told by the delegates showed broad commonalities: stolen land, stolen resources, cultural if not physical genocide…and 500 years of resistance. British Columbia's Native delegates spoke passionately about their land struggles, describing the newest assault on First Nations territory coming in on the coattails of the Olympics. Fighting the Olympics now became the rallying cry, and the delegates were asked to commit to the battle by coming to Vancouver in 2010, not to celebrate the Games, but to shut them down. One BC activist, Gord Hill, put it more bluntly: The Olympics is the very symbol of white oppression of native peoples. Stop the Games, and the system will be shaken to its roots.[14]

Could the groups now talking about indigenous resistance to the Olympics pull off a coup of this nature? Would non-natives support them? These are unanswered questions, but it is clear that Hill and others have found the Gandhian paradox to which Olympic boosters and government have no correct response. Better still, whatever they do or don't do will be played out for a worldwide audience courtesy of the Games themselves. Could the different levels of government block native peoples from congregating in Vancouver in 2010? Not easily, not without exposing their citizens to a major red pill moment. Could they tolerate any disruption of the Games themselves? No. How many native heads would they have to bloody to keep such disruption from happening? How would this look on world television? Whatever the authorities do is the wrong thing, casting the various governments, the Games organizers and the IOC into disrepute. Pulling off such a convergence of native protesters and supporters might not be the *coup de grâce* for the IOC, but it would be a grievous wound, one from which they might never fully recover.

As discussed, VANOC's center of gravity is their ability to provide the IOC the spectacle they need. Protests impact them as much as the IOC, but even without this, their vulnerability lies in one other key factor. It's not their credibility that is already shaky, it's not their fiscal honesty, equally in disrepute, that is their weak spot, rather VANOC's critical vulnerability lies with their volunteers, the thousands of unpaid workers who do all the chores that VANOC needs to be done for free in order to put on the Games. Take away the volunteers and VANOC's ability to deliver the Games in anything approaching a timely manner or to make money during the operating phase vanishes. Could VANOC hire people in place of volunteers? No, not without totally blowing their already over-the-top operating budget. Could the paid employees do all the joe jobs needed? No way. The critical vulnerability at the local level thus becomes one of knocking the volunteers out of the equation. There are endless ways to do this…all it takes is creativity to find those that work, ways to make volunteering as a corporate cog in the machine seem to be totally uncool, if not actually embarrassing.

The combination of taking away the IOC's television circus parade with protests and VANOC's ability to deliver a ready pool of free labor stops the Games in their tracks. Maybe they can still limp along in Vancouver, but the spectacle won't be pretty, and no city — at least those not run by totalitarian regimes — will readily flirt with the idea again. To survive, the Olympics will have to focus on sports, not real estate, to put the power into the hands of the athletes, not the oligarchy who run the IOC. In other words, the Olympics will have to cease to be the Olympics as we know them; the myth will have to become the reality.

Looking to the "End of History" for the Olympic Games

For the reasons cited above, the Olympic industry is unwilling, indeed unable, to reform itself if the changes to be made are more than merely cosmetic. The true frame doesn't allow it. The industry has become very rhetorically adept, able on demand to shape the media to its will. In addition to the mainstream media, the very athletes themselves and all the special interest groups feeding on the Games are too locked on to feeding from the Olympic trough to even contemplate changing the structure.

The elite "sports" organization created by de Courbertin and his band of nobles back in 1894 is long gone, replaced by an even more elite megacorporation now utterly addicted to wealth and power. The organizing committees in each bid and host city have taken Olympic "ideals" and the Games themselves as the golden path to corporate welfare heaven. They have no interest in re-forming themselves either, or of accepting even the most cursory regulation of their activities. There is only one future: The IOC has to be brought to an end. In connection to Sydney's Games, Helen Lenskyj writes this eventual solution to the Olympics in general:

> Overall...the Sydney Olympics made the world safe for global capi-tal, while the poor disproportionately bore the burden. This pattern will not change until the Olympic industry is dismantled, and interna-tional sporting practices are transformed.[15]

The dismantling of the IOC will require an international effort, one that may already be emerging as Olympic opposition groups of different countries share information and begin to link up.[16] Our own group in Vancouver has created a website called World Olympic Watch and will hold an anti-Olympics con-gress before 2010 to help solidify the growing rebellion. Just as the IOC plans for Games that are still a decade or more away, we too have begun to think of the anti-Olympic struggle in the same time frame. We couldn't stop Vancou-ver 2010 (yet), London's and Sochi's may be inevitable, but those that follow 2014 are not.

The View from 2008 to 2010 and Beyond

We have it in our power to begin the world again.

Thomas Paine, Common Sense, 1776

I can't think of a better Olympic legacy we can leave than a warning about the Olympic disease, and a manual on how to vaccinate against it. Prevention is the best medicine, and with enough effort, the world might be able someday to expunge itself of the Olympic blight entirely.

Kevin Potvin,
"Vancouver Should Help
Other Cities Avoid the Olympic Disease,"
Vancouver Courier, June 6, 2007

Beijing 2008

THIS BOOK will have come out while Vancouver's 2010 Games are still more than a year and a half away, but scant months before Beijing puts on its Olympic spectacle. And indeed, judging by the reports filtering out of China and by the hype of our own media, a grand spectacle it will be. The Canadian Broadcasting Corporation is already running commercials pumping their 2008 Games coverage. It will indeed be an event of gargantuan proportions, paid for by a sea of money and blood in support of something quite different than the simple love of sports. The People's Republic of China will use the 2008 Summer Games to unveil its new world image and launch China into the 21st century, which they clearly hope to own as the next dominant superpower. There is really nothing novel about this. The emergent

Nazi regime did precisely the same in 1936 as they kicked off their thousand-year Reich.

No one really knows how much Beijing has spent on the Games, but the final costs, if indeed they are ever unearthed, are certain to dwarf every Olympics of the past. One estimate puts the total at over $60 billion.[1] The Chinese have remodeled their capital, displacing over a million and a half residents in the process,[2] ignored numerous construction workers killed in the rush to build the Olympic venues and tried to hide the child labor used to produce Games souvenirs. They are also, in spite of promises to the contrary, actively suppressing any dissent about the Olympics or anything else.[3] Perhaps even more dramatically, they are running the risk of widespread environmental catastrophe by diverting water from agricultural areas toward Beijing and the massive Olympic developments.[4] As this book goes to press, a number of Tibetan Buddhist monks have been killed by Chinese security personnel in Lhasa, Tibet's capital.

For China, none of this seems to matter in their perception of the big picture. Simply put, what matters is re-engineering, or "imagineering" as we've already seen other Olympic cities do, the image of China in the eyes of the world. For the Games' 17 days, China will have the world's attention, and what they want to do — what they must do — is to create a new, kinder, gentler brand for their regime and its status as the emergent superpower. The masters of Beijing know that a skeptical world now sees their totalitarian state inexorably linked to generations of repression in Tibet and covered by the blood of 3,000 student protesters in Tiannamen Square and, more recently, by Falun Gong adherents. Some even link the Chinese government to the genocide in Darfur through Beijing's open support of the Sudanese regime and to the murder of pro-democracy protesters in Burma.

How to change these horrifying realities? There could be many ways, including foreign aid, charity and medical breakthroughs. But the fastest, most media-friendly way is to use the Olympics as the remarkable marketing tool that it is. In the months before the 2008 Olympics, stories about Beijing's Games will swell from a trickle to a flood as the world's athletes begin making their preparations. World leaders will pontificate on China as a new world power. The IOC will shower them with praise. The 17 days of the Games, followed by 10 more of the Paralympics, will then showcase all that China has been in its 5,000-year history. Moreover, it will provide a glimpse into what China hopes to become.

The Chinese have paid the money, cleared the neighborhoods, built the venues, diverted the water...and mobilized the Peoples' Liberation Army

(PLA). All they need now is a bit of luck that nothing unmanageable happens: a larger funding scandal, charges of athletes on drugs, more corrupt IOC officials or judges caught with their hands out, unpleasant protests or a security "incident." Doped-up athletes and the IOC's honesty are out of Chinese hands, of course, but everything else will be neatly locked down by government bureaucracy and the omnipresent PLA. The trick will be to do so discreetly, away from probing media eyes and ears. In China this should be remarkably easy to accomplish. A safe guess is that months in advance of the Games, pesky Falun Gong supporters, various "dissidents," and the newly displaced former residents of Beijing will be safely ensconced in "re-education" projects far away in Inner Mongolia or Manchuria.

If all goes according to plan, the world audience will emerge from 17 days of non-stop Olympic media bombardment with a much friendlier view of China and its government. China will have been re-branded as the gracious host of what IOC President Jacques Rogge will certainly declare as the "best Olympics ever." And, just maybe, the world will forget the image of a lone man standing in the path of a column of tanks, choosing to remember instead the immaculately swept streets of a reconstructed Beijing and the melody of "The East is Red" wafting from loudspeakers as Chinese athletes mount the podium to collect golden trinkets. These carefully crafted images will allow China to restore what they have long felt is theirs by right: the role of a world superpower. To think that the Chinese government sees the Games in any other light is to be naïve to the point of imbecility, yet one can already predict the happy headlines of the Western media as they extol the "enthusiasm and spirit of 2008" and sing along with the "One World, One Dream" anthem, composed specially for the 2008 Games.

The Chinese government will also use the Games for other purposes, economic as well as social. These will serve as joint statements to foreigners and citizens alike: China is more than open for business; it will do whatever it takes to get that business. On the home front, the message will be: Forget the past; look how the world sees us now. As always, the Games will fuel Olympic nationalism. And who knows, just like the Nazis, the Chinese military may even put the five rings on their military hardware for all the world to see.

As these words are written in the spring of 2008, there have already been protests by Westerners in Beijing who unfurled a banner calling for the freedom of Tibet. That there will be more such protests in Beijing and all around the world is certain. Already, calls for a boycott of the 2008 "Genocide" Olympics because of Chinese support for the Sudanese government and the repression in Tibet are being heard and may finally be achieving some traction.[5]

The IOC, the Beijing organizers, the Chinese government, indeed the entire Olympic Family, will decry the "politicization" of the Games by "those with an agenda," carefully ignoring that the Games are nothing if not political.

They always are, of course, but Beijing's usage of the Games for overtly political purposes may become so obvious that only the most cultish Olympic booster could miss it. Vancouver's Games will follow just two years later in February 2010, London's in 2012 and the new kid, Sochi, Russia, will be the hit of 2014. The IOC's franchise system is working seven years out and has no thoughts of abating their financial assault on the world. Why should they? They get their tax-free dollars and live the life of royalty; the host governments get prestige and, in the case of China, validation. And, local bid corp franchisers get their pet projects funded by a compliant citizenry. Those in the United Kingdom are already getting a taste of it as cost overruns reach for gold five years in advance of 2012. As Martin Slavin of London explains:

> Like all con tricks, it works best by arriving suddenly in the locality, promising "fantastic" outcomes to the greedy and the needy, getting a binding contract signed by the "urban elites" of the host cities (a contract which clearly says "the IOC is not responsible for the overspend, you are"), raising a political storm of protest amongst a vocal minority (who are eventually worn out from the effort of challenging the juggernaut), then departing to a new city to work the old con on a fresh set of startled punters. That's why the Olympics is always on the move. No one would let them do it twice in their lifetime.[6]

Sochi

The latest news on the future conquests of the IOC comes from the Black Sea resort of Sochi, the proud and bouncy host of the 2014 Winter Games. As with previous Games, the IOC will soon have another environmental disaster on their roster, one that might just conceivably exceed the damage that Vancouver has incurred.

Sochi was seemingly a strange choice since, unlike its competitors — Pyeongchang, South Korea and Salzberg, Austria, it had no winter sports infrastructure to speak of.[7] It is now primarily a summer resort. The surrounding mountains, however, are full of snow in the winter, leading some Russian Jack Poole to have a brainstorm, "Why not make Sochi a winter resort too? How to do it? Aha, the Olympics." And, coincidentally, the Russians had more than a little help from some special friends involved in the Vancouver bid. It turns out that the Sochi organizers turned to Paul Mathews of Whistler's Ecosign

Mountain Resort Planners whose company had been developing ski resorts for some time, including those in Russia since the 1990s. In 2000 the Russian government gave Ecosign the contract to evaluate the Caucasus Mountains for ski resort development.

The Sochi bid is the fourth successful Olympic and Paralympic bid that Ecosign has had a hand in, including Calgary in 1988 and Salt Lake City in 2002. In 2005 it developed a concept that became the basis of the Russian bid. In an interview posted on Ecosign's website, Mathews said, "The Sochi bid is excellent. What's interesting is that we kind of stole the idea from Vancouver and Whistler, because Sochi is on the Black Sea. Without the Vancouver-Whistler bid, we wouldn't have thought of a sea and mountains cluster for Russia, with the ice events by the sea and the snow events in the nearby mountains."[8] The modest Mr. Mathews was also quoted in regard to his remarkable success rate: "I guess we're a lucky charm for this thing." That, or really well connected. I'd be inclined to bet on the latter.

Another odd thing about Sochi was that, as in the competition for 2010, far stronger bids by the same two opposing cities have gone down to a crushing defeat. Both Salzburg and Pyeongchang already had their infrastructure in place, so what gives? Maybe, the conventional wisdom is looking at this all wrong: Having the infrastructure already built may not be a bonus, but a problem — for the developers. What Sochi's bid also had was the powerful lobbying efforts of one of the world's most powerful men, Russian President Vladimir Putin, who just happens to have a summer residence nearby. Putin, formerly a high-ranking KGB officer, has trampled on the nascent Russian democracy since coming to power in 1999, turning back the clock to the bad old days in the process. For the IOC, this is inconsequential, perhaps even an advantage. IOC President Jacques Rogge was clearly delighted with the choice of Sochi, noting that Putin had "guaranteed" that the Olympic venues would be on time and on budget. No doubt they will be, and God help anyone who stands in Putin's way. "This is very reassuring for the International Olympic Committee," Rogge said. "It guarantees us the support of the public authorities." True to form, the IOC is happy once again to swap spit with dictators, Hitler and the Nazis in the 1930s, China's blood-soaked regime in 2008 and now Putin for 2014. Former fascist-loving IOC presidents Avery Brundage and Juan Antonio Samaranch would be very pleased and proud.

Sochi's Games won't be cheap: Putin has pledged $12 billion to develop Sochi into a winter sports complex. With Russia veering back to the good old authoritarian days of the former Soviet Union, no one is ever likely to know the true costs. But the costs actually go far beyond monetary concerns. Once again, the environment stands to take the brunt of it. Mikhail Kreindlin of Greenpeace Russia says the impact of the construction will be disastrous. In a statement eerily reminiscent of the feckless Eagleridge protesters, Kreindlin said, "We're not opposed in principle to holding the Olympics in Sochi. But hosting them at the cost of destroying unique forests and animals, particularly in such fragile conservation areas which are protected by international organizations — we consider that to be totally unacceptable."[9] The species at risk include: "brown bears, deer, chamois, otters and the Caucasus wild cat." The area to be developed for Olympic venues in Sochi National Park and the Caucasus Nature Reserve are part of a World Heritage Site designated by UNESCO.

Curiously, just as with the Significant Projects Streamlining Act in British Columbia, the Russian parliament, or Duma, passed legislation in 2006 to turn over control of the mountains and forests surrounding Sochi to the Economic Development and Trade Ministry overseeing Russia's Olympic bid. Once again, cookie cutters make cookies, and it's hard not to see the hand of the IOC working in lockstep with local developers in Sochi's bid. The Sochi organizers even had plans for a high-speed train. Maybe they can borrow SNC-Lavalin's plans?

Regarding development of the area, Kreindlin said:

> Sadly, the Olympic bid is being used as a way for construction companies simply to get their hands on the most valuable land. For example, the last time the Russian government looked at this issue, which was in January, there was no mention made of the Olympic bid. They simply said that the land could be used for social infrastructure, whereas it was patently obvious that it would be snapped up by elite resorts and golf clubs, which have nothing to do with the Olympics.[10]

Kreindlin and his fellow citizens, like so many others in cities around the world, had fallen victim to the Olympic/developer machine. And, like so many others, they had doomed themselves, their cause and the forests around Sochi with the usual disclaimer that they weren't "anti-Olympic, but…." The failure to see that the Olympics are not apolitical, but the opposite, that they are not about sports, rather real estate, has led to the pathetic, obsequious hope that if they say that they don't oppose the Olympics somehow some remainder of the forest may still be saved. It won't, but they don't know it yet. When they do, Sochi's forests, like those of the Callaghan, will be so much "woody debris."

If it were only "woody debris" it would be bad enough, but as in so many other places, the Olympics are being used as a massive development tool by those who are identical in character, if not language, from their counterparts in Vancouver, Salt Lake City and Torino. Ecosign's evaluation of the region identified the Mzymta Valley near Sochi as having a 50,000 skier per day potential, with two sites being particularly promising: Rosa Khutor and Psekahko Ridge, both expected to open by 2009. The former is now the proposed alpine ski and snowboard venue, the latter planned for Nordic events. The village of Krasnaya Polyana is the proposed site of the alpine Athletes' Village. Moving into the area by invitation of the Russian government are the following companies: Gazprom, the state-owned natural gas and oil company that has invested $300 million in Psekahko Ridge, and Interross, a mining and forestry company that has invested $262 million in Rosa Khutor. This was all just dandy with the IOC's evaluation of Sochi's bid that said, "Sochi proposes a very good concept based around an ice cluster and a mountain snow zone 49 kilometers/50 minutes apart." Basically, as in Vancouver, the IOC doesn't really care about their third pillar of Olympism. As long as they get their Games, they're perfectly happy if you flatten the mountains.

Would all of this have happened anyway? It's likely, but even Mathews admits in the interview that the 2014 Olympics pushed development of Rosa Khutor and Psekahko Ridge along much faster: "The Olympic Games will move everything quicker, we'll have the funding in place a lot sooner, and timelines will have to be kept. Of course the market for the resorts will pick up quickly with three or four new ski areas down there, and all kinds of properties planned."[11] Once again, the Olympics remains in the service of the local developers, another "greenest Games ever" for IOC President Jacques Rogge's successor to boast about in 2014, as the organizers hand him his cut of the television revenues.

Mathews' last comment was telling: "There's money going in here like I can't think of anywhere else in the world."[12] He is no doubt correct: the Olympic party for the IOC and the developers just keeps getting bigger and better. Sochi may be the biggest windfall yet, but there are still plenty of potential Olympic host cities left to plunder, some perhaps for the second time if their memories have sufficiently faded.

Some Final Predictions
About Vancouver 2010 and Beyond

Finally, for Vancouver's 2010 Games, a few new observations and some predictions:

+ The street where VANOC headquarters is located, Graveley Street in East Vancouver, recently had a facelift courtesy of the City.

+ The City of Vancouver spent $368,941.03 for "road improvements."[13]
+ Property owners on the street were billed for the work.
+ VANOC, however, merely rents the building from the City at a subsidized rate and hence will have paid nothing.

- Duke Energy, a US firm, had seconded one of their staff to the Bid Corp back in 2002/03 to work as the bid's media liaison. This act of generosity seemed odd at the time. We now know that Duke, along with numerous power generation companies, have been given free rein to the streams and rivers along the Sea to Sky corridor, just in time for all the new condo development sprouting along the highway.

As for predictions:
+ Costs will continue to rise across the board, exceeding the $5.7 billion calculated in a previous chapter. The original $139 million "contingency fund," now down to about $27 million in late 2007, will vanish long before 2010, forcing VANOC to turn to government for more handouts. Some of these handouts will be direct expenses, others indirect. As an example of the latter, it seems that BC Place, the site of the 2010 Opening and Closing Ceremonies may need a new roof. Cost? $100 million to $250 million. David Podmore, chairman of PavCo and CEO of Concert Properties, proposes selling adjacent land to developers to come up with the money. (Does anyone want to bet on whether Concert wil have a role here...?)
+ Accountability by VANOC and government of all levels will remain at zero.
+ The environmental destruction of Eagleridge and elsewhere will engulf the Callaghan Valley.
+ There will be no social housing, rather gentrification; no "inclusivity," merely more homeless, more urban poor and more displacement.
+ Security will become a huge expense, serve to tarnish civil liberties during the Games and for years afterwards, yet fail to prevent an attack against the Olympics.
+ There will be major scandals as the shenanigans in the Callahan and the Athletes' Village are revealed.[14]
+ All told, each and every promise made in 2002 will be shown to be a lie.

It's too late for Vancouver. Because there is no end to Olympic rapacity, the IOC and the developers will continue to target cities worldwide until their citizens decide to stop it.[15] Business suits running globalization, those in track suits driving the Olympics: It's the same agenda. The Olympic machine — like that of the corporations that drive globalization — is not accountable and cannot be made so unless citizens can force it into something like a binding contract. The structure and promises of Bid Books and the other governing agreements, not to mention all of the official and unofficial promises, are contracts in name only. Alas, they are not contracts in law since they are not enforceable, at least not by the political entities that allow the IOC and local organizers free rein. Imagine, however, that Olympic organizers had to keep promises for fear of monetary and/or civil penalties. How many future Jack Pooles would there be if the prospects of financial ruin or jail time were realistic? How often would the IOC sponsor fraudulent bids if it knew it could be held liable?

That bid corporations, organizing committees and the IOC will not be made accountable in any country, notionally democratic or overtly authoritarian, any time soon thus seems a certainty. For this reason more than any other, the time has come to bring down the curtain on the Olympic Games by whatever means necessary. There may come a time when the Games can be reconstituted by the athletes themselves, perhaps along the lines of the Paralympics. Until that time, until they become what they have long promised to be, there is no place for them in a truly egalitarian, democratic and socially just society. How the Olympics can be stopped thus becomes a subject for debate on strategies and tactics, not a question of if, but rather when.

The answer to the question of "when" belongs to us.

Endnotes

page vi

1. Concerning the Circus Maximus: Cheating by participants and judges was common. See James Grout, "Circus Maximus," *Encyclopedia Romana*: penelope.uchicago
.edu/~grout/encyclopaedia_romana/notaepage.html). Some things never change…

Preface

1. Edward S. Herman and Noam Chomsky, *Manufacturing Consent: The Political Economy of the Mass Media*, Pantheon Books, 1988.

Part 1

1. Baron Pierre Fredy de Courbertin, founder and second president of the International Olympic Committee, was at least honest 100 years ago, correctly noting the cultlike attributes of the Olympics and eerily foretelling the later excesses.
2. George Orwell, "The Sporting Spirit," December 14, 1945. Orwell is best known for his darkly allegorical and futuristic novels *Animal Farm* and *Nineteen Eighty-Four*.

Chapter 1

1. Jack Poole is the current Chairman of VANOC, the successor organization to Vancouver's Bid Corporation. He is also chairman of Concert Properties, a successful real estate and development company. Here is the full context of Poole's comments as recorded by Frank O'Brien, editor of the *Western Investor* in his Western Perspective column in June 2002:

   > When Jack Poole addressed a room full of real estate developers this spring it erased any doubts of what the 2010 Winter Olympics bid for Vancouver-Whistler is really all about.
   >
   > At the risk of sounding naive, we had understood the bid was aimed at getting the Games, raising Vancouver's international profile and welcoming elite athletes to one of the world's best skiing locations.
   >
   > Wrong. The real purpose of the 2010 Olympics bid is to seduce the provincial and federal governments and long-suffering taxpayers into footing a billion-dollar bill to pave the path for future real estate sales. Whether the bid is successful or not is actually immaterial.
   >
   > "If the Olympic bid wasn't happening we would have to invent something," Poole, chair of the 2010 Vancouver Bid Corp and noted real estate developer, said in a most telling understatement.

2. Martin Slavin is a spokesperson for Games Monitor (gamesmonitor.org.uk), an anti-Olympic website concerned with the impacts of London's 2012 Summer Olympics.
3. Vancouver–Whistler 2010 Bid Society's directors: The following individuals served as directors at some period during the existence of the Society from 1997 until it was

dissolved by the Province in 2001. For simplicity, I have grouped the directors by profession.

Developers and resort owners. David Bentall: former president and CEO of Dominion Construction; played a leading role in GM Place development; **Caleb Chan:** developer of condominiums and the resort at Furry Creek along the Sea to Sky Highway; **Jim Gibbons:** President, Intrawest Resort Club Group, former owners of the Whistler–Blackcomb ski resort operations. Intrawest hoped to make millions for the use of Whistler–Blackcomb ski runs during the 2010 Games; **Arthur Griffiths:** President and CEO, Infotec Business Systems; CEO, Griffiths Milne Corporate Projects Inc.; former owner of the Vancouver Canucks hockey team; **Craig MacKenzie:** realtor, Sea to Sky Premier Properties; **Peter Ufford:** Former V.P. External Affairs, UBC; Director, Wall Financial Corporation; President and CEO, Sea to Sky Foundation; responsible for Sea to Sky University's capital funding and campus construction. The new university is also involved in significant real estate developments of their holdings.

Other business interests. Rick Antonson: President and CEO of Tourism Vancouver and the Greater Vancouver Convention & Visitors Bureau; **John Johnston:** Chairman, Delta Hotels; **Bruce Malcolm MacMillan:** former president and CEO of Tourism Toronto; former vice-president, Meetings and Events for Tourism, Vancouver; **Pierre Rivard:** founder and past chair, president and CEO, Hydrogenics; **Brian W. Thom:** lawyer, corporate commercial law; partner at Borden Ladner Gervais, the law firm representing the Bid Corp and later VANOC.

Politicians. Don Bell: Mayor, Municipality of the District of North Vancouver; currently MP for North Vancouver; **Iona Campagnolo:** recent Lieutenant-Governor for BC; **Philip Owen:** Mayor of Vancouver during the pre-bid period; **Hugh O'Reilly:** Mayor of Whistler during Vancouver's bid; **Ian Waddell:** MP, NDP, former BC Minister of Tourism.

Former Olympic athletes and related industries. Doug Clement: UBC coach, athlete, teacher and medical doctor, co-founded the UBC sports medicine clinic; participated in the Olympics as athlete and coach; **Charmaine Crooks:** Canadian Olympic runner; IOC Technical Team Member; **Silken Laumann:** Canadian Olympic rower; **Karen Magnussen-Cella:** Olympic figure skating champion; **Steve Podborski:** Olympic downhill ski medallist; **Sandra Stevenson:** President and CEO of Sport BC.

Labor. Ken Georgetti: President Canadian Labour Federation; Board of Directors of Concert Properties.

Unknown: Rob Cruickshank.

4. NDP Premier Glen Clark took over from Mike Harcourt in 1996. Clark also wound up resigning in disgrace in 1999 after the media whipped up an artificial frenzy about his "friendship" with a fellow who wanted to start a casino. After his rapid fall from the premier's office, Clark wound up working for the wealthiest and best-known entrepreneur in the province, Jimmy Pattison: So much for the real versus official difference between the BC Liberals and the NDP.

5. The timeline of key events in the history of the Vancouver-Whistler 2010 Bid Society. March 30, 1998: The Society incorporates under the Society Act of BC with a list of 5 Directors; Fiscal Year 1997–98: the Ministry of Small Business of BC contributes at least $50,000 to the Society; December 1, 1998: the Canadian Olympic Association awards the Society the right to represent Canada in the international bidding process for the 2010 Games; June 11, 1999: The Society incorporates as a "not for profit"

corporation under the Canada Corporations Act, Part II. Financial reporting require-ments under this part of the Act are minimal; August 3, 2001: the provincial Registrar of Companies issues a "Notice of Commencement of Dissolution" to the Bid Society's legal address by registered mail for failing to file Annual Reports required under Sec-tion 68 of the Society Act; November 2, 2001: the Registrar of Companies formally removes the Society from the government's registry for failing to file Annual Reports which were to include financial statement; 2002 to the present: There is no public re-cord of the Society dissolving its assets, of the Society holding an Annual General Meeting, of the Society submitting financial statements, of the Society submitting an Annual Report to the Registrar in accordance with the Society's Constitution, By-Laws and/or the Society Act of British Columbia.

The Bid Corp and VANOC were to continue in the same spirit of fiscal transpar-ency.

6. Vancouver–Whistler 2010 Bid Corporation members. As above, the members are listed by group with only a *partial* list of their various accomplishments and affili-ations is cited. Note that the following are directors of special interest due to their other affiliations. Fifty-five others are not shown here due to space limitations. Of these, 18 were Olympic athletes involved with the Canadian Olympic Committee; 3 were members of the Calgary Olympic Development Association (CODA) for the 1988 Winter Games.

Primary officers. Jack Poole: Chairman. He is also Chairman of Concert Proper-ties. **John Furlong:** President and CEO of the Bid Corp., former CEO of the Arbutus Club (belonging to Caleb Chan).

Other Directors

Business. Rick Antonson: President and CEO Tourism Vancouver, the Greater Van-couver Convention and Visitors Bureau; former vice-president of the Great Cana-dian Railtour Company, Ltd.; member of Convention Centre Expansion Task Force. **Peter Armstrong:** CEO of Armstrong Hospitality Group which owns Rocky Moun-taineer Vacations; Chair, Convention Centre Expansion Task Force. **Laurent Beau-doin:** Chairman of Bombardier, Inc., the third-largest manufacturer of civil aircraft after Boeing and Airbus; sits on the Canadian Advisory Board of the Carlyle Group; director, Alcan. **Suzanne Denbak:** Consultant with ConventionWorks, a global con-sulting group that specializes in the area of destination marketing and convention and exhibition facility development. Denbak is former president and CEO of Tourism Whistler (during Vancouver's bid). **France Chretien Desmarais:** daughter of Jean Chretien and wife of André Desmarias. She is linked through her father to Gordon Capital, owned principally by Richard Li (Li Ka Shing's son). Gordon Capital owns HSBC Securities. Andre Desmarais is President and Co-CEO of Power Corpora-tion of Canada, a management and holding company with financial services and com-munications. Their European affiliate Pargesa has media, energy, water, waste services and mineral interests. Both companies partner with Li Ka Shing in CITIC Pacific Limited (China's largest diversified Hong Kong company). André Desmarais is also a Director of Bombardier. **Doug Forseth:** Senior VP Operations, Intrawest, the company from which VANOC planned to rent Whistler–Blackcomb for the 2010 Games. **Greg Greenough:** Chair, McNab Enterprises, Ltd., the largest privately held residential property holder in Alberta and the Northwest Territories with multiple links to professional property management companies throughout Western Canada. **Rod Harris:** President and CEO, Tourism British Columbia. **Dan O'Neil:** President and CEO of Molson, Canada, Inc., the brewery with the huge sign supporting the bid. **Eric Major:** Managing Director of Global Immigrant Investor Programs at HSBC Capital (Canada) Inc.; linked to Li Ka Shing through HSBC. **Guy Savard:** Vice-Chairman of Merrill Lynch Canada and Chairman of Quebec Operations, former COO of Caisse de dépôt et placement du Québec, former vice-chairman and member of the executive committee of Midland Walwyn Capital Inc.; Merrill Lynch International is owned by Li Ka Shing. **Lorne Whyte:** CEO, Tourism Victoria. **Milton Wong:** Chair, HSBC Asset Management Canada, Ltd.; linked through HSBC to Li Ka Shing.

First Nations. Gibby Jacob: Chief, Squamish First Nation. **Lyle Leo :** Business Development Manager, Lil'wat First Nation. **Wayne Sparrow:** Councilor, Musqueam First Nation.

Labour. Tony Tennessey: member of Concert Properties board of directors and former union boss.

Politics. Malcolm Brodie: Mayor of Richmond. **Larry Campbell:** former Mayor of Vancouver. **Linda Mix:** Community worker; Tenants' Rights Action Coalition; Chair, IOCC. **Ted Nebbeling:** Provincial Minister of State for the Community Charter; Minister responsible for the Olympic bid. **Hugh O'Reilly:** Mayor of the Resort Municipality of Whistler during the bid. **Philip Owen:** Former NPA mayor of Vancouver. **Judy Rogers:** City Manager, Vancouver.

Real estate. Larry Bell: Chair of BC Hydro and the Canada Line (CLCO), Chair and CEO of BC Hydro from 1987 to 1991, and 2001 to 2003, past chair and president of the Westar Group, past CEO of Vancouver City Savings Credit Union, vice-chair of Shato Holdings (with links to Li Ka Shing) and a director of International Forest Products, Miramar Mining Corporation and Wheaton River Minerals. **Caleb Chan:** President and Chairman of Burrard International Holdings Inc., which develops and manages commercial properties. Burrard International is the parent company of GolfBC, which owns and manages golf courses in BC and Hawaii, including those at Furry Creek on the Sea to Sky Highway and in Whistler; Chan is on the Board of Directors of UBC Properties Trust and Belkorp Industries Inc., and is a trustee of the Canadian Hotel Income Properties Real Estate Investment Trust. He also served on the board of directors of HSBC Bank, Canada. **George Killy:** President, Harley Street Holdings. **Stanley Tun-Li Kwok:** President, Stanley Kwok Consultants, Inc., Director of Husky Energy, Inc., previous deputy chairman of Concord Pacific Developments, Ltd., previous president and CEO of BC Place, Ltd., past president of Pendboro Development Co., Ltd., non-Executive Director of Cheung Kong (Holdings) Ltd. (Li Ka Shing is Chairman and major shareholder). The principal activities of the group are investment holdings, property development and investment, hotel and serviced suite operations, property and project management and securities. Kwok is also linked to Li Ka Shing through Concord Pacific which owns Burcon International Developments, with the controlling shareholder being Marathon Realty, Gordon Campbell's former company. **David McLean:** Vancouver Board of Trade, 1992–93, founding chairman of the Vancouver Board of Trade Foundation, chairman of Canadian Chamber of Commerce for the same period, former chairman of the board and director of Concord Pacific, a public real estate company, director, McLean Group (real estate). **Peter Ufford:** Principal, Spectrum Marketing, director, Wall Financial Corp., Project Leader and Treasurer, Sea to Sky University.

Sports (and real estate). Charmaine Crooks: Olympic athlete, IOC member of the Technical Team. **Kerrin Lee-Gartner:** Gold medalist in downhill skiing at the 1992 Albertville Olympics; Lee-Gartner created Snow Creek Lodge in Fernie, BC. **Richard Pound:** IOC member; chair of WADA; partner, Stikeman Elliott, the firm that represents Li Ka Shing in Canada. **Nancy Greene Raine:** Gold and silver medalist at the 1968 Grenoble Olympics; with husband Al Raine was instrumental in the development and promotion of ski tourism in BC, first at Whistler and currently at Sun Peaks resort; they have also attempted to develop the Cayoosh Creek Resort at Melvin Creek on St'at'imc land against local opposition.

Chapter 2

1. Key dates: The initial preliminary application and completed questionnaire to the IOC for the 2010 Games was on February 4, 2002; the more elaborate application was due May 2, 2002.

2. Holger Preuss, *The Economics of Staging the Olympics, A Comparison of the Games 1972–2008* , Edward Elgar, Cheltenham, UK, 2004.

3. Philip K. Porter, "Mega-Sports Events as Municipal Investments: A Critique of Impact Analysis," *Sports Economics: Current Research*, John Fizel, Elizabeth Gustafson, and Lawrence Hadley, Eds., Praeger Press, 1999; Darren McHugh, "A Cost-Benefit Analysis of an Olympic Games," MA thesis, Queen's University, 2006.

4. Most of the actual fighting was on nearby Breed's Hill.

5. The notion that the Olympic Games is the only place where those from warring nations meet in peace is simply incorrect: Any of the hundreds of scientific and other professional meetings held annually does the same thing.

6. For a discussion of the ability of spectacle to influence public perception and behavior, see Michael Carter's review in the *Canadian Journal of History*, August, 2000, of Richard C. Beacham's *Spectacle Entertainments of Early Imperial Rome*.

7. Rafe Mair was a provincial cabinet minister in the 1970s, holding various portfolios including those of health and education in the Socred government. The Socreds became extinct in the 1990s.

8. Thomas Walkom, "The Olympic Myth of Calgary," *Toronto Star*, Feb. 8, 1999.

9. "Sutikalh and Skwelkwek'welt 2002 Submission to the International Olympic Commission" (original signed by Janice Billy). The document was copied to Richard Pound, head of the Canadian Olympic Committee. Both the IOC and Pound ignored the complaint.

10. The blockade at Sutikalh began in 2000. Numerous protesters were arrested, but the blockade held. It is still there. The Raines' ski resort remains on hold.

11. Vancouver–Whistler 2010 Bid Book.

12. The Crown Corporations backing the Bid Corp with taxpayer money included the Insurance Corporation of BC (ICBC), the Lottery Corporation and the Pavilion Corporation, the latter overseeing provincial buildings.

13. Linda Mix is a "housing activist" and a former chair of the IOCC. The Bid Corp would soon put her on its board of directors.

14. The defection of David Emerson from the federal Liberals to the Conservatives immediately after the results of the 2006 election shocked many people. Emerson, very new in the role of MP, slipped up in one interview in which he was trying to justify his defection, opining that it didn't really matter since "both parties are pretty much the

same" on most issues. Emerson had just given away the secret handshake and in the process disillusioned a lot of voters. I doubt the party insiders were very happy with this statement either.

15. As it turned out, they would have to finance a considerable portion of it themselves, but they didn't know that then.

Chapter 3

1. Centre on Housing Rights and Evictions (COHRE), Mega-Events, Olympic Games, and Housing Rights, 2007, cohre.org.

2. It seems that the famous car company, Fiat, was in the process of reinventing itself with their new ski resort, Séstiere, built just in time for the 2006 Torino Olympics. Stefano Bertone of the anti-Olympics group Nolimpidi! has documented the considerable public funding that made this transition possible.

3. Helen J. Lenskyj, *The Best Olympics Ever: Social Impacts of Sydney 2000*, State University of New York Press, Albany, 2002.

4. Vyv Simson and Andrew Jennings, *The Lords of the Rings*, Stoddard, Toronto, 1992; Andrew Jennings, *The New Lords of the Rings*, Pocket Books, UK, 1996; Andrew Jennings, *The Great Olympic Swindle: When the World Wanted Its Games Back*, Simon and Schuster, UK, 2000.

5. See the website 2010watch.com for this and other articles.

6. Ironically the IOC first offered the Games to Whistler, which declined.

7. *The Concise Oxford Dictionary*, Oxford University Press, London, 1964.

8. The promises alluded to in the Bid Book were laid out in more detail in "2010 Inclusive Winter Games Commitment Statement," a document long on platitudes, short on actual deliverables. Some salient quotes. Those marked with * are the more obvious examples where the so-called promises never came to pass. Of these, the promises of transparency and for protecting the residents of the Downtown Eastside are the most egregious:

> The Bid Corporation and its Member Partners are pleased to present the 2010 Winter Games Inner-City Inclusive Commitment Statement. This Commitment Statement builds from the attached Inclusive Intent Statement, endorsed by the Bid Corporation and its Member Partners, which speaks to participation and equity for all British Columbians, including low- and moderate-income people. The Inner-City Inclusive Commitment Statement outlines the goals and objectives in the planning for and hosting of a (sic) inclusive Winter Olympics Games and Paralympics Winter Games. The intent is to maximize the opportunities and mitigate potential impacts in Vancouver's inner-city neighborhoods from hosting the 2010 Winter Games.
>
> Also during the implementation phase, steps will be taken to ensure incorporation of the interests of different groups, such as aboriginal people, women, youth, people with disabilities, people of color, immigrants and other groups.
>
> *Business Development
> a) Develop opportunities for existing and emerging local inner-city businesses and artisans to promote their goods and services
> b) Develop potential procurement opportunities for businesses that employ local residents

*Employment and Training

a) Create training and a continuum of short and long-term employment opportunities for inner-city residents to encourage a net increase in employment

b) Provide reasonable wages and decent working conditions for any local
worker producing Games related goods and services before and during the
Winter Games

*Financial Guarantees

a) Provide adequate funds to maintain and operate the new or upgraded
public recreational facilities after the Games to maximize the number of facilities available to inner-city residents

b) Provide adequate programming funds for the new or upgraded public recreational facilities to encourage maintenance or increase in recreation programs

c) Provide disclosure of all financial aspects of the Games, including expenditures and revenues, in the bidding and organizing phase of the Games

d) Commit to a comprehensive annual financial audit

*Housing

a) Protect rental housing stock

b) Provide as many alternative forms of temporary accommodation for Winter Games visitors and workers

c) Ensure people are not made homeless as a result of the Winter Games

d) Ensure residents are not involuntarily displaced, evicted or face unreason-
able increases in rent due to the Winter Games

e) Provide an affordable housing legacy and start planning now

*Input to Decision-Making

a) Provide inclusive representation on the Bid Corporation's and Organizing
Committee's Board structures and all relevant Bid Corporation and Organizing Committee's work groups

b) Ensure inner-city inclusive work continues to operate under the Organizing Committee and its Member Partners

c) Work with and be accessible to an independent watchdog group that includes inner-city residents

d) Develop full and accountable public consultation processes that include
inner-city residents

e) Document opportunities and impacts experienced in inner-city neighborhoods in a comprehensive post-Games evaluation with full participation
by inner-city residents...."

9. Ariel J. Feldman, J.A. Halderman and E.W. Felten, "Security Analysis of the Diebold
AccuVote-TS Voting Machine," itpolicy.princeton.edu/voting.

10. City of Vancouver website on the voting machines at: vancouver.ca/ctyclerk/election
2005/accuvote.htm

11. Statement of union activist Gordon Flett.

Chapter 4

1. Pound was speaking about Atlanta's budgetary problems and the need for *guaranteed*
[italics mine] public funding.

2. Gordon Campbell, then BC Liberal opposition leader, speaking to the press about

the convention center deal between the governing NDP and Greystone Properties in the 1990s. Odd how a few years can change perspective: Greystone and Poole were now Concert, and Poole and the convention center goodie bag was now the Olympic venture. Only the ruling party was different. Campbell, however, had been right in 1999 about the dangers of cost escalation. Now, however, it didn't worry him. Justine Hunter, "Convention Centre Cost Worries Campbell," *Vancouver Sun*, March 1, 1999.

3. Diane Hartwick, personal communication.
4. Bob Mackin, "Powder Mountain Ski Resort Controversy Exhumed in Lead-up to 2010 Olympics," *Business in Vancouver*, August 14–20, 2007.
5. "Paul Desmarais and Corruption from Canada," *The Key Monk*, March 15, 2005, thekeymonk.blogspot.com/2005/03/paul-desmarais-and-corruption-from.html; Aker Kvaener, press release, "Aker Kvaener Wins Dalia Subsea Contract," May 8, 2003, rigzone.com/news/article.asp?a_id=6563.
6. "IOC's Kim to Face Corruption Charges," *ABC News*, Jan. 27, 2004.
7. 2010watch.com.
8. It is no coincidence that this book and the documentary share the same title. Conrad Schmidt and I had discussed both projects in the summer of 2005, seeing them as linked efforts to educate the widest possible audience.
9. Rod Mickleburgh, "Countdown to 2010: It's a Long, Long Way from Tipperary," *Globe & Mail*, March 31, 2004.
10. Charlie Smith, "City Misled Taxpayers in '03," *Georgia Straight*, Sept. 28–Oct. 5, 2006.
11. J. Andrews, "Redevelopment of Southeast False Creek," City of Vancouver draft report.
12. The new party even had many of the same financial backers as the NPA.

Chapter 5

1. Of the numerous histories about the ancient and modern Olympics, some of those consulted for this chapter were: Arthur Daley and Pat Jordan, *The Story of the Olympic Games*, Lippencott, Philadelphia, 1977; William O. Johnson, *All That Glitters Is Not Gold*, Putnam, New York, 1972; Judith Swaddling, *The Ancient Olympic Games*, British Museum Publications, London, 1980; David C. Young, *A Brief History of the Olympic Games*, Blackwell, Malden, MA, 2004.
2. The site of Olympia is about 20 km from modern Pyrgos, the capital of Ilia (Elis) Prefecture in the Western Peleponnese.
3. *Encyclopedia Britannica* online on "ekecheiria": britannica.com/eb/article-9404134/The-Olympic-Truce#857839.hook.
4. Andrew Jennings has documented in detail Juan Antonio Samarach's lust for the Nobel Peace Prize. See *The New Lords of the Rings*, Simon & Schuster, UK, 1996.
5. Joseph B. Verrengia, "Ancient Olympics Had Its Own Scandals," Associated Press, July 28, 2004.
6. For comparison to today's wages, Engen writes: "In Athens the typical wage for a skilled laborer was one drachma per day at the end of the fifth century and two and a half drachmai in 377…one drachma could buy enough food for 16 days for one person, four days for a family of four." Darel Tai Engen, "The Economy of Ancient Greece," E.H. Net* Encyclopedia: eh.net/encyclopedia/article/engen.greece.
7. Dave Zirin, *Welcome to the Terrordome: the Pain, Politics, and Promise of Sports*, pp. 135–37.

8. Ibid., p. 146.

9. Vyv Simson and Andrew Jennings, *The Lords of the Rings, Power, Money, and Drugs in the Modern Olympics*, Stoddard, Toronto, 1992, p. 59.

10. Andrew Jennings, *The Great Olympic Scandal, When the World Wanted Its Games Back*, Simon & Schuster, UK, 2000.

11. Stikeman Elliott is the firm that represents Hong Kong billionaire Li Ka Shing. Li Ka Shing's links to Vancouver's Bid Corp are detailed in chapter 2.

12. Pound was speaking to a *Los Angeles Times* reporter.

13. Jennings, ibid. Note that some of the characters nominated to be on NOCs have included some serious nasties, e.g., Uday, one of the sons of Saddam Hussein.

14. Others include: "Judicial, Sports for All, Women and Sport, Marketing, International Relations, Eligibility, Olympic Solidarity, Protection of Olympic Emblems, Press and Public Relations, Culture and Olympic Education, and Olympic Programme."

15. Helen J. Lenskyj, *Inside the Olympic Industry: Power, Politics, and Activism*, State University of New York, Albany, 2000, p. 41.

16. Ibid., IOC charter 1997, p. 8; quoted in Lenskyj, ibid., p. 43.

17. The IOC Charter. See an IOC website: olympic.org/uk/index_uk.asp search: ioc charter.

18. Ibid.: multimedia.Olympic.org/pdf/en_report_344.pdf.

19. Derrick Penner, "Courting Big Business," *Vancouver Sun*, Oct. 1, 2007.

20. Ibid.

21. International Olympic Committee 2006 Marketing Fact File: multimedia.olympic .org/pdf/en_report_344.pdf. Note that the numbers between the two data sets for television and other revenues post 2000 are similar but not identical, reflecting the fact that one runs from 2001–04, the other from 2000 to 2004.

22. Helen J. Lenskyj, *The Best Olympics Ever: Social Impacts of Sydney 2000*. State University of New York Press, Albany, 2002, p. 126.

23. Personal communication.

24. As of 2000 the number stood at about 125, according to Holger Preuss. Edward Elgar, *The Economics of Staging the Olympics: A Comparison of the Games 1972–2008*, Cheltenham, UK, 2004, Fig. 4.2, p. 30.

25. These include: "The use of all Olympic imagery, as well as appropriate Olympic designations on products, hospitality opportunities at the Olympic Games, direct advertising and promotional opportunities, including preferential access to Olympic broadcast advertising; on-site concessions/franchise and product sale/showcase opportunities; ambush marketing protection; acknowledgement of their support though a broad Olympic sponsorship recognition programme." olympic.org, the "official website of the Olympic Movement."

26. Jennings, ibid.

27. Naomi Klein, *No Logo*, Picador, London, 2001.

28. Vyv Simson and Andrew Jennings, ibid., p. 12.

29. Zirin, ibid., chapter 6: "The Olympics: Gold, Guns, and Graft."

Chapter 6

1. Vyv Simson and Andrew Jennings, *The Lords of the Rings, Power, Money, and Drugs in the Modern Olympics*, Stoddard, Toronto, 1992.

2. Andrew Jennings, *The New Lords of the Rings*, Simon & Schuster, UK, 1996.

3. Andrew Jennings, *The Great Olympic Swindle: When the World Wanted Its Games*

Back, Simon & Schuster, UK, 2000, pp. 11–12. Jennings was describing his testimony before the US Senate's Commerce committee.

4. Andrew Jennings, ibid.
5. Patricia Kidd, "Top 50 Sports Scandals," *Times Online*, Aug. 22, 2007.
6. Helen J. Lenskyj, *The Best Olympics Ever? Social Impacts of Sydney 2000*, State University of New York Press, Albany, 2002.
7. Details of the scandal and its aftermath are documented in detail in Andrew Jennings' book, *The Great Olympic Swindle*.
8. Helen J. Lenskyj, *Inside the Olympic Industry: Power, Politics, and Activism*, State University of New York Press, Albany, 2002, p. 49.
9. Andrew Jennings, *The New Lords of the Rings*, p. 56.
10. The IOC new recommendations for appropriate member behavior were adopted in 1998.
11. Helen J. Lenskyj, *Inside the Olympic Industry*, p. 105.
12. Helen J. Lenskyj, *The Best Olympics Ever?*
13. T. Sheridan, Report of the Independent Examiner for SOCOG, March 12, 1999.
14. Andrew Jennings, *The Great Olympic Swindle*, pp. 109–110; also cited in Helen J. Lenskyj, *Inside the Olympic Industry*, p 184.
15. Bob Mackin, "2010 Gold Rush, Powder Mountain Ski Resort Controversy Exhumed in Lead-up to 2010 Olympics," *Business in Vancouver*, Aug. 14–20, 2007, 929.
16. Mackin, ibid.; Nick Auf der Maur, *The Billion Dollar Game: Jean Drapeau and the 1976 Olympic Games*, James Lorrimer, Halifax, NS, 1976.
17. Jennings, all books cited above.
18. Gary Mason, "Not Even a Hint of Trouble," *Globe and Mail*, May 9, 2007.
19. Michael Liebreich, "Sydney 2000: Auditor Slams Costs." Jan. 28, 2003. Lieberich.com, liebreich.com/LDC/HTML/Olympics/London/Sydney.html.
20. George Monbiot, "The Olympic Games Myths Busted," Monbiot.com, posted July 5, 2007: alternet.org/rights/55928/

Chapter 7

1. Emerson has had quite a varied career in both the private and public sectors. Private: President and CEO of the Western and Pacific Bank of Canada (1986) (later the Western Bank of Canada); President and CEO of the Vancouver International Airport Authority (1992 to 1997); President and CEO of Canfor Corporation (1998), Canada's largest producer of softwood lumber. Public:British Columbia Deputy Minister of Finance; promoted to Deputy Minister to the Premier and President of the British Columbia Trade Development Corporation. Emerson was elected MP in 2004 as a Liberal. After the 2006 federal election, he crossed the floor to join the Conservatives.
2. VANOC website: vancouver2010.com/en/OrganizingCommittee/AboutOrganizing Committee/BoardDirectors/RichardTurner.
3. These include, in addition, to John Furlong (CEO): Kenneth Bagshaw (Chief Legal Officer), Ward Chapin (Chief Information Officer), Dave Cobb, formerly CEO of Orca Bay (owners of the Canucks) (Exec. VP for Revenue, Marketing, and Communications), Dan Doyle (Exec. VP Construction), David Guscott (Exec. VP Corporate Strategy and Government Relations), John McLaughlin (Chief Financial Officer), Cathy Priestner Allinger (Exec. VP Sport, Paralympics, and Venue Management), Donna Wilson (Exec. VP Human Resources, Sustainability, and International Client Services), Terry Wright (Exec. VP Service Operations and Ceremonies).

4. Kate Zimmerman, *Legacies of North American Olympic Winter Games*, 1–3. VANOC website: vancouver2010.com/en/OrganizingCommittee.

5. VANOC press release, "Civic Pride, Unity, a Key Legacy for Salt Lake 2002 Winter Games," May 14, 2007.

6. Philip K. Porter, "Mega-Sports Events as Municipal Investments: A Critique of Impact Analysis," *Sports Economics: Current Research*, John Fizel, Elizabeth Gustafson and Lawrence Hadley, Eds, Praeger Press, 1999.

7. Zimmerman website: katezimmerman.ca/writing.html.

8. VANOC's Vancouver 2010 Sustainability Report 2005–06 from their website. See also their "backgrounder" on the same subject, "VANOC releases report and action plan for sustainable 2010 Winter Games."

9. Clare Ogilvy, "Sustainability Report to be Released Today", *Province*, June 5, 2007.

10. Olympic Oversight Interim Report Card, 2010 Olympic Games, May 2007, Impact of Olympics on Community Coalition: info@iocc.ca.

11. The British Columbia government releases its annual budget in a so-called "lock-up" in which reporters and others are literally locked in a large room with their cell phones checked in. Each individual or group gets a copy of the budget that they can then study in order to prepare their stories. After several hours, the Minister of Finance comes on stage to present the highlights, illustrating it all with a power point presentation. The Minister takes reporters' questions, then departs, leaving the reporters to finish their stories. Not long afterwards, the Minister rises in the Legislature to present the budget formally, at which point the reporters are free to leave and release their stories. VANOC's attempt to manipulate the media in a pseudo-lock-up format was just ludicrous.

12. Enron, the ex-energy giant, began its precipitous fall from power by doing their accounting in much the same way as VANOC does.

13. "Host City" Agreement for Vancouver's Olympic, see: "Multiparty Agreement for the 2010 Winter Olympic and Paralympic Games.: canada2010.gc.ca/pubs/mpa/tdm_e .cfm.

14. Some additional clauses of interest: Clause 34 "Legacy Endowment Fund". Canada and the province of BC each contribute $55 million to Legacy Endowment Fund, to be managed by a 2010 Games Operating Trust. These monies are to be used for: "operating costs and related capital maintenance costs of [the] Whistler Nordic Centre, Bobsleigh, [sic] Luge and Skeleton Track in Whistler, and [the] Speed Skating Oval; athlete and coach sport development programs at facilities stated above; and for athlete/coach development elsewhere in Canada." That is if the money hasn't evaporated in cost overruns. Clause 36 is the "Whistler Legacies Society" clause. Here is what it says: "OCOG will establish WLS, the members of which will be, at their request, the Parties to this Agreement and the Lil'wat and Squamish First Nations." And, [the] "Purpose of WLS will be to own, manage or operate, or any combination of the preceding, as the case may be, the Whistler Nordic Centre, the Bobsleigh, Luge and Skeleton Track in the resort municipality of Whistler, the Whistler Athletes' Centre, and any other sports facilities for the Games in the resort municipality of Whistler whose ownership, management or operation has been transferred to the WLS." It would be a safe bet that such items wind up in the private sector not long after 2010.

15. Damian Inwood, "National Olympic 'Soul' Polls Stir Ire," *Province* , Aug. 2, 2007.

16. There are actually hundreds of words copyrighted by VANOC and protected by C-47.

17. Musi Alwand, owner of the Olympic, took over the downtown Vancouver restaurant in the 1980s. It was already in existence under the same name. Since 2003 VANOC's lawyers have demanded that Alwand change the name and take down the five rings, or face the legal consequences. Alwand, a firm supporter of the Olympics, is baffled by all of this, noting rather plaintively that, "I don't know why they are after me, I've been here almost twenty years…. I could work with them and it would be a positive thing for everyone." Obviously, VANOC can live with the negative publicity to enforce their copyright.

18. Kimberly Baker, "Creative License vs Copyright Law," *Common Ground*, Aug. 2007.

Chapter 8

1. "Furlong's Privateers" lyrics by Chris Shaw and Andy Vine with apologies to the late Stan Rogers.

> O the year it was two thousand two
> How I wish I was in the Callaghan now
> A letter of marque came from Lausanne
> To the greediest gang you could ever name
> God damn them all
> We were told we'd cruise the slopes for Olympic gold
> We'd spend no cash, shed no tears
> Now I'm a broke(n) man on Vancouver pier
> The last of Furlong's privateers
> O Johnny Furlong cried the town
> How I wish I was in the Callaghan now
> For twenty rich folks all business types who
> Would make for him the VANOC crew
> God damn them all…
> The Bid Corp Board was a sickening sight
> How I wish I was in the Callaghan now
> She'd list to the right with corporate hags
> And politicians in the trough with the staggers and jags
> God damn them all…
> On Jack Poole's birthday we clinched the bid
> How I wish I was in the Callaghan now
> Seven years to the opening day
> Lying like madmen all the way
> God damn them all…
> After Torino we launched again
> How I wish I was in the Callaghan now
> When a great big taxpayer hove in sight
> Armed with facts and prepared to fight
> God damn them all…
> The treasury lay way low with cash
> How I wish I was in the Calllaghan now
> Bought politicans had no fears
> But to catch it took VANOC seven whole years
> God damn them all…
> At length we stood one election away

> How I wish I was in the Callaghan now
> The corporate press made an awful din
> But angry citizens stove us in
> God damn them all…
> VANOC shook and pitched on her side
> How I wish I was in the Callaghan now
> Furlong was crushed by a pile of debt
> And the Auditor General began to fret
> God damn them all…
> Now here I am in twenty forty
> How I wish I was in the Callaghan now
> It's been forty years since we skiied away
> And we just paid it off yesterday
> God damn them all…

2. Samuel Johnson, from James Boswell, *Life of Johnson*, p. 615, 1970. Other wags have had fun with the term too: "In Dr. Johnson's famous dictionary patriotism is defined as the last resort of a scoundrel. With all due respect to an enlightened but inferior lexicographer, I beg to submit that it is the first." Ambrose Bierce, *The Devil's Dictionary*, at his entry for patriotism, *The Collected Writings of Ambrose Bierce*, p. 323, 1946, reprinted 1973. Not to be outdone, H. L. Mencken added this to Johnson's dictum: "But there is something even worse: it is the first, last, and middle range of fools," *The World*, New York City, Nov. 7, 1926, p. 3E.

3. The projection was based on Montreal's 1976 Olympic Summer Games debt of over $2 billion that was finally retired in 2006.

4. Alan Fotheringham, "House that Jack Built up for Sale," *Montreal Gazette*, Aug. 20, 1982.

5. Fred Lebolt, "Bell Unit Bid $150 Million for Developer," *Toronto Star*, Jan. 22, 1985.

6. "OSC Investigates Daon Trading with Bell," *Vancouver Sun*, Jan. 25, 1985.

7. Quote from Doug Ward's article, "Poole's Latest Splash," *Vancouver Sun*, Apr. 1, 1994.

9. It's funny how this works in the corporate mindset: Expo "created the boom," but the boom wasn't responsible for the loss of available housing; just like much later the successful Vancouver Olympic Bid drove the construction industry wild, but the escalation in costs of materials and labor was "unpredictable."

10. Union ownership is a great idea according to those who support "worker" capitalism. See Isla Carmichael, *A Case Study of Pension Power in Unions, Pension Funds, and Social Investment in Canada*," University of Toronto Press, 2005.

11. Frank O'Brien, "Vancouver Housing Project Draws Fire," *Financial Post*, Sept. 6, 1989.

12. Russ Francis, "Pooling the Funds," *Monday Magazine*, Oct. 2, 2002.

13. Podmore had come to VLC after a stint as President of BC Pavilion Corp (PavCo), a Crown Corporation. PavCo would later donate considerable funds to the Vancouver Bid Corp during the bid for the 2010 Games. Podmore would finally end up as the head honcho for the new convention center project.

14. Steve Wynn has been linked to the mob by at least one published report: Steve Miller, "When the Chicago Mob Sent Word Steve Wynn Should Be Turned Around," *Electronic Nevada*, 1996.

15. David Podmore, quoted in Crailes Communications, Sept/Oct 1999.

16. Justine Hunter, "Convention Centre Cost Worries Campbell," *Vancouver Sun*, March 1, 1999.

17. VANOC was unable to come up with a business plan until two and a half years after winning the bid, and when it did come out, it was remarkably long on business platitudes, short on actual details and full of flakey accounting practices. As an example of the latter, the document released in May 2007 avoids any suggestion that the capital costs associated with infrastructure of the Games, that is, RAV, the convention center, or the Sea to Sky Highway projects, are Olympic costs, yet in one appendix to the Plan, they call these same projects "Olympic Legacies." This sort of accounting was part of what got Enron into difficulty.

18. Miller, ibid.

19. Concert Properties Ltd. current board of directors:
Jack W. Poole, Chairman and Chief Executive Officer (also Vancouver 2010 Organizing Committee Chairman); David R. Podmore, President & Chief Executive Officer, Concert Properties Ltd. (amongst a few other things). Others: A. Gordon Armstrong, retired executive, Canfor Corporation Ltd.; Bruce Bell, President, Telecommunications Workers Union; Robert Beynon, VP of Benefits, Compensation & Operations, Telus Corporation; Nancy Curley, alternate business agent, Telecommunications Workers Union; John Davies, Chair, Board of Trustees, Carpentry and Workers' Pension Plan of BC; Gerry J. Forcier, Trustee, Pipefitters Local 170 Pension Plan; Leif Hansen, Trustee, United Food & Commercial Workers Pension Plan; Rodney D. Hiebert, Robert Matters, President, Steelworkers Local 1-405; Don L. McGill, Secretary-Treasurer, Teamsters, Local Union 213; Charles R. Peck, Chariman, Health & Welfare Pension Plan, International Brotherhood of Electrical Workers, Local 213; David Schaub, National Representative, Communications, Energy and Paperworkers Union of Canada; Brooke Sundin, President, UFCW Local 1518; Anthony A. Tennessy, Consultant, Operating Engineers' Welfare & Pension Plan; Bryan Wall, Trustee, United Food & Commercial Workers Pension Plan.

20. Actually, as we've seen from the discussions of VLC and other Poole enterprises, this dual nature is not unusual and appears structured to have a development as well as a real estate holding arm. So in fact, there were probably two companies with the same owners.

21. Jeff Lee, "Developer Drops out of Olympics Work," *Vancouver Sun*, Oct. 6, 2005.

22. The Malek brothers apparently further impressed Vancouver city councilors with claims that they had proposed building a massive Olympic training complex in the Iranian desert for Tehran's 1984 Olympic bid (Bob Mackin, personal communication)

23. It turns out that Barbeau resigned as president in January 2006, sort of perfect timing since the deal with the City was announced that April.

24. During the summer, Millennium had quietly re-registered in BC, first as "Millennium O.V." in June 2006; then with their current name in July 2007.

25. The Athletes' Village condos are now advertised from between $450,000 and $6 million in a recent *Georgia Straight* ad. See: millenniumwater.com.

26. While there had been various estimates for the total construction expenses for the Athletes' Village, the most realistic number is the following based on the City's own numbers: $153.4 site remediation (paid by the City) (Jody Andrews, Report to City Council, Administrative Report "Redevelopment of Southeast False Creek," April 4, 2006); $82.2 million paid by the City to Millennium for the City's 250 units; at the same ratio, an additional $279.48 million in construction costs to Millennium for the remainder of the 850 units. Total: over $515.08 million.

27. Future of village: 107 units of "middle income" housing will revert back to Millennium

after 20 years (Frances Bula, "Olympic Village Housing May Return to Developer," *Vancouver Sun*, Jan. 27, 2007.

28. I had been following this for 2010 Watch and the Work Less Party since the deal was announced in April 2006. Our first press release in February 2007 led to an article by Kent Spencer of the *Province*, "Games Watchdog Says Village Costs Are Being Hidden," Feb. 5, 2007. We put out a second press release on the story in May 2007 after our meeting with Vancouver City staff.

Chapter 9

1. Minister of Transportation Kevin Falcon speaking to the Lower Mainland Municipal Association's annual general meeting, comparing his "problems" with transportation projects to the eaze with which a 32-kilometer bridge that was recently built to connect mainland China to a new, island-based deep-water port. Quoted from an article by Sean Holman, *Public Eye Online*, May 17, 2006. [Italics, mine]. Falcon's attitude to those who defy his projects was amply highlighted at Eagleridge Bluffs. The same attitude is already on display in regard to the Gateway project.

2. One recent news report noted that some 72 percent of businesses along Cambie had suffered a loss in sales. Fourteen percent of these were considering closing. One local business owner was quoted as saying, "It's very hard.... Losing money and the stress.... I've lost a couple of years of my life, and it will be impossible to catch up." Jeff Hodson, "Survey Tracks Canada Line Pain," *Metro*, Oct. 23, 2007.

3. SNC-Lavalin is nothing if not diversified. Other than making Vancouverites crazy with the Canada Line, they are also helping to kill Iraqis and Afghanis by supplying bullets and other munitions to the US military. SNC has also been contracted for a variety of services by the Canadian Forces in Afghanistan. Their shareholders must love them.

4. The Work Less Party was founded by South African expatriate Conrad Schmidt in 2005 as a provincial party. A Vancouver civic version was created the same year, and a federal party (October 2007) has now been established. Schmidt is the author of the critically acclaimed *Workers of the World Relax*.

5. Schmidt and his partner, Chantal Morin, produced and directed the Olympic documentary *Five Ring Circus*.

6. Glen Clark was BC's opinionated premier in 1993, the year that saw large-scale protests and arrests in Clayoquot Sound on Vancouver Island's west coast.

7. I obtained a copy written by West Vancouver's environmental coordinator and municipal arborist, Stephen Jenkins, which talked about the development of the Ridge. The letter had been sent to provincial and federal environmental protection officers. Both ignored it. I, in turn, passed my copy of the letter to Kent Spencer of the *Province* who wrote an article about it, "1,800 Homes Envisioned on Eagleridge Bluffs," *Province*, June 5, 2006.

8. Freedom of Information legislation at the provincial level mirrors federal Access to Information legislation: Both allow delays in compliance, both can come with hefty fees for "staff time" and both allow the agency being questioned to "sever" information that they simply don't want to reveal. My experience is that agencies will often use all of these tactics to frustrate any information request. The onus is on the person seeking information to complain through the office of the provincial or federal information commissioner for resolution.

9. Stephen Jenkins, ibid.

10. Nahanee was originally from the Pacheedaht First Nation.

11. Kiewit and Sons are based out of Omaha, Nebraska. When not destroying endangered habitat in British Columbia, they also build bases for the US military.

12. The Hartwicks have reams of documents exposing those involved in swiping the Callaghan project. The coverup of wrongdoing here has been so massive, involving so many in government, that much of the press have simply been scared off. Most recently, Bob Mackin of 24 Hours had his story on the Hartwicks killed by his editor, but it ran in Business in Vancouver, "Powder Mountain Ski Resort Controversy Exhumed in Lead-up to 2010 Olympics," Aug. 14–20, 2007.

13. The BC government gave the Squamish and Lil'wat bands 122 hectares of land in eight parcels in exchange for allowing VANOC and Whistler to go ahead with development of the Callaghan. Clare Ogilvie, "Olympic-sized Land Deal 'a Winner,'" Province, May 11, 2007.

14. Jeff Lee, "2010 Olympics Come to Callaghan," Vancouver Sun, Feb. 15, 2006.

15. Andrew Jennings, The Great Olympic Swindle: When the World Wanted Its Games Back, Simon and Schuster, UK, 2000.

16. Andrew Jennings, ibid., chapter 3, "There's Jim and Earl and Frank and Nick and Spence and Bob and All Those Fellows Doing Deals in Salt Lake," pp. 38–48.

17. A curious sidebar to all of this is that the Hartwicks have never been against the Games, but merely want "their" project back. They thus joined the protesters at Eagleridge Bluffs in being pro-Games but against the outcomes that the Games routinely deliver, a failed strategy if there ever was one.

18. Mackin, ibid.

19. Charlie Smith, "Think Vancouver: Convention Centre II: Boon or Boondoggle?" Georgia Straight, March 3–10, 2005.

20. Donald Gutstein, "Developers Are the Games' Real Winners," Georgia Straight, May 31–June 7, 2007.

21. Vaughn Palmer, "Dobell's Rationale: He Sees No Conflict of Interest, Thus He Doesn't Have One", Vancouver Sun, May 1, 2007.

22. Some of Ken Dobell's official roles (VANOC, 2010 Legacies, and the Canadian Public Service Agencies websites) include: Former Chair of the Vancouver Convention Centre Expansion Project (he was recently replaced by Concert Property's David Podmore); Director of VANOC and chair of VANOC's Finance Committee; Director of the 2010 Legacies Now Society; Director of the Canadian Council for Public Private Partnerships. From April 2006 to the present, Dobell held a contract as advisor to the City of Vancouver and the City Manager in regard to social housing developments. Dobell registered as a lobbyist in October 2006, six months after the contract began, and in violation of guidelines under the Lobbyist Registration Act. Past roles: 1999 to April 2001, Chief Executive Officer of the Greater Vancouver Transportation Authority; June 1990 to December 1998, Vancouver's City Manager. He was first appointed as Deputy City Manager in 1978.

23. Ken Dobell's paw prints are all over the Gateway project, too, as "special advisor" to Premier Campbell.

Chapter 10

1. A direct quote from a CBC radio reporter from an eastern province after an interview I did in the spring of 2003. She was clearly afraid for her job if she ran anything related

to the conflicts of interest of her boss, CBC Chair, Carole Taylor. Given that the job might still be in jeopardy, the reporter will remain anonymous.

2. Taylor has since gone on to run as a "star" candidate for the BC Liberals in the provincial election of 2005, easily won her seat in the legislature and now serves as Finance Minister in Gordon Campbell's Liberal government. She had frequently been named in the mainstream press as a future successor to Premier Gordon Campbell. She now plans to leave politics before the 2009 provincial elections.

3. Heiberg duly lost, at least in part because of the allegations of conflicts of interest.

4. Peter Mansbridge is CBC's chief anchor of the nightly national news hour.

5. Laura Lynch is now one of CBC's regular European-based correspondents.

6. My alleged "conflicts" were presented on CBC Radio and their website: "Ethical Questions Raised about Anti-Olympic Campaign," July 4, 2003: cbc.ca/canada/british-columbia/story/2003/07/04/bc_shaw20030704.html

7. Here are some CBC reporters, in no particular order, who've done some credible work on Olympic issues: Pierre Martineau (French CBC), Natalie Clancy, Alan Waterman, Eric Rankin, Chris Brown and Maureen Palmer. Thanks to you all, but imagine what we'd know and the service to the public that would have been served if CBC/Carole Taylor had really let you do your jobs instead of kowtowing to the Olympic gods of television broadcasting rights.

8. Jeff Lee, "2010 Games' Venue Deals Revealed in Court," *Vancouver Sun*, May 4, 2007.

9. Kent Spencer, "Unsigned 2010 Deal Raises Fears: Watchdog Says Arena Owners Have Committee 'Over a Barrel,'" *Province*, April 28, 2006.

10. The real story ("Games Watchdog Says Village Costs Are Being Hidden") was buried in pretty pictures of the Athletes' Village and the main article: Kent Spencer, "Athletes to Have Royal Stay," *Province*, Feb. 5, 2007.

11. Bob Mackin, "Powder Mountain Ski Resort Controversy Exhumed in Lead-up to 2010 Olympics," *Business in Vancouver*, Aug. 14–20, 2007.

12. Mackin was, however, able to eventually get some stories about the growing anti-Olympic movement into *24 Hours*.

13. In the summer of 2007, Conrad Schmidt and I had put out a press release with an extensive backgrounder detailing how much Olympic security was really going to cost. Only the *Georgia Straight* reported it. In October 2007, we did a detailed press release with backgrounder showing the amount of carbon dioxide, the number of trees cut down, habitat destruction, etc. for the Games (see chapter 15). We'd held a press conference to present these numbers, had brought up the American environmental group Guard Fox Watch to support our conclusions and thought we'd really made an impact. Lots of reporters came to the press conference, but neither the *Sun*, *Province* nor English CBC reported a single word of it. Against such harsh facts, there was no room even for "balance."

14. For a good depiction of corporate journalism and what happens to reporters who buck their managers, see *Into the Buzzsaw: Leading Journalists Expose the Myth of a Free Press*, Kristina Borjesson (Ed.), Prometheus Books, 2002.

Chapter 11

1. John Carlos speaking about the Olympics. From an interview with David Zirin, quoted in *Welcome to the Terrordome: The Pain, Politics, and Promise of Sports*, Haymarket Press, Chicago, 2007, p. 126.

2. Ibid.

3. Jeff Lee and Gary Kingston, "Win Medals, Earn $$$," *Vancouver Sun*, Nov. 20, 2007.

4. And for once, the *Vancouver Sun* agreed in an editorial, "Cash for Olympians Sends the Wrong Message about What's Important in Sports, *Vancouver Sun*, Nov. 24, 2007.

5. Andrew Jennings, *The Great Olympic Swindle: When the World Wanted Its Games Back*, Simon & Schuster, London, 2000.

6. Stars on Ice and IMG Sports and Entertainment.

7. The firm of Hill and Knowlton is mentioned in relation to the Salt Lake City crisis (as cited in Jennings; see chapter 7; they were used again to manage problems with Sydney's bid. See also Helen J Lenskyj, *The Best Olympics Ever? Social Impacts of Sydney 2000*, State University of New York Press, Albany, 2002.

8. C.M. Hall, *Tourism and Politics*, Wiley, 1994; cited in Lenskyj, ibid.

9. Lenskyj, ibid., p. 98.

10. Ibid., p. 66.

11. Varda Burstyn in regard to Salt Lake City Olympic scandals in her foreword to Helen Lenskyj's book, *Inside the Olympic Industry: Power, Politics, and Activism*. State University of New York Press, Albany, 2000, p. xiii.

12. Ibid.

13. Ibid. p. 99.

14. Thomas Walkom, "The Olympic Myth of Calgary," *Toronto Star*, Feb. 8, 1999.

15. "The Importance of the Olympics," *Globe and Mail* editorial, 1996, quoted from Lenskyj, ibid., p. 100.

16. Kevin Potvin is the controversial editor of the independent East Vancouver newspaper *The Republic of East Vancouver*. He found himself tarred as an Al Qaeda supporter after an article he had written for *The Republic* after 9/11 created a delayed firestorm. Potvin's article, "A Revolting Confession" (vol. 28, 2002), owned up to his conflicting emotions on watching the twin towers fall: One part of his psyche was appalled and saddened by the loss of innocent life; another part saw in the attack just comeuppance against an empire that had suppressed much of the planet with its military and economic clout. The 2002 article was well known in East Vancouver's activist circles. It was "leaked" to the press by individuals/political parties unknown (but suspected) in 2006, shortly after Potvin announced his intention to run for the Green Party of Canada. In their frenzy to lynch Potvin for allegedly supporting the massacre of the 9/11 victims, some in the press saw an easy link between Potvin's/*The Republic's* anti-globalization stance and his supposed support for Al Qaeda.

Chapter 12

1. Mitt Romney is the former governor of Massachusetts and was, until recently, candidate for the Republican presidential nomination in 2008. Back before 2000, Romney was the replacement CEO for the Salt Lake City Organizing Committee (SLCOC) after the organization floundered under the IOC bribery "votes for scholarships" scandal.

2. Holger Preuss, *The Staging of the Olympics: A Comparison of the Games 1972-2008*, Edward Elgar, Cheltenham, UK, 2007.

3. Intrawest was bought out by the Fortress Investment Group of New York in August 2006 for a reported $2.8 billion. A subsidiary of Fortress, Fortress Credit Corp is one of the project lenders for the Vancouver Athletes' Village project.

4. Ibid, pp. 15–18.

5. Ibid., p. 276, Figure 12.1.

6. Athens costs were actually $14. 2 billion officially, but could have been up to $20 billion; Beijing costs are $60 billion according to a CBC radio news report on Sept. 10, 2007.

7. Philip K. Porter, "Mega-Sports Events as Municipal Investments: A Critique of Impact Analysis, *Sports Economics: Current Research*, John Fizel, Elizabeth Gustafson and Lawrence Hadley (Eds.), Praeger Press, 1999.

8. Preuss, ibid., pp. 62–64.

9. Ibid, p. 253, Fig. 10.4.

10. The Los Angeles Games showed a $222 million surplus overall. Much of this went to youth and national sports federations.

11. Thomas Walkom, "The Olympic Myth of Calgary," *Toronto Star*, Feb. 8, 1999.

12. Kent Spencer, "Hidden Costs in Details of Olympic Contracts," Kent Spencer, *Province*, Apr. 14, 2006; Daphne Bramham, "Wimpy Local Politicians' Olympism Digs Us in Deeper, *Vancouver Sun*, Feb. 10, 2007.

13. Damian Inwood, "Athlete Center Over Budget," *Province* , Aug. 17, 2007.

14. Ibid.

15. Damian Inwood, "Yaletown Park to Become Party Zone," *Province*, Sept. 13, 2007.

16. Vaughn Palmer, "Dear Taxpayer: Here's Your Olympics Bill," *Vancouver Sun*, June 14, 2002.

17. Daphne Bramham, "Olympic Budget Keeps Growing", *Vancouver Sun*, Jan. 31, 2003.

18. Marvin Shaffer, Alan Greer and Celine Mauboules, "Olympic Costs and Benefits: A Cost-Benefit Analysis of the Proposed Vancouver 2010 Winter Olympic and Paralympic Games," Canadian Council on Policy Alternatives (CCPA), 2003; Canadian Taxpayers Federation (CTF): The following is only one example of the concern the CTF feels about the entire Olympic project from a fiscal perspective: Maureen Bader, "Olympic Security Cost Explosion Result of Blank Cheque, news release, July 26, 2007, CTF website: taxpayer.com/main/news.php?type_id=1&topic_id=5. The Fraser Institute's Niels Veldhuis called the Bid Corp and the BC governments rosy economic projections for Games benefits "nonsense." The office of BC's Auditor General also points out numbers the Bid Corp didn't like: "Review of Estimates Related to Vancouver's Bid to Stage the 2010 Olympic Winter Games and Paralympic Winter Games," 2002/2003 General Report.

19. None other than Jeff Lee of the *Vancouver Sun*.

20. In the movie *The Matrix* , Neo (Keanu Reeves) is offered the choice of two pills, one blue and one red. If he takes the red pill, he will be launched into the real world in which a tiny group of rebels battle a machine culture that has enslaved most of humanity if he takes the blue, he returns to ignorance. Neo takes the red pill, his eyes are opened and he more-or-less willingly joins the resistance.

21. Kevin Potvin, "There Is Sufficient Money for Global Warming," *The Republic of East Vancouver*, Aug. 16-29, 2007.

22. David Eby of Pivot Legal had come up with some novel uses for the City's hoped-for profit from the Athletes' Village: the $64 million windfall, along with some other funds, could be used to pay for the construction of 3,200 housing units that the city's homeless urgently need. Eby presented his proposal to City Council in June 2007. One Vision Vancouver councilor found it "interesting." The ruling NPA ignored it.

23. Helen Lenskyj, *The Best Olympics Ever? Social Impacts of Sydney 2000*, State University of New York Press, Albany, 2002.

24. An ad for a seminar put on by the National Foreclosure Institute, *LA Times*, July 27, 2007.

25. The Gross Domestic Product (GDP), the most commonly used indicator of economic success, is "outcomes" neutral: GDP can increase if the country is hit by a disaster like hurricane Katrina, just as it can if business is more productive in producing necessary goods and services. Notably, some folks did really, really well out of the misery the storm left in its wake.

26. As of September 18, 2007, the US Federal Reserve lowered the prime interest rate by half a percent. This emergency measure may buy the industry some time.

27. Lenskyj, ibid., p. 93.

28. Ibid., p. 95.

29. Ibid., p. 90.

30. Helen Lenskyj, "The Olympic (Affordable) Housing Legacy and Social Responsibility," in N. Crowther, R. Barney and M. Heine (Eds.), *Cultural Imperialism in Action: Proceedings of the Eighth International Symposium for Olympic Research*, 2006, University of Western Ontario, London, ON, pp. 191–199.

31. Helen Lenskyj, *The Best Olympics Ever?*, p. 2.

32. VANOC had yet to come up with their mascot for the 2010 Games. The betting was that they would choose a furry animal like the unusual white Kermode bear of northern B.C. If it weren't so politically incorrect, one might expect that VANOC's long-awaited mascot would be to be a Native baby, rather than a cute furry animal. We at NO GAMES picked one for them to save them the trouble: a skunk with Jack Poole's face on it. In the end, they came up with three mascots: A sasquatch; a bear-thunderbird-like thing; and another weird hybrid — the companion to these was a Vancouver Island marmot.

33. The Auditor General did it himself, but was unable to figure out where all the money went, cited in Helen Lenskyj, *The Best Olympics Ever? Social Impacts of Sydney 2000*.

34. Lenskyj, ibid., p. 61.

35. Lenskyj, ibid., p. 56.

Chapter 13

1. Joe Moulin's 2007 documentary, *Citizen Sam*.

2. The list includes: the American Hotel, Burns Block, Marr Hotel, Pender Hotel and Picadilly Hotel. The APC's Anna Hunter estimates that the total number of lost units of low-income housing is over 800 since 2003. Pivot's David Eby's guess is closer to 500 rooms. See official City estimates at city.vancouver.bc.ca/commsvcs/housing/pdf/2007SRAsurvey.pdf. Eby notes that these estimates "don't count student conversions or rent inflation putting rooms beyond welfare rates as rooms closed to low income people."

3. The numbers are from Anna Hunter and David Eby. Eby cites the "GVRD Homeless Count," which can be found at gvrd.bc.ca/homelessness/pdfs/HomelessCount2005 Final.pdf

4. John Bermingham, "Coleman Touts New Strategy for Downtown Eastside, Sending Homeless to Other Parts of BC a Possibility," *Province*, June 24, 2007.

5. An upper-middle-class enclave almost directly south across False Creek from the Downtown Eastside.

6. Francis Bula, "Housing Promises in Olympic Bid Unlikely to Be Kept, Report Says," *Vancouver Sun*, June 25, 2007.

7. Carlito Pablo, "It's a Bad Time to Be Poor," *Georgia Straight*, May 31–June 7, 2007.

8. Project Civil City website: mayorsamsullivan.ca/pdf/project-civil-city.pdf.

9. See *Georgia Straight*: straight.com/article/sullivan-bullish-on-disorder.

10. Richard Rosenberg, professor emeritus at UBC and a board member of the BC Civil Liberties Association, argues that the cameras are unlikely to vanish after 2010. See Vancouver Public Spaces website: vancouverpublicspace.ca/index.php/campaigns/surveillance.

11. Bob Mackin from *24 Hours*, quoting from an interview with VANOC CEO John Furlong.

12. Bula, ibid.

13. Dharm Makwana, "Poverty Gaining Ground: Envoy," *24 Hours*, Oct. 17, 2007. The Carnegie Community Action Project and other anti-poverty groups reported the situation to the UN's Special Rapporteur Miloon Kothari. Kothari was writing a report on homelessness and poverty in Canada for the UN.

14. Clare Ogilvie, "Olympic Venues' Progress Report," *Province*, Feb. 11, 2007; Dan Raley, "Olympics a Natural Fit for Whistler, Boosters Say," *Seattle Post-Intelligencer*, Aug. 31, 2004.

15. Helen Lenskyj, *The Best Olympics Ever? Social Impacts of Sydney 2000*, State University of New York, Albany, 2002, p. 10.

16. Helen Beatty, "Atlanta's Olympic Legacy," *Progressive Planning*, 161, 2004.

17. Lenskyj, ibid., p. 138.

18. Wendy Petersen of the Carnegie Action project has documented rising rental prices throughout Vancouver, including in the Downtown Eastside where many of the poor live.

19. Lenskyj, ibid., p. 3.

20. COHRE report: cohre.org/mega-events.

21. Ibid.

22. Reed Eurchuk, "Olympics Cause Displacement," *The Republic of East Vancouver*, July 19-Aug. 1, 2007.

23. Ibid.

24. Lenskyj, ibid., p. 114.

25. These included: Janet Austin, YWCA; Carole Brown-Ray, Cam Community Centre; Tung Chan, S.U.C.C.E.S.S.; Nancy Chiavario, Mt. Pleasant Community Centre Association; Ken Clement, Lu'ma Native Housing Society; David Eby, Impact of the Olympics Community Coalition; Maureen Enser, Urban Development Institute; Robert Funt, Salient Group; Paul Gauther, BC Paraplegic Association; Al Kemp, BC Apartment Owners and Managers Association; Kim Kerr, Downtown East Residents Association; Martha Lews, Tenant Resource & Advisory Centre; Andrew Mak, Strathcona Community Centre; Karen O'Shannacery, Lookout Emergency Aid Society; Peter Simpson, Greater Vancouver Home Builders' Association; Terry Soper, Gather Place DTS; Jean Swanson, Carnegie Community Action Project; Krista Thompson, Covenant House. Shayne Ramsay, BC Housing, ICI Housing Table facilitator; Cameron Gray, Celine Maboules, City of Vancouver Housing Centre (Celine Maboules is one of the staff people who drafted the City's response to the report); Steve Hall, Canada Mortgage and Housing Corporation; Greg Steves, Heather Brazier, BC Housing Policy Branch; Andrea Long, Service Canada; Suzanne Bell, BC Residential Tenancy Branch; Enzo Guerriero, VANOC; Elizabeth Bowker (recording), VANOC.

26. Report of the Inner-City Inclusivity Table, March 2007: vancouver.ca/commsvcs/housing/pdf/icihousingtablemar07.pdf

27. David Eby, "A Plan to Achieve the 2010 Olympic Housing Commitments," presented to Vancouver City Council.

28. Helen, J Lenskyj, "The Olympic (Affordable) Housing Legacy and Social Responsibility," in N. Crowther, R. Barney and M. Heine (Eds.), *Cultural Imperialism in Action: Proceedings of the Eighth International Symposium for Olympic Research*, University of Western Ontario, London, 2006, pp. 191–199.

29. Lenskyj, ibid., p. 8.

30. Helen, J. Lenskyj, *The Best Olympics Ever?*, citing David Whitson and Donald Macintosh (1996), p. 292.

Chapter 14

1. Charlie Smith, "2010: It's the Terror, Stupid," *Georgia Straight*, Aug. 11, 2005.

2. "Legacies of North American Winter Games," VANOC website: vancouver2010.com/en

3. Holger Preuss, *The Economics of Staging the Olympics: A Comparison of the Games 1972–2008*, Edward Elgar, Cheltenham, UK, and Northhampton, MA, 2004, p. 226.

4. Peter Severinson, "2010 Olympics Will Need Extra Money for Security," *Province*, June 6, 2006.

5. Security costs for 1984, 1988, 1992, 1996 and 2000, *Wall Street Journal*, Aug. 22, 2004, cited in mindfully.org/Reform/2004/Olympic-Games-Security22aug04.htm; for Montreal's 1976 Summer Olympics: Holger Preuss, *The Economics of Staging the Olympics: A Comparison of the Games 1972–2008*; Salt Lake City's security cost estimate ranges between $330 million, Charlie Smith, "2010: It's the Terror, Stupid," to $350 million, "Legacies of North American Winter Games," VANOC website: vancouver2010.com/en. The cost of security at Nagano in 1998, about $180 million, represents a mid-range of estimates from various sources; the cost of the 2004 and 2006 Games is cited in Zellen, note 21; projections for 2012 are from "2010 Olympic Security Costs Soar," UPI, Dec. 11, 2007: newsdaily.com/Sports/UPI-1-20071211-10284800-bc-oly-budget.xml.

6. "2010 Olympic Security Costs Soar," UPI, Dec. 11, 2007: newsdaily.com/Sports/UPI-1-20071211-10284800-bc-oly-budget.xml.

7. From mindfully.org; ABC Australia website, Olympic Index.

8. The City of Sydney and Salt Lake City's bid contracts required a high level of security for key Olympic Family members, especially those classified as "visiting dignitaries." Helen J. Lenskyj, *The Best Olympics Ever? Social Impacts of Sydney 2000*, State University of New York Press, Albany, p. 44.

9. 142.36.102.61/2010Secretariat/Downloads/CostSharingMOA_e.pdf

10. A Canadian Forces (CF) memo in February 2006 noted that the headquarters for the CF contribution would be at the Esquimalt naval base on Vancouver Island. CF security preparations and operations for 2010 will be called Op PODIUM. Officially, it was to begin in Ottawa in March 2007.

11. CSIS's actual track record in dealing with real versus imaginary threats is legendary in Canada: They utterly failed to track Sikh terrorists who would later blow up an Air India jetliner with 329 people aboard; at the same time, they were investigating "radical" groups such as student anti-globalization protesters and the Raging Grannies, a group of grandmothers who show up at political protests and sing satirical songs.

12. Which just got a $30 million upgrade for 2010, adding more hidden costs.

13. There were rumors that the IOC was unhappy with the official security numbers and said so at a meeting in Guatemala City just before Harriman left his post. His replacement, Chief Superintendent Bud Mercer, was appointed in late October 2007.

14. For those unfamiliar with the application processes at federal, provincial and municipal levels, the take-home message is this: It's not meant to be simple, accessible or even free. All levels of government retain the authority under existing legislation to obtain long extensions before providing requested information, can "sever" material they don't want to reveal and can charge for processing. This can be thousands of dollars, usually a significant barrier to individuals or social activist groups.

15. Jeff Lee, "Olympic Security, What Will It Cost?" *Vancouver Sun*, July 8, 2006, quoting Senator (Canadian) Colin Kenny, head of the Senate Committee on Security. Lee cites the following figures: costs of at least $350 million; numbers of personnel, 500 Vancouver Police Department, 1,150 other police; RCMP, 3,700 constables; volunteer law enforcement, 1,500; contract security, 3,000; civilian volunteers, 2,500; military, unknown. The total expected, according to Lee, is 12, 350.

16. rcmp-grc.gc.ca/.

17. rcmp-grc.gc.ca/.

18. The 2010 Winter Olympics will run from February 12 to 28, 17 days. The Paralympics take place from March 12 to 21, 10 days. While the latter may not require the same security presence, those staying on for Paralympic security are unlikely to be released in the in-between period. Thus, whatever savings may be realized by cutting personnel will be more than offset by the additional time for overall coverage that is now closer to six weeks in duration. With a month pre-deployment before the February dates and a month of clean-up and teardown afterwards, the total period in question is now about three and a half months.

19. In another related matter, the Air Force chief has said there is a need to integrate unmanned aerial vehicles in the Air Force that he said can be used in time for 2010.

20. At the G8 summit in 2002 in Calgary/Kananaskis, all of the police on the streets had brand new mountain bikes.

21. Barry Zellen, "Olympic Security in the Age of Mass Terror," securityinnovator.com, June 15, 2007.

22. IOC Guatemala City meeting, ibid.

23. I have to thank Wendy Petrik of the Vancouver Port Authority (VPA), since once she realized what I wanted, she quickly supplied the required information. The VPA response is in marked contrast to most of the other agencies that I wrote to with Freedom of Information or Access to Information requests. The other shining example of cooperation came, to my surprise, from the RCMP.

24. "So what" questions are an army technique to figure out contingencies and what you can do about them. For example, say you identify that one major threat to the movement of athletes in 2010 arises from having to cross bridges. So what? Well, blocking a bridge means you have to get the athletes where they are going in another way. So what? So, you have to drive them along a different route. So what? It may take a lot more time; it may face more obstacles, etc. So what? Schedules are now out of whack. So what? Disrupted schedules lead to more security headaches as the security personnel struggle to adjust on the fly. Et cetera. The result of such an exercise is meant to be a conclusion that some particular action needs to occur, leading to a job or task for some unit to perform in order to ensure that any contingencies have been covered.

25. John Colebourn, "RCMP documents warn 2010 Olympics Security Budget Inadequate," *CanWest News Service*, July 27, 2007.
26. Jeff Lee and Miro Cernetig, "Fortress British Columbia," *Vancouver Sun*, Aug. 4, 2007.

Chapter 15

1. Richmond Oval Art Plan, presented to Richmond City Council, April 25, 2006.
2. Rafe Mair, "Let's Learn from Eagleridge Bluffs Protest," *The Tyee*, March 5, 2007.
3. The dimensions of the road equate to 120,000 square meters. A hectare is 10,000 square meters. Hence the area destroyed is approximately 12 hectares. According to Joe Foy of the Western Canada Wilderness Committee, a hectare in this area will contain about 400 trees of all types (old growth and secondary) of different species and ages.
4. The number of trees cut depends on calculating the volume of the logged wood per truckload. Eckhard had figured 575 truckloads, but at the 30 cubic meters volume this is more like 633 truckloads or 19,000 cubic meters of wood for a total of 18,990 trees. Note that these estimates do not include the loss of secondary growth, so the total number of trees destroyed is likely far higher than presented here.
5. VANOC: vancouver2010.com
6. VANOC "Sustainability Report" can be found on their website: vancouver2010.com/en/Sustainability/SustainabilityReport.
7. This was the letter sent by West Vancouver environmental officer Steven Jenkins to his provincial and federal counterparts in which he mentioned the 1,800 units slated for Eagleridge Bluffs.
8. ec.gc.ca/pdb/ghg/inventory_report/2004_trends/table3_e.cfm
9. Wendy Cox, "Defining the Olympic Cost," *Canadian Press*, Sept. 16, 2006. All of the numbers in this list are estimates based on various published reports that often vary considerably. It is important to note that, once construction begins, costs tend to creep upwards. The numbers given here are, if anything, low-end estimates. In reality, no one will ever be able to determine the actual true costs.
10. vccep.bc.ca
11. The Do RAV Right Coalition estimates the cost at over $2.5 billion, a likely underestimate given the contributions from the different players to date: doravright.ca.
12. CTV website, Feb. 4, 2006.
13. Charlie Smith, "City Mislead Taxpayers in '03," *Georgia Straight*, Sept. 28, 2006.
14. VANOC's contribution to the skating oval is now estimated to be at least $61 million (ctv.ca/servlet/ArticleNews/story/CTVNews/20060914/Olympics_costs_060914/20060914?hub=Canada) and up to $63.1 million according to VANOC's Business Plan (whistlerblackcomb.com/olympics/index.htm). The rest of the cost, about $115 million, is borne by the citizens of the City of Richmond.
15. This was the initial estimated cost that the Resort Municipality of Whistler would have to pay above and beyond VANOC's projected contributions (see VANOC's Business Plan: vancouvercondo.info/2006/08/olympics-are-expensive.html). Newer information suggests that the cost to Whistler could end up between $45 million and $50 million (Vancouver Condo Info: vancouvercondo.info/2006/08/olympics-are-expensive.html).
16. This is a minimal number based on the City of Vancouver's site remediation costs and the cost of construction for the 1,100 units.
17. As in note 15.

18. Dave Rudberg, administrative report RR-1a, Dec. 21, 2006, presented to Vancouver City Council. Rudberg is Vancouver's "Olympic czar."
19. A safe number (see chapter 14) for local security personnel would be about 1,000 reservists, 1,000 Vancouver Police Department and 1,000 RCMP. Of the estimated total of 15,000, this means some 12,000 persons will be brought to BC from elsewhere in Canada.
20. From the Terrapass website: terrapass.com
21. Ibid. One cross-country flight/passenger is equivalent to 4 months of driving, or 100 gallons of gas. The calculation for CO_2 as a result of air travel goes like this: 5,391 miles (1 mile = 1.61 km or 8,679.5 km) gives 2,102 lbs CO_2 or 955.5 kg. (1kg = 2.2 lbs). Hence a flight of 8,679.5 km gives 955.5 kg CO_2 or 0.11 kg CO_2/km. Based on trip length:
   Air short haul: 3,540 × 0.11 × 90,333 (visitors) = 35,175,670.2 kg CO_2/1000 = 35,176 tons (rounding up); Cross country: 10460 × 0.11 × 102,333 = 11,774,435 kg = 117,744 tons; International flights: 20,920 × 0.11 × 90,333 = 207,874,300 kg = 207,874 tons.
22. C.W. Schmidt, "Putting the Earth in Play: Environmental Awareness and Sports," *Environmental Health Perspectives*, 2006, 114, A 286–295.
23. Time for Change: timeforchange.org/CO2-emissions-by-country.
24. The GHG intensity of GDP in BC in 2004 was 0.52 kt CO_2 per/$million of GDP, 520 tons per million dollars spent in the BC economy. It's probably a little more than that today in 2007, but not by much: ec.gc.ca/pdb/ghg/inventory_report/2004_trends/table3_e.cfm
25. "Meeting the Challenge: A Carbon Neutral 2010 Winter Games": davidsuzuki.org.
26. R. S. Cowles, E. A Cowles, A. M. McDermott and D. Ramoutar, "Inert Formulation Ingredients with Activity: Toxicity of Trisiloxane Surfactant Solutions to Twospotted Spider Mites (*Acari tetranychidae*)," *Journal of Economic Entomology*, 93, 2000, pp. 180–188.
27. VANOC "Sustainability Report," vancouver2010.com/en/Sustainability/SustainabilityReport.
28. The recommendations were produced by Guard Fox Watch, an environmental watchdog group based in San Francisco: planetdrum.org/guard_fox_watch.htm.
29. Personnal communication, Stefano Bertone, spokesperson for Nolimpiadi!
30. Helen, J. Lenskyj, *The Best Olympics Ever? Social Impacts of Sydney 2000*, State University of New York, Albany, 2002.
31. Poole is apparently quite ill with pancreatic cancer. Whether he will be around to collect his ultimate reward is thus debatable.
32. Bob Mackin, "Powder Mountain Ski Resort Controversy Exhumed in Lead-up to 2010 Olympics," *Business in Vancouver*, August 14–20, 2007.

Chapter 16

1. "Red Emma" (1869–1940), an anarchist opponent of both capitalism and Marxism, was an early feminist, social activist, editor, writer, teacher and rabble-rouser. My own daughter is named after her. If my Emma could add one more descriptor to Goldman, it would be "rascal."
2. Helen J. Lenskyj, *The Best Olympics Ever? Social Impacts of Sydney 2000*, State University of New York, Albany, 2002, p. 87.
3. The quote is from an Anti-Olympics Alliance member quoted in R. Henschke, "Olympic Impact," *Vertigo*, 2, 26, 2000, cited in Lenskyj, ibid., p. 182.

4. 2010watch.com.

5. Native elder Harriet Nahanee died of pneumonia shortly after serving 14 days in Surrey Pretrial Centre. Members of the Native Youth Movement took the IOC's flag in her memory.

6. The Work Less Party now has three wings: civic, provincial and federal.

Chapter 17

1. The *Vancouver Sun*'s editorial in response to 2010 Watch's call for a true referendum, Sept. 29, 2006. Also the *Sun* was mistaken (about this and much more): the original vote in 2003 was a plebiscite, not a referendum.

2. Richard K. Moore, "Escaping the Matrix," *Whole Earth*, Summer 2000.

3. Moore, ibid.

4. The Fraser Institute is a private, neo-liberal think-tank in Vancouver.

5. This was analogous to the 2006 Canadian federal election in which a prominent Liberal minister of the governing party, David Emerson, jumped to the new Conservative government within days of the Liberal's loss. Many in the riding, especially those who had voted for Emerson as a Liberal, were simply outraged. Emerson, clearly not at all understanding why anyone would be peeved, made a famous statement to the effect that it didn't really matter since the parties were all alike anyway. The shock was palpable, not only amongst ordinary citizens, but also within the leadership of all major parties. One could almost hear them panicking as they realized that Emerson had given away the secret "handshake."

6. The full list is: "1. Public participation and full democratic accountability (full public disclosure of all aspects of Olympic preparations; public meetings and consultations, and neighborhood meetings, particularly in areas near venues; intervenor funding to allow independent community groups to conduct their own social/environmental impact studies; an ongoing independent watchdog to monitor all Organizing Committee, NOC, activities; IOC and other Olympic structures to be fully and democratically accountable to the residents and voters of the city and province/state; 2. Financial guarantees (firm financial commitments from government and the private sector; all public funds to be recovered; all direct and indirect costs to be fully and publicly accounted for; independent financial assessment, including cost/benefit analysis; no tax increases: corporate sponsors to share financial and social risks; the IOC and NOC share financial risks; functional rather than extravagant games). 3. Social equity (Olympic committees to be representative of the gender, racial and social cross cultural makeup of the city/state/country; Olympic housing to be 100% affordable and 60% social housing; rent protection; housing for the homeless; new and upgraded and affordable recreational facilities; affordable tickets to all events; free or low cost tickets for low income people). 4. Full social impact assessment (Olympic revenues to be put in a social investment fund, controlled by the community, for socially useful projects; non-harassment measures for street homeless people; measures to protect civil liberties, including freedom to peaceful assembly; sex equality and equal opportunity; environment; sexual parity on all committees, staffing and so forth; correcting the gender imbalance in Olympic sports; employment equity in hiring; accessible Games). 5. Environment (full environmental assessment and strategies at the bid stage; detailed plans for air/water quality and protection; detailed waste disposal plans; environmental assessment of traffic and transportation plans; green construction materials; recycling/reusing strategies). 6. Employment (no job loss; award wage

policy; no volunteers replacing paid workers; no loss of volunteers to existing charities). 7. Lasting standards (Olympic standards should be in effect throughout the bid,
preparation and staging of the Games; financial, social, and environmental impact assessments should cover at least a five year term from the end of the Games). From *Toward a Socially Responsible Olympic Games, Bread Not Circuses Coalition*, 1998, cited in
Helen J. Lenskyj, *The Best Olympics Ever? Social Impacts of Sydney 2000*, State University of New York Press, Albany, 2002, pp. 228–231.

7. As cited by Helen Lenskyj, the full list includes: 1. Reform of the IOC's structure
and function (to include: an open membership selection process; ending elitism and
sense of entitlement demonstrated by most IOC members and the overall lack of accountability to citizens of host cities; ending the IOC's exemption from conventions
regarding corruption and bribery; providing a transparent host city selection procedure, including listing visits of IOC members and officials). 2. Public oversight (no
more exemption by the IOC or bid organization from freedom of information legislation, full disclosure of all agreements demanded by business interests or sponsors;
an end to misleading budgets that hide or diminish taxpayer funded infrastructure
projects; and eliminate the secrecy and frank deceit in bid and organizing committees' communications with citizens). 3. Public relations campaign mounted by IOC
and bid and organizing committees. [Ending the media's complicity with the Olympic
industry that serves to stifle public debate and critique; allow the release of information on negative social /economic/environmental impact suppressed or preempted
by "Olympic spirit rhetoric" and the myth of the "pure athlete" and "pure sport."] Not
least, Lenskyj adds a crucial item to the third category, but one that just as well applies to the first two: Stop "assuming that citizens are unreflective dupes whose support is easily secured through Olympic propaganda". From Helen J. Lenskyj, *Inside the
Olympic Industry: Power, Politics, and Activism*, State University of New York, Albany,
2000, p. 192.

8. Helen J. Lenskyj, *The Best Olympics Ever: Social Impacts of Sydney 2000*.

9. Andrew Jennings, *The Great Olympic Swindle: When the World Wanted Its Games
Back*, concerning the OATH (Olympic Athletes Together Honorably) group's calls
for IOC reforms after the scandal of 1998. Lenskjy called the IOC's evental "reforms"
"new wine in old bottles."

10. Dave Zirin, *Welcome to the Terrordome: The Pain, Politics, and Promise of Sports*, Haymarket Books, Chicago, 2007, p. 218.

11. Brian Martin, "Ten Reasons to Oppose All Olympic Games, *Freedom*, 57, (15), Aug. 3,
1996, p. 7.

12. Rogge may, however, be getting complacent: In 2004 he put his son, Philippe, on the
Belgian Olympic Committee as a chief "administrator." See, "Philippe Rogge Rejoint
Son Père", Dec. 17, 2004: sport.fr.

13. The *encuentro* ("meeting") was called by the Zapatista National Liberation Front
(EZLN) and held in Yaqui territory on the outskirts of Vicam, Sonora, from Oct. 11
to 14, 2007. Over 1,500 delegates and observers were present. Subcomandante Marcos
gave the opening and closing remarks. At the end of the meeting, delegates adopted
a series of resolutions, including one committing them to fighting against the 2010
Olympic Games: zapateando.wordpress.com/2007/10/16/culmina-en-vicam-el-en-
cuentro-hemisferico-de-pueblos-indigenas/.

14. "No Olympics on Stolen Native Land," *Warrior*, 3, Summer 2007.

15. Lenskyj, ibid., p. 231.

16. Some organizations and their websites: World Olympic Watch, worldolympicwatch
.org/; 2010 Watch (Vancouver), 2010watch.com; see also no2010.com; London anti-
Olympics group, nobid@mayor-of-london.co.uk; and gamesmonitor.co.uk.

Epilogue

1. CBC gave the estimate of $60 billion in the fall of 2007.
2. COHRE report: cohre.org/mega-events.
3. Aileen McCabe, "China Charges Human-Rights Activist," *Vancouver Sun*, Feb. 2, 2008.
4. Richard Spencer, "Water Diversion Hurts China's Struggling Farmers," *Vancouver Sun*, Feb. 2, 2008.
5. Eric Reeves, "Holding China Accountable for Complicity in Darfur's Ongoing Genocidal Destruction," Dec. 17, 2006: sudanreeves.org/index.html.
6. Martin Slavin is an anti-Olympics activist in London: gamesmonitor.org.uk.
7. "Olympics: Russia Wins 2014 Winter Games," *Associated Press*, July 5, 2007.
8. Bob Barnett, "Next: 2014 Olympic Bid Putting Sochi on the Map," *Pique Newsmagazine*, June 28, 2007.
9. Ibid.
10. Chloe Arnold, "Russia: Environmentalists Oppose Sochi's Olympic Bid," Feb. 15, 2007: rferl.org/features/features_article/aspx?m=07&y=2007&id=20234E99-1493-4047-AFAB-00B2AD7DADCB
11. Barnett, ibid.
12. Ibid.
13. This was in response to an FOI filed by the author.
14. Some of the funny business about the latter includes the constantly escalating site remediation numbers (originally near $153.4 million, now mysteriously grown to $159.1 million. Also, reporter Bob Mackin and I were able to view the minute books for Millennium as well as Armeco Contruction. Here is what we found: Millennium holds no board meetings, has issued no shares and to date has not filed the required annual financial reports with the provincial Ministry of Finance. The documents cited previously did not show who the project lenders were. However, the City of Vancouver finally provided the required information after I filed a request under FOI legislation. What the City is calling "mortgage" holders are Fortress Credit Corp, a subdivision of Fortress Investment Group which bought the Whistler-Blackcomb resort from Intrawest in August 2006 for $2.8 billion, and the City itself. Ken Bayne, Director of Financial Planning and Treasury for Vancouver denies that being a mortgage holder is the same as a project lender, a distinction that seems awfully subtle. The minute books for Armeco revealed that the Malek brothers had indeed been directors of Armeco in the past, conclusively showing that the relationship was not as casual as they had stated earlier.
15. Delhi, India, is now building the venues for the 2010 Commonwealth Games. It's the same story as the Olympics: massive displacement of the poor and small businesses and environmental destruction, all driven by many of the same corporate interests. Indeed, India sees the Commonwealth Games as a trial balloon for a run at the 2020 Summer Olympics.

Index

About the author

CHRISTOPHER A. SHAW is a professor of Ophthalmology and the Program of Neuroscience at the University of British Columbia. The research in his laboratory focuses on identifying the causes of neurological diseases such as ALS and Parkinson's. He has published extensively in his field and is the author of over 200 peer reviewed articles and co-editor of three books. Shaw was a founding member and lead spokesperson for the No Games 2010 Coalition. Currently, he is the lead spokesperson for 2010 Watch and a policy and media analyst for the Work Less Party.

If you have enjoyed *Five Ring Circus*, you might also enjoy other

Books to Build a New Society

Our books provide positive solutions for people who want to
make a difference. We specialize in:
Sustainable Living ✦ Ecological Design and Planning
Natural Building & Appropriate Technology ✦ New Forestry
Environment and Justice ✦ Conscientious Commerce
Progressive Leadership ✦ Resistance and Community ✦ Nonviolence
Educational and Parenting Resources

New Society Publishers

ENVIRONMENTAL BENEFITS STATEMENT

New Society Publishers has chosen to produce this book on recycled
paper made with 100% post consumer waste, processed chlorine
free, and old growth free.
For every 5,000 books printed, New Society saves the following
resources:[1]

33	Trees
3,020	Pounds of Solid Waste
3,322	Gallons of Water
4,334	Kilowatt Hours of Electricity
5,489	Pounds of Greenhouse Gases
24	Pounds of HAPs, VOCs, and AOX Combined
8	Cubic Yards of Landfill Space

[1]Environmental benefits are calculated based on research done by the Environmental
Defense Fund and other members of the Paper Task Force who study the environmental impacts of the paper industry.

For a full list of NSP's titles, please call 1-800-567-6772 or check out our web site at:

www.newsociety.com

New Society Publishers